The Good Paper

The Good Paper
A handbook for writing papers in higher education

2nd edition

Lotte Rienecker and Peter Stray Jørgensen

With contributions by Signe Skov, Vanessa Sonne-Ragans, Lotte Thing Rasmussen, Charlotte Wien, Kirstin Remvig and Ida Klitgård

Samfundslitteratur

Lotte Rienecker and Peter Stray Jørgensen
With contributions by Signe Skov, Vanessa Sonne-Ragans, Lotte Thing Rasmussen, Charlotte Wien, Kirstin Remvig and Ida Klitgård

The Good Paper
A handbook for writing papers in higher education
2nd edition, 2nd print run 2022
(The book is a translation of *Den gode opgave*, 5th edition from 2017)

© Samfundslitteratur 2018

Editor: Henrik Schjerning
Cover: Imperiet (Annette Borsbøl)
Typeset: Ane Svendsen, SL grafik (slgrafik.dk)
Print: Totem

ISBN: 978-87-593-2994-8

Activities at: samfundslitteratur.dk/tgp

Samfundslitteratur
info@samfundslitteratur.dk
samfundslitteratur.dk

All rights reserved.
No part of this publication may be reproduced by institutions or companies without prior agreement with Copydan Writing, and then only within the provisions of the agreement. Brief extracts for review are excepted.

CONTENTS

FOREWORD TO THE ENGLISH EDITION 17
    Use 17
    Changes in this edition 17
    Activity book 18
    Other books on writing by the authors of The Good Paper 18
    Contact the authors 18

READER'S GUIDE 19

1. GOOD PAPERS IN HIGHER EDUCATION
   – GENRES AND QUALITY CRITERIA 21
    The research paper as a genre 21
    The research genre investigates a subject-specific problem 23
    The research paper meets scientific and scholarly requirements 24
        Research means bringing factors into play 25
        The research text is hierarchical 25
        Research is both the knowledge and the inquiry of the field 26
        Academic speech acts 26
        Requirements and qualities of the good paper in higher education 28
    Avoid common misconceptions of what constitutes a good paper 29
    Other types of papers and genres you as a student will have to write 30
        Other types of papers: Popularising papers, practice papers, tests 31
    The foundation of your research – the paper's pentagon 32
        What can be included in the pentagon's corners? 33
        Examples of good papers in the pentagon model 33
        Use the pentagon model 40
    The good paper's quality criteria 40
        A teacher's comments on a paper 40
        Rhetoric of science 41
        1. In the good paper, the writer is professional and displays independence 42
        2. The good paper uses the field's knowledge and tools 43
        3. The good paper is focused 45
        4. The good paper is "written" on the top of the taxonomies of educational
            objectives. 46
        5. The good paper is an argument 50

6. The good paper is critical of its own material, its field and of itself	50
7. The good paper communicates on a meta level	51
8. The good paper meets the curriculum's parameters	52
Examples of qualities in bachelor theses	53
Nuances?	61
The different purposes and ideals of the Anglo-American and Continental research traditions	61
Advice to students writing in the Continental tradition	64

2. WRITING PROCESSES OF RESEARCH PAPERS ... 67

Choice of topic	67
Your interest in the topic	67
The useful topic	68
The good topic	68
Theoretical, abstract or concrete topics?	69
After choosing a topic, the first thing you should do is write	69
You have started writing, yes, but what?	69
Write before and while you read	70
Write backwards – start with the conclusion	71
Begin with the central aspects	72
Put off in depth studies of theory and history, summaries and descriptions	72
Be flexible when writing	73
More revisions?	74
Introductory writing is writing to think	75
The techniques of writing to think	76
Brainstorming	76
Mind mapping	76
Non-stop writing	78
Broad writing	79
Display (visual representations) i.e. drawing the central content of your paper	79
Why write to think?	80
From writing to think to drafts to finished papers	81
Writing with or without an outline	81
The texts of the writing process: Notes, drafts and finished text	83
Should you write with a reader in mind?	84
Revising a text	84
Take a break	86
Revise on paper	86
Criteria for revision	86
From writer based to reader oriented revision	88
Get feedback	88

  Know your supervisor's criteria 88
 The process of project planning 89
  Your (pre)conditions 89
  Use calendars and schedules 91
  Plan backwards from your deadline 91
  Logbook 93
  Reading for papers 93
 Experiment! 93

3. SMALLER HOMEWORK ASSIGNMENTS, ONE-WEEK ASSIGNMENTS, SET EXAMS – ESSAYS 95
 What is the purpose of essays in the first year of study? 95
 Quality criteria 96
 Restrictions and possibilities: What are you *required* to
  do and what would be wise to do? 98
 Progression and independence 100
 If you are set an assignment question 101
 Introducing your paper: What should you include? 102
 Structure and presentation 103
 The writing process – if you only have six hours, three days or a week 106

4. FORMULATING A RESEARCH QUESTION – FROM TOPIC TO FOCUS AND QUESTION 109
 Definitions: "Problem" and other problem related words 110
  Other words for research question 112
 Must there be an actual problem (and for whom) to write a research paper? 113
  How do you formulate a research question? 115
 Research questions in "hard" and "soft" disciplines 116
 A question? 116
 A good research question helps you to write the good paper 117
 A bad research question – what is that? 119
 The process: From topic to research question 120
  How to move from topic to research question 120
 Formulate your research question on the basis of the answer 123
  An observation 124
 Use wh-words 124
 Fill out a template 125
  Be inspired 126
 1. The research question guides the paper's pentagon 126
 2. Formulate a research question that is knowledge-transforming according to
  the taxonomies for learning goals 126

What-, why- or how-questions 127
What 127
Why 128
Commentary 129
How 129
3. The research question governs the paper as an argument 129
4. The research question's broadness vs. narrowness 130
The research question guides the paper's delimitation 132
5. The research question's main point must be evident 133
Divide into main question and necessary working questions 135
6. The research question must be precise 135
Vagueness 135
Watch out for plural terms and broad concepts 136
Watch out for the absence of actors and sources 137
Using the words and terms of the field 137
Write a short research question with clear layout 138
7. Consciously use open/closed questions in the research question 138
Supervision and formulating research questions 141
Keep you supervisor informed 141
Get input from your supervisor and fellow students/others 141
A good research question is no guarantee 142
Unanswered questions and unfinished research questions 143

5. **LITERATURE AND INFORMATION SEARCH FOR YOUR PAPER** 145
By Lotte Thing Rasmussen, Kirstin Remvig and Charlotte Wien
What am I looking for? 145
Where do I search? What search tools should I use? 146
Information searches in the context of writing a paper – what and where? 148
How do I search? 149
How much of the literature should I read? 150
Use good reference works 150
Research question and search profile 151
Core concepts, language and synonyms 152
Substitute concepts – superordinate and subordinate concepts 154
Translate the search profile into a search language 157
Boolean operators – and/or/not 157
Phrase searches 161
Truncation 162
Help functions and tutorials 163
Use the database's indexing in your search 163
How do I use the search profile? 164

Chain searches/citation searches 167
    How do I chain search? 167
    Retro- and prospective chain searches 168
    Why can't I settle for a chain search? 169
Use your supervisor and information specialist effectively 169

6. READING AND TAKING NOTES FOR YOUR PAPER 171
Curricular reading and reading for your paper require different reading and note-taking strategies 171
    Reading and writing go hand in hand 172
Reading for papers 172
Ways of reading 173
    Skimming – reading to gain an overview of the topic 173
    Selective reading – goal-oriented reading for writing papers 174
Taking notes for your paper 176
    Notes for the paper: Files 177
    How should you store notes? 178
Note-taking software 178
    The more processed the notes, the better the paper 179
    Highlighting and referential notes 179
    Processed notes 180
    Notes for contextualising 180

7. PHILOSOPHY OF SCIENCE IN THE PAPER 183
By Vanessa Sonne-Ragans
Why philosophy of science is relevant for writing a paper 183
    Philosophy of science and field of study 184
    The purpose of philosophy of science in the paper 184
    What are the challenges? 185
How much philosophy of science should your paper contain? 185
    How little philosophy of science is enough? 186
    When is there too much philosophy of science? 186
Philosophers of science and paper writers do different things 187
What is required when a paper uses scientific knowledge to conduct research? 188
    Science is 188
    Philosophies of science engage in a methodological reduction 189
    Central scientific concepts 190
Elaboration of theory, model, method and methodology 193
    Theories 193
    Models 195
    Method and methodology 195

How to use philosophy of science to substantiate the premises for a good paper .. 197
The three basic research approaches 200
Basic evaluation criteria in the philosophy of science: A theory's view of
    knowledge and reality 203
Two fundamentally different views of reality: Materialism and idealism 206
    Pros and cons of the two positions 207
Three fundamentally different views of knowledge 209
Papers are enhanced when the choice of theories and methods is grounded in
    a view of knowledge and reality 212
    Are you in doubt about where the philosophy of science fits into your paper? ... 213
    Where do you write about your paper's view of knowledge and reality? 214
    *How do you write about your view of knowledge and reality when it is
        ambiguous?* 214
    Philosophy of science enhances your paper's argumentation 215
How you tackle philosophy of science through a dialogue with your supervisor .. 217

8. SOURCES IN YOUR PAPER 219
Sources' functions in and for the paper 219
    Applied sources 220
    The professionalism and scholarliness of sources 221
Why use secondary sources? 221
    Using secondary sources in papers – which and how 222
How many sources? Your research question is the guide and measure for
    handling your sources 224
    Where are different sources placed in the pentagon? 225
When and how should you refer to secondary sources in your text? 226
    *Source qualification, source argumentation, source discussion and source
        criticism* 227
    Qualify secondary sources 227
Literature review: Materials, sources, state-of-the-art 231
    What is a literature review? 231
    Why a literature review? 232
    How? 233
    Delimitation 233
    What sources and materials can you include, and how? 234
    The literature must be qualified in relation to your study 234
Discussing sources – advanced! 235
Source criticism and review 238
    Checklists for source criticism 238
    Use of the source as a criterion 241
    Quality control as assessment criterion: The academic hierarchy of authority 242
How should you represent sources? 244

  Quotes 245
  Quotation technique 247
  Paraphrasing and summarising 248
 How to reference sources 248
  Which sources must be referenced? 251
 Distance to sources 252
 Contagion and plagiarism 254

9. DATA IN THE PAPER 255
 Qualitative and quantitative data 256
 Before choosing data: Research question and supervisor 257
  Always prepare collection carefully 257
 Presenting data in your paper's introduction 262
 Including data as documentation in your paper 263
 Data can be discussed in discussion sections 264
 Collecting and using human data 265

10. THEORY, CONCEPTS, METHODS AND RESEARCH DESIGN (= THE METHOD OF YOUR RESEARCH) 269
 Theories in your paper 271
  Concepts are often drawn from theories 272
  You must define concepts and state why you use them in your research 272
  Problems with a paper's theory 273
  Too much or too little theory 273
 Choice of theory for research papers 274
 How to find theories 277
 Theory section 277
 Method and method section 279
  Turning a theory into method (analytic tool) 282
 Where in the paper do you write about theory and method? 283
  Introduce theory in the introduction or theory section 284
  Where in your paper should you present critique of theory and methods? 285
 Discussion, evaluation and critique of theory 285
 Discussion, evaluation and criticism of methods: Research method 289
  Validity and reliability 294
 The paper's research design, the procedure 296
 From research question to theory and method and research design – in a linguistic sense 297
  Use your supervisor for selection, use, qualification, discussion and criticism of theory and method 297

11. THE PAPER'S STRUCTURE AND ELEMENTS ... 299
When and how to structure ... 299
Use the research question as a structural guideline ... 302
Structure is determined by genre ... 302
The structure contains elements of the argumentation ... 308
General – concrete – general, up-down-up ... 310
End your paper at an upper, general level ... 312
Consider your paper from a bird's-eye view – 3 activities ... 313
The structuring process takes place throughout the entire writing process ... 314
Structuring problems ... 314
Text types – the building blocks of the academic text ... 315
Definitions ... 316
Summarising and paraphrasing paragraphs ... 317
Descriptive, characterising paragraphs ... 318
Narrative and descriptive paragraphs ... 318
Comparative, juxtaposing paragraphs ... 319
Analysing and interpreting paragraphs ... 320
Discussion sections ... 322
"What do I think?" ... 325
Reflecting sections ... 325
Evaluating sections ... 326
Discussion and critique of method ... 327
Design and perspective paragraphs ... 328
Introduction ... 329
The introduction as a template ... 330
The introduction reflects the entire paper ... 332
Choice of topic, problem definition, motivation and research question ... 334
Hypotheses ... 335
The paper's purpose ... 336
Point of view ... 336
Theory ... 336
Method ... 337
Philosophy of science ... 337
Concept definitions ... 337
Data ... 338
Delimitation ... 338
The paper's research design and structure ... 338
Introduce your project, not your reservations ... 338
Conclusion ... 339
The conclusion must relate to the research question ... 339
Write your conclusion as you go ... 341

Perspective 341
The paper's formal sections 341
   Front page 342
   Table of contents 343
   Use headings to demonstrate the structure 343
   Appendices 344
   Notes, note sections and references in the text 345
   Abstract 346

12. THE PAPER'S ARGUMENTATION 347

Argumentation in papers and other genres 347
Argumentation in research papers 348
Argumentation forms part of the unfinished disciplinary debate 352
What should your paper argue for? 352
Your paper as a cohesive argument 353
Disciplinary context 355
Conclusion 356
   Conclusions in papers do not have to be long 356
   The perspective contains points about the literature and your own research 357
Documentation 358
   What can you use as documentation – and for what? 359
   Placement of theories and methods in the paper's argumentation 360
   Research argumentation 360
Research design and procedure 360
Use the argument model in your writing process 361
Argumentation is shown in the structure 363
Argumentation in language 365
   Use argumentation signals 365
   Objectivity 365

13. CLEAR AND ACADEMIC LANGUAGE 367

First of all: Language changes from think text to draft text to product text 368
   Text to supervisor, project- or feedback group 368
Clear and academic language 369
   Clear language in papers – a virtue rather than a requirement 370
Choose precise, unequivocal and argumentation terms 371
   Precise and unequivocal terms 373
Carefully choose the subject and verb of a sentence 374
   The subjects – what is in focus? 374
   The verbs of the sentence must be specific 375

The good paragraph's beginning, middle and end 376
   Use academic keywords to demonstrate coherence in the section 377
Write metacommunicatively 378
   Research metacommunication 380
   Textual metacommunication 381
   Too much metacommunication? 382
Detachment and contagion in language 383
Watch out for "hidden" translations from foreign-language sources! 385
  By Ida Klitgård
   English into Danish – Anglicisms 385
   "Colouring and discolouring" 388
   A question of credibility 389
FAQ 390
   Use of evaluating terms? 390
   Variation in language? 391
   Literary language 391
   Popularising language 391
   Spoken language, everyday language, slang? 392
   Difficult language 393
   Using "I", active and passive 395
   Nominalised style? – both yes and no 396
   "What do you think?" 397
What can you do? 398

14. SUPERVISON, INDEPENDENCE AND OWNERSHIP 399
How much supervision can you receive? 400
Independence and ownership 400
Good supervision 401
Seek information about supervision 401
   First meeting – as early as possible 402
   Your initiative! 403
   Preparing for supervision 403
   Calibrating expectations 403
Emailing your supervisor 405
Several supervisions 406
   Good text for supervision 406
Feedback from macro to micro level (top-down) 407
Forward-looking and retrospective feedback 408
   The supervisor and the – your – good paper 408
   How to receive critique 409
Working through supervision 410

    Get feedback on all papers – and give feedback on the feedback 410
    No supervision or unhelpful supervision? 411
    Alternatives to supervision 411

15. RECOMMENDED LITERATURE FOR WRITING PAPERS AND ON STUDY SKILLS 413
    Read more about 413
        Examples of papers 413
        Research papers in general 413
        Writing process 413
        Research question 413
        Searching for and incorporating information 414
        Argumentation 414
        Popularising papers 415
        Study skills 415

BIBLIOGRAPHY 417

INDEX 423

ABOUT THE AUTHORS 429

Foreword to the English edition

We are pleased and proud to publish this 2nd edition of *The Good Paper*. The book has been read and used for a generation now (since 1997 in 5 Danish editions) by students pursuing higher education as a handbook and a reference work for writing papers and projects. It has also been used by quite a few supervisors and librarians, and it is to a high degree their reports back to us and the publisher that have shaped each new edition. In this edition, we have added 5 new co-authors to provide contributions for their areas of expertise. *The Good Paper*, thus, has become even better!

Use
The English version targets primarily foreign students studying in Denmark. The translation is a close one-to-one to the Danish 5th edition from 2017, so that users may refer to the same page number in the English and the Danish version.

Changes in this edition
The biggest and most important changes in this edition are:
- A new chapter, written by Vanessa Sonne-Ragans (an external lecturer in the philosophy of science at the University of Copenhagen), on the philosophy of science and how you incorporate it into a good paper. It is a recurring theme throughout the book that integrating premises, considerations, and discussions from the philosophy of science can make a good paper even better. Much of the feedback the book has received – especially from teachers at institutions of higher education – has expressed a desire for *The Good Paper* to deal with the philosophy of science since the inclusion of philosophy of science has become a mandatory requirement in some higher education programmes.
- The book's chapter on literature and information searches has been replaced with a newly-written chapter penned by Lotte Thing Rasmussen, Kirstin Remvig and Charlotte Wien, all from the University Library of Southern Denmark.
- In the chapter on language, Ida Klitgård, associate professor in English at Roskilde University, has added a section on contamination from English when you write papers in Danish.
- A section on the literature/state-of-the-art section has been added to the chapter on sources for the paper.

Many other minor changes and updates have also been added, and there are a number of new titles and internet resources in chapter 15 on recommended literature.

Activity book
The Good Paper is an activity book. This means that our workshop activities on paper-writing throughout the years are included in the book and on the publisher's homepage as Word files, so you can download, modify and fill out the forms or use them for workshops. Most of the activities and forms are related to the writing process in the sense that they can be used as drafts for your text that can be copied from the form. They are work *on* your paper, not work *about* your paper. The activities are also meant as preparation for working with your supervisor, for information searches, and for interaction with those who are giving you feedback. There are also a number of new activities in the book's new chapters.

You may find all the activities together and download them at *samfundslitteratur.dk/tgp*

Other books on writing by the authors of The Good Paper
We refer in *The Good Paper* to *Scribo – værktøj til informationssøgning og problemformulering* [Scribo – A tool for information searches and research questions] as an online tool that the paper writer can use to answer questions about the basis of the paper. For people just beginning their studies, we have written *Studiehåndbogen – for studiestartere på videregående uddannelser* [The Study Handbook: For people beginning higher education] (2011) and *Bundne opgaver* [Writing Essays] (2008); and, for thesis writers, *Specielt om specialer – en aktivitetsbog* [What's special about theses – An activity book] (2011) is geared toward writing theses and builds on the principles set forth in The Good Paper. *Problemformulering på videregående uddannelser* [Research questions for higher education] (2014) elaborates on various types of research questions, and *Studielæsning på videregående uddannelser – læsestrategier og læseteknikker* [Studying for higher education – reading strategies and reading techniques] (2007) delves into reading. You can't write a paper without reading! *Klart sprog* [Clear language] (2014) provides guidelines for good language in papers.
    Many more specialised study method books may be found in the bibliography.

Contact the authors
We are happy to receive inquiries or development ideas about *The Good Paper* either personally or through our publishers, Samfundslitteratur – see samfundslitteratur.dk.

Copenhagen, November 2017

Peter Stray Jørgensen psj@samfundslitteratur.dk
Lotte Rienecker lrienecker@gmail.dk

Reader's guide

The Good Paper is a reference book and therefore does not need to be read chronologically from cover to cover. However, we do recommend that you read the whole of chapter 1 on the research paper genre and quality criteria as we here introduce the general ideas and concepts used in the rest of the book.

The book is structured, so that each chapter can be read on several different levels:

- You can read the headers and the boxes in each chapter which offer good advice and suggestions and briefly present points and guidelines.
- You can read texts that explain and argue for the reasons behind our recommendations.
- Finally, if you would like to see theory carried out in practice, you can read the annotated examples.

The chapters include numerous activities that can strengthen and encourage the writing process. These activities can also be found on *The Good Paper's* website: samfundslitteratur.dk/tgp. Here you can also find the accompanying question sheets in Word format, so you can adapt them to your own research paper.

We have not been able to avoid repetitions and cross-references in the book. Repetitions only occur when something is presented from a different angle or appears in a significantly different context. Cross-references are either supplementary or included to avoid repeating the same phrase more than once.

1. Good papers in higher education – genres and quality criteria

This book is about learning how to write a research paper. Not all papers you write will be of this type, but they will be a step on the way towards it: that is, they will, in different ways, prepare you for and teach you how to meet the requirements of a particular genre.

In this chapter and the next, we will describe the different types of papers people write in higher education. We will especially make an effort to describe the conditions and requirements of the independent, investigative (scientific) paper. We will not just describe how to meet these requirements; we will also explain how to write a good paper. We devote a lot of time to explaining and defining the book's concepts and points of view.

Genre – a definition

The concept of genre is central to this book. A genre is a group of texts that share similar elements, structures and possibly language and therefore have the same purpose, function and speech act (i.e., something you do using words, for example, describing, analysing, evaluating)

The research paper as a genre

By "research papers", we mean texts written by students that in principle must meet the same requirements and criteria as academic texts in general.

Research papers are modelled on academic genres: these are texts that are, for example, written by teachers in the field for the purpose of academic progress and research. A research paper requires a high level of independence from you as a student. When writing a research paper, students (in collaboration with a supervisor) must themselves choose a subject area, formulate a research question, search for and choose literature (theory), choose an epistemological perspective and a suitable method and research design, and analyse, evaluate and draw their own conclusions.

A bachelor thesis is an example of a research paper. In a bachelor thesis, independence can mean that the writer analyses data or discusses subject-specific points of view. By writing research papers, you will train yourself in treating material in a professional manner.

However, the demands for independence can be limited by the fact that some decisions regarding the paper will already have been made by your teacher or institution. This will be made clear in the assignment question or the curriculum. These limitations could be requirements regarding subject matter and/or the research question and/or choice of sources. Later in this chapter, we will expand on how to qualitatively demonstrate independence in papers.

Research papers in higher education especially include
- dissertations, master's theses
- MA papers
- projects
- bachelor theses, including professional bachelor theses
- smaller papers and assignments at BA level.

At some institutions, projects and research papers are used as general terms for dissertations. What we write about research papers largely applies to projects as well.

With regard to genre, projects do not differ from research papers. They contain the same elements and are both based on research, argumentation and documentation. We have read many projects from Roskilde University and Copenhagen Business School (for example, when acting as external examiners), and the only difference is that projects ordinarily take practical societal and commercial challenges as their starting point and are the result of group work. However, requirements and criteria for the text of projects and research papers are the same. Higher education also includes other types of assignments. We discuss these on pp. 30-31 and in chapter 3.

When having to write a text, knowing what genre to write in or which genre you have chosen will prove a great help. The more clear this is to you, the more equipped you will be to make each individual decision down to word level.

The research genre investigates a subject-specific problem

Common to research papers is that they research a single, subject-specific problem in a disciplinary context in a professional way. Here is a definition:

The research genre – a definition

- Documentation
- of research
- of a single subject-specific problem
- on the basis of a given field's (or adjacent fields') literature, "state-of-the-art",
- by using the theories and methods of the field (or another relevant field)
- with the purpose of arguing/persuading
- peers
- of the accuracy of the results, conclusions and perspectives of the research
- presented in a way that is acceptable to peers.

Most researchers will agree with this definition. In the box below, we account for the individual concepts.

Concept definitions

- *Research* is the guiding concept in scholarly writing and is the most important academic speech act (see pp. 26f.). However, *doing research* does not necessarily mean *solving* the chosen problem: in the humanities and social sciences, you are usually expected to analyse, interpret, discuss, or evaluate (you can read more about this in chapter 4 on research questions).
- *A single problem* means that several problems may only be treated in the same paper if they can be united by a single focus.
- *A subject-specific problem* is a problem that belongs to a given field. To ensure that it does, your supervisor must confirm that your subject matter is connected to the field. The expression "a subject-specific problem" does not mean that a research question must be based on something highly problematic. Instead it should be understood as something that requires a subject-specific answer; a single problem that needs to be explored within the given field. You can read more about what a problem is in chapter 4 on research questions.

- *The field's literature, the state of the art,* is a field's best and most up-to-date knowledge at a given time.
- The field's *theories and methods* refer to the concepts and skills used in your research. Concepts are basically the same as "theories", and skills the same as "methods". When writing a research paper, you must select concepts and methods from the field's "toolbox" specifically suited to the problem. In research papers, theories and methods are tools for problem solving – not a goal in themselves. However, papers that are purely based on theories and methods do exist. Here problem solving consists in treating problems in or between theories and methods.
- The goal is to *argue for/persuade your reader of the accuracy* of your research's conclusion, results and perspectives. Ideally research must contribute something new to the field; new knowledge, new procedures, etc. – however small it may be. But the reader must find the new aspect credible, and therefore research papers must always *argue for* this new aspect.
- Argumentation *(making arguments for/persuading)* is aimed at peers who can use and develop the results further. Your paper must therefore comply with the conventions and scientific and scholarly practices within the professional community. When considering who your reader is, take a look at the box below?"

The target audience for papers written for higher education is deemed to be non-specialised peers.

Who is your target audience?

The target audience may best be described as professionals within your discipline, who do not possess the same specialised knowledge about the field or subject-specific problem discussed in the paper.

The research paper meets scientific and scholarly requirements

Understanding what research is provides the background for the genre's definition.

Research means bringing factors into play

A central feature of research is that you investigate how at least two factors (or even 16 or 144 factors!) affect each other, for example:
- How do these concepts (factor 1) explain phenomenon X (factor 2)?
- How has historical development X influenced Y?

When writing a paper you must therefore always bear in mind that factors must be brought into play with each other; typically theory is brought into play with data – but theories can be brought into play with each other or method and theory. In practice, however, most papers examine data by means of the field's methods, theories and concepts with the purpose of analysing, explaining, discussing, evaluating, constructing data/objects/phenomena/texts in order to solve a problem or construct/design something new. But there are variants. Students may also write purely theoretical papers, in which theoretical positions are analysed, discussed and evaluated (see pp. 352f.). It also has to do with bringing factors into play with each other and investigating how they can contribute to a mutual understanding of one another.

The research text is hierarchical

The research paper is a hierarchical text where the research question is placed at the top of the text's hierarchy. Ideally, the formulation of the problem should be the determining factor for all the writer's choices in regards to documentation, theories and methods as well as linguistic choices on micro level. This is described as the higher and lower levels of a text.

The levels of research texts	
• Higher levels of the text:	The foundation, the text's main guiding principles: Research question, purpose, materials, philosophical/epistemological starting point, theories, methods, literature, application of knowledge, argumentation, subject-specific content.
• Intermediate levels of the text:	Form: Textual elements, structure, order, introductions, conclusions, etc.
• Lower levels of the text:	Execution: sentence and word level, referencing, etc.

These levels demonstrate what you, both as writer and reader, should give high and low priority to in the writing process, and when receiving feedback and being assessed. But it is not quite that simple; language is more than writing correctly; language is also content and meaning and it indicates whether the paper has been written in the right genre and in a scholarly manner.

Research is both the knowledge and the inquiry of the field

As mentioned before, science is research. It is important that research is carried out within the subject-specific context which constitutes the knowledge, methods and theories of the field and which is rooted in the literature of the inquiry

The distinction between researcher and scholar is important to note as it emphasises the two main skills involved when carrying out research. You must be able to use, read and know the literature of your field (scholarship) as well as conduct research and investigations (researcher).

The two sides of research can be presented like this:

Knowledge of the field's literature ("scholarship", "being well-read", "other's material"):	Carrying out research ("research", "using other's material"):
- Philosophy of science - Knowledge, data - Research methods, procedures - Central concepts - Theories, models - Disciplinary underpinnings - Most suitable sources - Criteria of selection - Alternative sources - Critical reading of sources and critical perspective.	- Research question "identification of the problem" - Purpose, the relevance of the research - Motivation - Selection and collection of material - Operationalisation of theories and methods - Analysis - Themes for discussion - Argumentation, points - Evaluation of research - Coherence, structure - Presentation, language.

Academic speech acts

All text genres employ distinctive text types (textual elements such as summaries, analyses, comparisons, etc. Read more about these on pp. 315ff.), and the distinctive speech acts that are related to these. In academic writing the most important thing is to understand the academic speech act to research. When writing a paper, you must know which speech acts your paper is meant to perform – and which it should avoid.

The following is a list of our suggestion of acceptable and non-acceptable speech acts in research papers:

Acceptable and unacceptable speech acts in the research paper	
It is acceptable in research papers to - analyse - argue - categorise - cite - concretise - consider - construct - contextualise - criticise - define - describe - differentiate - discuss - evaluate (based on subject-specific criteria!) - interpret - make probable - paraphrase - prioritise - problematise - prove - qualify - reason - reflect - relate - research - review - select - specify - show - substantiate - synthesise.	It is unacceptable in research papers to - agitate - believe - converse - degrade - entertain - experience - feel - lecture - plagiarise - popularise - postulate - praise. However, you may believe or have an opinion about something if it is on the basis of academic argumentation.

In short: a research paper performs the speech act of researching and speech acts that follow therefrom.

Requirements and qualities of the good paper in higher education

On the whole, requirements and quality criteria can be presented like this:

Characteristic features and quality criteria of the research paper

Focus and context
- The central speech act is to research
- Focus, purpose and relevance is defined
- The writer positions himself as a researcher in the field.
- The principal sender-receiver relationship is from peer to peer.

Theory, method, concepts
- It always includes theory, concepts and/or method – and, perhaps, a philosophy of science.
- Theory has been selected and substantiated on the basis of functioning as a tool for analysis and/or model of explanation – and/or as the object of analysis/discussion/evaluation.
- Method is selected, systematically described and substantiated on the basis of the extent and form of the material as well as the focus and purpose of the paper.
- All important concepts are defined.

Argumentation and reasoning
- Acceptable documentation of (i.e. basis and grounds for) the central claim/point.
- Its reasoning, argumentation and procedure can be replicated.
- All important choices and decisions regarding the content, procedure, etc., are substantiated.
- There are no internal contradictions or inconsistencies – unless these are explained.
- It considers relevant counter arguments, is fair and avoids bias (preconceptions).

Structure and elements
- It is structured around a number of (often) obligatory textual elements; its basic structure is unremitting and the research procedure is described.
- The conventional norms of how to write an introduction and conclusion are complied with
- It is often in the form of an argumentation.

> **Use of sources**
> - Sources are up-to-date.
> - It relates to the work of others in an analytical and critical way and by actively using it
> - It qualifies and evaluates its sources.
> - It complies with the accepted rules and norms for treating secondary literature, references, referencing styles, notes, etc.
>
> **Language and presentation**
> - It employs the language of the field
> - It uses subject-specific and academic speech acts (text types)
> - In regards to concepts, its language is clear, precise, consistent as well as correct, timeless and metacommunicative.
> - It includes the relevant formal requirements (abstract, introduction, notes, bibliography, etc.)
> - Typography and layout support the (overall) presentation.

These are high ideals, and therefore they are rarely fully observed in every text. However, students in higher education should be able to handle these ideals, and all teachers in higher education should strive towards these and keep students accountable for them. Although this may seem overwhelming, you will learn through working with your paper, and this book will inform and teach you about these particular characteristics of the good paper.

Avoid common misconceptions of what constitutes a good paper

Unfortunately, there are a number of misconceptions of what determines the quality of a paper. These misconceptions may all impede or block your writing. Among others these include:
- That your paper must be shaped by personal, not just professional, engagement
- That extensive and broad knowledge is rewarded the most
- That you must be original and innovative
- That the most important thing is to agree with your teacher
- That as long as the content is good, the form is unimportant
- That writing in an especially abstract and complex academic language is rated highly.

Other types of papers and genres you as a student will have to write

During your time as a student you will undoubtedly have to write (and read and speak) in a number of different genres. On the following "genre map", each different branch represents a different text group, which each performs the same basic speech act. A speech act is something you do with words, for example, promising or lying. You must primarily be able to write within the genres presented on the left-hand side of the map. As a student, you will rarely have to write in the remaining genres (unless you are asked to).

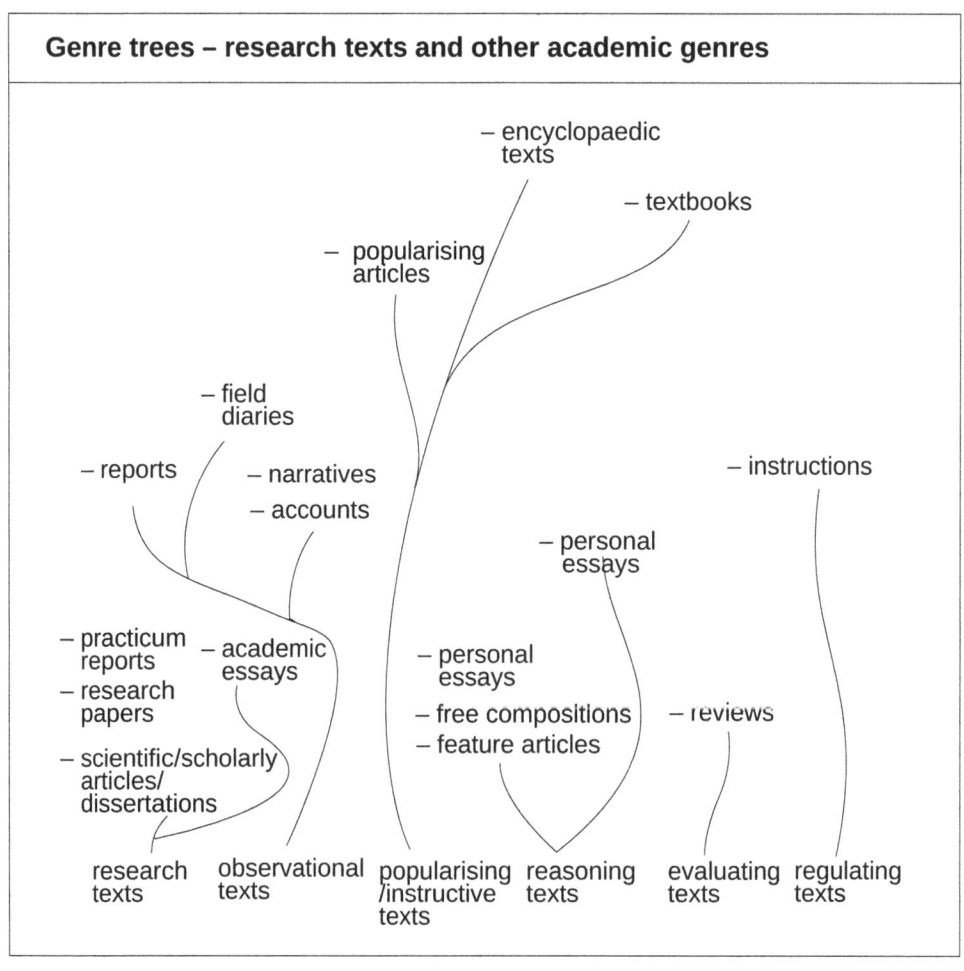

When writing a research paper, you must avoid the genres in which research is not the main speech act and/or the genres with other target groups and purposes. This is an important point, because students at all levels of education end up writing in the wrong genres, especially the textbook or instructive text genre. This poses problems when it comes to the research and documentation your paper must be based on as well as in regards to purpose, target group and sender. Presumably, this is because most of the texts students read are not the type of text they are asked to produce such as textbooks, online portals, encyclopaedias, special popularising papers (unless required to by their curriculum). These genres are written by teachers and/or researchers, and require research and documentation. Only then is popularisation possible.

Other types of papers: Popularising papers, practice papers, tests

Popularising papers are not actual academic papers, but are texts that belong outside the academic sphere. We have chosen to include them, as many disciplines consider it important that students are familiar with this type of text. In general, there is an increasing focus on teaching students "professional writing", i.e. writing genres used in practice in institutions and companies. Although this text type falls outside the main scope of this book, it briefly discussed in the next chapter. See chapter 15, p. 413 for a referral to useful literature on professional writing.

Practice papers train students in the skills and textual elements (text types) they must master when writing a research paper, for example for summarising, analysing, evaluating.

Tests evaluate academic skills and disciplinary knowledge, for example, by means of set exams.

Both practice papers and tests belong in the educational sphere and are dissimilar to genres outside this sphere. However, the research paper resembles the scientific and scholarly article. You can read about practice papers and tests in the chapter: "Smaller homework assignments, one-week assignments, set exams – essays".

> **Activity: Determine the genre of the articles you have read**
>
> - Determine the genre of articles from your curriculum
> - Are we dealing with research papers, popularising papers or an academic essay, etc.?
> - Which text type is most prominent? (summary, analysis, discussion, etc.)
> - What is the function of each section? What do the sections *do* in contrast to what they *say* (content)?
>
> This activity is suited for study groups.

The foundation of your research – the paper's pentagon

Some elements must be present before being able to determine whether a research paper's basis is acceptable. We have illustrated this with a pentagon.

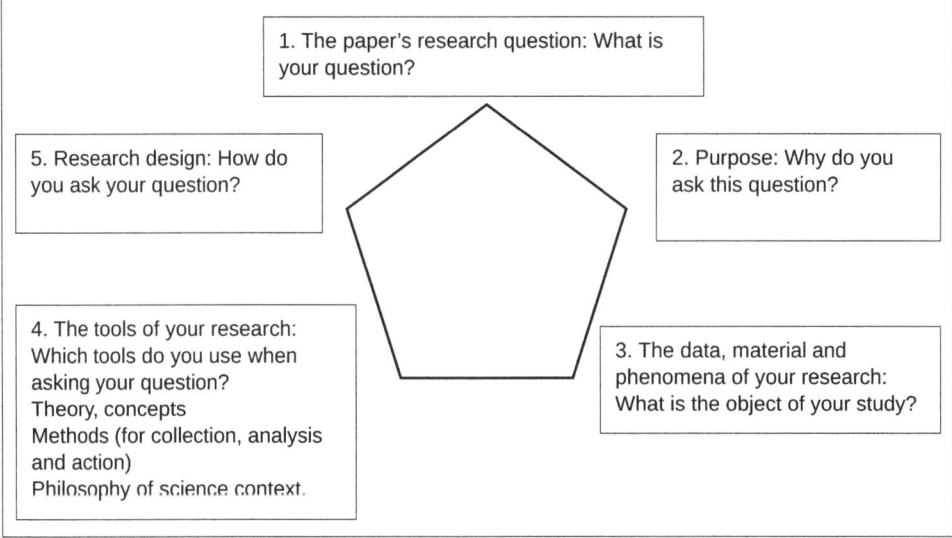

The pentagon points out the basic cornerstones of all research. The model is central to understanding research writing and for guiding the writing process. Throughout the rest of this book, we will frequently return to the pentagon in order to place and relate other elements and activities of the writing process to the foundation of the paper.

Some research papers do not include data in the conventional sense, but examine theories, concepts or methods. If this is the case, theories are included in the third corner of the pentagon (see example 4 in the following).

What can be included in the pentagon's corners?

In the following, we give examples of what to write in each of the pentagon's corners.

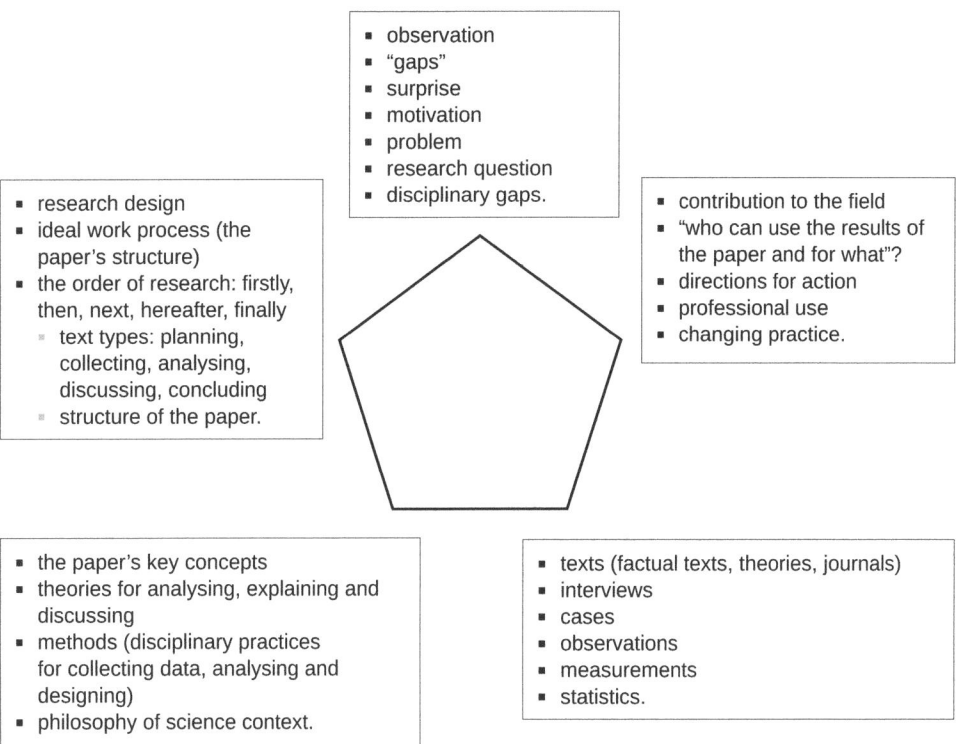

Examples of good papers in the pentagon model

We will now give six examples of pentagons based on good papers (however, as we point out in our comments, these papers still include problems). The papers are selected from different subjects and fields.

Example 1: Paper in Literary History (Bachelor degree in Danish)

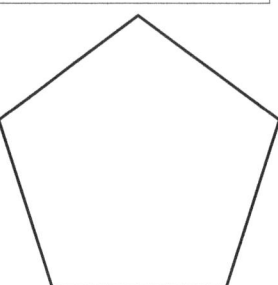

5.
1. The literary historical problem area
2. The approach of the classical literary theorists
3. Analysis of the interesting in texts from before 1870
4. Analysis of texts from after 1870
5. Conclusion supporting the research question.

1. "In the following I aim to prove that psychology is not a product of naturalism, but is a general characteristic of 19th century literature."

2. "The aim of this paper is to view 19th century literature through a wide lens in an attempt to reveal a connection which is not apparent from traditional period divisions [before and after the modern breakthrough, ca. 1870]". [At first glance, the purpose is subject-specific, however the paper's perspective connects the problem to teaching literary periods in high school].

4.
Theory: The statements of literary theorists [analytic tool], i.e.:

Method:
- The concept of "the interesting"
- "Generally available psychological terminology", which is used as an analytic dimension.

3. Literary texts and meta texts (reviews etc.) from before and after the modern breakthrough.

Comment: A historical problem area that questions a previously established period division. We often come across more narrative historical papers asking: What happened? This is a good example of a problem oriented history paper. The research question is in fact a hypothesis, i.e., a claim the writer seeks to prove. Many papers take a hypothesis as their starting point rather than a question. However, the hypothesis can always be turned into a research question which the paper answers. Read more about hypotheses on pp. 110, 193 and 336.

Example 2: Paper in Nursing (Professional bachelor degree)

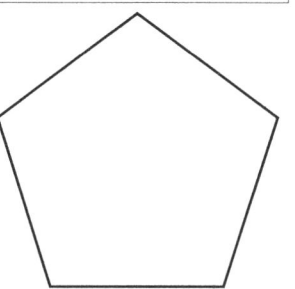

1. "As an anesthetics nurse, how do I reduce anxiety and communicate with a patient who is to undergo general anesthesia and who has previously experienced awareness during anesthetics?"

2. "[I want to investigate how communication with patients who have undergone traumatic experiences is carried out] in the hope of being able to reduce patients' fear of anesthetics."

3. Practice description (patient NN) + other's data.

4.
Theory: Literature on awareness. Anxiety-theory. Theory about communicating with patients. American theories on communication strategies.

Method: The theoretical concepts are used as a model for analysis.

5.
1. Account of theory
2. Analysis of practice descriptions using concepts from theory
3. Conclusion of practice descriptions
4. Perspective: Suggestions for procedures in connection with awareness.

Comments: The purpose of papers for professional bachelor degrees is often practical and professional, targeted at how to improve job performance. The point of departure is a practical problem within the profession, which the writer suggests how to solve.

Example 3: Paper in Political Science (Bachelor degree)

1. "This paper aims at examining how knowledge drawn from evaluations leads to changes in practice […]. Why do evaluations often have no impact? […] Which conditions must be met before evaluations can lead to learning? Were these conditions met in connection with the social housing policies from 1993-2004? How could these policies have prevented evaluations from leading to learning?"

2. "It is therefore relevant to research what can be done, when you want to evaluate as well as acquire new knowledge."

3. The data of the paper is the so-called "social housing policies" initiated during Poul Nyrup's government's Urban Development Committee and which, from the beginning, included a number of evaluations.

4. *Theory*: "Our researched is based on theories about learning in organisations, which focus on how you move from knowledge to practice."

Method: Methodological literature, e.g. Bryman: *Social Research Methods*; Christensen: *Kvalitativ analyse* [Qualitative analysis]; Kvale: *Det kvalitative interview* [The qualitative interview] [and many more]

5. "By way of introduction, we will account for our method and introduce our case in section 2 […] in section 3 we account for the evaluations used […]. In section 4, we introduce the analytic terminology we wish to employ […] we adjust the theories to this […] In section 5 we operationalise the model of learning through evaluations and develop five hypotheses […] In section 6, we test the five hypotheses [through semi-structured interviews]".

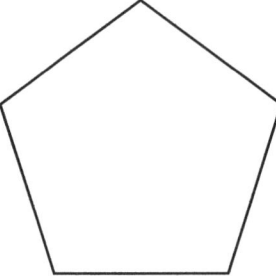

Comments: In this paper, all the guiding principles are in place. We would like to emphasize corner 5: Here, the procedure is a clear progression in the research toward a testing of the hypotheses.

1. GOOD PAPERS IN HIGHER EDUCATION – GENRES AND QUALITY CRITERIA

Example 4: Paper in Library Science (Bachelor degree)

1. "I aim to uncover which meanings the concept of discourse is ascribed in organisational communication. Furthermore, I wish to describe which ideas of construction are included in the different meanings and uses of the concept of discourse. This will lead to a discussion of whether there is a connection between the concept of discourse, the idea of construction and the understanding of organisations."

2. Because the concept of discourse has several meanings, it is important to distinguish between these to know which meaning the concept of discourse is ascribed and to know which idea of construction constitutes the basis for the use of the concept of discourse." –
"It is assumed that the conclusions regarding the relationship between discourse and construction can be transferred to other fields …"

5.
1. "First I will examine the three texts and describe each author's theory …
2. Then I will compare the three approaches. I attempt to place each author within the different theories with the purpose of comparing their concept of discourse and understanding of organisation.
3. Finally I wish to uncover the relationship between the concept of discourse and the idea of construction."

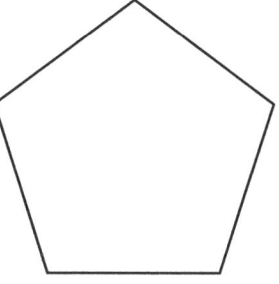

3. "Three texts by theorists in the field of organisational communication" (theories about organisational communication).

4.
Theory: Søren Barlebo Wenneberg's theory about social constructivism.

Method: Analysis, comparison and categorisation of the three theorists' definitions of the concept of discourse on the basis of Wenneberg's theory of social constructivism.

Comments: This paper is special in that it contributes to the field's methods, concept definitions and concept understanding as a basis for later analysis.

Example 5: Paper in Social Work (Professional bachelor degree)

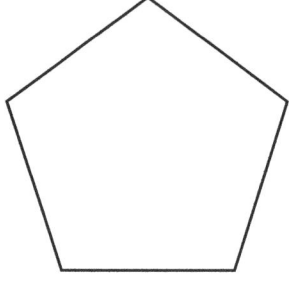

1. "From the perspective of inclusion/exclusion, how does having to live on the lowest welfare benefits rates affect newly arrived refugees in the areas of social life, leisure time and political life? Can a social worker influence families' inclusion/exclusion within these areas through acknowledgement or lack thereof?"

2. "To research how low income levels influence their lives in general […] Gather information to present factual criticism."

3. Interviews with 3 refugee families and 2 social workers.

4.
Theory:
Henning Hansen on 5 areas of life. Luhmann through Nils Mortensen on the concept of inclusion/exclusion. C. Juul Kristensen's concept of marginality. Høilund and Juul's concept of acknowledgement on the basis of their normative theory of social work.

Method:
Semi-structured, qualitative interviews.

5.
- Economic/legal framework
- Selecting families for interviews
- Methodological and theoretical framework: Inclusion/exclusion
- Question guide based on Henning Hansen
- Model of analysis based on theory
- Analysis of family interviews
- Social measure: The concept of acknowledgement is introduced and interviews are analysed on the basis of this.

Comments: The purpose of this paper is to present factual criticism of existing conditions. The research aims to collect knowledge to support this criticism. Note, that the research question poses two questions and lists two purposes. In both cases, the latter is the main question and purpose. The first are prerequisites of the last. We suggest that you always clearly indicate your main research question and purpose if several are included.

1. GOOD PAPERS IN HIGHER EDUCATION – GENRES AND QUALITY CRITERIA

Example 6: Paper in Teaching (Professional bachelor degree)

1. I wish to investigate how working with objectives and evaluations may upgrade Physical Education so it clearly comes across as an educational subject.

2. Furthermore, I wish to include the concepts cultivation and practical competences to discover whether including these may contribute to upgrade Physical Education further (the development of practical competences as an ideal of cultivation).

3.
- Evaluation report from "Idræt i skolen" [P.E. in school] from the Institute of Evaluations 2004
- Questionnaire: The significance of P.E. for boarding school students
- Experiences from own teacher training.

4.
Concepts:
- Objectives, evaluations, cultivation, practical competences

Theories:
- Mølgaard and Klausen: Evaluation theory
- Rønholt: Model for practical competences
- Klafki: Categorial cultivation

Methods:
- Quantitative questionnaire
- Analysis on the basis of theoretical concepts.

5.
1. Historical background
2. Questionnaire
3. Analyse evaluation report and questionnaires
4. Discuss results in light of central concepts (cultivation, practical competences, etc.)
5. Discuss the future of Physical Education and professional possibilities for action
6. Conclusion.

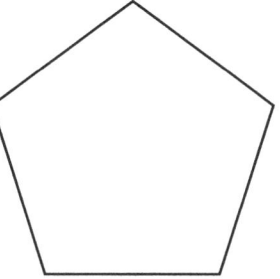

Comments: This is a really good paper where the pentagon has been filled out with relevant information. An objection could be that the paper lacks a precise definition of "upgrade" and "educational subject" which are central concepts in the research question and yet do not appear in the fourth corner. At times concepts appear to be implicitly understood in the paper. However, it is important that concepts are understood correctly and defined explicitly.

Especially in this type of paper, where the concepts are crucial to the research question.

Use the pentagon model

If you can write something relevant in each of the pentagon's corners to use as guiding principles in a paper, a project, etc., you are well on your way. If you are unsure of how to fill out a corner, at least you know what to look for. If you have no research question, data, method, etc., the first question is: Do I need it? What does my object of research dictate? What does my curriculum say? As an interpreter of the field, what does my supervisor say? For example, is it relevant to write about the paper's underlying philosophy of science?

The next question is: How do I find the missing elements for my research? From my supervisor? In the literature/data? Among my fellow students? In the project catalogue? From external projects? When working on papers and projects, one of the most important things is to conceive of realisable and interesting ways of conducting research; this is just as important as obtaining broad subject-specific knowledge.

As a student, you should take as your example good texts written by professionals: your teachers and their peers, who are experienced in conducting research, as well as good papers by previous students. Research papers, which you can find in peer-reviewed journals, are especially good examples of the genre. Texts by students must resemble these, but be of a smaller scope both in breadth and, as a rule, depth. In the rest of the book we will elaborate on the book's two keywords genre and research on the text's higher levels.

The good paper's quality criteria

Meeting the research requirements of your paper is one thing; but how do you carry out this task well?

A teacher's comments on a paper

The following is a teacher's comments on a literature paper written for Spanish at BA level.

> A paper with a *clear structure* and many good observations in *both form and content*. The fact that you test your *methodological skills* in this paper is good, and demonstrating that you have a *conceptual framework* and *subject-specific insight* for approaching your material is good as well. However, next time think more about prioritising: do not necessarily comment on all stylistic features, but focus on those that can *substantiate the analysis of content*, i.e. can *act as a premise for the overriding argument,* for example in your claim that the text illustrates the conditions of modern man. Here you could have *examined the connection between form and content:* I.e. why is this form used (fragmentation – breakdown)? Is this connected to the thematisation of the individual's loss of centre and identity and perhaps also to the mental breakdown you claim introduces the short story? And remember to *proof-read!*
>
> (Our italics)

The teacher's criteria are focus, structure, observations, methodical and academic argumentation and proof-reading. These are wholly expected, common and good criteria. The teacher takes as his starting point general requirements for research papers; the pentagon (see p. 32) and the paper as an argument, and finally the teacher assesses how the student manages these requirements ("clear structure", "good observations", "good that …", etc.). Moreover, the comment points ahead toward similar papers: "But next time think a bit more about …"

Rhetoric of science

It is remarkable that the qualities mentioned by the teacher are in no way specific to different subjects or fields. When asked, teachers in all kinds of higher education, for example, professional education programmes, mention the same textual qualities across disciplines. This is due to the fact that science rhetoric (the study of how to write/speak about science) are the same across the entire system of higher education, faculties and nations (in the West), and science rhetorical requirements are crucial to the way papers are assessed. Many students and teachers call for subject-specific instructions for writing papers. However, it is our experience that teachers often present general guidelines in the different fields. For instance, we once listened to five university teachers and one external examiner from the same field give a lecture on their field's "the good paper". Out of the three hours the presentation lasted, ten minutes were spent on subject-specific advice. The rest of the lecture could have applied to any other subject in higher education.

The next pages treat the research paper's most important quality criteria in more depth.

1. In the good paper, the writer is professional and displays independence

The question of how much of yourself to include in your paper always poses a problem. It is easy to err on either extreme.

Many students lose their motivation because they find the research paper genre too impersonal, and they cannot include themselves in it. Many receive feedback such as: "We have no interest in your subjective, personal or private views – the important thing is to present the views of the text". However, if you cannot relate to what or how you write, you will stop caring about your writing; as if you are separated and alienated from your paper.

Including too much of yourself in a paper is a typical problem for new students. For many graduate students the opposite is true. They collect heaps of documentation without daring to use or assess the material. Finding the proper balance consists in understanding that you should only avoid including your private person in papers. You are more than welcome to incorporate your professional self – in fact this is how to demonstrate independence. You are always welcome to present your evaluations, as long as these are prefaced or followed by valid, academic documentation. "I think/choose ..." (regarding the use of "I" in papers, see the section "Use of "I", active and passive", pp. 395f.). Academic reasoning and arguments clear the way for presenting your own opinions and evaluations in a legitimate fashion.

At times, you will be able to use your own experiences in papers (for example when writing a practicum report). However, like all material, personal experiences must be subjected to academic and methodical analysis. For this reason, including matters of a personal nature requires professional detachment as being too closely attached to your subject matter may lead to a limited analysis. In contrast, great detachment will lead to apathy and demotivation, especially when it comes to disciplines that deal with people and where the students expect to be personally involved. If you find a paper boring or irrelevant, increase your involvement by focusing on your own personal and professional interests where ever possible. Naturally, it is problematic if you consider the work and your paper completely irrelevant; if you do not question what you read; or if your paper does not enter into dialogue with your own common-sense opinions and evaluations. The student, who reputedly wrote that the Danish Great

Belt Bridge was 2 1/2 mm long, was neither reflective nor critical when he wrote his paper: he did not stop to ask himself whether his statement seemed likely based on a common-sense judgment.

> **Writers can become visible as professionals through**
>
> - their choice of topic and choice of philosophy of science, materials, sources, theories, methods, etc., based on the research question
> - their own decisions in treating the material: Problems, analyses, interpretations, conclusions, evaluations, perspectives and practical precepts
> - their own experiences etc., which can be used purely as illustrations or as objects of methodical analysis.
>
> Writers must not include themselves as:
> - private persons with personal interpretations and evaluations with no professional basis or personal experiences that have not been treated methodologically
> - a basis for generalisations.

Independence
As a writer, you show independence, *inter alia*, by selecting or combining different options, for example, methods, sources, points of view and in the way you do things, for example, by

- choosing
- controlling
- sorting
- applying
- analysing
- discussing
- proportioning
- prioritising
- evaluationg.

But you cannot achieve independence alone and without the assistance of others. Including your teachers, fellow students and other people who can contribute to improving your paper also constitutes independence.

2. The good paper *uses* the field's knowledge and tools

There is a crucial difference between papers that are predominantly knowledge-telling and knowledge-transforming. Roughly speaking, all research papers awarded the grade of C/[Danish grading scale 7] or better are to some extent knowledge-transforming. These terms were coined by the important American researchers, Bereiter & Scardamalia (1987). They characterise the two styles of writing as such:

Knowledge-telling papers	Knowledge-transforming papers
- are topic oriented - are narrative - relate *everything* known to their writers - consider the heading (topic) not the problem - chapters and/or sections are internally cohesive – there is no cohesion between chapters/sections/elements - are writer based.	- are purpose oriented - research a problem, analytical - are selective, treat information - relate to the problem as their point of departure - there is cohesion between the different elements - are reader oriented.

We often experience that students with a narrative style of writing end up having problems. These problems are typically related to the fields of history and languages. Students must keep in mind that retelling "stories" does not make for interesting material in higher education. The interesting thing is how these "stories" have come to be, whether their narrators are reliable and which status and significance they are ascribed by different agents; in short, different fields' construction of knowledge is what is interesting, rather than the actual content of a field. Being a good storyteller may prove to be an excellent skill for communicating the content of your field in the future, but papers and assignments are genres that cultivate selective purposiveness and problem orientation. For an example of a problem oriented, literature historical paper set up in the pentagon model, see p. 34.

Knowledge-telling papers remain close to their sources. In a research paper, however, the writer must *use* the sources and have a sensible purpose for including particular sources in a chosen context. At some point, descriptive papers must become more analytical or interpretative. Due to our experience with poor knowledge-telling papers, we place great emphasis on the research question. Knowledge-telling papers are essentially about "what the books say". These papers do not consider what the acquired knowledge can be used for in either the writer's field or the so-called real world. The knowledge-telling student will typically read too much and write too little, asking too few questions on the way. So, if you would like to write a paper that shows you are able to use elements from your field, the important thing is to base your work on questions such as:

- How do I analyse/interpret/challenge current understandings, evaluate or design new ways of acting in connection with x, by means of relevant elements (concepts, theories, methods)? And how do I subsequently analyse/interpret/evaluate these employed concepts, theories, methods, etc. from my field?

We will return to this in chapter 2 on the writing process, as this knowledge can encourage work processes which in turn encourage detachment to and intimacy with sources.

Knowledge production
Knowledge production is a third and higher level placed above both knowledge telling and knowledge transformation. It is important to be innovative when writing a PhD dissertation; although innovation is allowed in a master's thesis, it is not required – and it is certainly not a requirement when writing a bachelor's thesis. Knowledge production is always welcomed, but far from required. Many students demand too much of themselves – too early on.

3. The good paper is focused

Even in papers of 80-100 pages, there must only be one focus. A paper will never benefit from a scattered focus. In the same way that researchers' articles and theses do not focus on several subject-specific problems, a paper is expected to treat one topic, one problem and to be cohesive and coherent. If you do not stick to a single focus, you will quickly end in the text book genre, where several subject-specific foci can be included in one book. Let us imagine that you are set the assignment: "Give an account of x's historical development over the past few years". This paper could easily end up becoming unfocused. This is our advice: Create your own focus. Select a theme you wish to focus on and argue for and make it your central point: What could be a characteristic perspective on the particular development, which example is representative?

Generally, focusing, delimiting and making substantiated choices will pay off. Furthermore, working with narrower texts is easier. Broad knowledge is acquired through overview-reading, and is best demonstrated in written and oral exams. If you attempt to demonstrate broad knowledge in a paper, you will easily wind up in the textbook genre.

Poor papers (which have received low grades) are typically too wide-ranging and summarise without applying knowledge, facts, theory and methods. They also use textual elements without relating them to each other.

4. The good paper is "written" on the top of the taxonomies of educational objectives.

In the Danish system of education, two taxonomies are used in particular: John Bigg's SOLO-taxonomy and Benjamin Bloom's taxonomy of learning goals. These can act as guiding principles that ensure a paper's quality.

Both taxonomies set forth goals which higher education should strive to meet in terms of what needs to be taught and what exams are meant to assess. Moreover, the taxonomies form the basis of the quality criteria for many papers and assignments in different educations. It is important to know these taxonomies, because if your teacher or external examiner is at all familiar with the "system", they will be looking for the level on which to place each text (as well as evaluate the individual levels of your paper). We have added an extra step to Bloom's taxonomy, because *perspective* and *action* can be important objectives for a research paper. When it comes to papers, the perspective and action column should be added to the SOLO-taxonomy as well. It is important to emphasise that these levels do not indicate a paper's level of difficulty.

SOLO taxonomy (Structure of the Observed Learning Outcome)				
Prestructural	**Un-instructural**	**Multi-structural**	**Relational level**	**Extended abstract level**
Using irrelevant knowledge or answers, which make no sense.	Answers are focused on a single, relevant aspect.	Answers are focused on several relevant features, but no connections are made.	Different parts are integrated into a cohesive whole; individual parts are connected to conclusions; the meaning is understood.	Answers generalise the structure underlying existing information; a higher order of principles are used to include new and bigger questions.
• Not understanding the point	• Dentifying • Carrying out simple procedure	• Enumerating • Describing • Listing • Combining • Calculating algorithms	• Comparing • Contrasting • Explaining causality • Analysing • Relating • Applying	• Setting forth theories • Generalising • Setting forth hypotheses • Reflecting • Putting into perspective
(From Biggs & Tang, 2007)				

> **Bloom's Taxonomy of Educational Objectives**
>
> **Action**
> - Formulating norms/designs
> - Putting into perspective
>
> ↑
>
> **Evaluation**
> - Evaluating based on different criteria
>
> ↑
>
> **Synthesis**
> - Combining parts into a whole
> - Interpreting
>
> ↑
>
> **Analysis**
> - Breaking down into parts, separating
> - Noticing systems/structures
>
> ↑
>
> **Application**
> - Testing, using
>
> ↑
>
> **Comprehension**
> - Explaining with own words
>
> ↑
>
> **Knowledge**
> - Summarising, paraphrasing, accounting, describing
>
> (Adapted from Bloom, 1974 [1st ed. 1958])

With these taxonomies, it becomes clear that knowledge-telling is the most modest of learning goals. The levels more or less correspond to the academic text types (see pp. 315ff.).

The levels build on top of each other. It is impossible to imagine a well-written paper without a summarising section on which analyses are based (however, in many cases only a short summary is needed). A summary that is good, faithful, sufficient, but not too comprehensive is an essential cornerstone of any paper. But summaries are only included so they can be used later in the paper. Similarly, analyses are a prerequisite for evaluation etc.

Thus, when writing a paper your objective should be to place your text on the far right side in SOLO and as high up on Bloom's taxonomic ladder as possible at your particular level of study and as the material and project allows. However, adjustments must be made depending on your subject and field: The Humanities are based on interpretation, discussion and perspectives, while papers in Engineering, Natural and Social Science often include concrete designs, which are also an obvious part of pedagogical, health and tech(design/construction) papers.

At a general level, this means your research question should be as taxonomically advanced as is possible in your field and given your subject and material. At a secondary level, this means the material and sources you include should not just be described, but must be commented, analysed, interpreted, evaluated or used for new solutions – at least with respect to the paper's most important sources.

In practice, the best research papers always contain a lot of material which as a minimum is placed on the level of use/analysis. Poor and failing papers almost always contain too much summary material, and if evaluation is included, it will be subjective and not made on the basis of predetermined and academically accepted criteria.

To practice and demonstrate advanced qualifications when writing your paper, you must be relentless in reducing the amount of summary material you may be tempted to include.

In practice, this knowledge can be converted into this advice:

Do this to write a better paper	
Maximise text where you: • select and substantiate choices • use concepts, models/theories for your own purposes • analyse, interpret – specific material is a good thing • discuss • combine, compare, conclude, put into perspective • evaluate other's/your own text • design, formulate specifications, describe solutions.	Minimise text where you: • describe • paraphrase • summarise.

5. The good paper is an argument

Research consists of questions and answers, and takes on the form of an argument: The paper constitutes an argument for the conclusion. All research is based on a question the researcher, or the student, wants answered, and papers pose questions and document answers. The answer, or the conclusion, is an argument. The explicitness of the argumentation varies, but argumentation and documentation are an integral part of producing a text that researches, asks and answers. Arguing for an overriding point (conclusion) is a feature of the genre, see "What should your paper argue for" p. 352.

Argumentation is an important and crucial theme in all textbooks on writing papers known to us. Therefore, we have also dedicated an entire chapter to argumentation in papers (chapter 12).

6. The good paper is critical of its own material, its field and of itself

The purpose of writing papers is to motivate students to identify more with their discipline. The good research paper must be the students' attempt to work as a professional and as a researcher; not just to document subject-specific knowledge. It is important that students consider whether the information they include in their

papers is not merely disciplinary, but also true. Furthermore, the students must consider how much importance and priority they wish to assign each bit of information. This is not done by simply using the material, but by
- evaluating the claims of your sources and their foundation
- evaluating your own selection of data
- evaluating the system and method behind the of collection and processing of your own and your sources' data (see chapter 8 on the inclusion and evaluation of sources).

In practice, we see that really good papers comment on concepts, theories and methods (both its own and other's), criticise sources and especially substantiate every choice the writer makes.

7. The good paper communicates on a meta level

The good paper metacommunicates to the reader, i.e., the writer conveys
- what he/she does
- why
- how
- and in this way establishes cohesion between the paper's separate parts.

Metacommunication demonstrates that each of the paper's parts are connected and that the writer has a good grasp of disciplinary connections and is capable of conveying this to the reader. Thus metacommunication has several functions (Stray Jørgensen, 2001):

Metacommunication
- demonstrates how the writer relates to the field (research)
- signals to the reader how information is to be understood and thus provides an overview
- includes a "self-pedagogical" function as the use of metacommunication forces the writer to consider and decide what to use information for and thereby avoid merely describing, reproducing or narrating.

We will consider this in more depth in chapter 13 on the language of a paper.

8. The good paper meets the curriculum's parameters

The previous quality criteria are all global: They apply to all research papers. But the individual paper is written against the backdrop of a concrete curriculum, which furthermore is "administered" by a teacher and/or supervisor.

At different educational institutions, scholarliness and genre make general demands on research papers. In addition, papers include an educational aspect. You will write many papers while studying because by doing so you will learn to

- prepare and carry out a research design under supervision, thereby learning how to
- evaluate sources and research by employing and including sources in your own work
- practice applying methods and theories to material
- write professionally.

In Denmark, the aim of making students write so many papers is research-based education in which students try their hand at research in the form of student-(mini)-research. The intention is also to develop proficiency in academic writing, which can only be learnt by practicing.

Read your curriculum
When your work is assessed, you should always find out what your curriculum says about the knowledge, skill, qualifications and competencies you are expected to demonstrate in a given exam. The curriculum will describe the learning goals or competencies that are to be gained from each paper and the work involved. These could be presented as such

- analysing (the most common competency mentioned in curriculums at all levels of study)
- discussing
- measuring, calculating
- being critical
- substantiating
- reflecting
- posing research questions
- evaluating
- being aware of, knowing, being able to, designing, constructing, innovating.

You must acquaint yourself with the local terminology, so you understand what your supervisor tells you. Consult your supervisor. Also, you should take a look at good papers written by previous students. This can give you a sense of the texts on your level of study and of how you can benefit from the academic qualifications and competencies gained from writing the paper in question.

Examples of qualities in bachelor theses

The following examples are taken from the first page of different theses. Usually you will be able to identify the papers qualities, or at least the paper's expected qualities, from the first few pages. The first three examples were awarded high marks; the fourth was given a low mark, but still passed. The last example is an abstract, which nevertheless reveals qualities of the paper. All these examples demonstrate how the quality criteria described earlier are used.

1. The Translated Laugh – Calvin & Hobbes – a case study

(Bachelor thesis, English, top mark)

1. Introduction

Half a year ago I discussed with a friend whether or not the Danish version of Calvin & Hobbes was a good translation. To my great surprise he claimed that the Danish version was more amusing than the original American. I have wondered since if this could be true and now the possibility of researching the matter more closely has arisen. In doing so I have discovered that many more questions come to the surface: what is humour? how is humour translated? what restrictions or privileges does the comic strip offer?

The purpose of the paper is not to thoroughly examine a Calvin and Hobbes album for translation mistakes but to suggest an appropriate strategy for conquering the typical hurdles of translating a humorous comic strip. The strategy presupposes that a translator's most important tool is to be able to identify the functions of the comic strip and the functions of humour.

Translation theory, humour theory and comic strip theory have provided the necessary background. An important part of this paper is to highlight their functional use for the translation process. The benefit of a cross-disciplinary paper is that each individual area which has been researched in great depth, in unity, brings to light new perspectives regarding translation.

The appendix of Calvin and Hobbes comic strips and their translations provides the paper with concrete exemplification. Three professional translators have been asked to translate four chosen Calvin & Hobbes comic strips and answer questions related to the process of having done so. The results of this exercise serve to verify the argumentation presented in the paper.

First of all, I will locate those aspects of the comic strip which have an impact on the translation process such as author, form, structure, readership and macro and microcosmos in order that the aforementioned restrictions and privileges can be defined. A paragraph on image and text cooperation has been included so as bring focus on an otherwise overlooked aspect in the translation of polysemiotic texts. Consequently, I will delineate a set of proposed strategies which form the basis of the subsequent discussion. The discussion draws on a comparison between source and target text, examples which appear in the appendix, and on contributions from theorists within the three areas. The examples have been chosen for their representative value of the authorship and according to their humorous diversity. In the final part of the paper I will evaluate the proposed strategies as to their potential in translating humorous comic strips.

• •

Our comments:
- The first pages of this paper set the scene for focused research of a problem based on observation/surprise.
- All the corners of the pentagon have been included (research question, purpose, object, theories/methods, procedure).
- The paper constitutes an argument.
- The paper is knowledge-transforming.
- Theories are selected according to their function, i.e., chosen on the basis of the research.
- The paper aims for the taxonomies' higher levels. This is demonstrated by the fact that the paper largely consists of the writer's own analyses, and it will end by *suggesting an appropriate strategy.*
- There is a clear structure (the following text types are mentioned: *locate, define, bring focus, propose strategies, discuss, evaluate*).

An outside reader will not be able to assess whether the elements are well chosen in regards to their connection to each other: Have relevant theories/methods for treating Calvin & Hobbes comics and the particular research question been chosen? Does the argument itself constitute a reasonable conclusion? Only professionals can assess the content. However, the presence of these different elements informs the reader that the basic understanding of genre is spot-on.

••

2. The Chinese Postman Revisited

(Bachelor thesis, geography, high mark)

Introduction

0.1 Problem

A classic problem in graph theory, widely known as the Chinese Postman Problem[1], is the challenge of planning a least-cost route traversing all edges in a network at least once [2] [9]. In reality it is not that simple. There are, of course, multiple postmen who must divide the road network into routes of similar impedance based on criteria such as physical length, types of dwellings, amount of mail etc.

While the Danish national mail company PostDanmark is showing signs of moving away from its image as a state monopoly behemoth and embracing new technology like GIS[2], the mail route planning is taken care of by middle management and experienced mailmen, who cooperate to divide the road network into routes. Apart from being somewhat random, the procedure builds to a great extent upon the knowledge of employees, knowledge which cannot be supposed to be invariable (experienced employees have a tendency to retire).

Therefore, it would seem that there is a basis for developing a method of GIS-assisted route planning that, while heuristic, will be more precise and stable than the trial-and-error method used today.

0.2 Methodology

I plan to use the postal district 2400 NV in Copenhagen as a case study and benchmark for my results, since I myself have delivered mail in the area, and thus feel fit to judge the usefulness of the routes computed. Data to be used are road network (DAV), types of dwellings (BBR/VAP). Other factors affecting the mail delivery, such as distance and mail quantity, will also be considered. Impedances will be assigned to network edges following a weighting of the different factors. Then, edges can be grouped into routes, each of which has to satisfy a number of demands such as being somewhat continuous and of suitable size.

1. so called because it was first formalized in 1962 by Chinese mathematician Mei-Ko Kwan [9].
2. See for example http://www.postdanmark.dk/postkassen

••

Page 1 shows that
- the paper promises to design a foundation for GIS-assisted route planning based on an observation of a problem, i.e., the paper's purpose is problem solving/designs/construction
- all corners of the pentagon are represented

- the paper is knowledge-transforming: The writer personally calculates routes in his former postal district on the basis of the presented methods and variables.

In this kind of paper, method, systematism and calculations are important quality parameters. It is a paper based in the natural sciences and actual theory is absent, however, the paper includes "graph theory".

3. Can Volatility in Stock Markets Be Predicted Using a Statistical Model?

(BA level, Economics, high mark)

1. Introduction

Over the years, there have been many attempts to establish statistical models for the development in yields of various financial assets, mainly stocks. However, in accordance with the hypothesis about efficient markets, it has only proven possible to predict an infinitesimal proportion of future yields, which in turn has limited the applicability of such models.

Apart from yields, the variance of yields, also known as volatility, is an important aspect of a financial asset. This factor is interesting because volatility can be interpreted as a risk and is thereby crucial to risk-averse investors, facing a trade-off between yields and risk. Being familiar with volatility is thus relevant in many contexts in the financial sector, as investment decisions, where the size of future yields is uncertain, are constantly being made. Moreover, volatility constitutes a central element in risk assessment, which for example is used in connection with portfolio control. Furthermore, future volatility is essential for price fixing options, which is an increasingly used financial instrument, and whose value is directly related to the volatility of its underlying asset – typically in form of shares.

Since 1963, it has been a known fact that volatility in the stock market is not constant, but that the stock market experiences both turbulent and stable periods. The question is then whether volatility, unlike yields, can be predicted. This is the topic of this paper.

Provided that volatility is predictable, it will not clash with the efficient market hypothesis. This means there should be more reason to expect that volatility can be predicted in relation to future yields.

Research question/Structure and delimitation of the paper

Can volatility in stock markets be predicted using a statistical model?

In order to answer the above research question, I will base this paper on ARCH-models; a popular group of volatility models. Because of the limited scope of this paper, I have chosen to place main emphasis on the theory, but I will continuously shift between data and theory. However, this is mainly done to underline the theory's relevance to reality.

I will start by briefly explaining the idea behind the ARCH-models in order to provide an overview of the subject. Then I will describe characteristics of data of yield on shares, taking data from the stock market as my starting point. This is done to demonstrate why volatility to some degree can be predicted, but also to show what a good volatility model should take into account.

Then I will demonstrate how the ARCH-model is technically constructed and how it can be generalised for the more practicable GARCH-model. In order to evaluate the GARCH-model's ability to make predictions in practice and its underlying assumptions, I will assess the model for a number of share indexes to obtain results for comparison. In conclusion, I will consider a possible expansion of the GARCH-model as well as present examples of appropriate areas of application.

••

The first pages of this paper show that
- the subject-specific problem and its relevance are described in clear terms
- the aim of the research is made clear
- all corners of the pentagon are represented
- the description of the research procedure is aimed at application (for example, the student has written "in order to" four times)
- field terms are introduced and explained.

Although the text may be incomprehensible for people without an understanding of economics, it is still clear that the student has included the proper elements, uses subject-specific tools and structures and designs his paper appropriately.

••

4. Mozart's life

(1-week assignment, BA level, Music, low mark)

Introduction

In this paper I will describe the life of Wolfgang Amadeus Mozart and his career as an opera composer.

Then I will write about some of the composers who influenced Mozart. I will then describe the opera genres Mozart composed and whether any development occurs in his choice of genres. Based on this I will shed light on his characteristics and significance as an opera composer.

The life and career of Wolfgang Amadeus

The Mozarts

Wolfgang Amadeus Mozart was born in 1756. He came from a family with a great interest in music. Wolfgang's father, Leopold Mozart was a composer and taught Wolfgang Mozart and his sister Maria Anna. Mozart's father relates how Mozart learned to play his first piano pieces when he was four[1] and wrote his first compositions at age five.

The family lived in Salzburg, but Leopold traveled extensively with his two children and showcased their talents. These travels are documented in the father's diaries and the letters he sent to his mother.[2]

Wolfgang Mozart's career as an opera composer

In 1767 W.A. Mozart wrote his first dramatic piece (Apollo et Hyacinthus). A couple of years later, the piece received high praise from an English philosopher, who described how the emotional level of Mozart's compositions was very well-developed despite Mozart only being 11 years old at the time.

Leopold continued to take his son traveling. He wanted the now 12-year-old Wolfgang Mozart to compose an opera for the carnival in Vienna. Here Mozart wrote his first opera (*La finta semplice*); however it proved to be in vain. The opera was not performed and they had to return home.

1. Gad's Musikhistorie, p. 332
2. The New Grove Mozart, p. 1 and 3

• •

This is a first-year paper and was awarded a pass mark, albeit a low one. It is an example of a poor paper.

On page 1, we see that:
- There is no problem.
- There is no focus but several unrelated research questions.
- The paper presents a knowledge-telling approach on the lower levels of the taxonomies: describing, telling, illustrating as well as sections that are not interrelated.
- There is no theory/concept/method.
- There are no possibilities for analysis or knowledge-transformation.

- The sources used are encyclopedias. This may be acceptable in a first-year paper, but after the first year, it is expected that at least one academic reference is mentioned on the first page.

The paper could have reached a higher level by
- focusing – for example by concentrating on "genre development" and not including the reception and appraisal of Mozart (his significance, etc.)
- including the pentagon's concept/theory corner. For example *development* could function as the basis for a theory section. There must be theorists who define the concept of musical composers' *genre development*, for example, by finding disciplinary answers to questions such as:
  - How is the concept of composers' *development* understood in the field of music?
  - How does Mozart's genre development manifest itself in selected operas used as points of reference in the argumentation?
  - How is genre development analysed?
  - How can the development in Mozart's lifework be evaluated?

In this way, the paper would have moved away from being predominantly summarising and become more analytical/evaluating on the basis of theory. This would have heightened the level. Presumably this paper passed because it was written in the first year. However, in later years of study, the requirement for knowledge-transformation is not easily avoided.

The criteria for good papers are not all equally important. General criteria (content, focus, knowledge-transformation, argumentation) are considered more important than formalities and linguistic correctness and elegance. Assessing texts – which are not measurable entities – is always a question of overall evaluation and deliberation.

· ·

5. MR-protocols when scanning the cerebrum for multiple sclerosis – clinical practice and theoretical basis

(Bachelor thesis in radiography, high mark)

Abstract

The basis of this project is an interest in the application of different MR-protocols when scanning the cerebrum for multiple sclerosis (MS).

<u>Research question:</u>
How do clinical wards' MR-protocols differ in the scanning of cerebrum for DS?

Why do the sequences applied in clinical practice affect the picture quality in DS-scanning of the cerebrum?

What does the research recommend in regards to the composition of the MR-protocol used when scanning the cerebrum for DS?

Method:
A positivistic and quantitative method is applied.

Information is partly collected from 12 clinical wards from different regions of the country and partly found through literature searches and studies of subject-specific, relevant literature and research papers.

Conclusion:
Differences in MR-protocols consist of sequence types, the number of sequences, body planes and the application of I.V.-contrast.

Because they are constructed to highlight or suppress certain types of tissue, the sequences employed affect the picture quality. Therefore, different sequences will result in differences in picture quality.

Research-based recommendations focus on consistency in the composition of MR-protocols. A standard protocol when scanning the cerebrum for DS is recommended. In addition, a uniform positioning of patients is recommended for first time scans and subsequent control scans.

••

This abstract contains all the following information ensuring the reader is given a concrete and precise overview of the paper:
- The paper's point of departure (surprise)
- The research question, which consists of three questions. The first two are prerequisites for the latter which constitutes the overriding research question
- Data and method (and the underlying background research (theory))
- Conclusion and recommendations that constitute the actual answer to the research question
- The main content of the paper
- All corners of the pentagon are represented.

We are dealing with an abstract, which means the information presented here will be of a more general nature than information in an introduction. It is unusual for an abstract to be divided under headings, but it provides clarity.

Nuances?

Are your ideals different than the ones presented here? In that case, writing down your ideals and discussing them with your supervisors, fellow students and examiners would be a good idea.

Do your examiners have other ideals? Ask them about their role models and read your curriculum's description of the paper in question. It is our impression that the research paper or term paper is a global and stable genre throughout the Western world. Research and documentation must still be carried out, and this is what the old-fashioned research paper does best.

If the individual writer demonstrates his knowledge of the conventions, he can also challenge the limits (for example, by using speech acts that are not among the "accepted"). These are not merely conventions, but textual attitudes necessitated by the conditions of research. You must therefore be familiar with the conventions and your examiner must be certain that you know them. If this is the case, you can play around with them and go beyond their limits. In the end, all communication is about showing what you know and what the recipient in question allows the sender.

The different purposes and ideals of the Anglo-American and Continental research traditions

Distinguishing between research texts' different purposes is important, as these differences may strongly affect the way students write their papers. There are a number of different research traditions.

In Western academia there are two significant, and principally different, ways of writing. Firstly, there is the Anglo-American research tradition (problem based, often data-based) secondly the Continental (Romano-Germanic) research tradition (theory or theorist based, or data based with no or a small extent of problematisation). The Anglo-American tradition is predominant in subjects dealing with facts and concrete matters, such as the natural, tech, medical and social sciences as well as psychology, linguistics and social scientific disciplines within any field. The Continental tradition is associated with subjects such as aesthetics, philosophy, history of ideas (and culture), i.e. subjects that interpret cultural, aesthetic, religious and philosophical concepts and which are concerned with the theorists behind these concepts. However, the Continental research tradition also applies to fact-based disciplines such as archaeology and can be found in the field of pedagogy, which forms part of a number of programmes in higher education. In general, the Anglo-American research tradition is gaining ground, also in the humanities.

These different ways of writing reflect the fact that scientific and scholarly texts can serve different purposes. There is a distinction between

- the *epistemic* purposes of the hard disciplines, i.e. creating/producing new knowledge and solving problems
- the *epideictic* purposes of the soft (especially humanist) disciplines, which point to, emphasise and underline the value of existing conditions (phenomena).

One of the epideictic tasks of the humanities is to point to and preserve culture by continuously writing and displaying it etc. without necessarily problematising it every time. Epideictic papers are written in soft disciplines, where many consider words like problem, method and linguistic economy etc. unfamiliar.

In the Anglo-American (problem-based, empirical) tradition, typical research questions are:

- With which method can we best research phenomenon X?
- How can phenomenon X be interpreted by means of concept/theory Y? (I.e. focus is on the phenomenon and not the theory)
- How can the problem be solved using X?
- How can X be constructed, created?
- How can X be treated?

In the Continental (theory and theorist based or empirical with a lesser degree of problematisation) tradition, typical research questions are:

- What does concept/theory X actually mean?
- What and who has inspired and influenced theorist X and in which direction?
- How does theorist X's influence on others manifest itself?
- A biography or monograph of X
- X seen in light of Y or in combination with Y
- The historical development of X
- An interpretation or reading of X.

Continental papers are more expository and interpretative in comparison with Anglo-American research papers and focus on a concept, theory, work or theorist and often do not include a problem. In Denmark, Continental papers are often written about the major (and especially) Continental figures such as Bourdieu, Giddens, Foucault, Lave & Wenger, Habermas, Luhmann, Beck, Kierkegaard, Freud, Barthes, Eco, Lacan, Derrida, Heidegger and a countless number of other philosophers, theologians, psychoanalysts, cultural theorists and sociologists and their theories.

There is thus a connection between research traditions (rather than nations and fields) and writing conventions. Research traditions are cultivated in disciplinary environments. Therefore, texts and ideals may vary. We advise that you:
- Be aware of which tradition your sources, your supervisor and you belong to and
- Be aware of obeying the particular writing conventions and how to do so.

Typical features of the two traditions are listed below:

Research traditions ←——— "a continuum" ———→	
Continental (Romano-Germanic) research tradition	**Anglo-American research tradition**
- Philosophy, history of ideas, epistemology, culture	- Facts, observable conditions, data
- The arts	- Academic "craft"
- Essays	- Investigative texts
- Philosophising essays, textbooks, monographs	- Research paper
- Concepts, theories	- Methods
- Culture-bearing, historical tradition	- New understandings and actions
- Gradual "erkenntnis"	- Guided, goal-oriented cognition
- Sources constitute the point of departure	- Problems constitute the point of departure
- Many points, covering the topic, width	- One point, one focus, one claim, narrowness
- Often non-linear structure with digresssions	- Linear structure
- Requires systematism in the writing process.	- Requires posing a research question early in the writing process.

It is here made evident that this book is based in the Anglo-American research tradition.

Roughly put, the most important difference is that the *writer* alone is responsible for intelligibility of the text in the Anglo-American tradition (reader or receiver oriented), while the Continental research tradition places all responsibility for understanding the content on the *reader*, who is expected to either keep up with the writer or be left behind. The ideals of Anglo-American research, texts and language are clarity, precision, transparency and linearity (writing "one thing at a time", textual development).

So, if you think science and research is difficult, abstract, theoretical and full of digressions, you are probably thinking of Continental science.

These two opposing ideals necessarily lead to very different texts and writing and research processes. This forms a continuum: many texts and many researchers place themselves between the two extremes or vary between different ways of writing and researching depending on the topic and on whether they can write continentally. This is the real challenge; if you are not sufficiently ingrained in a specific writing tradition, there is a big chance you may fall through. But if you are up to the challenge, you should just get started; everyone has to begin somewhere.

Textual ideals reflect the purpose of the text down to word level. Teachers in higher education are carriers of these different ideals; they each work very differently and for different purposes. All you can do is consult them; establish your own direction based on your papers' purposes and then stick to the supervisors that can teach you what you want to learn, also as a writer.

Advice to students writing in the Continental tradition

Our experience shows that it is harder for students to write in the Continental tradition than in the Anglo-American. Students writing in the Continental tradition often encounter genre-related problems. Many Continental primary texts belong to the genre of philosophising, reflective essays. However, these texts were published as books; they were never handed in and assessed at a university. In contrast, many Anglo-American publications were written as a direct step in furthering academic qualifications and therefore obey all academic conventions, such as, documentation, methodological procedures or explicit method specifications, unequivocal concepts and concept application, unambiguous, non-associative language and a general intersubjective controllability. Using the language of argumentation (see chapter 12), many

Continental texts contain interesting and broad claims; however, their weakness is often related to documentation and method. Of course, these sources should be read and discussed, but with critical detachment.

Many of the Continental texts treated by students and researchers are not university texts. Therefore, it may be worth considering writing in a different genre than the primary Continental texts, as it is common to be influenced by the genres you read. It is important to remember that reflective, academic essays is one of the hardest genres to master, and in our experience, the genre is mainly suitable for fully qualified academics and less suitable for students. Our advice to Continental writers can be found below:

If you choose to write in the Continental tradition …

- Use your supervisor as much as possible and read his/her texts. Writing style will usually be inspired by the theorists you have chosen, and you should therefore study the discourse of the given field. For this reason, it is especially important to be in close, professional contact with your supervisor.
- Consider writing about Continental subject matter in an Anglo-American format. I.e., basing your research on a clear problem.
- Be aware of your reading material's genre and which genre your paper should be in (see the genre-forest on p. 30).
- Never let your sources seduce you to write claims without documentation, eschew being critical of a statement's basis, include everything about a topic without discernment, include content without structure, use introspection as a principal method (unless the curriculum asks you to), employ associative writing, ambiguity, metaphors or jargon. Professors can perhaps get away with this, but students rarely will!
- Think and discuss with your supervisor how you can keep an appropriate linguistic distance to your sources; this proves harder when writing in the Continental tradition.
- Under all circumstances, remember that you are not meant to write like the theorists you are writing about.

2. Writing processes of research papers

As we discussed in chapter 1, it is crucial that research papers demonstrate knowledge-transformation and argumentation. This chapter describes how you can keep these aspects in mind throughout the writing process; from choosing your topic to placing the last comma. This chapter is mainly concerned with the independent, research paper. Instructions on how to approach essays are presented in the next chapter.

Choice of topic

Many find it hard to come up with a good topic, especially for dissertations and other large assignments. We often hear people say they need to feel "passion for it". One way of discovering where your passions lie is by looking at a whole slew of topics. You might

- run through a catalogue of papers and theses from your field – these may often be found at the library
- go through a thesaurus listing topics from the articles of your field. A thesaurus is an organised list of words, terms, concepts and the relationship between these.

Every time you come across a topic that makes you think: "If only this were my topic" or which sparks the slightest interest, you should write it down. Continue doing this to establish which patterns and reoccurring themes appear in the things that interest you. From this you can construct one or more topics or titles that might hold your interest.

Your interest in the topic

Having an interest in the topic you are writing on is usually conducive to the writing process. At any rate, being strongly motivated is a good thing. Writing from a "point of privilege", i.e. from having special access to particular knowledge (on the basis of personal experience etc.) will serve as impetus.

However, being passionate about the topic is not a condition for writing a good paper, but do try focusing on the aspect of the topic you find most interesting, controversial, least researched, etc. If you have no ideas, you can

- ask you supervisor for ideas
- read papers from you field
- look into whether your teachers offer topics from their own area of research.

The useful topic

Some programmes have "science shops" offering projects ordered by external partners for example from the business world or public institutions. Working as an "employee" on this kind of project can be exciting, challenging and educational. Some students delight in writing a project that is useful to others than themselves.

The good topic

To find out whether the topic of your research paper or thesis is viable ask the following check questions:

Activity: Check your topic

- Can you identify a subject-specific problem?
- Is there neither too much nor too little material?
- Can you build on others' work?
- Can you analyse or discuss on the basis of others' work?
- Can you find a procedure for carrying out the research?
- Do you know how to fill out all the corners of the pentagon (see p. 32)?
- Can someone within or outside your field make use of your results/conclusions?
- Does your teacher understand your project (preferably on the basis of your first talk)?

You do not have to answer all the questions, but if your answer is no more often than yes, you should consider finding a different topic.

Activity: Talk to your teacher/supervisor and fellow students about possible ideas for a topic

Theoretical, abstract or concrete topics?

It is difficult to write about purely theoretical topics! The material of theoretical papers is the subject area's existing theories, models and methods which can be compared, opposed, combined, refined, developed, problematised, etc. Theoretical topics may seem alluring, because all the material you need is contained in a few books, which will easily fit on your desk, and you can get to work without even leaving your chair. However, it is not that simple. It appears that writing about a topic that can be concretised is easier. A concrete topic is often based on data or deals with a phenomenon that can be concretised and which you can apply theories to (for as you know, theory and method must be included).

After choosing a topic, the first thing you should do is write

When starting a paper, you can either begin by writing down what you already know or believe about your chosen topic or you can start by reading plenty of literature. It is always best if you have something to write about from day one (and you always will, as you can begin by explaining why you have chosen your particular topic).

You have started writing, yes, but what?

It is important to start writing *independently*. Therefore, we suggest that you immediately start writing on the basis of your approach to the topic, your points of view and your own ideas.

> **Activity: What parts of your paper can you write on the first day?**
>
> - Write about your motivation (as background) and what sparked your interest in the topic
> - Write about the most interesting aspect of your paper
> - Outline the principal argumentation: What are you arguing for? What objections could be made against your arguments? What documentation is there or could there be imagined for these objections? (See chapter 12 on argumentation)
> - Write down what you would like to change or develop
> - Write down at least one – preferably, more – good examples. Examples are the best way to make data concrete and there is nothing more illustrative in the introductory description of the problem or more suitable as material for analysis as using examples

- Write down your factual knowledge: What do you already know about the topic?
- Write down any prejudices you may have about the field
- Suggest
  - data
  - method
  - key concepts
  - theory
  - a framework within a philosophy of science
  - delimitations
  - perspectives.
- (Temporarily) define the way you use important concepts
- Begin by writing a draft of your introduction or conclusion (see chapter 11 for templates for introductions and conclusions): The introduction because it includes the guiding principles in your area of research; the why and how, questions those are good to consider throughout the writing process. The conclusion because you often have it in mind already at the beginning of the writing process
- Write a list of keywords of central themes, dimensions, persons and parameters, etc.

Finish the sentence: "What I really want to say is …".

Several of these points can be written in a single day and end up in the finished paper (though presumably in a more complete and polished form). They could be included in the paper as an introductory "problem and phenomenon description", which does not have to be lengthy, but can be written and completed immediately after choosing a topic.

Write before and while you read

As a starting point, the first thing you write will not end up in the paper; it will be used to determine what to ask from the literature or what the data is meant to answer. The writing process can begin immediately after you have chosen your topic. You can even go as far as to make it a rule not to read anything before you have written down what you already know about the topic and your head has been emptied of any knowledge of the topic. So:

- Write as much as you can, before searching for literature and reading.

Your purpose for writing in the beginning is
- to question the literature, in order to be more equipped to choose relevant literature
- to put the basis of your original interest in the topic in writing: What do you want to know/learn? (Your original interest may change, but this is absolutely fine)
- to immediately start writing and drafting potential text sections, so these are ready – for yourself or for supervision (the further you have come in your studies, the more likely this is to be a real possibility)
- to discover possible research questions.

Preliminary research questions constitute the first important stopping point or intermediate goal of the process. Without these, you are more likely to become lost in the large amounts of information. Regardless of whether you start work on your paper by writing or reading, you should never stop searching for a suitable research question. However, the best way of finding a research question is often through writing – but you should not for that reason consider the research question a condition for being "allowed" to write. It is a good idea to write down different research questions every day until you have one or more to base your reading and writing on. Your research question can be changed until the day your paper is due. But begin the writing process with questions you want your reading to answer immediately.

You should also be aware that, in some fields, your research question must be approved by your supervisor or some other authority. This will appear in the curriculum, or you may ask.

Your paper should guide what you read, not the other way round: you should read material that can help you answer your research question. Furthermore, you should not read without writing. While you read or during breaks between reading, write down points that are of interest and use to your paper.

So, when should you stop writing on the basis of what you already know? You should stop when you start repeating yourself and going round in circles – when you have reached this stage it is time to include new knowledge.

We return to how you can work with your research question in chapter 4.

Write backwards – start with the conclusion

If you already have an idea of what your conclusion will be, it can be a good idea to write it first and thus write your text backwards, so to speak: Which documentation will I need to come to this conclusion? Naturally, this requires that you are not restricted by anything you have written earlier and that you are completely willing to scrap what you have written if it turns out that the material does not support the conclusion. It is guaranteed that you will have to rewrite your conclusion and introduction in the end, but you can still write good drafts of these sections from the very first day, although they will need to be continuously revised.

Begin with the central aspects

Another good idea is starting with what is central to the problem area and basing your paper on this. When you have written down the most central and crucial points, you should ask yourself: "When I've presented this analysis or argument, what must the reader be introduced to in order for the central points to be understood in their proper context?"

All paper's documentation must be part of the conclusion, i.e., part of the argument for accepting or rejecting one or more views, etc. Writing about something that is directly pertinent to your paper's conclusion will often provide you with the best direction.

Put off in depth studies of theory and history, summaries and descriptions

Beginning your paper by writing about theory and history will rarely pay off. These sections are the hardest and require the most preparation to write. In practice, these are the parts that are most likely to bring you to a standstill when writing. If you start with conditions and documentation, you will end up treating these in relation to their later function in analysing and arguing. If you believe the first chapters of the paper (especially chapters on prerequisites and literary reviews) also should be written first, you will have to postpone writing actual coherent text until you have read most or all of your literature. And this will cause you problems!

It is possible to get started on your paper quickly and still write usable text as long as you are willing to

- start where your material allows you
- start anywhere in the text
- work on the same text later, when you have acquired more knowledge.

You should not write summaries and descriptions before you know what you will be using them for, i.e. when you have written the main sections of which the summaries and descriptions are a part. The key characteristic of a good summary or description is selectivity; identifying what is important. This is only possible if you know which context they are to be a part of, for example causal analysis, argumentation, interpretation, evaluation. As we already mentioned, you should generally consider summaries and descriptions to be "subordinate" material, which should only be included if absolutely necessary or pertinent to the paper's purpose. First and foremost, you should focus on knowledge-transforming and independent material.

Research paper design

- It is a problem that … (point of departure, "initiator").
- It especially constitutes a problem for … (who does it concern?).
- It should be used by … for … (who is meant to use it and for what in which situation?).
- The problem is caused by … (possible causes).
- Therefore I will … (your aim: You wish to research, find an explanation for, interpret, analyse, discuss, create designs …).
- I wish to study this material … (data).
- I wish to research the problem in this way … (method).
- Important words and concepts are … (concept definitions).
- I understand the problem on the basis of … (theories).
- I will only include … because … (delimitation).
- I will only treat the topic in light of this … (point of view).
- At this point I imagine the following structure of sections … (content and structure).

Write as much as you can. In a meeting with your supervisor this outline can form the point of departure even if you have not filled out all the points.

The goal is not to present your supervisor with a finished product, but rather to initiate a dialogue on the basis of something written by you.

Be flexible when writing

Much research has been carried out on students' writing processes. In the box below we present the most important findings of this research.

> **"The research corner" – empirical research findings about research writing processes**
>
> - Most writers work recursively rather than in phases
> - Notes that process (ask, comment) make for good papers
> - Structuring your paper before writing a rough draft is just as effective as structuring it while drafting
> - Writers who produce several drafts are better prepared for writing large papers
> - Before finishing their papers, good writers know and consider the target group's criteria for good writing
> - Receiving good feedback before your deadline is the most effective learning method.
>
> (For example, Hyland, 2002; Bereiter & Scardamalia, 1987)

Writing and reading seldom takes place in as orderly and linear a fashion as it appears on paper. You will often have to go "back" and revise an earlier step once you have reached a more informed level. Similarly, very few people will move directly from drafting to revising – rather alternating between producing new text and revising is very common and known as a "recursive process". You write a text that makes you think and learn (research) something new and this enables you to write more. One rule of thumb is: The longer your text, the more revising it will require.

More revisions?

While some consider any text incomplete until it has been handed in, others would rather come as close as possible to finishing their paper first time round.

At a number of writing courses, we asked the people who write several drafts and the people who only write one draft, respectively, to put up their hands. There is always a small group of people who only write a single draft (usually less than a third, depending on the field: the more tech the field, the more single-draft writers) and who then merely revise words, characters and layout. These people often tell us that the longer the text becomes the harder being a single-draft writer becomes. Writing a 10-page paper poses no problems, but it becomes nearly impossible when writing a 100-page thesis. This is also why research into textual revision shows that the more skilled writers are, the more they revise.

Being a single-draft writer requires that you have planned your entire text before writing it. Only a few are able to do this and most people are wise to expect that a text will always require several rewritings. Writing 60 pages for a 20-page paper is perfectly normal.

Above all other things, we recommend flexibility. There is no reason for making any description of the writing process a model to follow. Descriptions can at most serve as suggestions. Planning and writing your paper in one go requires you to meet a number of prerequisites before you can write, not least read or have a general overview (before you have even written anything to have an overview of). Furthermore, you are at risk of being limited by a planned outline and the books you have read. This may prevent you from discovering new ways of using the material and may result in you dependently summarising "what is written in the books". Flexibility when writing forces you to participate actively (and demonstrate independence) so that you include the texts in research you are constantly developing. A process oriented approach requires extensive revision, but it makes it easier to get started.

Introductory writing is writing to think

Academic writing can be divided into two types of writing: Writing to think (process writing) and writing a "finished" text (product writing).

Writing to	
... learn involves:	... present involves:
- Writing to think - Discovery - Creativity - Personal integration of knowledge - Writer based - Readers: Yourself and a trusted few - Language: Personal - Genres: Drafts, notes.	- Popularisation - Revision - Analysis/criticism - Presenting knowledge - Reader orientation - Readers: Distant - Language: Formal - Genres: Finished professional texts.
(Adapted and expanded from Young, 1994)	

These two types of writing are radically different, especially in regards to purpose and form, but also in regards to content.

The techniques of writing to think

There are a number of writing techniques that can help you get started. Here are five ways of writing in order to think:
- Brainstorming
- Mind mapping
- Non-stop writing
- Broad writing
- Displays (visual representations and drawings of the paper's coherence).

Brainstorming

Brainstorming on a topic means writing down any ideas, thoughts and associations you get from the topic in random and no particular order and without being critical. It is important that you do not evaluate or give yourself time to think about your ideas. Setting a time limit of 5, 10 or 20 minutes for a brainstorm is a good idea.

We cannot stress enough the importance of beginning all papers by writing lists, keywords, schedules, timelines, etc. Start with lists as these provide an overview! This also applies to papers that stay close to the text. Even Husserl's phenomenology can be turned into a list, where dimensions are listed from memory, for example, based on your last read through. This allows you to put things in your own words, which means you are adapting material rather than simply paraphrasing it on the basis of your notes.

> **Activity: Write quickly for 10 minutes without stopping or editing**

Mind mapping

Mind mapping consists of creating a visual network of your ideas, thoughts and associations. Write your topic in the middle of a piece of paper and note your associations in lines or circles drawn from the topic in the middle.

Do the same with the sub topics. Do not give too much thought to content or placement. Nor should you be critical of what you write. You can also set a time limit for mind mapping, for example 10 minutes.

Compared to brainstorming, mind mapping outlines connections and relationships between the different points you write down. You will get further than with a linear and incoherent list. (In this section, we have treated mind mapping as a tool for writing to think, however, mind mapping can also be used for taking notes and structuring material).

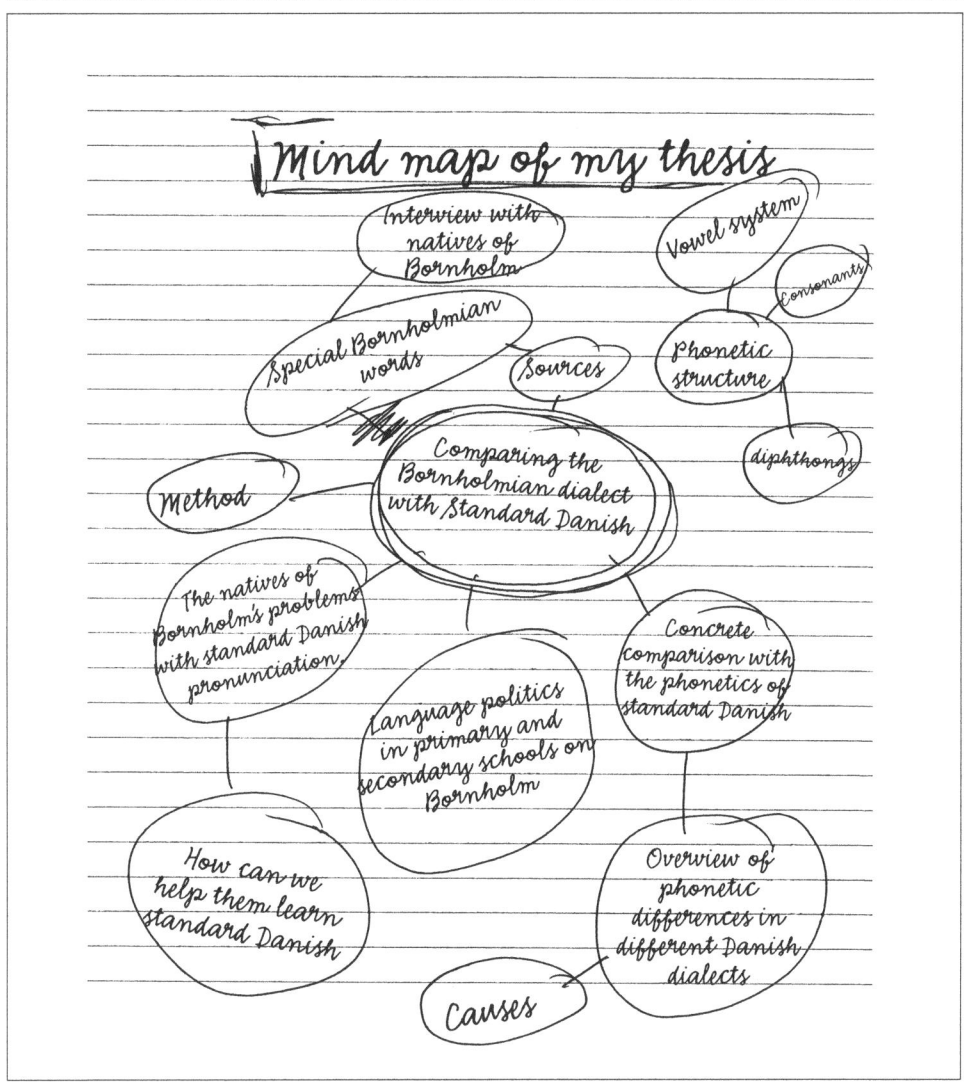

There are many free mind mapping programmes available. Try googling "mind map".

> **Activity: Make mind maps every time you need to generate and structure ideas**
>
> - Instead of using a sheet of paper or a programme you can construct your mind map from post-its which can be moved around
> - Find a mind mapping programme online.

Non-stop writing

Non-stop writing is to write about a topic within a set time frame, for example, 15 minutes, without a structure or without revising. Furthermore, you should not stop to think or plan while non-stop writing, nor should you edit your text while writing. The point is to let go of any control so that ideas and thoughts can flow freely without planning or critical revision.

The most important rules for speedwriting are to
- write cohesive text – not bullet points or keywords
- continue to write without thinking about what you are writing
- not revise what you have written and not correct words or punctuation
- continue writing even if you have nothing more to say about the topic – if this is the case, write about your lack of material, repeat the last sentence again and again or if worst comes to worst, write "blah blah blah" until you think of something that is relevant to your topic.

Writing on a computer with the screen covered is a good way to do non-stop writing.

> **Activity: Use non-stop writing before you start writing new text**

Broad writing

Broad writing is writing smaller, unstructured pieces of text about various aspects of the topic even though these text sections will eventually end up in entirely different places of the paper. This means you can write about the material you have and can jump from one subtopic to another.

Display (visual representations) i.e. drawing the central content of your paper

It may be a good technique to create a display of your paper. Peter Dahler-Larsen defines a display in this way: "A display is a visual or tabular representation of qualitative data in concentrated form" (Dahler-Larsen, 2002). A paper display can help you get an overview of and see the relations among the paper's most important elements.

Displays can be
- figures consisting of bubbles/boxes connected by keywords
- timelines
- tables
- graphs in a coordinate system
- diagrams (process diagrams, tree diagrams, etc.)
- combinations.

In all cases these drawings (along with associated words) represent elements of the paper's research through the connections between text and data or a table of results. A display is a cross between a mind map and structuring the paper's basic idea.

Below you will find a display of a paper with the research question: "Which conditions must be met before evaluations can lead to learning? Were these conditions met in connection with the social housing policies from 1993-2004? How could these policies have prevented evaluations from leading to learning?

A display of the central coherence of the paper could look like this:

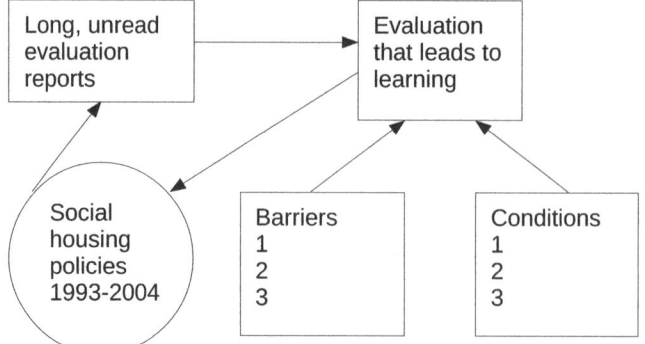

To make the relationships between the elements visible, the arrows between the boxes should also be named. A (edited) display is a very suitable tool for communicating your paper's main idea to your supervisor.

Displays can also be used to structure parts of your paper, for example, chapters and sections:

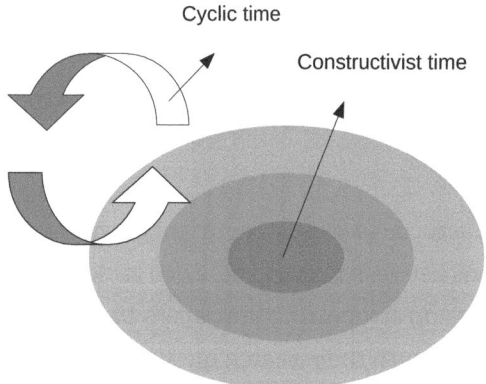

Figure 4: The dimension of time
NATO constitutes the core of stability surrounded by circles of increasing uncertainty.

The arrows indicate the conception of time. The core presents options – constructivist time. In the surrounding circles there is an increasingly cyclic understanding of time.

Why write to think?

Writing to think is especially useful at the beginning of any writing process in which the ideas the paper is to be based on must be found or conceived. The principle is that writing makes you think whereas thinking does not necessarily make you write. Our recommendation that you dive straight into the writing process and begin by writing what you are most ready for is really a form of "think writing".

If you ask a group to "think write" about their topic for 10 minutes and then ask if anyone had an idea while writing, many will answer yes. But how many get new ideas from following a detailed outline? Very few!

Ideas and new connections appear when you alternate between letting go and holding on tight. A good, purposeful piece of writing naturally requires you to produce "finished text" at some point. If you start in reasonably good time, you will have time to write more loose, contemplative texts to begin with and more finished, polished texts later on.

Writing to think is first of all for your personal use and it should only be handed in in very rare cases. Once you know what you want to present, you can start writing finished text. But you will naturally still think and develop new material while writing with a target audience in mind. All writers should allow themselves at least one session where they write to think when dealing with material they still lack knowledge about.

Many students only expect to have to write a single draft, which then only requires minor corrections and proof reading. In this way, they begin with writing to present, which is a shame, as they will have cheated themselves of the privilege it is to write to think: writing without thinking about the reader and writing just to develop one's own ideas.

From writing to think to drafts to finished papers

Writing with or without an outline

To make an outline that is more than a list of keywords, important prerequisites are
- that the writer is aware of some of the many elements the text will include
- that the writer has an idea of the paper's central point. In practice, this means the writer must have a focus or even a research question.

If writers are able to structure their finished paper early on, they have come far in their contemplation and deliberation of content. Some are even able to structure their paper immediately after having written the first version of their research question, whereas others spend a long time working on their outline and restructuring their paper until the very end. We recommend deliberately working in the following order:
- Content – the research question reveals the central content

- Form, structure – as indicated by the outline
- Presentation – language, layout, etc.

Activity: Write back and forth

When you have chosen a (temporary) focus (a research question), write down as many points for the structure as possible. From here start drafting a part of the paper you can write about. Whenever necessary, go back and adjust the research question and structure. You should frequently check whether your point of departure has changed or the plan for your paper requires adjusting (the recursive part of the process)

You will continuously need to write to think – also when beginning new sections.

Even though all roads may lead to Rome, our experience suggests that stubborn, deeply-rooted writer's block and delays in studies are always caused by

1. forcing work into a form (i.e. an outline) and forcing the production of finished material before having enough to write about in regards to content, i.e. not deliberating content when writing and instead writing finished text from the beginning. It is common for students with writing problems to have a strong product-oriented working style.
2. or reading too much for too long, thus delaying writing.

It is always worth using your work processes to experiment. The goal is always productivity as well as good products.

Advantages and disadvantages of beginning to write with and without an outline

Outline before writing (structure – write)	Writing before structuring (write – structure)
- The writing of cohesive texts is delayed	- You will be able to start writing cohesive texts early on
- You will gain an overview early on, however there is a risk that this overview is a purely fictional, pro forma outline	- You will generate material for content and structure by writing

• Form before content • Supervisor-friendly.	• Content before form • Inconvenient for your supervisor.

The precondition for writing to think is the fact that writing is the same as rewriting, i.e., writing your text many times!

The texts of the writing process: Notes, drafts and finished text

In the finished paper, the various parts must naturally all be completed in regards to structure and formulation as well as be revised and controlled. However, while being written, the paper's different components do not need to be on the same level or have equal status. On the contrary, these differences will often be the mark of a successful writing process. This indicates that you have focused your energy on the material you had and on your most fully developed thoughts, and that you have been able to prioritise, evaluate and be flexible in your writing process. The following table is based on Sharples' (1999, p. 75) suggestion of how to categorise the status of texts.

The status of drafts in the writing process:

Rough drafts	Working papers	Reader-oriented drafts
are collections of data, unrevised papers, documentation, anchoring – for your personal use, for example: Notes, texts from speed writing, brainstorms, mind mapping, unfocused summaries (paraphrasing).	are edited and knowledge-transforming texts – to be read by you and your supervisor, for example: Analyses, interpretations, argumentation, evaluations, focused summaries, drafts, compilations of information.	are texts aimed at readers, papers that are ready to be handed in and read – for the reader (supervisor, external examiner), for example: Revised and completed text, finished papers.
Focus on content (writer based text)	→	Focus on form (reader oriented, finished text)

Organising each of these kinds of drafts into separate folders on your computer or in binders will be worth the effort.

> **Activity: Prepare your paper on your computer**
>
> - Create a folder with subfolders corresponding to each new central section of your paper and name these folders according to the name and status of each section ("working paper" etc.).

In this connection, the task of the writer is
- to assign drafts their correct status
- to understand that only knowledge-transforming texts can form the basis of a research paper
- to know which kinds of drafts your supervisor can read and respond to.

Always inform your supervisor and group members of the status of a text and what you want them to comment on.

Should you write with a reader in mind?

We have all been told to "write with your reader in mind", and of course you will have to consider your reader sooner or later. However, the question is when should you start considering your reader in order for it to be beneficial to your paper and writing process?

To be able to develop your ideas, a general piece of advice when writing is to ignore the reader for a short while. Peter Elbow, the famous American writing pedagogue, described (in a famous article "Closing My Eyes as I Speak" (1987)) how he closes his eyes when teaching and giving talks to an audience because he is unable to develop a line of thought while at the same time being in contact with his audience. By dismissing any thoughts of the reader, you will alleviate the pressure of an imagined, critical reader's expectations of you. The idea is to first write your text for the sake of your own learning, before considering the wants of your reader.

Revising a text

Revision (literally "seeing again") means to read and process what you have written in contrast to producing new text. Some writers revise while or alternately to producing text. Others start writing and then revise later. Finally, there are writers who basically only revise formalities.

> **Research on revision**
>
> - The more writing experience a writer has, the more thorough his/her revision will be.
> - Revising other's writing is easier than revising your own, you discover more mistakes and flaws.
> - Revising other's text is the best way of learning to revise.
> - Most writers are only able to consider few parameters of revision at a time. Instead they must revise several times.
> - Effective revision requires consciousness of the textual criteria of the given genre and contact with the reader's criteria).
>
> (Hyland, 2002; Schriver, 1987; Sharples, 1999; Sommers 1980)

Students' revision of papers is something that has been researched extensively in the hope of finding the key to good revision strategies.

Research on writing has shown that untrained writers often underestimate the importance of revising a written text. Often new students only revise on word and sentence level (especially deleting repetitions and inserting better words), while practiced and good writers revise much more and much more radically (they will for example include new sections, delete others and move around sections of text). The best thing is to start revising at the most general levels and revise the lower levels later (when the first levels are settled). Read about the text's levels on p. 25).

Separating production and revision can be an advantage (if you are able to!) especially if you tend to speculate too much, too early on, about "which requirements you must meet", "what the teacher wants", "which criteria apply to the paper". You could separate the two by producing text for a few days and then revising your text for the next few days. Or you could produce as much new content as possible in the morning (when you are most awake) and spend the afternoon improving what you have written.

However, you can also revise too much and for too long. Unending revision is a sign of writer's block. If your text no longer surprises you; provides you with new insights, or you no longer come across actual mistakes or gaps, it is time to take a chance and hand in your paper.

Take a break

It is worth remarking that the longer you wait between writing and revising your text, the more potential changes will become obvious to you. Therefore: Take as long a break as possible between writing a draft of the entire text and the revision and editing that will lead to your finished text.

Revise on paper

In practice, it is best to revise on print-outs of your text and not on your computer. Revising anything beyond word level will prove difficult on a computer, as you are not able to get an overview of a larger amount of text. You should print out your paper every time you need an overview both on micro and macro level.

Criteria for revision

You may have been able to write a draft of you paper without specifying a research question or a purpose. However, revising without a research question or purpose is difficult. To revise a text, you must employ these general guiding principles:

- What is written in the pentagon's corners? Have these become clearer in the text?
- Who is the target group: What does it already know about the topic and what does it expect and want?
- According to the curriculum and your teacher's interpretation and concretisation, what is the purpose of your paper?

Activity: Check the local quality criteria

- Compare your paper to the requirements set out in the curriculum, the course description and your teacher's/supervisor's particular understandings and criteria. Note the requirements' and criteria's relevance for your paper.
- Make note of how you will meet the requirements and criteria in your paper.

You cannot make all the small, but crucial, decisions (such as "does this piece of information belong here or should I delete it?") without considering each decision in light of your paper's focus (research question). In your paper, only include the things that directly aid in answering your research question. At the latest when the text is to be revised, you should write out your research question, and, if necessary, write your research question at the top of each page as long as you are still in the drafting stage!

It is wise to revise several times: First content, then form, and lastly language and formalities. I.e., use the same order for revising your text as you did for writing it. Begin by reading your draft focusing on whether the text is arguing for or against what you wish to prove, and whether the text includes sufficient and well-chosen documentation. Order and language are unimportant as long as you are still deciding which text sections are going to be included in the finished paper.

A good principle when revising others' texts, is to move from higher to lower order concerns. This is called revising top-down in contrast to bottom-up. This corresponds to what we wrote about the text's higher and lower levels, p. 25.

In the following we suggest which textual features belong to content, form and formulation, "top" and "bottom":

Revision in three steps

1. Firstly, make the big changes: Content = higher order concerns
- Research question
- Purpose (target group)
- Argumentation
- Documentation
- Use of examples
- Prioritisation of material.

2. Then smaller changes: Structure/form
- Order
- Transitions
- Beginnings and endings
- Repetitions.

3. Lastly, small changes: Formulation and formalities = lower order concerns
- Language, style, "tone"
- Spelling and punctuation
- Citations
- Notes

- References
- Titles and subtitles
- Layout and typography.

Before you hand in your paper, take a look at the lists of criteria presented in this book and use them for your draft (you can find the collected lists on samfundslitteratur.dk/thegoodpaper). But first and foremost: Consider the local criteria presented by the curriculum and your supervisor's written/oral interpretation and description of what is emphasised by your field.

From writer based to reader oriented revision

When you have reached the stage of revising more than producing text, you should put yourself in the reader's place – or alternatively ask someone to read your text and help you revise it. The crux of the matter is to shift from being writer based to being conscious of your reader in your text (see the text box on p. 83).

In writing groups, the most frequent comment is: "Write more about ..." When you have written for a short time, your text can quickly become difficult for anyone but yourself to understand. It is therefore a good idea to take a break from the text to detach you from it. After a couple of days, or even weeks, revising dispassionately will become easier – being detached is vastly easier when revising others' texts. Asking someone else to help revise your text is therefore a very good idea.

Get feedback

When the time has come to revise your text, it is also a perfect time for you to read up on the criteria that apply to the genre of your text. These criteria are best obtained through your supervisor's feedback on your draft commenting on what is already well-written and what can be improved. Commonly, supervisors will not read more than an extract, but even feedback on a few pages can prove crucial, as many features will be characteristic of the entire text.

Know your supervisor's criteria

Although there is a general core of consensus, teachers and supervisors will always have different ideas and concepts about what constitutes a good text. Many students and teachers feel provoked by the idea of having to obey the criteria of the reader and writing a text the reader will like. They believe it is "conformity and dependency" and if students followed their own ideas and judgment, it would perhaps lead to something more independent and original. Although this may be a sensible strategy for geniuses, for everyone else a lack of knowledge of the criteria will simply lead to writing poorly for too long. Writing something that is unapproved will not lead to useable qualifications. If the teachers' assessment criteria are unclear, the assessor is free to make idiosyncratic assessments – and students will not benefit from this type of "freedom". We believe students, individually and collectively, are wise to insist that assessment criteria be made as explicit as possible, in order that revision can be based on these criteria.

Persons with an academic degree will often have to write professional texts for different target groups who must like and be able to use the text. Some educations provide training in writing during the writing process. Students should accept this offer and use it to their full advantage.

Finally, one of the points this book makes is that papers fall into a formatted genre which involves a number of general conventions, considerations and restrictions, but which can also be locally defined and negotiated. This is where the teacher must help students.

So, examine the criteria before and while revising and discuss them with readers and teachers.

The process of project planning

We highly recommend that you always plan and manage your writing process. Below we suggest tables and principles for organising and completing your paper expediently.

Your (pre)conditions

First you must discover the best conditions for writing:

Activity: Discover when you write the best – a quiz

Check the answer that applies to you:

When do you write best?
- In the morning
- In the middle of the day
- In the early evening
- at night.

How do you write best?
- Undisturbed and alone
- In places where there are other people, e.g. the library
- While listening to music
- With a friend
- Never.

What is your best writing practice?
- Long, undisturbed stretches of time (how long?)
- Short sessions with regular breaks.

Where is your favourite place for writing?
- Somewhere quiet and undisturbed
- Somewhere with room for the books and materials you need to for your paper.
- Somewhere with good seating and lighting.

How do you motivate yourself?
- With rewards
- With "punishments"
- By updating your Facebook status
- With manageable intermediate goals, e.g. writing for half an hour at a time.

How do you plan your writing?
- On a long-term basis
- On a short-term basis
- Not at all.

> **What do you do if you encounter problems while writing?**
> - Consult my supervisor
> - Talk to my friends
> - Nothing – and start panicking.
>
> When you have answered, consider whether you should change your writing conditions and writing practice.
>
> (Adapted from Davies, 2011)

Use calendars and schedules

We recommend that you use tools for planning and managing your writing. In the following we offer a number of suggestions which must be adjusted to your own work.

Plan backwards from your deadline

Start with an ordinary calendar.
- Mark your deadline and all the days and times before your deadline where you will not be writing, e.g. because of classes, meetings, holidays, birthdays, hobbies and work.
- Then make a schedule similar to the one on the next page, but adjust it to your own paper and your style of working. Consider whether your plans are realistic.

Activity: Plan your entire writing process

- Cross out any points that are not relevant and add any points you feel are missing
- Fill out the plan working backwards from your deadline.

Activity ↓ Week/day →						
Choice of topic						
Check requirements for paper						
Information and literature search						
Informative reading						
Selection and collection of data						
Selection of concepts, theories, and, as appropriate, philosophy of science						
Selection of methods						
Research question/point						
Delimited literature search						
Reading + introductory writing						
Concept definition						
First analysis of data						
Method section						
Theory section						
Discussion						
Introduction + conclusion						
Specification of requirements						
Calculations and treatment of numbers						
Experiments and tests						
Models, tables, designs and illustrations, text for figures						
Bibliography + notes						
Supervision, feedback, supervisor meetings						
Revision af draft						
Proofreading						

Logbook

You can also keep a log of what you have written throughout the day, which ideas and thoughts you have had, what you plan to write, etc. The logbook can be adjusted according to your plans so you can gain an overview of the writing and assess the situation.

Reading for papers

Reading for papers is different than reading for courses or independent studies. Normally reading for a paper will be guided by the paper's research question: Your reading must contribute to answering the paper's main question.

Also consider which type of information you need: Do you need concrete information? Data? Theories and concepts? Methods? Etc.

Read more on pp. 172ff. Read more in Stray Jørgensen (with the assistance of Harboe), 2007.

Experiment!

Generally, there is much to be gained from experimenting with your writing processes and continuously observing which processes and work routines you find fruitful. This will also prove useful after you graduate.

3. Smaller homework assignments, one-week assignments, set exams – essays

This chapter is about smaller papers, which are often assigned during the first year of study and which lead to and prepare the ground for the research paper. Depending on your particular discipline or programme, these papers will be called different things, e.g. essays, 1-week assignments, homework assignments, set exams, academic essays. However, common to all these papers is their aim to train students in some of the skills needed for writing a research paper. In this book, we will mainly use the term *essays*.

Here, you can read about the common features of this type of paper; the requirements and criteria involved and how these papers can best be written.

Writing papers on the first year of study trains skills for
- documenting knowledge (knowing and using the theories, methods and subject areas of the field
- focusing and formulating problems within a given topic on your own
- involving and using the sources of the field
- academic text types (describing, summarising, analysing, discussing, evaluating)
- structuring (the paper's structure)
- writing in clear and academic language
- referencing tech, handling footnotes, etc.
(From Skov, 2008)

What is the purpose of essays in the first year of study?

The first papers you write are often about approaching the subject area. Writing a paper is thus a central learning object.

This preparatory writing is also about acquiring the particular fields' ways of communicating knowledge, and here writing is central. This means that students must assimilate to the writing traditions of the different fields as well as academic writing in general. Finally, writing a paper serves as a form of documentation for assessment and exams.

The primary purpose of preparatory papers is to help you

- *acquire* subject-specific material and methods
- *learn to learn* in an educational context
- *document* that you have acquired these skills
- *demonstrate* your acquisition in a way that is accepted within the discourse of your academic field.

In preparatory papers, you are not required to produce new knowledge or make independent contributions to disciplinary discussions. The existing knowledge and methods of the field constitute the basis for first year papers, and students must document their understanding and skills within this knowledge and these methods. Students must also demonstrate proper and correct use of and reference to sources (read more about sources in chapter 8).

Quality criteria

The quality criteria that apply to many first-year papers can be summarised as such:

Essays – quality criteria

The paper must
- answer the assignment question/requirements of the curriculum/the teacher's questions and criteria
- be focused on the topic, question, curriculum
- include and use relevant literature, sources, methods and concepts (from the curriculum)

- explain all choices (theories, methods, structure, presentation, etc.)
- argue and relate to the material
- demonstrate correct and proper treatment of sources
- place main emphasis on analytical and argumentative elements and focus less on summarising material (to the extent possible in regards to the paper's formal requirements)
- be clearly structured and employ correct, subject-specific terminology
- use field terms and concepts
- observe formalities.

(From Skov, 2008)

As previously mentioned, international literature on academic writing distinguishes between the phenomena of "knowledge telling" and "knowledge transformation" (Bereiter & Scardamalia, 1987). But although the main purpose of obligatory papers is to acquire and present the existing knowledge of the field, meaning main emphasis is placed on "knowledge telling", it is always good to try to demonstrate a more independent approach to the subject-specific material, i.e. "knowledge transformation". Approaching material independently and professionally is an important quality criterion of more authentic academic texts, like bachelor theses and dissertations, and is furthermore a central learning goal in educations where academic writing is required (read more about independence and quality criteria in chapter 1). An independent approach to the material is thus also conducive to high marks. Using knowledge in a new way is more demanding than simply reiterating it.

Activity: If you are about to write your first paper, you should check

- which existing knowledge and skills you are expected to possess
- how you are required to present it
- how you can (even to a small degree) demonstrate independence.

The rest of this chapter is about how to check these aspects. In regards to the requirements for presenting your knowledge, we refer to the chapters on sources (chapter 8), text types (chapter 11) and on clear and academic language (chapter 13).

Restrictions and possibilities: What are you *required* to do and what would be wise to do?

Many of the essays you will write in your first years of study are characterised by being more restricted than papers in your later studies. These restrictions may be related to content, research questions and procedure. This is because there are certain subject-specific requirements for essays, while independence in relation to the subject-specific aspects is emphasised in later years of study.

Where these restrictions apply can be illustrated by a version of the pentagon model made especially for *essays*.

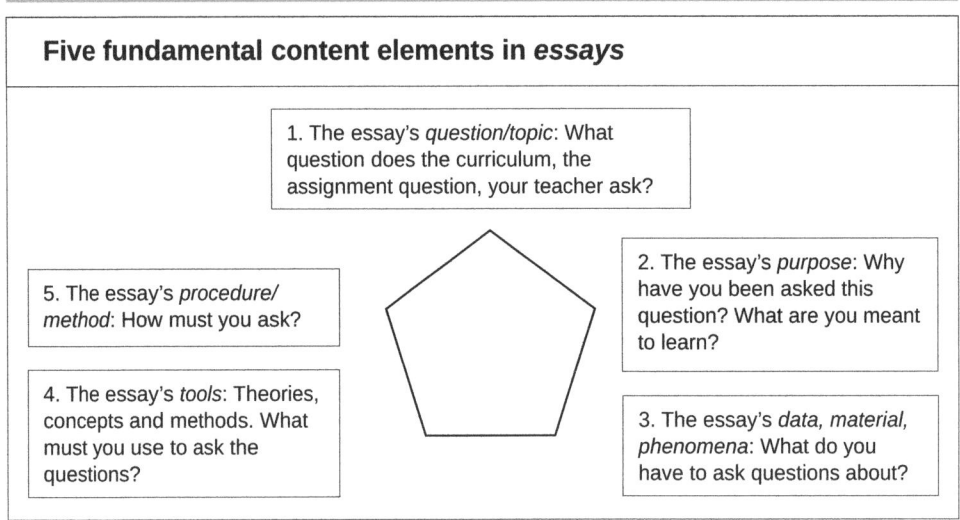

The restrictions are related to the five fundamental elements of the corners, depending on which type of paper you have to write. Set exams will typically include an assignment question, which means restrictions are placed on the first corner. Term papers will often include restrictions on the material being examined (corner 3) and/or on how it is researched (corner 4).

Take a look at this extract from an Anthropology curriculum, where the learning goals for BA level are defined as following:

Example: Anthropology

- *Give an account of and compare* different texts in preparation for identifying differences and similarities in the ways the texts view the topic.
- *Identify and summarise* different anthropological problems in the curriculum.
- *Apply* analytical concepts presented in the course to an *analysis* of the empirical material presented in the course.

From this it is evident that the paper is restricted in regards to choice of topic (the course's subject matter), the material on which to base your work (the texts received and the curriculum) as well as procedure (you must account for, compare, identify, summarise, apply and analyse). To get a good result, it is crucial that students are aware of which requirements their paper must meet – and that these are then met.

Another example of restrictions is shown below. The example is taken from a set exam on module 3 of a nursing education. According to the exam criteria the aims are to:

Example: Nursing Education

- *Identify* a problem in nursing related to one or more fundamental physiological needs: nutrition, excretion and movement as well as the patient's reaction to illness.
- *Describe and analyse* the problem by including all disciplines involved in the exam.
  In the description and analysis, you must include knowledge based on practice, development or research.
- *Deduce and substantiate* relevant nursing interventions related to the chosen problem.

In this example, restrictions consist of the requirement to identify, analyse, deduce and substantiate in relation to a specific problem and by including specific knowledge.

Progression and independence

Apart from the restrictions on and requirements for content, as exemplified above, with you must comply with as a student, it is a good idea to consider how you can show more independence when choosing, substantiating, using and relating to your field and material.

In the example from nursing education, it is thus important not to spend too much time and space on those parts where you must "identify and describe" a problem. Instead you should place main emphasis on those parts of the paper that require most independence, i.e. the parts in the example that ask you to "analyse" or "deduce, substantiate and relate". However, you should not leave out the aforementioned, prerequisite levels when writing your paper.

When asked to substantiate and relate or discuss and evaluate as in the examples, ensure you have the necessary, subject-specific foundation for doing so. Personal opinions and beliefs are not valid in scientific and academic texts. Only evaluations based on academic documentation and argumentation count as legitimate contributions to the professional debate of for example analyses, theories or research. Read about evaluations in the chapter about the language of your paper on p. 390.

In most cases, curriculums and assignment questions will directly or indirectly propose that first year papers be structured so that these begin with more descriptive, summative sections, followed by more classifying and analysing sections and finally sections that discuss or create designs. This corresponds to the progression found in the SOLO-taxonomy and Bloom's taxonomy (see chapter 1) and the progression in academic text types (see chapter 11). It is once again important that you do not spend too much time and energy on the lower parts of the taxonomies, i.e. summarising and describing sections (the text types summary and description).

> **Good advice for furthering progression and independence when writing**
>
> - Produce the text types required by the curriculum and/or assignment question and/or supervisor's Instructions. But remember, above all, to include analysis.
> - Consider the possibilities for reaching the higher levels of the hierarchy of text types, which include discussion or evaluation (see chapter 11 on text types).

- Be aware of how you prioritise text types; make sure you use your limited number of pages wisely and prioritise the text types that require you to be most independent (see the taxonomies on pp. 47-48 in chapter 1).
- Begin your writing process from behind – i.e. start by brainstorming/drafting the analyses. Working on the more independent parts of the paper early on can be an extremely effective writing tool. In this way you ensure that these parts are prioritised and you gain an overview of the paper's direction and point(s). (Read more about the writing process later in this chapter).
- Make sure you communicate on a meta-level, i.e. describe which text type you are using and explain your choice. (Read more about metacommunication in chapter 13 on clear and academic language).

(From Skov, 2008)

If you are set an assignment question

In many programmes of study, students are assigned papers where the question has been set by their supervisor. The students then have three or six hours or a week to write the paper. When writing this kind of paper, you should not only have read the curriculum carefully in order to know which requirements and restrictions you must comply with – you must also carefully analyse the assignment question you have been set.

Activity: Analyse your assignment question

- Which text types are you asked to use (e.g. define, summarise, compare, analyse, discuss, relate)?
- Which concepts, problems and phenomena are you asked to consider?
- Which material must you include?
- Where can you best demonstrate independence?
- Where will you place your main focus?
- Which overriding problem connects the sub-questions?

It is important to be aware of which overriding problem area connects the sub questions in a given assignment question. This will help your paper form an answer and cohesive argument for the assignment question you have been set or have had to formulate yourself.

The example below is an assignment question from a writing exercise on the first year of Philosophy.

Example: Philosophy

Rawls' difference principle

Taking chapter 3 in Kymlica's "Liberal Equality" in *Contemporary Political Philosophy* as your starting point, you must:

1. Introduce and exemplify Rawls' difference principle understood as the principle that "social and economic inequality is only just if it benefits the least advantaged in the best possible way".
2. Account for Rawls' two arguments supporting the principle.
3. Discuss two possible objections to Rawls' theory.

It must be clear from the paper that supplementary literature has been used. Find articles on kb.dk. The paper must be about 6 pages long.

While the first two questions make precise demands on topic and material, question 3 requires more independence as the student must participate in a disciplinary dialogue and find objections to Rawls' theory. In the writing process, you must therefore set aside time for the last question and not spend all your time and energy on answering the first questions. Also, be aware that assignment questions do not always specify which text types you should use.

Introducing your paper: What should you include?

In your introduction, you should clearly indicate which text types are used. If your paper includes a table of contents, you can also present the different text types here. In this way, you demonstrate your grasp of the paper, knowledge of academic text types and of the requirements your paper must meet.

> **Activity: In your introduction, you should**
>
> - Include the questions you wish to answer in your paper.
> - Explain how you will proceed and with which materials (theories, concepts, data, methods).
> - Use terms and expressions from your curriculum and assignment question if one has been set.
> - Describe how your paper is structured, including which text types you have employed.

Read this introduction from a set exam from teacher education (subject: Danish) which was awarded a high mark.

Example: Teacher education (Danish)

The aim of this paper is first of all to concretise the importance of language when teaching Danish. This is firstly done on the basis of an analysis and evaluation of Morten Søndergaard's exhibition *LOVE*. Through this I will concretise the *Word Pharmacy* and argue for its applicability in teaching Danish. I will especially focus on *Adjectives(R)* where I will include form and content. I will connect this to a concrete teaching situation and here consider and reflect on how *Adjectives(R)* can be included in 6th grade Danish lessons. Finally, I will criticise and discuss the professionalism of Søndergaard's project.

This introduction states the paper's aim, structure, cohesion, material, text types as well as focus. This is all done with clear reference to the assignment question constituting the paper's starting point. The reader (teacher and external examiner) is left in no doubt as to what the paper comprises and will be convinced that the student has grasped what she wants and must do in her paper as well as why. These are important signals to send in your introduction, as the introduction is the first thing your reader sees.

Structure and presentation

The table of contents is another important way of signaling and aiding the reader – in so far as you have written a paper long enough to need a table of contents or in which a table of contents is required. As a rule of thumb, we suggest you include a table of contents if your paper is 5 pages or longer.

As mentioned earlier in this chapter, most papers will be structured according to a progression of text types: Texts will move from being descriptive and summarising to being classifying and analytical and finally to the text types that discuss and create designs. This is shown in the box below in which the left column contains keywords for a typical and classic structure of academic papers. The right column indicates which text types the different subsections usually correspond to.

The connection between content elements and text types	
Content elements (outline)	Test types
Introduction, assignment question, procedure	Describe, summarise
Theory and method	Describe, account
Research	Analyse (refer, cite)
Results	Interpret, compare, categorise
Discussion	Discuss, argue, evaluate
Conclusion, answer	Sum up, present perspectives
(from Skov, 2008)	

The following is a classic example of a table of content taken from a political science paper awarded a high mark.

> **Example: Political science**
>
> | | |
> |---|---|
> | The media's effect on the possibilities of non-governmental organisations for influence | 2 |
> | NGO's appearances in the media | 2 |
> | Theory | 3 |
> | Method | 4 |
> | Is corporatism decreasing? | 5 |
> | Corporatism vs. pluralism | 5 |
> | Delimitation of the research area – the Internet | 6 |
> | Discussion – on the media's, systems and citizens' terms | 7 |
> | On the media's terms | 7 |
> | Corporatism on meso-level | 9 |
> | Entering into dialogue with current and potential members | 10 |
> | Conclusion | 11 |
> | Bibliography | 13 |

The table of contents contains both a direct and more indirect introduction to the use of different academic text types (description, analysis, discussion) placing main emphasis on the discussion as indicated by the page numbers (pp. 7-10). The table of contents also includes classic content elements (introduction, theory and method, delimitation, research, discussion and conclusion). Finally, this table of contents presents a single, cohesive statement about and discussion of NGO's possibilities for influence, i.e. as a single argument.

As is the condition for many essays, this paper is on the one side very specific in regards to the phenomena researched in the paper (that is, NGO's possibilities for influence), on the other side the paper's procedure is described in very general terms (theories and methods are not specified). The table of contents thus clearly illustrates the purpose of most essay writing on the first years of study, i.e. that students meet certain specific requirements in regards to content as well as simultaneously demonstrate a more general academic and scientific approach to the content. The challenge for students is thus to strike the right balance between being specific without becoming esoteric and being general without being "vapid".

The end of this chapter is about how to organise your writing process according to the time limit you have been set.

The writing process – if you only have six hours, three days or a week

When your teacher, at the beginning of term, introduces you to the paper(s) you must write during or for completing a course of study, you can already start investigating which type of paper you have to write.

> **Activity: What you can do when starting to write a paper**
>
> - Read your curriculum so you know which knowledge and which skills you are *required* to demonstrate
> - Read your curriculum to acquaint yourself with the learning goals and thereby with the purpose of the paper
> - Use the points and priorities of the teaching as a guide for which texts, discussions, dimensions are important in your field of study and thus also for your paper
> - Ask your supervisor about the quality criteria as well as assessment criteria that apply to the paper in question
> - Read similar and well-written papers by other students
> - Study the literature about writing papers in higher education
> - Fill out a provisional pentagon for your paper.

The above advice applies no matter whether you are writing a term paper, 1-week assignment or a six-hour set exam. Furthermore, chapter 2 provides general advice for the writing process, reading process and the revision of papers.

When you only have limited time to write a paper, it is a good idea to consider which subtasks are involved and how much time to devote to each subtask. When time is scarce and your paper must meet the specific requirements of an assignment question, it is especially important to organise your time to ensure that you answer all the questions asked.

As suggested earlier, you can begin by writing your paper backwards, i.e. start by writing a draft of the last assignment question(s). This ensures that you

- write something related to the knowledge-transforming questions
- become aware of which knowledge you must account for in order to answer the last question(s).

In this way, you avoid spending too much time and space on material that does not demonstrate enough independence or which may not be relevant or necessary for your paper.

Below we suggest how the subtasks involved when writing papers are connected to the time available. As with all planning the important thing is to make room for flexibility so you keep to the schedule even if a task takes longer than planned. Feeling like you have not come as far as you wanted or planned is not constructive.

Activity: Suggestions for organising your time when writing six hours, three days or one week papers			
Time consuption **Subtasks**	6 hours	3 days	1 week (7 days of 7 hours)
1. Interpret the assignment question	1 hour	1 day	2 days
2. Non-strop write and brainstorm			
3. Focus and write a research question			
4. Gain an overview, structure			
5. Plan the writing process			
6. Read and write			

7. Write	4½ hours	2 days	4½ days
8. Revise			
9. Proof read	½ hour	in the hours before handling in your paper	½ day
(From Skov, 2008)			

In practice, the phases of writing do not progress as linearly as the table suggests. It is important to be flexible and alternate between reading, writing, revising, structuring and gaining an overview both for the sake of the paper and the writing process (read more about writing processes in chapter 2). The table is meant to provide you with an overview of the relationship between subtasks and the time available and help to make you aware of stopping up and moving from one phase to the next.

4. Formulating a research question – from topic to focus and question

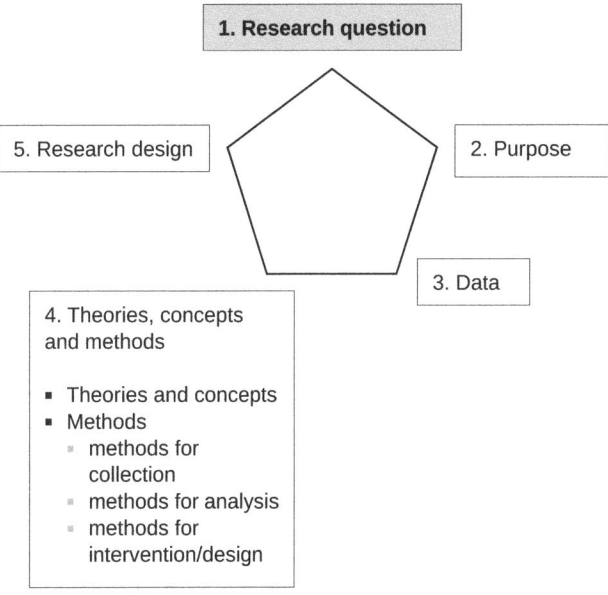

The good paper is guided by its research question. Not by the literature and theory. When researching a subject-specific problem in a research paper, it is crucial that you choose which subject-specific problem to write about sooner or later. However, this is not to say that there is a specific time during the writing process where you must have made this choice. If working with the material reveals that the problem is different than initially thought, the writer can (re)write the research question after having written the entire paper.

In this chapter, we define the research question and characterise and give examples of both good and poor research questions. Hereafter we provide suggestions for the work processes that can lead from choosing a topic to formulating a research question.

> **A research question is**
>
> - one or more connected questions you want to answer
>
> or
>
> - one or several connected phenomena you want to:
>   - describe
>   - categorise (divide into categories or groups)
>   - analyse – interpret
>   - discuss, argue for or against
>   - synthesise (make into a whole) integrate
>   - evaluate
>   - design, construct, create
>
> or
>
> - a claim you want to argue for/against.

Definitions: "Problem" and other problem related words

In chapter 1 we established that in higher education a research paper is about researching a disciplinary problem.

A problem could be a gap in the knowledge of a given field; that expectation and reality do not correlate; that a phenomenon breaks a system or the like, i.e. something does not seem right; perhaps a phenomenon has not yet been categorised or a disciplinary "truth" you may disagree with. Many good research questions are based on the discovery of these types of anomalies.

The problem (the observation of an anomaly) is the point of departure for the research question.

> **A real problem is**
>
> - a gap in the field's knowledge
> - something the field has not or should not have finished researching
> - an unexplained observation, an outlier finding

4. FORMULATING A RESEARCH QUESTION – FROM TOPIC TO FOCUS AND QUESTION

- something that has not yet been categorised, analysed (with these particular methods/theories; this systematism; this degree of detail or from this particular angle)
- something that does not seem right
- contrasts that can still be discussed
- something that is currently being debated in the field
- something that can and should be argued for (or against, i.e. all representatives of the field are not already familiar with or agree with the argumentation)
- something that is in conflict with the general view
- something that must be (re)evaluated, changed, transformed, constructed or needs new designs.

The research questions on pp. 117-119 are all problems in this sense.

A problem can be found in those places where the field can do more than refer to already known facts and established dogma. Often a problem can be identified as a gap:

Problem identification: Which "gap" is your research meant to fill?

There is a lack of:
- qualification of …
- documentation of …
- evaluation of …
- interpretation of …

- categorisation of …
- explanation of …
- description of …
- design for
- …

And vice versa: What is your contribution, i.e. your solution to the gap?

Note that we have here described gaps using text types as in Bloom's taxonomy and the SOLO-taxonomy for educational objectives, see pp. 47-48.

Generally different words and terms are used in connection with research questions. In this book, the concepts are used as such:

Problem related words – definitions

- **Topic**
  - A delimited subject area
- **Problem**
  - Something in the subject area that lacks an answer/solution.
- **Problem area**
  - A description of the context in which the problem exists (there can be several problems within a problem area)
- **Research question**
  - A concrete question posed within a problem area.

Other words for research question

Many people use the words "problem area" or "purpose" or "aim" instead of "research question", however we do not find either of these suitable:

- Problem area is a broader, thematic "collection of problems", which means there can be several research questions within the same problem area. Problem area is more of an everyday term which is also used in numerous non-educational contexts.
- The research question is a question you want an answer to. Research question is a field term which only applies to the focus of papers, dissertations and research articles.
- The paper's purpose specifies why you want an answer to the question the problem raises: What is the answer/text meant to be used for? Which academic or professional interests could there be for researching this particular question?

The following example shows how the different elements appear in the introduction of a dissertation (Linguistics, high mark):

The fact that we do not know what happens in the brains of aphasia patients when their language improves, poses a problem for the planning of effective rehabilitation programmes. Is the improvement caused by other braincells taking over the linguistic functions of the damaged braincells? Or are we dealing with other mechanisms?	Problem area
The answer to these questions will be greatly significant for the way rehabilitation of aphasia patients is planned and made effective, and thereby how the given temporal and economic resources can be best be utilised to improve aphasia patients' circumstances.	Purpose
It is not clear which functional or biological cerebral changes are connected with linguistic improvement, but there are a number of different theories about this.	The problem
These theories constitute the topic of this dissertation as I aim to evaluate which theory or theories are most tenable.	Research question

This is a good example of the difference between the research question and the formulations that lead to it. (The research question focuses on evaluating the tenability of the theories, which is a big ambition for papers on any level of study. It would have been better if the research question had also included the *basis on which* the tenability of these theories is to be evaluated).

The next question is *who* must consider it a problem for the research question to be deemed good in an educational context.

Must there be an actual problem (and for whom) to write a research paper?

Many students ask this question. It could be posed like this:

> For whom must it be a problem? If I think it is a problem that I do not know when the Napoleonic wars ended, can I not make this the research question of my paper?

Our answer is that this is not enough – not even for essays in high school – unless the end date of the Napoleonic wars is still under academic debate. But it is not; the answer to this question is a known fact which can be looked up on the Internet. For material to be appropriate for a research paper, you must be able to analyse, interpret or argue for or against it. The angle and the question must include something that has not already been established by scholars, i.e. something that is still being researched or debated. For example, something that is still unsettled or discussed in the field's texts; different views and discussions; something that has not yet been treated in systematic academic texts or if you disagree with the existing view.

Take a look at this research question from a bachelor thesis in linguistics.

> It is supposed that among speakers of standard Copenhagen Danish, the language of young people contains more glottal stops than that of middle aged and older people. However, research has yet to be carried out in this area. The purpose of this paper is therefore to investigate whether age is a decisive factor for standard Copenhagen Danish speakers' use of glottal stops in two-syllable Danish words that end on -el, -en and -er.

This paper (which was awarded a high mark) poses a question which had not yet been answered exhaustively in the field of Linguistics. Thus, the writer poses a question which requires her to research and explain her results on her own; she must pick out knowledge from a number of different texts to answer her own question. Thereby the question is not alone a question for the writer herself, but also a question for (some) linguists.

However, in her introduction, the linguistics student does not write what a linguist's possible purpose for this research might be: Why is it interesting? What is the disciplinary perspective of researching the development of glottal stops in Copenhagen Danish? Being able to answer and write about this is the next step towards a well-chosen, motivated basis for a paper or a project. The paper writer's ambition is to develop his or her writing skills from being able to pose and answer questions to being able to demonstrate and research actual disciplinary problems.

The key to posing a question which is not merely a problem to you because you do not know the answer, but which is also a problem for at least a couple of professionals, is for many students to base research questions on the *new aspects* of the field, but by using *known methods:* How can I analyse the poem Søren Ulrik Thomsen (Danish poet) wrote yesterday? How can I assess a new practice in occupational therapy? The important thing is to spot something that has not been done yet and then to conduct research that corresponds to the expectations of your particular level of study. In practice, it seems that a number of students at bachelor level and above succeed in posing and researching real problems (in some cases even high school students succeed in doing so). This should be your ambition, as this is how you acquire "research competencies" and learn how to analyse.

How do you formulate a research question?

The table below demonstrates when it is possible to pose a research question and when it is not.

The field has already provided an answer: "Problem-free area". There are only subject-specific facts. Here you cannot formulate a research question.	There is no final answer in the field, but the field (or adjacent fields) has research methods and explanatory models (theories) relevant to the problem. Here you can formulate a research question.	The field or related fields include no viable research methods. There are only professional and unprofessional speculations. Here you cannot formulate a research question.

An example of a problem that cannot be researched is:

....

What did people think 50,000 years ago?

....

There is no documentation and no methods for answering this question (even though it is a good one!). Therefore, a BA paper based on this research question was reduced to pure, unprofessional speculation.

Research questions in "hard" and "soft" disciplines

Different disciplines deal with different topics and objects and therefore also deal with different types of research questions. The greatest difference is between the natural and human sciences. Below they are presented as opposites (although many educations combine soft and hard disciplines and there is thus a continuum):

Research questions in hard and soft disciplines	
In hard disciplines:	**In soft disciplines:**
• the problem is defined at the beginning of the writing process	• you often write your way into the problem
• you choose the question from the discipline's reservoir of problems	• you find the problem in the specific topic's fields/texts
• the problems often belong within the discipline's well-defined and conventional problem types.	• the problems are unique and defined according to the concrete case
• the writing is guided by the research question	• a clear direction may not be necessary or possible until late in the writing process
• you seek *the* explanation	• you seek possible explanation(s)
• you look for answers that can be generalised and applied to other, similar disciplines	• you seek specific answers which apply only to the case at hand
• you arrive at definitive answers in the form of absolute knowledge which principally end all research of the subject (for the time being).	• you reach new views of the topic, but leave the conclusion open for later research.
(Based on MacDonald, 1987)	

A question?

The research question does not have to be formulated as one or more questions. It could for example be: "An argument for". However, it is often easier to write a conclusion for a research question formulated as an interrogative. And even if it is not, it must always be possible to rephrase a good research question as one (or more) interesting questions. If there are several questions, there must be one main question.

A good research question helps you to write the good paper

In the following, we present 14 good research questions from a number of different educations. The good research question is a guiding tool that helps the writer research a problem by means of disciplinary tools consistently throughout the paper and which communicates clearly to the reader. This is how we identify the good research question.

Examples of good research questions

1. Danish culture course, BA

Research question chosen by student on the basis of the topic: Analyse an aspect of Copenhagen (history, politics, architecture, etc.) of your choice.)

From Orvar Lofgren's view of the relation between man and his cultivation of nature ("mindscape" and "landscape"), I want to analyse the historic development of the landscaping of the parks of Copenhagen.

2. Nursing, BA

How does the nurse's experience of the phenomenon "the difficult patient" affect interaction including the relation and communication between herself and a patient with a chronic kidney disease and thereby the quality of care?

3. Philosophy, MA

[…] Today the individual state can no longer be seen as an isolated entity. Furthermore, many of the elements that characterise the liberal, democratic state are now global phenomena. Traditionally, the state has been viewed as a sovereign entity both internally and externally, but this too is no longer the case. The state's sovereignty is put under pressure externally by the process of globalisation and internally by minorities' requirements for group-specific rights and self-governance. These conditions make it necessary to rethink political philosophy and adapt it to a modern, internationalised world. This project is divided into two chapters: The first offers a more trivial account of traditional, state-centred political philosophy. The second chapter deals with the new aspects of world development which political philosophy should take into account today.

4. Art History, BA

The period of Mannerism has been much discussed and is difficult to define. It is widely disputed what the concept involves as well as what characterises this period following the High Renaissance. The focus of this paper is not art as a form, but rather spatiality as it manifests itself in the 16th century's urban and garden spaces in Italy. I want to investigate whether there are general features that can be said to characterise the Mannerist composition of space. Taking analyses of three Italian 16th century buildings and two gardens as my starting point I will attempt to define these. Where it is necessary I will include other examples of Mannerism architecture. In my analyses, I will draw on Werner Hager's theory on Mannerism spatiality in "On the Mannerism Structure of Space in Italian Architecture". Throughout I will include observations by John Shearman, Nikolaus Pevsner and Arnold.

5. Spanish, BA

Why does a new regulation in region X in Spain demand that all employees must be bilingual? Regulation xxx seen as a politically strategic use of the concept minority discourse.

6. Engelsk, bacheloropgave, litterær

Raymond Carver's characters do not seem to communicate very much, nor very well. How does the communicative void between Carver's characters affect the structure of his novels? The effect of the lack of communication on the content and structure in Carver's novels are analysed through the Bakhtinian concepts of monologue versus dialogue.

7. Teaching, BA

I wish to investigate how working with objectives and evaluations may upgrade physical education so it may clearly appear as an educational subject.

8. Dansk, bacheloropgave, litterær

Hvordan er fallos blevet ændret/blevet mindre i udvalgte litterære værker, fra strukturalisme og psykoanalyse til dekonstruktion og kønskritik?

9. Social Science, level unknown

Starting from an analysis of the policy process from the Structural Commission's report from January 2004 of the agreement to organise the employment area as part of the Budget agreement for 2009, you must discuss and evaluate possible explanations of Denmark getting a unified, communal employment system.

10. Library and Information Science, BA

[…] I aim to uncover which meanings are ascribed to the concept of discourse in the area of organisational communication. Furthermore, I wish to describe which views of construction are contained in the different meanings and uses of the concept of discourse. This is meant to lead to a discussion of whether there is a connection between the concept of discourse, idea of construction and understanding of organisation.

11. Engineering, electronic tech, M.Scs.

A study of how the electronics sector can reduce emission of greenhouse gases by reducing polluted power station units. Wind power alone will replace the reduced electricity production.

12. Pedagogy, MA

How can the concept of evidence be applied in psychological research?

13. Medicine, BA

In this project, I wish to limit the location of the binding site between IFN--λ3 and its receptor chain IL-10R2.

14. Sociology, M.Scs.

How does Donna Haraway's theory of situated knowledge differ from radical social constructivism and the feminist standpoint theory? How do these three theories relate to the researcher's role in science production and do they qualify a critical science?

What makes these research questions a good point of departure for a research paper is that they
- pose a real problem, something not yet clarified or a yet unused perspective, there is a reason for conducting this research
- prepare the ground for knowledge-transforming and a selective choice of data, concepts, theories and methods subject to the research question
- form a basis for seeing the paper/project as an argument
- pave the way for using the tools of the field (concepts, theories and methods) for analyses, discussions and designs, i.e. most examples clearly show what is being questioned as well as what is used to pose the question – the paper's main content will thus be placed high on Bloom's taxonomy and on the right on the SOLO-taxonomy.

There are other factors that are worth considering when posing a research question. It is important to consider the consequence of posing open and closed questions, of expressing yourself precisely or unclearly, and the research question's length and clearness of its layout.

A bad research question – what is that?

Look at this research question:

What happened at the battle of Agincourt?

This is a bad research question unless the events in the battle are in need of re-interpretation. Then, the research question should contain the word "new interpretation" and preferably some names of the old sources/interpretations that are to be challenged. The paper here can be nothing but pure summarisation, albeit of many sources. If the research question can be reformulated as "What's in the book(s)?" rather than "What can I analyse on the basis of something that is in the books?", then it is a bad research question for a research paper.

This weak research question will not lead to a focussed, professional, analytic and well-reasoned research project.

The process: From topic to research question

In principle, you can start pursuing a research question, once you have chosen a topic. It is a good idea to start finding your focus using the activities (mind maps, non-stop writing, etc.) described in chapter 2 on the writing process.

Ideally you should strive to formulate a working research question that can guide your writing process as soon as possible. Giving yourself time and space to formulate a research question is especially important because the wording of your research question will reveal your paper's degree of disciplinary knowledge. Looking for your research question in your sources and textbooks is a classic work pattern. We would like to warn you against doing this! First of all, this is where you find other's questions and not your own (unless they are the same). Secondly it may take a long time before something appears.

> **Activity: Immediately start writing several research questions**
>
> You should start writing possible research questions for you topic immediately, and you should enter these into an academic dialogue with your textbooks, your teachers and your fellow students.

How to move from topic to research question

Formulating a research question *is a process*. It will often take a long time before you finally discover your focus, and this focus can change once you get acquainted with the material. However, this should not prevent you from beginning to formulate research questions as soon as you have chosen your topic. Even though you probably will not be able to formulate a finished research question on the first day, we suggest that you

- attempt to formulate temporary research questions as soon after choosing your subject as possible. The purpose of this is to make a preliminary sorting of your information search and enter into dialogue with your supervisor and others on the basis of the draft of your research question
- continuously relate to what needs adjusting to ensure the research question always encapsulates your paper's central point.

It is important that you get started quickly. In the following we present an overview of a number of suggestions for formulating your research question.

One way of reaching an actual research question is by thoroughly describing the problem itself.

Activity: Problem description

As a starting point for your research question, describe the problem you are writing about thoroughly and concretely. The description must be at least a half A4 page.
- What is the problem?
- In which situations is it a problem?
- For whom is it a problem? E.g. for the field's researchers, professionals, interpreters because they lack (the right) knowledge?
- Where do you observe the problem (in reality or in texts)? Exemplify the problem
- Why is the problem problematic?
- In which (types of) texts is the problem described?
- In what way does your field engage with the problem (with theories/methods/concepts/actions)?

The problem description must be included in your paper's introduction as a motivation and concretisation of your agenda. A detailed problem description will only motivate your reader to read your paper. Too many papers do not describe the problem well enough, but still assume the reader will acknowledge the problem. However, this will leave the reader thinking: "Why should I bother to read this?"

Pointing out the problem and problem owners in aesthetic disciplines can be especially difficult. However, again it applies that a disciplinary problem is not necessarily problematic, but is something that has not yet been researched before or in that exact way. Even the seventh interpretation of the same poem or artwork will fill a gap in the field's knowledge and thereby constitutes a problem. If something within a given field has not yet been completed, it is a problem that can be researched.

Activity: Formulating a research question early in the writing process

- Write one/several research questions as quickly as possible on the basis of your topic
- Write about the knowledge you currently have. Use brainstorms, mind maps, displays and non-stop writing (see chapter 2 on the writing process)
- Search and skim literature (for a short time to get ideas)
- Quickly get a response from your supervisor and others
- Choose a preliminary research question
- Continue to update your research question in line with searches, reading, research and writing
- Write a possible conclusion (if you have an idea of where you might end up) then ask the question the conclusion answers.

Activity: From observation to pentagon

Write about:

1. Observations (what have you observed in practice or in the literature?)
2. Surprise – which subject-specific problem is your observation an expression of? ("how can it be that …?")
3. What is the disciplinary purpose of researching the problem? In which disciplinary context can a "solution" of the problem be used?
4. Actual research question – how can you explain, interpret, argue for, suggest, organise, set up, evaluate, etc. xxx-material with yyy-systematism (concepts, theories and methods)?
5. Material that needs to be researched
6. Possible concepts, theories and methods
7. What will lead you to the answer of the research question – how have you thought to complete the research (design and procedure) and explain the results by means of models for explanation, theories, and methods?

Fill out the pentagon model for your paper's most important guiding principles – feel free to do so even if you do not feel ready!

> **Activity: Insert as many fundamental elements of your paper into the pentagon as you can before you begin the writing process**
>
>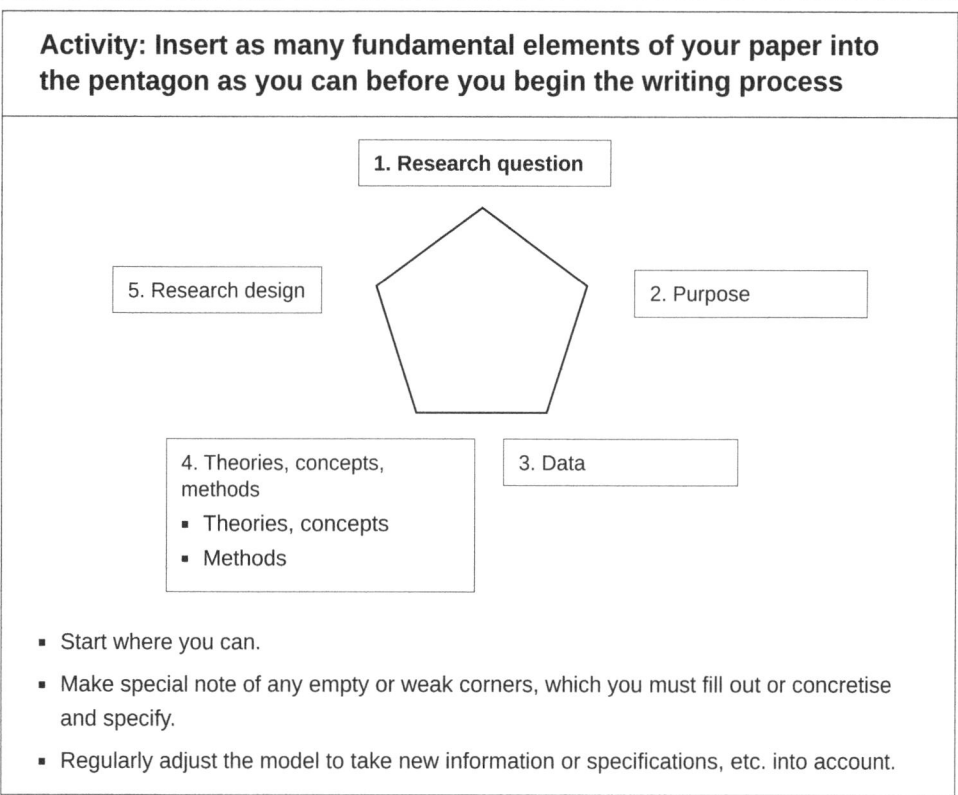
>
> - Start where you can.
> - Make special note of any empty or weak corners, which you must fill out or concretise and specify.
> - Regularly adjust the model to take new information or specifications, etc. into account.

Formulate your research question on the basis of the answer

Conversely, you can take the answer (which must be written in the conclusion) as your starting point and base your research question on this:

> **Activity: Write from answer to question**
>
> - Write for 10 min (or more – but setting a time limit is important) about what you consider the most "pressing topic/question", or at least what you want to say at some point in your paper or what you have observed about your research area. Write without thinking or planning in advance and without revising, write quickly and "on autopilot".

- When you have finished non-stop writing, write one sentence and one question: What is the point in what you just wrote or the point you wish to make?
- If you had to hand in your paper in 24 hours, what do you think your conclusion would be at this time? What are your points? Explanations of your observations? Possible connections between your observations? Etc. Feel free to answer these aspects.
- Now write the question the conclusion is the answer to. This is your current research question!

An observation

A good research question is very often based on an observation, which is then researched, substantiated, documented, explained and the significance of which is argued for in the paper.

Try writing a temporary draft of your observation and the point/conclusion/claim you can attach to it early in the writing process.

Here you may ask: Does having an answer early on have anything to do with an academic, open attitude? Yes, it does. Remember that research is frequently based on hypotheses, i.e. the observations the researchers presume to have made of the order of the world. In your text, you must document and argue for what you believe you can demonstrate, and naturally include any material that may argue against you. Working on the basis of an early, temporary point does not mean that what you have written earlier cannot be changed. You have to be willing to change your claim/conclusion if you find documentation that changes the situation.

Writing papers as well as doing real research work consists in being goal-oriented and open at the same time.

Use wh-words

Ask using wh-words. Remember that interrogatives will specify where your paper's focal point is placed: On descriptive, explanatory/interpretative material or material that evaluates/puts into perspective/creates designs (read about the text types on pp. 315-324).

> **Wh-words**
>
> - Ask *how*
>   - and write an evaluating, normative and design oriented text.
> - Ask *why*
>   - and write an explanatory, interpretative, analytical and discussing text.
> - Ask *what, which, where, who*
>   - and write a descriptive, classifying, categorising text.

Note that these question groups directly correspond to the levels of research questions shown in the overview on p. 134.

Fill out a template

There are a number of other templates to inspire you to formulate a research question according to its particular context:

- Write a standard introduction (see p. 330).
- Fill out a "research paper design" (see p. 73).
- Write an abstract of your imagined, completed paper (base the abstract on the pentagon model and outline the "results/conclusions").
- Use the research question programme *Scribo* (Rienecker & Bay, 2014).

> **Activity: Use Scribo**
>
> The programme *Scribo – a research question and literature search tool* poses a number of systematic questions about the research question, so that you end up writing research question in the process of answering the questions. The programme helps you formulate a research question as well as search for literature.
>
> *Scribo* is freely available at a number of educational institutions (universities, university colleges, etc.) – see scribo.dk.

Be inspired

One way to get ideas for good research questions – both in terms of content and formulation – is to look at how others have formulated good ones.

> **Activity: Find good research questions**
>
> Find 10 research questions from good papers in your field/from your supervisor and use the inspiration you might draw from their content or form.

1. The research question guides the paper's pentagon

The research question is the element of the pentagon (see chapter 1) that guides the elements in the other corners.

The examples from the section on good research questions were selected because they all included these elements (although you sometimes have to look carefully for the "theoretical words"). By including all the corners of the pentagon, the writer sends the right signal to himself, to his supervisor and other people giving feedback who will read the research question, to the librarian/information specialist, who is meant to advise you on the information search, and lastly to the reader. Many people will start by reading the research question to find out what is being researched and with which tools.

> **Activity: Specify your research question**
>
> In your research question, you might both include the specific object of your research (usually data/phenomena, but also theories/methods) and the tools with which you conduct your research (concepts, theories, methods). In this way, the research question will provide a precise description of your research.

2. Formulate a research question that is knowledge-transforming according to the taxonomies for learning goals

Using knowledge selectively for delivering your own research results is always considered an expression of greater qualifications than simply demonstrating knowledge by retelling already known research. Research questions can be arranged on a stepladder which corresponds to Bloom's stepladder of learning goals or the SOLO-taxonomy (see pp. 47-48):

Research questions – levels

3. Design → How to evaluate/act?

Evaluation

Synthesis

Discussion

↑

2. Interpretation → Why are things this way?

Analysis

↑

1. Description → What is this?

Description

What-, why- or how-questions

Research questions can be categorised according to where they place the paper's focus: on description, analysis or evaluation/design/construction.

What

If the research question begins with the word "what" or can be rephrased to "what is ..." or "what happened ...", and if your research is purely based on what-questions (no matter which specific words you use), or if you use words like "description" or "account" and words like "analysis", "interpretation", "discussion", "evaluation", etc. do not occur, the readers of the paper will expect the text to be descriptive.

From this type of research question, we can expect to be told about "what happened once" – and nothing more:

> **History, BA**
>
> The topic for this paper is how these different strategies were conceived and formulated. The aim is to describe the intellectual currents and sociological changes resulting from the development of military technology initiated during the Second World War and continued during the Cold War.

So, when is writing a expositional paper ever a good idea? If you can describe something new that has not yet been described in the field, a descriptive paper can be a good thing.

Why

The reader of your paper will expect the text to analyse cause and effect, influences, backgrounds and explanations and connections. Many research questions start with: "Analysis of ..." which indicates that analysis is the paper's most important contribution.

Below is a typical, good why-research question from a nursing paper:

> My workplace, the transport agency Movia, focuses on health and fitness through a number of health promoting offers and policies. It is my clear impression that the employees make use of many of these offers, but how do these initiatives affect the employees? How conscious are they of leading a healthy lifestyle at and outside of work, and how much of this is due to Movia's efforts?
>
> I have often wondered whether investing in these health initiatives influences employees to lead a healthy lifestyle at and outside the workplace and what the reason for this could be.
>
> This paper will be structured as a single case study meant to analyse the influence of health promoting initiatives in Movia. The purpose is to create knowledge that can inductively generalise the significance of these health initiatives at similar, public workplaces.
>
> The research question below constitutes the point of departure of this case study:
>
> **1.1 Research question**
> Which influence and role does Movia's health initiative have in relation to employees' awareness of leading a healthy lifestyle in regards to the four factors, diet, smoking, alcohol and exercise?
>
> Why do these health initiatives have this particular influence and role?

Commentary

This paper enquires into causes and explanations, which it later documents through the answers of the interviewees but also by means of theory that goes behind the interviewees' explanations. Why-research questions require analysis and interpretation of causes.

How

The aim of many research questions is construction/design. This especially applies to professional bachelor's programmes: Engineering, design, teaching, pedagogy, nursing and many other professional disciplines. This research question from an engineering paper is a classic example of this:

> By employing an electromagnetic field and signal therapy, we wish to develop a system that can automatise and specify the process for determining the calorific value of a truckload of wood chips.

Note that methods which must be constructed on the basis of employing an electromagnetic field and signal therapy are explicitly included. This sort of specification of method is good; it explicates how the research is carried out.

A well-written paper based on a how-question, evaluations, designs and constructions always builds on the inclusion of description and analysis as prerequisites for the later evaluations and designs.

3. The research question governs the paper as an argument

As already mentioned, the conclusion's main claim constitutes the answer to the research question.

Just like a research article or dissertation, a paper argues for its conclusion. Therefore, clearly presenting the text's argumentation in the research question is a good idea. Many books on essay writing and research emphasise that argumentation is the actual purpose of the text (argumentation in the sense of reaching a conclusion through documentation).

The Purdue Online Writing Lab's prestigious website advises that a good research question consists of a topic *and* a specific point or claim (see Purdue's website owl.english.purdue.edu). Before a topic can become a research question there must be an unsettled disciplinary question; a hypothesis, or a point to put forward, which the text will now present grounds to explore and document academically. This also fully applies to the softer disciplines of the Humanities. This is exemplified below by a research question taken from a bachelor thesis (physical education, teacher education).

> As in all other subjects, demands are also made on the teaching of P.E. in regards to the goals of the subject areas that pupils must work with and evaluations of this. The P.E. teacher faces a dilemma, as the pupils, parents, management and other teachers' expectations of the subject do not correspond with the ministerial demands. It is therefore necessary to upgrade P.E. so that it may clearly present itself as an educational subject.
>
> In this paper, I will examine how focusing clearly on goals and evaluation impacts P.E. The point of departure of this research is my own experiences from teaching practice on the 3rd and 4th year of teacher training. Furthermore, I will include the concepts cultivation and action competences to investigate whether an inclusion of these can contribute to a further upgrade of P.E.

In Anglo-American research and study environments, a "thesis statement" is often used instead of an inquisitive research question. Thus there is an expectation that the point will be presented already on the first page. In Denmark, the "point-first model" is becoming increasingly more common in relation to the "point-last model".

4. The research question's broadness vs. narrowness

The research question must reflect the narrowness and width of the object, data (or the aspect being researched): Should your answers be quantitative or qualitative, specific or generalising? Even in qualitative humanities, it is common that the research question promises to provide an answer that applies to the entire category of the treated phenomenon, i.e. the writer generalises. This is the case in the following example taken from a bachelor thesis in film studies:

> In this project, I want to examine pop music's function in films and analyse the aesthetic conditions that apply in this connection. Furthermore, I will describe the historical development of this aesthetic tool.
>
> [The table of contents reveal that 4 examples are analysed. Our comment].

When making inquiries about a large category of phenomena, you can expect to get the following answer: Many things apply in this case, the world is big, the phenomena are different. And the answer becomes so unspecific that it no longer matters. How has the film studies student selected the examples? Are they typical and representative of something? Can many or all other films that include pop music be generalised based on these examples? Which function do the examples have in the text? Is it possible to generalise on the basis of them or are they only meant to be examples of some of the many tendencies discussed in the paper? In brief, the writer should have chosen a far narrower research question.

> Which function does pop music have in four selected films?

If you pose a broad and general question, you only have one methodological option for researching the question, i.e. by reading wide-ranging texts you can refer back to. Broad questions generally lead to descriptive texts because their only documentation comes from secondary literature.

It is exceedingly common for papers to want to generalise about all objects/phenomena in a group: all children, all men, women, etc. However this requires a foundation fit for quantifying questions (for example, statistics, comprehensive surveys, general theoretical observations, etc. See chapter 12 about argumentation). Many students writing papers feel bound to the Truth with a capital T and rightly so. However, Truth is often nuanced and hard to generalise – especially if it is concerned with mankind or something manmade.

Take care not to pose a research question that leads to generalisation on the basis of one or few instances. However, if you consider statements to be interesting even though their validity is not applicable to all objects in the given category, it does not matter that your material is insubstantial. At any rate, you can include all about how and whether what you have described and interpreted can be generalised in your conclusion and perspective. The conclusion is this advice:

- Do prepare the ground for small claims (i.e. "in these cases, this and this applies". If the claims become too broad, they become unspecific.
- The conclusion's main claim must correspond to the documentation.
- Formulate your research question to suit the scope of the material (data).

Many research questions are broad and generalising to begin with and are later narrowed down as both writer and supervisor come to realise the necessity of doing so. It is very uncommon that the reverse will ever occur. Our advice is *always to formulate your research question as briefly, narrowly and concretely* as possible. You can always expand it later.

The research question guides the paper's delimitation

So, how can a research question be sufficiently narrowed down? This can be done by formulating a research question on the basis of only one or a few cases, one instance, one specific problem/phenomenon which you research using few and defined disciplinary tools. You can especially delimit the pentagon's data corner (3) and the theory and method corner (4):

What can you delimit?

Data/material can be delimited in terms of
- time
- space
- persons
- phenomena.

Theories/methods can be delimited by stating which, although relevant, (parts of the) theories and methods you do not include.

You can delimit in terms of
- what your methods/documentation allow
- which question is the most important
- what you are most interested in
- your best example, which must be included.

Delimitation must be substantiated. Why have you chosen to make the cut exactly there? You should only delimit material that the reader may expect you to include. Read about introductions, pp. 329ff.

The following is an example of delimitation (from a 2nd year group project, Humanistic Technology, Roskilde University):

Delimitation

We have delimited our project by excluding several aspects and areas although these could have been relevant to the chosen topic. First of all, we have chosen to exclude animated as well as interactive data visuals, even though we acknowledge that these elements will be increasingly important for the digital media of the future. Instead we have chosen to focus on statistical visuals, which make smaller, technical demands on us as designers, but which today are more accessible and commonly used.

In regards to the part of the project focused on design, we have chosen to delimit ourselves by excluding more technical approaches to the production of graphic design, for example theories on chromatology, shading, typography, etc. Instead we have chosen to focus on the communicative aspects of data visuals as well as the cognitive and perception-based aspects of interpretation that are significant for the understanding of these.

This is a good example of how to substantiate delimitation and focus.

5. The research question's main point must be evident

Research questions commonly consist of several questions. Naturally, these questions are interrelated and one of them usually constitutes the main question. Take a look at this research question from literary studies

> [...] Taking the above as the starting point, my research question is thus:
>
> a. How did Dostoyevsky relate to *The Double*?
> b. How is *The Double* constructed?
> c. With which means does Dostoyevsky generate a horizon of expectation in the reader?
> d. How is *The Double* narrated?
> e. How is time structured in *The Double*?
> f. How does spatiality appear in the work?
> g. Which role does language play in *The Double's* composition?
> h. What consequences does the work's composition have for the reader?
> i. Is it possible to deduce an overriding artistic principle from *The Double's* composition?
> j. What is *The Double's* message?

When reading a research question that consists of a number of questions, you can get the impression that these are all level and will be treated equally. Hopefully this is not the case or else it is likely that a focus is lacking. Here all the working questions of the paper have been presented as the research question. The actual research question, i.e. the central point of this paper, is a combination of questions i, j and g. For example:

> What is the connection between *The Double's* message and the artistic principles that underlie the novel's composition and language?

The research question should only cover the paper's central point. It is for example implicit that concept definitions will be included in the research and there is therefore no reason to include a separate question on "what is understood by ...", unless this is the text's main point. If there are several questions, you should preferably demonstrate how the different questions are interrelated. A series of disjointed questions will arouse an experienced reader's suspicion that this is a knowledge-telling paper in which a large number of elements have been included because they are related to the topic; not because a single problem is being researched.

Divide into main question and necessary working questions

In the classic three-part research question (known from assignment questions in high school), the last question is often the actual research question whereas the first two are working questions:

1. What is x? (description)
2. Which elements does x consist of? (analysis)
3. How can x be evaluated? (evaluation)

The third question is the actual research question. Question 1 and 2 are necessary for answering question 3.

In this example from a sociology paper, the last question is the main question while the others are prerequisites for an answer to the last one.

Which requirements characterise the modern labour market under information and communication structures? How do these requirements interact with the individual's social position in society? And are we in fact dealing with new liberating structures?

We suggest that you choose a main question and include all other questions as subordinate, but necessary working questions that must be answered before the main research question can be answered.

6. The research question must be precise

Linguistic precision is more important in the research question than anywhere else in the paper: The words you choose to use are promises and the reader will expect you to follow up and keep your promises.

Vagueness

Being vague and imprecise goes against academic ideals of unambiguity, replicability, clarity and accuracy.

Problematic, vague phrasing in research questions	
Do not use words and expressions such as	
"give an account"	"look at"
"be about"	"what is understood by …"
"attempt/try to …"	"describe to which extent"
"illuminate", "shed light on"	"touch upon central concepts"
"pin down"	"some", "certain", "one", "all"
"approach"	I.e. avoid imprecise, unspecific, generalising expressions.
"view …"	
"deal with"	

It is better to formulate a longer research question, using more words and clarifications, than to formulate one that is imprecise.

Watch out for plural terms and broad concepts

Examples of plural terms are "factors", "processes", "information", "all people", "women", etc. You must always consider whether broad concepts and plural terms in your research question really apply. Do you want to give an answer that applies to many/all elements of a category or only a few specific elements that you have defined? A general piece of advice is to always consider whether you can

- specify a few particular examples
- or attach plural terms to sources that claim there is a such tendency or similar.

Take a look at this formulation from a research question (teacher education):

> … how can pupils' understanding of x be developed … […] to describe today's adolescents?

Because of the research question's vague phrasing, the introduction to the paper becomes far too generalising. The paper actually deals with pupils in puberty and specific 9th grade pupils.

Watch out for the absence of actors and sources

It must be clear to whom you ascribe statements and observations, concepts, theories, etc. – i.e. who are the actors in your text and when you "say something" yourself. This means, for example, that even though the research question is relatively brief, you must pay attention to when you blur actors by using the passive form. Read more about the use of passive and "I" in chapter 13 about academic language, pp. 395f.

Using the words and terms of the field

Precisely because accuracy is important, we recommend that you use field terms as tools (theories and methods) for conducting research. Generally, we suggest that you consider how the corners of your paper's pentagon can be formulated in subject-specific terminology. Take a look at this example (bachelor's thesis, linguistics, high mark):

> How can Hawkin's processing theory account for the diachronic occurrence of a marginal type of relative sentence in Japanese?

For most non-linguists, the field terms in this research question will be gibberish. However, they will be extremely clear to the professionals at which this paper is targeted.

You will presumably have to search for literature both before and after formulating a research question. You will first be able to carry out a narrow search on the basis of (the right) disciplinary search words once you have chosen your field terms. If you want to send your research question to an information specialist at your library, the field terms will have to be included in the research question. If you have to search for literature on your own you will also need to use field terms that can lead to narrow searches in combination with other words, for example names of what you are researching (data).

Apart from being precise and subject-specific, the terms must be used consistently throughout your paper.

> **Use the same terms**
>
> - As search words in your literature search
> - In the research question
> - In the abstract.

Remember that you will need to include search words in order to upload your papers online and for future readers to be able to search for them.

Write a short research question with clear layout

In connection with the phrasing and wording of you research question and for the sake of clarity, you should also make your research question as short as possible and accentuate it, for example typographically.

A research question will become too long if it includes material that might as well be included in the introduction (see pp. 329ff. on introductions). However, it can also become too short if it does not include field terms or indicate which disciplinary lens is applied. A single line is often not enough to present a longer, more complex paper's research question. The research question must be able to stand alone as the essence of the three most important corners of the pentagon: The research question (1), data (3) and theories and methods (4).

The overriding purpose of everything we have written about formulating a precise and accurate research question is to prevent the writer from painting himself into a corner from the beginning. A research question is a promise like a speech act, and when making promises, you should express yourself as precisely as possible and promise only as much as you can keep.

Read more about precise language on pp. 372-373.

7. Consciously use open/closed questions in the research question

The following examples are taken from a PhD dissertation and a master thesis respectively:

History:

Did foreign minister Per Hækkerup potentially sell a Danish oilfield to Norway for a bottle of whisky?

Psychology:

Can coaching be used as a tool to improve performances in X?

These are both closed questions, which can be answered with yes/no, either/or. Closed questions can be identified grammatically by the fact that they do not start with wh-words, but with a verb: Can …? Is …? Did …?

The point is that the question about Per Hækkerup is a good, but narrow, closed question, whereas there is no apparent benefit in not using the open question: "Why/how can coaching be used …" in the psychology example.

The closed question in the Per Hækkerup example, which according to the press constituted the research question of a PhD dissertation, is validated by the fact that historians at the time did not, in fact, know whether Per Hækkerup had sold Danish territory to Norway while drunk during a negotiation. However, the rumour had been going on for decades. Only a thorough and comprehensive examination of all documents, witness accounts, etc., would be able to answer the question, and this answer can be either yes/no, unless the phrase "Did he sell" can be softened: "Well, he might have done it to some degree of the word". However, a sale is usually easily defined. Incidentally, the answer to the question was "no". When a yes/no answer can in fact be documented, it is completely natural to pose a yes/no question.

Is it, on the other hand, possible to imagine flatly rejecting that coaching can be used as a method for improving performances in a given area: "No, coaching is a completely useless method in this situation". In the soft disciplines, the likely answer would rather be: "Yes, under some circumstances techniques from method X can be used, but it depends on … etc.". Here, research is about acquiring knowledge about conditions, contexts, nuances and combinations, not about absolute confirmation or refutation. Being able to give as short a yes/no answer as possible, does not make a research question interesting. What makes it interesting is being able to develop and describe the procedure employed and evaluating its applicability and the possibilities for its dissemination. The answer reveals whether open or closed questions are appropriate.

If you have initially formulated a closed question, try to rephrase it as: "In which way/under which circumstances/why/how does it happen, when it happens?" – this can prove more fruitful and less restricting.

Activity: Check your research question regularly and revise it if necessary

You can use this checklist for your research question:

Questions to the elements of the research question
- Is there a disciplinary problem, an unexplained observation, something that does not correspond with conventional views, a knowledge gap, an observation that sticks out?
- How high does the paper place itself on the taxonomies (see pp. 47-48) which you will be assessed according to?
- Do you prepare the ground for the paper as an argument?
- Do you clearly use/relate to the concepts, methods and theories of your field?
- Can you fill out an entire pentagon and is there internal cohesion?
- Is your contribution visible however small?

Questions for operationality
- Is there a relation between x and y (or more variables) that you wish to research?
- Are you able to provide an answer to the research question as a result of your research?
- Is the narrowness/width of your research question fitting to the material and methods available to you?
- Can the research be completed within the time limit?

Questions to the phrasing
- If you have several questions, is there one clear main question?
- Are questions formulated openly, i.e. not as either/or, yes/no-questions?
- Is the research question
    - subject-specific and precise?
    - clearly highlighted?
    - as short as possible?

Be sure to check your research question regularly to ensure that your paper is on the right track. Be prepared for discrepancies between your text and your research question, which can easily mean that the research question must be adjusted or changed.

Remember that a research question is first final, when you print out your paper to hand it in!

Supervision and formulating research questions

A crucial part of the process of formulating a research question is to get your supervisor's opinion of the draft of your research question.

Few supervisors (but there are some) will help students formulate a research question. However, they will presumably respond to a research question proposal for a longer research paper. In practice, the supervisor's role is often to help delimit and narrow down research questions that are too broad.

Keep you supervisor informed

The research question and the continuous work of keeping it up to date in relation to your paper are your responsibility and not your supervisor's. However, you should keep your supervisor informed and part of the process, so that he or she can provide you with good disciplinary and methodological ideas and objections which you can relate to and incorporate. Keeping your supervisor informed about your research question in practice means that every piece of paper you send to your supervisor must include an attachment of the updated research question (or written in the header of every page!), as well as a message of how it has been changed since the last supervision. It is impossible to relate to a paper without knowing the research question.

Get input from your supervisor and fellow students/others

On the levels of study where you are entitled to a supervisor, you should always discuss drafts of you research question with a teacher in the field. Otherwise you may risk wasting time on a paper that is doomed to failure. If you have made one or more subject-specific observations or if your answer at this point is a controversial one, you should consult your supervisor about whether your idea is viable. In some schools and universities, the teacher must "approve" research questions. However, we believe this often leads to students making their supervisors largely responsible for their research question and then resting on their laurels because they think: "My research question is done because my supervisor has approved it!" As we have said earlier, you should never consider your research question to be finished before the text is completed. Research questions must regularly be adjusted in a dialectic relationship with the problem, sources, data, theories, methods. Finally, it may become necessary to rewrite your research question when you compare it to your conclusion. A shift in focus can occur during the writing process and it is infinitely easier to change the research question than change the content of 25 pages.

Approval of your research question means that …
… it appears fine to you supervisor at this point, but that … • (radical) changes must be reported to your supervisor • approval of the foundation is not the same as approval of the execution • you must still continuously evaluate whether your research question needs adjusting.

Activity: Consult your supervisor
Consulting your supervisor is fundamental: "Will this research question lead to an academically acceptable paper if I in addition carry out my research well enough, or is the paper doomed to failure?

If your supervisor rejects your research question, listen and make sure you understand your supervisor's reasons and alternative suggestions. Ask for quick feedback on your next draft.

While reading this chapter, you may be unsure whether your supervisor agrees with us and our suggestions. If in doubt, ask you supervisor, read the curriculum, read previous students' (good) papers. At your educational institution, there may be special writing traditions that you need to be aware of. In brief:

Obtain knowledge about the requirements and traditions you are subject to at your educational institution or faculty.

A good research question is no guarantee

A good research question alone does not guarantee a good paper. There are excellent texts without actual research questions (but which then include some other form of defined focus) and there are examples of excellent research question which are then followed by poor texts. The research question does no guarantee a good paper, but it makes it more probable that you will end up with a good paper and a work process that is less frustrating. From our supervision, we know that a text rarely causes trouble as long as it includes a really good research question. Therefore, if a paper runs into problems, we always look at the research question first.

Unanswered questions and unfinished research questions

What do you do if you reach a negative, invalidating answer: "It turned out that, it does not apply that …/it could not be done … and the hypothesis has been negated, so the introductory research question cannot be answered"? This answer can in fact be just as qualified, intelligent, sharp, analytical and significant as a corroborative answer. It may show something interesting about the sources and methods and what the applied data and tools can be used for, etc. You must articulate this in your discussion and conclusion to answer why the data, sources, research design, execution, etc., has led you to a negative answer to your research question.

At the same time, this is a really good issue to discuss in supervision: "I can't answer my research question, what do I do? Rewrite it, redo all my research or write that I have no conclusion?" This situation requires supervision.

At the end of your paper, in your conclusion or perspective, you can also formulate new research questions as a result of the higher level of understanding of the field's answers and questions you have now reached.

The research question and the conclusion's answer do not meet as a fully formed circle. Instead the research and its answers or lack of answers enable new ways of asking. Here you must remember that there is a big difference between writing papers and real research: When writing papers, the student is not expected to *provide finished answers*, but "only" to show that he or she is able to *ask and search for answers in a methodical, analytical and reflected way.*

5. Literature and information search for your paper

By Lotte Thing Rasmussen, Kirstin Remvig and Charlotte Wien

Many librarians find regularly that students reel off research questions when they are looking for literature and then ask: "Do you have a book about that?" Consider for a moment that, if the answer is "yes," then there is no need to write the paper. When you are writing a paper, you have to search through a lot of different material and information for something you can use in your paper. When you put it all together in a pile, what is in the pile should only be there because it is a part of your overall answer. If you were to give the pile a title, it would be the same thing your research question is about.

You should think about your information search on the basis of three questions:
1. What do I need to know to provide an answer for my paper?
2. How do I find the material I need to be able to provide an answer for my paper?
3. And how do I search for it?

What am I looking for?

There is no one final key with the literature for precisely your paper. So, "what" is important. Part of the task of an academic paper is to be able to limit, search, assess, select and use the literature you find relevant in relation to answering the research question you have formulated. "What" also covers all the various types of material that might have relevance for you.

Types of material may include

Books, different types of periodical articles, news sources/newspaper articles, research results, studies undertaken by researchers, public authorities and/or businesses, conceptual definitions, statistical materials, handbooks, theory, philosophy of science, methodological literature, and much more.

Regardless of what *you* choose from the material to answer *your* research question, the choice of the basic literature and how you use it is half the job of writing a good paper.

Throughout the entire paper phase, it is important to keep to the question "what do I need to know right now?" During the process of writing an academic paper, various questions will appear for which you will need to find an answer/justification/probability. You will be able to find these answers in your own data (primary data), other studies (secondary data) and in different types of literature.

Where do I search? What search tools should I use?

All information and all literature "live" in certain places and are made searchable in certain ways. However, no search machine is complete. Therefore, you also need to search in different places. Most academic literature by far (academic articles are most often published in professional periodicals – either physically, in electronic form, or both) is contained in various databases, and research libraries pay for a license to many of these databases. Therefore, use the access to the library at your school to find out which databases your research library has purchased a license for. Academic databases may be found in narrow disciplinary and broad interdisciplinary forms.

Google Scholar and Wikipedia are search tools that are accessible to anyone. At your research library, you can also get access to different search tools you can use to find materials that are aimed at researchers and students. The many different types of search tools contain different types of information and academic focus:

- *Library catalogues,* which you can search from your computer. The library records in its catalogue its collections of materials: books, periodicals, etc., so you may find information, see whether a book is in the stacks and where it is located on the shelves. If your own library does not have the book you are looking for, you may search at www.bibliotek.dk, which contains all the libraries in Denmark. If you have a library card to one of them, you may order the material from other libraries to be sent to your local library.
- *Fact bases* contain information in the form of numbers, raw data, statistical information or definitions of concepts – occasionally with short texts as compendia and encyclopedias do. Examples of this are statistical data bases such

as, for example Statistics Denmark and StatBank Denmark or databases with information about companies – for example, Passport or Bisnode MarketProfile.
- *Full text/bibliographic databases* contain references to books and other documents such as reports, periodical articles and patents. A bibliographic database may be a pure "catalogue," in which you can only see the reference (for example, the Danish National Research Database), or it may contain the documents themselves in full text (for example, JSTOR). Full-text databases may be part of one of the large database hosts that provide several databases under the same "roof," such as, for example, Web of Science, EbscoHost, Proquest, Science Direct (which are all scientific article databases) and InfoMedia and Lexis-Nexis (news, newspaper, subject-specific databases).

What are you searching?	Search tools	What can you find?
- Definitions - Short explanations of terms and concepts - Short description of a topic/problem area	- Reference words - Wikipedia - Compendia - Encyklopædias - Dictionaries - Handbooks	- Definitions of concepts - Explanations of words and, perhaps, their origin and development. - Translations - Concise overview articles
- Academic periodical articles	- Academic periodical databases - Google Scholar - bibliotek.dk	- Academic periodicals and/or periodical articles as reference or in full text
- News sources - Newspaper articles - Trade journals - Magazines	- InfoMedia - Databases with foreign press materials – for example, Lexis Nexis, Factiva, PressReader, Retriever, WISO - bibliotek.dk	- News, newspaper, or subject-specific articles in full text - News and archive materials - Electronic format or microfilm

• Academic materials from researchers at universities and institutions of higher learning	• Library catalogues • Danish National Research Database • Universities, etc., homepages	• Working papers • Reports • Conference papers • Dissertations
• Literature on the paper's theories, methods and philosophy of science	• Your library's catalogue • bibliotek.dk • Academic databases	• Textbooks • Academic dissertations • Academic articles

Activity: What do I need and where can I find it?

- What do I need to know right now? Consider what types of material will be ble to give you the knowledge you need? In what corner of the pentagon model (see p. 32) do you find yourself in the process right now?
- Where can I find the material? Think about where the type of material you are looking for might be indexed. Use the overview above. Investigate, for example, the array of databases within your research area to which your university library has purchased a license.

Information searches in the context of writing a paper – what and where?

Information and literature searches are "hidden" in all corners of the pentagon model. Corners 3 and 4 cannot be done without an information search, but you will also typically benefit in 1 and 2 if, for example, you orient yourself in reference works and search for in inspiration in earlier treatments of the same and/or related topics. (We recommend the research question and literature search tool *Scribo* with which you can work your way through the pentagon).

The pentagon can help you gain an overview of *what* you need to know and *where* you can look for it:

1. Research question –
What are you asking?
Often, people start by searching a general topic relatively broadly in order to determine how the topic has been investigated before. Orient yourself, for example, in reference works, encyclopedias or Wikipedia in definitions of the most important concepts, look for inspiration in earlier treatments of the same and/or related topics.

2. Purpose – Why are you asking?
The academic purpose of the investigation – i.e., its use. For this, you may do some searches for inspiration, illustrations of your case, why the topic is important and relevant. Here, all sorts of sources may be relevant. A current debate, for example, can show a need for – and thus give you an idea and motivation to do – a study.

3. Data – What is the object of your study?
The study's data, material, phenomena, subject matter. Your subject matter (data) may be one or more texts (primary sources) that you have ordered from the library. There may be reports, studies, research results that may help illuminate your field (secondary data), or you may collect or create data (primary data) through measurements, observations, interviews, questionnaires, your own experiments, etc. In that case, you may need literature about how this can be done.

4. Theory, philosophy of science, methods – What tools are you using to ask the question?
The tools of the study: Philosophy of science, theory, concepts, academic methods. Textbooks, primers, academic articles, handbooks, methodological books.
We write "books" here regardless of whether they are analogue or digital materials and resources.

5. Research design – How do you ask your question?
The investigative method/research design. The method of the paper is the paper's recipe in which ingredients and sequence must be clear and follow in a logical order. Therefore, you should consider whether you have found sufficient information to answer your research question. Use, for example, *Scribo* (www.scribo.dk): "Research design → question 19 → explanation/tip", where you can find some good advice for your considerations.

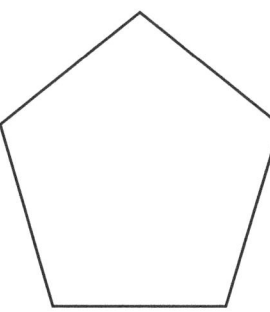

How do I search?

The third and last important question you should ask yourself in connection with the information and literature search for your paper is "*how* do I search the literature". This question is also of a practical nature and goes to the technical search skills you need to develop. It is important to emphasise that searching requires craftsmanship, and practice makes perfect. You can read how to do it, but you must also do it. Most people start with so-called "unstructured searches" in which they search a little here and there – often without any more specific goal than to orient themselves in the way the databases deal with topics and conceptual clarifications. In this section, we develop a more structured approach to information searches.

You should very probably use some of the literature you have read and will read about the specific subject and other subjects in your studies for your paper – and you must build on the lessons and recommendations of your teacher/supervisor. Pay attention to the core literature of the discipline/field – is there anything you absolutely must read? However, it is rarely enough if you are to write a paper. You must also search out supplemental literature.

How much of the literature should I read?

Students are rarely assessed on *how much* they have read but on whether they can demonstrate the connection between the literature and their own research and how they have limited and used what they have read. Therefore, it is most often a reasonable prioritisation to use some time to write and rewrite, to structure and edit. Better to do a thorough written presentation on the basis of fewer texts than a quick last-minute paper on the basis of many texts. What is important is whether the *choice and use of the literature* are justified and seem appropriate.

Use good reference works

If you have a topic but have not yet focussed it or formulated a research question, it is a good idea to start by identifying the most important concepts and terms within the field. Using a compendium or an encyclopaedia/Wikipedia can help clarify terminology and jargon with respect to the topic, and they can also provide an overview of the entire field – for example, academic disagreements and various standpoints in any debate. In certain instances, you can also find references to the important literature respecting the topic. You can find compendia and encyclopedia in general and subject-specific versions. Common to the former is that they strive as an ideal to collect all the knowledge into one volume. Examples of general reference works are *Den Store Danske Encyklopædi*, *Britannica Online* and *Wikipedia*.

The free encyclopeida, Wikipedia, is today among the world's most visited homepages: Several hundred thousand people around the world write, edit, quality-check, and utilize its content. Despite the fact that Wikipedia is a democratic and dialogue-based tool for academic communication and exploitation of the "wisdom of the crowd", you should be aware that a Wikipedia entry may be overly influenced by the understanding or critical interest of its users. So, use your critical sense.

In subject-specific reference works, you find far more nuanced information than in general reference works. An example is the *Encyclopedia of Human Rights.* Many of them are published electronically. So, you can consult them from home.

Activity

- Look up the important concepts and terms for your topic (research question) in a general reference work
- Then look up the same concepts/terms in relevant subject-specific reference works to which your school grants you access.

Research question and search profile

Once you have become familiar with the terminology and core concepts in your field and have gone through the steps that are described in chapter 4, you should be ready to formulate your research question – not in its final form, perhaps, but precisely enough to devise a "search profile." The search profile serves two purposes:

1. It helps you to limit and define your topic.
2. And it helps you plan and guide your searches and, thus, focus on the topic about which you are seeking information.

A good search profile

Contains a limitation of the topic, a series of search words that cover the topic and a strategy for what you will do if you find either too many or too few documents.

Of course, you do not need to devise a search profile to do a quick fact search on the Internet or some preliminary searches on the topic you are thinking of writing about. But the search profile is useful if you want answers to a more complicated question and would like to search several or all aspects of your research question at the same time. As a rule, the research question includes several different concepts. Once you have your research question pretty much in place, you may begin to do searches in a more structured way. In the following, we illustrate the process with a starting point in this research question:

"What stereotypes do researchers have about journalists?"

Core concepts, language and synonyms

Three words leap out in the research question: *Stereotype, researcher* and *journalist*. The first word, *stereotype* (which, in Danish, might be described as *forestillinger*) links to theories about stereotypes that are a central field within social psychology. *Researchers* and *journalists* link to the case or the data to be investigated. In order to answer the research question, we are looking for literature that contains all three words. The starting point for the search, therefore, must be a combination of these three concepts. The search words that almost leap up in the research question we call *core concepts*. We begin our search profile with these three core concepts.

| Core concepts | stereotypes | researchers | journalists |

The research question has three core concepts. If your research contains question contains a different number, you should adapt your search profile.

> **Core concepts in the research question – the PICO model**
>
> In the health sciences, people – especially in the clinical field – work with the PICO model. Each letter may be seen to stand for a core concept in a research question and can, thus, be used in a search profile:
> - P: Patient, population, problem
> - I: Intervention
> - C: Comparison
> - O: Outcome

> There are several models in relation to PICO, but you can also try to use *who, what, where, how* and *when* as a substitute for each core concept in order to see whether you can work with them. This type of model may be splendid for the development of a research question within the respective fields, but be aware that it may limit you in your search process if you put your trust in a fixed model for your search profile.

It may be relevant even at this point to consider what language you want to search in.

Do you want to find documents in English, German, French, Swedish, Norwegian? The answer depends on your specific research question and your language skills. Most people will presumably try to meet their information needs primarily in one language. But might not German, French, Swedish or Norwegian texts provide a broader perspective on the topic?

The search language may be an important source in distorting an information search since we have to sort out results from languages that we cannot read. Certain subject areas, however, are primarily nationally anchored. If you investigate, for example, the implementation of the Danish 2014 school reform, Danish language literature will be important, but search also outside the country's borders. The Scandinavian countries and Germany with which we have historic ties may be able to provide interesting comparisons. And even though the Danish school system is far from the American or the English, other countries have, of course, researched the implementation of their school reforms. So, consider thinking broadly. You might be inspired, for example, to describe a new method that has not been tried before. Many of the major international databases contain literature mostly in English. So, you will not find much if you use Danish search terms.

In our example, we are interested in international research since there is little research in Denmark on stereotypes. Therefore, we have chosen to translate our three core concepts into English. The Danish word *forskere* translated into English gives us another concept because, in English, 'forskere' may be either *scientists* or *researchers*. In our search profile, therefore, we change the language, add *researchers* – and place an OR between the terms (more on this, pp. 157ff.).

Core concepts	stereotypes	scientists OR researchers	journalists

In our example, both *scientist* and *researcher* turn up when we translate a concept into English. But these sorts of synonyms are found in all languages – even in Danish, of course. Therefore, you should pay attention to whether there are several words for the same concept for each of your core concepts.

Core concepts

Always discuss your paper's core concepts and their translation into other languages with your supervisor. It is crucial for your search process that you use the correct terminology within your chosen area. In addition, be careful to identify synonyms for your concepts, so you do not miss any relevant literature.

Substitute concepts – superordinate and subordinate concepts

Unfortunately, you cannot know in advance whether a search for obvious core concepts will provide you with a sufficient quantity of relevant literature. Therefore, it is a good idea to have some "substitute concepts" ready. That is, some extra search words you can use if it is necessary to find more or less material. In addition to synonyms, you can work with superordinate and subordinate concepts: Superordinate concepts if a search of the core concepts gives too few results and subordinate concepts if the original search gives too many results.

The question now is how you find your superordinate and subordinate concepts: The starting point again is the research question because, even though the core concepts do not provide a reasonable number of results, you must still be able to answer your paper's research question. Therefore, it is a matter of finding what you might call "topical synonyms" for each core concept. And, here, preliminary work in reference materials may prove to be useful.

The concept of *stereotypes* is, as we said earlier, a theory within the field of social psychology. So *social psychology* might be an obvious superordinate concept for the search profile. If you were to search even more broadly, you could also add *sociology*. A quick Wikipedia entry (Danish version) on social psychology reveals that it "deals with topics such as attitudes, postures, identity, attribution, groups and social reality". An entry in the English Wikipedia shows that a central area within social psychology includes *prejudices* and *stereotypes*. *Stereotypes* we have already, but we can add *prejudices* as a subordinate concept to the search profile.

The Danish word *forestillinger* (which might be translated as *preconception*) could also inspires core concepts, but it is a word with many meanings. Does it mean performances, expectations, imaginings, conceptions)? In your work with the research question, it is easy to use such ambiguous words. This may make sense in relation to the paper; but, in the search process, it can be clear that the word contains several different meanings, and you may need to specify your concept by substituting something more specific or to add an adjective to pin down the meaning.

In the same way, the next core concept, *researcher*, has superordinate and subordinate concepts. The Norwegian Wikipedia, which has the most precise definition of the Nordic versions, writes: "A researcher is a person who is occupied with research and, as such, is a broad, generic designation of a number of different types of scientific positions." Thus, obvious superordinate concepts might be *science* or *research*, *research institutions*, *universities*, while subordinate concepts could be different titles within the university world or concepts taken from individual disciplines (*professors, doctors, associate professors*). To the last core concept, *journalists*, you could add *mass media* or *news media* as a superordinate concept and *reporters, science journalism* and *news journalism* as subordinate concepts.

Wikipedia and encyclopaedias

NB: You may use Wikipedia, for example, as a reference work in your work process. But if this version were to contain a definition of, for example, *stereotypes*, a subject-specific encyclopaedia such as the *Encyclopedia of Social Psychology* would be a far better reference.

Superordinate concepts may prove to be especially useful if you are looking for a very specific concept. If, for example, you are searching a narrow concept or a new field of research about which there are only a few publications, it can be practical to increase the number of possible search results. However, be aware that superordinate concepts can also open the floodgates for a lot of unnecessary results that do not contain what you are looking for. Subordinate concepts can likewise prove useful if your core concepts contain a number of relevant subordinate aspects. Sometimes, you might discover that it can be rewarding to substitute a core concept with a subordinate concept in the search profile (and, thus, also in the research question) because it sharpens and limits the problem area and the search. There does not need to be a real logical connection between core concepts and super- or subordinate concepts. The only requirement is that they must be related in a topical sense.

As search concepts gradually fall into place, you can begin to write them down in a "search profile schema". The search profile can be used in all types of databases that contain academic and scientific literature. It is permissible to get smarter as you go and add or remove search words. Remember in that case to write down your choices in your schema. Then, you can subsequently account for your search better if that is a part of the paper's requirements.

Our search profile now looks like this:

Core concepts	stereotypes	researchers OR scientists	journalists
Superordinate concepts	social psychology OR sociology	research OR science OR universities OR research institutions	mass media OR news media
Subordinate concepts	prejudices	professors OR doctors OR associate professors	reporters OR science journalism OR news journalism

> **Activity: Make your search profile**
>
> Identify your core concepts from your research question/your topic, and begin a search profile in the same way as the previous schema.

Translate the search profile into a search language

With a search profile like the one above in hand, you are well-equipped to meet with a librarian. The librarian can help you to choose the right search tools and supervise you in the execution of your search. However, if you have a little bit of insight into search theory, you can easily do it yourself. The next pages contain a quick introduction to some of the most important tips and tricks in information search theory.

When you are looking for information for your paper, it is fundamentally about working with the search profile until you have found an appropriate number of relevant documents in the database(s) you have selected. Often, however, you will find you get a mixture of relevant and irrelevant documents. Most often, it is the case that the more documents you find, the greater number of them are what we call "noise", that is, irrelevant for your paper. Therefore, you need to be able to control the number of found documents and adjust the search results up or down. You can work to find a number of synonyms and make use of your super- and subordinate concepts, but there are several other techniques that can help you on your way.

Boolean operators – and/or/not

When you combine search words, you use so-called "Boolean logic". Boolean logic consists of three operators: *and, or* and *not*. You combine your search words with these three terms. We shall return to the operator *not* in a bit. First, we shall focus on *and* and *or*.

> **Activity: Consider the following two propositions**
>
> - Carrots and potatoes
> - Carrots *or* potatoes
>
> Which proposition will provide the biggest result on your plate and in a database search respectively?

In a database search, the second proposition will provide the most documents. However, many people in a hurry make a mistake because Boolean logic cuts against linguistic logic. This logic is illustrated in this figure:

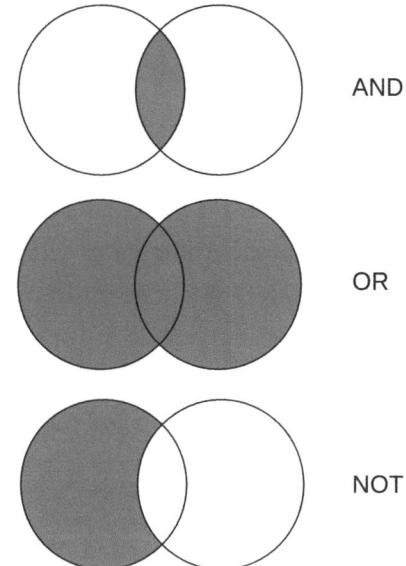

When you search with *and*, you "cross" one search word with another and get the documents that contain *both* search words at the same time, in union. The Boolean operator *and* narrows the search result. On the other hand, if you search with *or* between two search words, you expand the search result and get an intersection. By using *or* between two search words, you get documents that contain *either* one or the other search word. *Or* must, then, be used when you are searching for words that are equally valid or have the same meaning (synonyms). Therefore, we have placed an OR between the synonyms in our search profile schema (p. 156).

Most databases do not understand meanings but simply search for a string of letters. If you search with the word "researcher", you will not find documents in which the word "scientist" is used instead. Therefore, it is important that you have thought through the synonyms that cover your search words.

Health databases

In the health databases PubMed, Medline and Cochrane Library, it is possible to search with so-called MeSH terms and thereby avoid overlooking relevant synonyms. MeSH stands for Medical Subject Headings, and by using them you can search these databases very precisely.

The important thing here is that an *or* must be used when you are searching for a concept and its synonyms. *And* is used when you are searching for two search words that are not synonyms but each has its own meaning; and, therefore, you want *both* words to be present in every search result.

Not is also a Boolean operator. We have kept this until last because it must be used with circumspection. An example illustrates best why: If we were to write a paper about political Islam but not the fundamentalist segment of political Islam, it would be obvious to do a search of "Islam *not* fundamentalism" and, thus, cleanse your search result of any talk of fundamentalism. But if there is a book in the library called *Political Islam: Something Different and More Than Fundamentalism*, you would not find it even though it would definitely be relevant. So, unless you are very sure about your case, you should avoid the Boolean *not* and, instead, use combinations of *and* and *or*.

Boolean operators are used in almost all databases, but there can be a difference in the way they are written. Most by far accept using AND or OR (in English and with capital letters). Other possibilities are uncapitalized letters or a "+", an "&" or a ";". You can always look up in the database's help or information function how the database supports search operators.

> **Activity**
>
> Experiment with some simple searches in a database, so you can get an idea of how it works.

It is relatively easy to follow what the database does when you combine, for example, just two concepts with AND or OR. On the other hand, if you have more than two words that are to be combined with both AND and OR, you can easily lose oversight. In most large databases, you can use the database's search history function, so you can search for one word at a time and then combine them with OR for synonyms (vertical in the schema). Then combine the results of your OR searches with AND (horizontal in the schema). The advantage of searching for one concept at a time is that you minimise the risk of mistakes – typos, spelling mistakes or lack of quotation marks around phrases. You will quite simply have an easier time keeping track of the results and controlling your search when you search one column of concepts at a time.

In your search profile, you can keep track of your process by inserting Boolean operators as in the figure below. We have also added in the figure quotation marks around the concepts that are to be searched together (see "phrase searches" in the next section, p. 161f.).

If you cannot select a search history function, you will need to combine AND and OR in the same search of a longer search string. Here, again, you must first connect synonym search words with OR and then combine them with AND. You keep track of the process by putting a parenthesis around the OR searches and then place AND between the parentheses. A search string containing all concepts from the search profile will, therefore, look as follows:

(stereotypes OR "social psychology" OR sociology OR prejudices) AND (researchers OR scientists OR research OR science OR universities OR "research institutions" OR professor OR doctor) AND (journalists OR "mass media" OR "news media" OR reporters OR "science journalism" OR "news journalism")

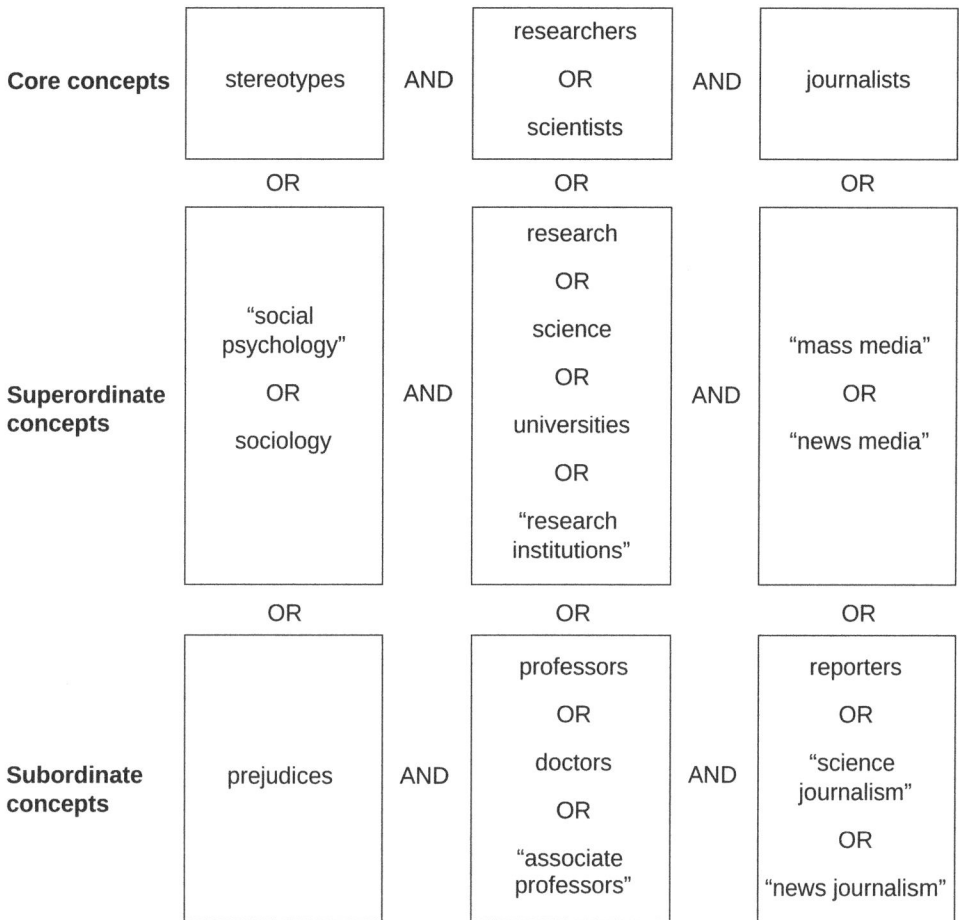

Phrase searches

In some cases, you may need to search a series of words in a particular order – for example, if you search a concept consisting of several words or you are searching for a particular person. If, for example, you are interested in finding something about *social media* and type this into the database's search field, the database will find results with the word *social* and results with the word *media* and, most often, put the two results together. You will get results about *social benefits, social skills*, etc. Of course, you will also get hits on social media, but you will get many hits you cannot use – that is, noise. In this case, you should do what is called *phrase searching*. This search option is accessible in almost all databases. In most, you do the search by placing quotation marks around the words ("… …"). Phrase searches are suitable for searching for concepts consisting of several words that are unequivocal strings of words. However, they can also be used to search for specific people or titles if, for example, you want to search for a particular theoretician or find a specific title in the literature.

Activity

- Try to search a concept of several words – for example, social media. First, search the words without the quotation marks – social media. Then try with quotation marks – "social media".
- Try social AND media as well and social OR media.
- Take note of the number of results in your search and compare them.

Truncation

Many databases only search exactly what you have written – i.e., the string of letters you have typed. Therefore, in most search tools, you may *truncate* your search word in order to correct for different endings the search word may have. Truncation is a sign that tells the database that it should ignore everything following the truncation sign. If you are searching for *journal**, you will find *journal, journalism, journalist*, etc. Here, we use the asterisk sign * to indicate a truncation. The asterisk sign is often used for truncations, but you can also use the §,!, #, $,? signs and even @.

The effect of a truncation can be great. If, for example, you are searching for *journal** at www.bibliotek.dk, you will find 274,383 documents as opposed to 166,675 (as of December 2016) if you did not truncate. Truncation also makes your searches broader. At the same time, it increases the risk that you will get more unusable results. Nevertheless, more and more databases automatically truncate search words. This may produce a lot of noise. Therefore, you should consider turning off the automatic truncation if that is possible.

Activity

- Consider whether some of your concepts should be truncated if you want more results.
- Test one of the concepts with and without truncation and compare.

Help functions and tutorials

The language of search engines is quite simple: It is easy to understand the purpose of phrase searches, truncation and Boolean operators. But in practice it is hardly so easy to use these different search tools optimally. The problem is that the commands you give search engines are expressed differently from search engine to search engine and that search engines are altered on a running basis. For a good search result, therefore, it is important that you are familiar with the way you express the individual commands in each search tool. Look under the database's help function or search on YouTube by searching for *tutorial* combined with the search engine's name. Both will give you a quick and easy overview of the options you have to make your searches more precise in various search engines.

Use the database's indexing in your search

Your searches can be made much more precise and directed if you know a little about how the databases are constructed. When you search in a database, the database does not "read" its content from one end to the other. You search its indexes. Databases often have many different indexes: title, author, abstracts, complete text, etc.

Most search engines by far provide the option of addressing different indexes. How you do this practically varies from search engine to search engine. In many of the larger databases, you limit by choosing an "index field" for the words you have written. Then the database adds an abbreviation for the index you have chosen – for example, TI for title, AU for author and SU for subject. Quite often, you can also write the abbreviation yourself. In bibliotek.dk, you can, for example, write *ti=informationsearch*, and you will get all the materials in bibliotek.dk that include *informationsearch* in the title. A similar function is found in Google. Here, for example, you can write *allintitle:* before your search word and only get results where your search word is included in the title. There are many options for this kind of addressed indexing. Try to google *search operators google*, and you will get relevant results.

As mentioned, some databases contained so-called topic indexes. A topic index is distinguished from other indexes in that someone has described the material's topic by adding topic words to it. Topic indexes may be called different things such as, for example, *topic words, thesaurus terms* or *subject terms*. When you do limited searches through topic indexes, you can be certain that the documents you find will deal with the concept you are searching. Many of the topic indexes are constructed as a so-called thesaurus in which topic words are placed in a hierarchy with the option for searching, respectively, broader and narrower related concepts. The idea is that you can move up and down in your level of generalization according to need – if you need more hits, you can search with more general topic words and vice versa if you have too many hits. If you do not find anything on what you are searching, you can take inspiration from the database's thesaurus. The database may call your concept something other than what you think. If you are searching for something on *school reform* in the American database ERIC (Education Resources Information Center), you will discover, for example that the concept *educational reform* is to be searched under *educational change*.

It is quite ordinary that concepts in the 'soft' disciplines such as the humanities and social sciences are not as precise and well-defined as in the 'hard' disciplines. In natural science, health science and technology, it may be easier to search for specific (perhaps, Latin) concepts because the automatic topic indexing systems work better when the academic concepts are unequivocal.

How do I use the search profile?

We have reviewed the most fundamental things about information searches for academic papers. In the following, we shall show how you can use the method in practice by doing the search for which our search profile is devised. We have decided to do the search in the database Communication Source, which focuses on media research and is hosted by the database host called EBSCO Host. The choice was made to use Communication Source because we wanted a media studies tint to the topic. The search was conducted on 25 November 2016. The first search string was as:

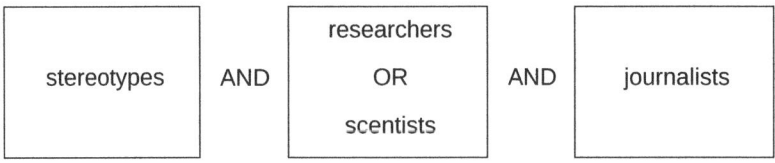

stereotypes AND (researchers OR scientists) AND journalists

This provided seven results, but we thought that was too little. So, we wanted to raise the number of found documents. We did this with the help of our super- and subordinate concepts and by truncating some of the search words. When we searched for *professo**, the database also searched for everything that contained *professo*. The same was true for *journalis**. Therefore, we deleted *associate professor, science journalism* and *news journalism*. We searched *news media* and *mass media* together under *media*. The next search string, therefore, looked as follows:

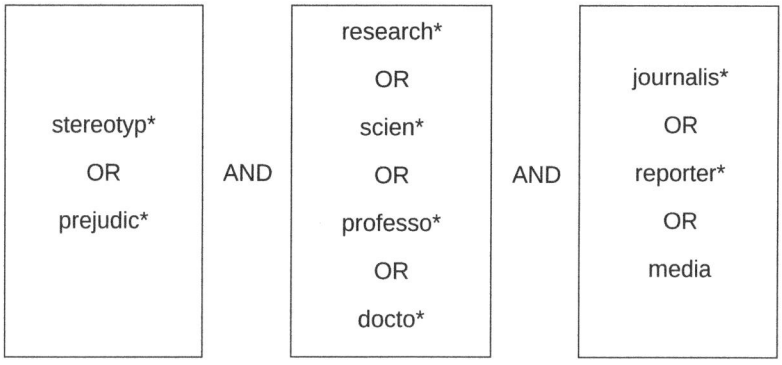

(stereotyp* OR prejudic*) AND (research* OR scien* OR professo* OR docto*) AND (journalis* OR reporter* OR media)

This provided 1,254 hits. We could increase the number more by utilizing superordinate concepts in the search string, but we assessed that we had an appropriate number and that we now had to work on making our search more precise. We could increase precision by addressing different indexes or limiting the search in relation to language, time and document type. On p. 163, we described how one can limit the indexing of the database – for example, with TI, AU or SU. Thus, we started by limiting the search to the SU index, which in this database was indexed for topic words.

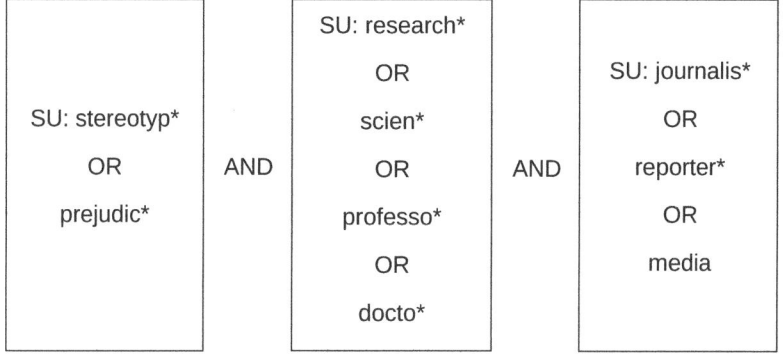

SU (stereotyp* OR prejudic*) AND SU (research* OR scien* OR professo* OR docto*) AND SU (journalis* OR reporter* OR media)

This gave us 90 results. In this example, we were interested in articles from peer-reviewed academic articles and, therefore, decided to limit our search to peer-reviewed periodicals. Thus, the results were reduced further down to 69. By quickly scanning through the results, we could see that the concept *Research** had provided some noise in the search. It turned outthat this topic word was used to describe research generally. Therefore, we removed it from the search.

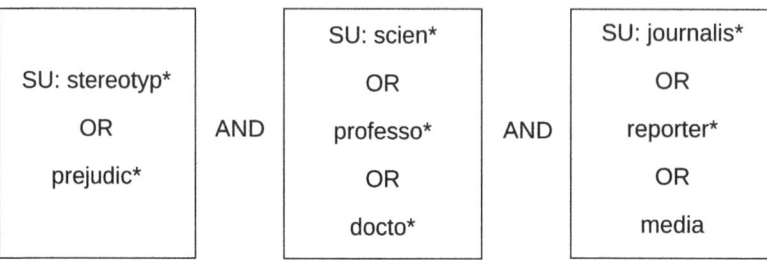

SU (stereotyp* OR prejudic*) AND SU (scien* OR professo* OR docto*) AND SU (journalis* OR reporter* OR media)

This search gave 12 documents. None of the 12 documents provided an answer to our research question, but that was not the idea. If we had found an article that contained the answer to the research question, there would have been no reason to write the paper because the answer was there in advance. So, it was a good sign. It was also clear that all 12 articles touched on the topic and contained references to literature from social psychology and media studies and that they contained – or referred to – studies of the relationship between journalists and researchers.

In the example above, we have searched an academically relevant database. There may be a number of databases that, in different ways, may meet your information needs. Thus, the search should be repeated. Here, it is important to consider how far you need to go. We find more and more students who are told by their supervisor to investigate what can be found with respect to current research on a topic. Here, as a student, you need to inquire into what the supervisor means: Is a systematic, exhaustive search in all relevant databases expected? Or, rather, are we talking about a smaller state-of-the-art cross-section in which you are to demonstrate briefly that you are familiar with the most important theoreticians within a given field. Clarify, too, what expectations there are for documentation of the search process.

Within the health sciences, for example, there is generally more focus on a systematic search and documentation of the search process, which makes sense when you have an evidence-based approach. There is no reason to repeat a study of a particular combination of medical treatments if the results of your information search show that the treatment has already been tested and patients became more sick than well.

Chain searches/citation searches

There is another way of doing searches in academic literature – namely, *chain searches*. When researchers publish their work – for example, in academic articles, they always cite other academic books and articles on which they draw. This is true for both direct citations of others' texts but also broader references to the conclusions, methods or ideas of others – therefore, they are also called citation searches. This type of search is effective when you need to search the literature within a particular area, but chain searches cannot stand alone. Therefore, you should also be sure to orient yourself broadly in order to be certain that you do not unintentionally limit yourself in relation to your topic.

How do I chain search?

The idea behind the chain search is that you re-use the bibliographies of others. If you happen upon a relevant article or book, there is a high probability that you will also find this work's references interesting. The article you have, in turn, builds on the research that is referenced in the bibliography. Ergo, your own work may be logically seen, to a certain degree, to build on the texts that are referenced. The system may best be illustrated with a diagram like the one below.

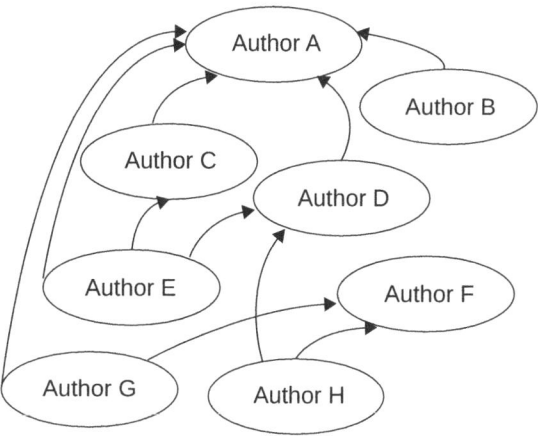

Author A has written an article. Author B has read it, and he writes an article in which he cites A. Authors C and D have also read A's article, but they disagree with the conclusion A reaches. Therefore, they both write – independently of each other – a critical article. Author E has read the articles by C and D and also author A's. E believes that both C and D misinterpret A and that A is actually right. Yet another article is published. And so it can continue for many years.

If you search the literature to look at others' references, you are fundamentally doing a topic search in which the authors over whose shoulders you are looking have selected carefully the literature they have found most relevant for their work. If you use others' references to delve into a topic, you know you have covered it well if you do not run into new, relevant references when you find a new bibliography.

Retro- and prospective chain searches

This form of chain search is retrospective because, in the first instance, you will only find references to literature that is older than the work in which you have found the reference. However, the great thing about chain searches is that you can also search prospectively – that is, forward in time. In this way, you are not cut off from access to the latest research.

If, for example, you have read a landmark book that is five or ten years old, it will probably be used and discussed by a whole series of authors afterwards. In the databases Web and Science, Scopus and Google Scholar, you can do a forward-looking chain search based on an old book or article by choosing *Cited by* or *Times cited*. In this way, you will find all the books and articles that refer to it. These were, by their very nature, written later. If, once again, we return to the previous figure (p. 167), you can by taking your starting point in author A's work find author G's more recent article because G refers to A.

This form of forward-looking chain search has a number of advantages: As mentioned, this ensures that you do not overlook the most current literature. But, beyond that, it provides an opportunity to investigate how influential a given work is. The logic is simple: the more a work has been cited, the more interest (positive or negative) it has created. Finally, we can investigate how a given theory, method or approach has developed forward in time.

> **Activity**
>
> - Try to do a search in Google Scholar.
> - Select one of the results that is cited most often (Cited by).
> - Click on Cited By and see who has cited the reference you have selected.

Why can't I settle for a chain search?

It is not enough, however, to settle for a chain search because you risk being dazzled by a single paradigm or an entirely unique research tradition and, thus, overlook other – and, perhaps, more fruitful – approaches to the topic. When you take your starting point in a single reference and search back in time, you are naturally guided by that starting point – and you cannot reliably know whether the article's author has systematically avoided other relevant texts. So, even though you have searched the works referenced and, perhaps, also their references and thereby gained an overview of the topic, you may risk overlooking parallel discussions. When you do a forward-looking chain search, the situation may be the same: Here, you also find only newer works that cite the original work. You cannot be sure you will find more recent – relevant – works that, for one reason or another, do not mention the original work.

Use your supervisor and information specialist effectively

Information specialists and librarians are experts in search techniques, while your supervisor is the expert in assessing the literature and placing it in a specific academic/theoretical context. Always ask your supervisor about the core literature within the area about which you are writing your paper. Perhaps, your supervisor is also familiar with certain periodicals with which you might want to acquaint yourself. However, this is no guarantee that you will get the most important things since supervisors are not able to scour all the nooks and crannies of a subject area. This is where the librarian or information specialist at your library comes into the picture as an important resource in your paper-writing.

> **Get help from an information specialist/librarian, for example, if you**
>
> - get stuck in your search process
> - find way too much/too little, or if you do not find anything you think is sufficiently relevant
> - are in doubt about the extent to which you are looking the most suitable databases.

Most probably, your bibliography is in the process of preparation throughout your paper-writing process, and your final bibliography will be an expression of how you have chosen to answer your research question. It is a misunderstanding to believe that the bibliography is simply a part of your paper's formalia, which never gets read. Your supervisor or censor *reads* the bibliography, and they will refer repeatedly to the bibliography to orient themselves along the way as they read your paper because the bibliography is the basis for your documentation.

> **Get supervision for the bibliography**
>
> It is a good idea to take your bibliography to meetings with your supervisor – even when it is just in a preliminary version. The bibliography provides a supervisor with a nice insight into how you are working with your research question, and your supervisor may be able to advise you if any relevant types of material are missing.

Remember what we wrote at the start of the chapter: your bibliography must ultimately be an expression of the material you have found relevant and selected to answer your research question. Your supervisor can support you in determining whether it is satisfactory in relation to this purpose.

And check your library's homepage for courses and guidance on information serches.

6. Reading and taking notes for your paper

Curricular reading and reading for your paper require different reading and note-taking strategies

In higher education, you need to read literature in at least three different ways:
1. *Curricular reading* for oral and written exams "when you need to know it all".
2. *Topic oriented reading* – when you consider writing a paper within a particular subject area.
3. *Targeted reading* – for writing papers.

The point made in this chapter is that the content of your reading and accompanying notes depend on their later function. We will not consider curricular reading further in this book, apart from advising you against reading in this way when writing papers. In the following we will offer advice on how to read and take notes for your paper.

First and foremost, reading academically for papers means reading strategically, i.e., being selective about
- what you read
- how much time you spend reading each source
- which parts of each source you read.

To take good, useful notes for a paper, you must decide on a question you want to answer in your paper. The purpose of reading and taking notes for your paper is to formulate and answer your research question and any additional questions derived from it. Reading for your paper also means posing questions you aim to answer through your reading.

Reading and writing go hand in hand

All reading must be followed by writing! Preferably you should write the same day you read, as writing on the basis of your reading is the best way of understanding the material; material is stored in your long-term memory and not just in your short-term memory from which it will quickly disappear again. A long reading phase before you start writing is therefore not advisable. Here, writing means cohesive text (not tantamount to completed and correct text). The result of a reading phase that is not also a writing phase is usually that sources must be reread before being able to write.

Reading for papers

We have seen many students read too much, too early, and too thoroughly!

Apart from reading to gain a general overview of the topic, it is a good idea to postpone reading, at the very least, until you have taken certain strategies into consideration and preferably described what you want and hope to use your literature for (however, this does not need to take a long time). In chapter 2 on the writing process, you can find suggestions on how to start writing early on.

In relation to both scope and method, reading for your studies must be purpose-oriented.

An exception: Literature that does not have to be read purposefully the first time

Literary and philosophical works are an important exception. These types of works are read to enter a different world and you must read carefully to understand the whole work. You may not take notes when reading it the first time – however, you must do so if you decide to include the work in a paper. To start by reading fiction and works that interpret culture or philosophical works in a purely purpose oriented way would be a shame, as these texts also operate on emotional, associative and subconscious levels. In order to reap the full benefits, you must allow these texts to affect you on all levels and this takes time and requires immersion.

However, all other literature must be used, commented on and extracted from, and as long as your observe the established rules for using literature, you can treat it as you want.

Ways of reading

You must read your texts in an appropriate way. You can read in different ways:

> **Ways of reading – what is the purpose?**
>
> - Overview-reading – flicking through a book and e.g. reading the preface, table of content and blurb to gain an impression of the text
> - Skimming – reading to gain an overview of content (scope, type and level) and form (presentation and language)
> - Normal reading – reading to understand and appropriate the content and meaning of a text
> - Thorough/intensive reading – reading to learn in detail
> - Selective reading – reading to find particular information.

Overview-reading, skimming and selective readings are especially relevant when it comes to reading for papers.

Skimming – reading to gain an overview of the topic

There are two stages of choosing which literature to read:
- The first choice is made when skimming titles and abstract of possible literature: Here you choose from existing texts. However, you should not read all the literature you have found nor should you read it equally thoroughly.
- The second choice is made once you have the text in hand or on the screen. This is done by skimming books and articles before reading them. You form an overview of what the text is about, what type of documentation it uses (e.g. renowned theorists, new data) and which conclusions it reaches.

> **Skimming**
>
> - Skimming: A superficial way of reading with the purpose of:
>   - gaining an idea of content (scope, type and level) and form (presentation and language)
>   - preparing for a more thorough form of reading (or rejecting the text).
> - Skimming can be compared to a tourist's first visit to a city (reading about the city in advance is a good idea).
> - You skim by letting your eyes glide down the pages and stopping at "interesting places".
> - "Interesting places" are especially found in:
>   - the beginning and end of all passages
>   - headings
>   - highlights, e.g. italicised words
>   - long words (which are often meaningful and significant)
>   - keywords related to the text's topic.

The purpose of skimming is to assess whether you should spend time reading the text and whether you want to read it from cover to cover or perhaps just parts of it. Textbooks should rarely be read from beginning to end like novels.

Always take notes when reading to gain an overview of your topic. They are used to pinpoint where in the text interesting angles for a paper appear.

Selective reading – goal-oriented reading for writing papers

Create good conditions for goal-oriented reading by

- writing down one or more temporary research questions (as mentioned previously these must simply be sufficiently interesting and narrow so that you can base a literature search on them, as they can always be changed once the material has provided you with more insight)
- writing down everything you know before beginning your literature search.

Reading for the purpose of writing a paper – suggestions

Before reading: Is the text relevant?
- Know why you are reading the text for your paper. On the basis of your (temporary) research question, write down questions you want answers to:
    - Background information, detailed facts
    - The author's research, points of view, evaluations
    - Methods, philosophy of science, theories, concepts, data?
- Check the text's status:
    - Age, subject-specific relevance, whether it has been cited in other texts, where it is published – can it be used?
- Quickly get an impression of the text whether it is electronic or printed. Look at:
    - The blurb, headings, illustrations, references, table of contents (structure), preface, abstract, band, introduction in composite work, introduction to web texts, links.

Now you should be able to assess whether a text is relevant or whether you should put it away immediately.

When reading: Use the text
- Gain an overview of the text:
    - Read the table of contents and index closely: Which topics/themes are prevalent?
    - Read the first and last paragraph/chapter (introduction and conclusion).
    - In long texts: Read the beginning and end of each paragraph.

Now you should be able to assess whether a text is relevant to your paper.
- Skim the text with your research question in mind, locate the places that are relevant to your paper, and note or write comments, questions, etc. on post it's.
- Then read purposefully and selectively to find the information you need for your paper and make notes – not just about content, but also about how to use it in the paper. Make note of this in the files you need for structuring your paper. See the bottom of p. 177.

After reading: Evaluate the result
Evaluate the result of you reading in relation to what you were looking for. Did you find it? Do you need to read the text again? Do you need to search for new texts?

Sometimes reading the same text several times, each time with a new pair of glasses, can be necessary – as in this example: A students had to write a paper on a novel which she had to examine from three different perspectives. After several failed attempts of reading the novel while focusing on all three aspects, it became necessary to read the novel three times and take notes to each of the three aspects individually.

A brief comment on reading speed

Many students ask for courses on reading skills as they would like to learn how to read faster. There are techniques for this – see, for example Elbro & Nielsen (1996): *Videregående læsning* (a short but authoritative version). However, a good reading course will not focus on speed alone, but also on which parts of the text you should read carefully or less carefully. We believe practice should be focused on this: The goal is not to read much as possible as fast as possible, but rather to be able to select relevant material to study for a given task. Without reason, many students worry about reading too slowly according to their conception of the curricular requirements. However, if you are worried, it might be a good idea to test yourself after a lesson in *Videregående læsning* or simply by doing a simpel test with your study group after class. If you read much more slowly than most, you might consider taking a course. There are also. apps you can use to train how fast you read. Just use "speed reading" as a search word.

Finally, you should take stock every once in a while: What is the most interesting thing I have read and learnt about my topic so far?

Taking notes for your paper

You should take focused notes for your paper, in which you write down everything in relation to your own questions to the text, which must be relevant to your paper. This is why taking notes is much easier once you have formulated a research question. If you follow this method, your note taking will to a greater extent be guided by the literature's purpose and what is relevant in that context. When writing a research paper, you must read with the intention of being able to reproduce, use, insert, analyse, discuss and evaluate. A writer will likely come across minor details that he/she needs or wants to make note of. However, you should not limit your note-taking to what seemingly has relevance for your paper. You must be goal-oriented and open at the same time. Perhaps other and more relevant themes will appear, and as a result you may have to change the way you problematise the field and thus change your temporary research question.

Notes for the paper: Files

We recommend putting at least some of your notes into files during the writing process. This is the most practical way of storing your notes, because from here, turning your notes into finished text will only require a small step. If your notes are good, your paper is already half written. In downloaded documents, you can usually take notes directly In the document, but you must also remember to transfer them to your files. See below in the section entitled "Note-taking software".

Creating the following folders for a paper before reading and taking notes can prove practical:

Activity: Takes notes in files for each section of your paper

Immediately make a folder for these files, for example:
- Introduction
- Research question
- Concepts
- Theories
- Philosophy of science
- Methods
- Data
- Examples
- Analyses
- Discussions
- Criticism and discussion of method/theory
- Conclusion
- Perspective
- Bibliography
- Appendices
- Relevant key words

… and *not* for topics or authors!

Each folder represents a fundamental element of the paper, so by organising your notes in this way, you have already begun structuring your paper. You should regularly add notes, references, more or less completed text and ideas to the respective folders. Thereby you will already have gathered and written many sections, by the time you start drafting.

How should you store notes?

You can take notes in the margin of the book or by highlighting text, on paper or in files.

The latter methods are clearly better than the first. Consider how long you want to keep your notes for. Personally, we have used notes from our student days well into our working life. This requires that notes are written and stored so they are still understandable after a decade.

You must also remember to immediately note down all information about your sources for later references and bibliography:

For all notes, note, copy, download:

- Author(s), editors
- Title
- Publisher
- Edition

- Year of publication
- Place
- Articles, volume, no., page numbers (from – to)
- The page number from where your notes are taken.

This information (apart from page numbers) can be found in the book's colophon, on the title page or online. Download/take photo copies of longer passages and the title page of sources.

Note-taking software

There are note-taking programmes that have different functions for ordinary notes and mind maps. Some may be especially suited for paper-writing.

There are many advantages to taking computer notes, first and foremost:
- Quick access to other Internet-based resources
- Easy to take multimedia notes
- Easy to locate and save your notes.

If it is a matter of linking your notes to the text you are writing, it is often easier and more practical to use the comment function (for example, in Word) or you may use brackets, highligh colours, etc. Other programms are especially useful in digital texts in Word and pdf formats. Here, you can underline, overwrite with yellow, for example, add comments, etc. These notes can be put into your paper along with, for example, portions of the digital source from which you would like to quote. You can read more about digital note-taking software in Stray Jørgensen (2014c): *Notattaknik for studerende på videregående uddannelser*, and google, for example, "note taking freeware" to see graphic programmes.

The more processed the notes, the better the paper

Research into the connection between notes and papers shows a correlation between how well processed the student's notes were throughout the semester and the quality of the paper: The more processed the notes, the better the paper in general (Slotte & Lonka, 2001). Conversely, students accused of plagiarism were more disposed to merely highlight or photocopy pages of texts. This was demonstrated by an interview study of expelled university students (Angélil-Carter, 2000). These students have not used note taking for both appropriating and distancing themselves from texts. The results of the surveys confirm our recurring experience that you must begin relating to your sources as soon as you search and read the first one. Problems with note taking skills will often result in problems in papers. This is therefore a good reason to learn how to take processed notes.

The degree to which the content of notes is processed can include progression: From highlighting important passages to taking notes for constructing ideas and innovation. In the following, we describe the different types of notes for papers and set exams on the basis of how processed they are.

Highlighting and referential notes

The least refined type of notes is highlighting the texts you read. Highlighting and taking notes in the margin of books is of limited value as storing your notes in the books is unmanageable, and the material will first impress itself on your mind once you rewrite it (or speak about it). If you highlight and take notes in books' margins, you should also take other types of notes, to avoid having to leaf through numerous books and articles to find information or to summarise the reading of the semester. You can use post it's to mark interesting places and supplement with your own comments.

Referential notes include summaries of the main points of a text or lecture and nothing more.

Processed notes

Your comments constitute knowledge-transformation, and comments made while reading are worth their weight in gold when drafting. A student quotes her teacher for offering the following advice on notes: "Take notes on Bourdieu every time you find him sexy!" And better yet: "Then analyse why you find these particular passages sexy. You must be able to explain why". These are processed notes. Too many and too subjective notes are better than no comments, even if you do not use them in your paper. Your initial reactions the first time you read a text are fleeting, but form part of being able to qualify, comment and evaluate sources. They will often be forgotten shortly after, and for this reason immediately writing down your initial processing of a text is extremely important. Feel free to add to it throughout the writing process.

Often it will turn out that you need notes on sources, lectures and much more. It is a good idea to take plenty of notes each time a text presents interesting perspectives, as this constitutes inspiring sources you can continually add to your professional "baggage". As a student and a professional, these are what you base your work upon, and which inspire and serve as the foundation for later papers.

Notes for contextualising

As mentioned earlier, many papers, including essays, research papers and set exams, are about relating different elements to each other, e.g. different theorists' view of the same theme or phenomena, or the way texts relate to one another. Many write these elements separately and do not relate them to each other until the end. The most skillful way of preparing for the paper's analysis/discussion is to take notes on the relation between elements during the semester, instead of or in addition to sequential "each-theorist-on-his-own"-notes.

The following is an assignment question for a 1-week paper:

••

Describe the relationship between modernism and postmodernism by including F.J. Lyotard's and F. Jameson's writings on the topic.

••

"The relationship between" are important words in this assignment question.

If you had to write this paper, you would benefit from having notes on the following before the assignment week begins

- the two movements and the cultural dimensions they relate to
- the required texts and their context
- the authors and their context (who, when, which background, the texts' purposes, target audiences)
- the movements in light of the course's other themes, e.g. for perspectives on the significance of the texts
- the movements in light of the subject (in this case, Modern Culture).

The paper's focal point must be the discussion and overview of relation and development. Therefore, notes on the relationship between elements are a greater step towards writing a good paper than sequential notes. See the section on displays pp. 79f. as illustrations and visual notes also constitute note taking techniques. Tables and displays are suitable for taking notes that relate elements to each other and selected contexts.

7. Philosophy of science in the paper

By Vanessa Sonne-Ragans

Philosophy of science is theory about what a science or research is – i.e., theories, methods, concepts, etc. – and about the norms that should apply in doing research in a particular field.

Using philosophy of science in a paper ensures
- that you formulate the foundation for your paper in the proper way
- that you are assessed as a qualified practitioner in your specific field
- that you optimise the opportunity for your peers to assess the quality of your professional competence
- that you live up to the way people normally contribute knowledge within your field
- and that you seem conscious of the particular requirements that exist for scientific knowledge.

Why philosophy of science is relevant for writing a paper

In this chapter, we guide you through the use of philosophy of science by pointing out how you should and should *not* use it in written papers. In light of the various traditions and methods in different fields and disciplines, this chapter provides a general overview of the most distinctive differences in the views three basic scientific approaches have of knowledge and reality around which you should, then, frame your own grounding for your paper. You may use the chapter's introduction to various aspects of the philosophy of science to formulate the basic premises of your paper. This will provide you with an overview of how the theories and methods you use in your paper are founded in the philosophy of science. We show you, for example, how to work with the views of knowledge and reality that are central in any argument or explanation within a particular discipline.

By way of introduction, we shall explain how you may use philosophy of science in your paper to strengthen the argument for your paper's choice of methods, theories, analytic strategies, etc. We provide you with a schematic to use and a series of activities, each of which in its way safeguards the use of philosophy of science in your paper.

Philosophy of science and field of study

You should use philosophies of science or aspects of them with respect to the specific topic you have defined. This is to ensure that your use of theory and knowledge lives up to the requirements for independence, the norms of the discipline, and the forms of argumentation required for the production of academic knowledge. These requirements reflect the fact that you must write about your investigations in a professionally relevant way and the fact that there are particular requirements for papers that make use of academic knowledge. This means that you may not simply use any possible form of knowledge in your paper but must make use of a specific form of knowledge. This knowledge consists, in particular, of theories, concepts, methods (quantitative or qualitative tools), models, systematically collected measurements and methodologies (guidelines that direct the choice of method), all of which have been developed within academic disciplines to explain and understand *selected* parts of reality.

Philosophy of science may be viewed as unnecessarily difficult – and it *can* be difficult, but you must believe that your use of philosophy of science actually makes a difference for you and your paper. You are expected to be able to write confidently, taking your starting point in an argumentation based on a philosophy of science, because it provides you with stronger professional credibility. It makes you into a better practitioner.

The purpose of philosophy of science in the paper

The philosophy of science is a discipline that discusses what science in general is, and it does so by advancing norms for scientific practice (Sonne-Ragans, 2012). Philosophy of science contains considerations that make for a qualified and solid discussion of the research within a specific discipline. You need to incorporate philosophy of science into your paper because it ensures better quality in all five corners of the pentagon. The philosophy of science can connect all the corners together: from the formulation of your research question to the formulation of the method and procedure of your paper. It is important that the incorporation of philosophy of science into your paper does not turn into an "ism" section. Rather, you must show that you can write about the knowledge you use and produce in a relevant way. One of the points of this book is that good papers do not consist of every possible consideration or speech act but of *particular* modes of argumentation, explanations, considerations and speech acts that must be a part of the text in order for it to become, in fact, *scientific*.

What are the challenges?

Incorporating philosophy of science into papers is not easy; it requires direction and guidance, and many students and writers of papers who may not have an opportunity to get it also find it to be difficult. Typical considerations are:
- What can you use philosophy of science for as a student?
- Is it necessary to write about philosophy of science?
- When is it relevant?
- Where can it be incorporated?
- How is it linked to problems of a practical nature?
- How can it make a difference in concrete results?
- When have you written enough about philosophy of science?
- Is it better to omit it if you don't feel up to the task?

The answers to these questions depend on the field or discipline involved. Some fields have great expectations, others do not. So, you should start by getting a handle on the specific requirements of your discipline. Find papers and theses that demonstrate how others have done it, or ask your teacher or supervisor how they think it should be done. But curricula, good advice and examples are one thing. How you sit down with the paper and start writing about and working with a philosophy of science if you have never done so before is something else. How do you get started? How much do you include? How little philosophy of science is enough? Can there be too much in a paper? That is what the next section with deals with.

How much philosophy of science should your paper contain?

Essentially, you should include a separate section on the paper's foundation in the philosophy of science. This section is typically included as an introductory section (see the section on paper structure, pp. 329ff.) or in the methodological and theoretical section that is the basis for your choice of methods and theories. Often, it is logical to include your basic presuppositions in the discussion and conclusion sections and to incorporate them into your discussion of the literature you have used. But if, for some reason or other, you do not feel it is possible to incorporate the basic premises into other parts of your research, it would be a good idea to communicate it on a meta-level by briefly explaining that your chosen philosophy of science is only used to place your research within the proper professional and theoretical context and that you will not go into additional considerations about how these presuppositions affect the results of your research.

How little philosophy of science is enough?

In many cases, it is enough to explain why your research question (see chapter 4) calls for a particular selection of data or analytic method and precludes others, i.e., that you

- can argue for how a given problem cannot be solved with existing theories and methods but requires, for example, the use of theories from other disciplines
- view with a critical eye the results you reach and see them in the context of existing knowledge in the field
- have done the relevant literature search, which documents that you have a sense of the delimitations of your topic (which is shown in your choice of search terms)
- in your introduction, for example, mention the theories and methods that constitute the basis for your research.

In other words, if you show that you know what kind of knowledge you are dealing with and can discuss and explain your choices, then you are in good shape. When you begin to write a text that grounds your paper's components in relation to each other at the same time that you ground your choices from knowledge of the field, then you are actually well on your way toward writing a paper that will be able to be accepted by the professional and scientific community you are addressing.

When is there too much philosophy of science?

You should check how much philosophy of science is expected in your field. Above all, you should make sure that what you include has relevance for your research question in a clear and distinct way. In other words, you need to make sure that you do not mention trends or -isms that have no clear connection to the problem you are researching and the methods and theories you are using in your research.

Philosophers of science and paper writers do different things

Philosophers of science are concerned with the establishment, development, and methodological foundation of sciences and research; they want to understand and investigate how research produces knowledge.

In the following table, you can see how philosophers of science and practitioners and paper writers such as you use philosophy of science to understand and analyse practice. Paper writers belong exclusively to the right-hand column. The point of the table is to provide you with guidelines for how you as a paper writer should work with philosophy of science.

Philosophers of science	Practitioners af science
Are often philosophers or others concerned with scientific forms of knowledge. They establish and discuss rules for good scientific practice (genuine science).	Are researchers, practitioners, and students, i.e., those who use scientific knowledge in a systematic study of some segment of reality. Practitioners of science must use knowledge for something. Not simply reformulate it.
Problem area: The development, history, philosophy, and sociology of the sciences.	Problem area: A limited segment of reality that one investigates via theories, concepts, and methods developed within a specific discipline.
Are concerned with: Establishing norms for scientific practice and understanding the conditions for its development.	Are concerned with: Solving practical problems, changing reality, creating new possibilities for human life. Use models, methods, theories, results, hypotheses, formulas, and concepts with the aim of understanding practical problems.
Relationship to science: Philosophers of science reflect on the norms for good science through discussions of views of knowledge, reality, truth, objectivity, etc.	Relationship to science: Practitioners of science are not blind to the fact that science is both a phenomenon and a practice but are most oriented toward using philosophy of science to make sure their practice is professional.

Focus on:	Focus on:
Discussion and assessment of whether scientific knowledge is consistent in relation to the framework within which it is produced. I.e., whether it is logically coherent within its own framework.	Assessment of whether the knowledge that is used is suitable in relation to the specific problem to be solved in the discipline. I.e., that a good theory or method is one that works in practice. A theory may well cohere internally, but if it does not work, it cannot be used.

In this table, we point out that you as a paper writer should not discuss philosophical theories disconnected from practice and the problem you are investigating. For paper writers, the point of using philosophy of science is to be able to produce a text that is conscious of its scientific basis and standpoint within the framework of the discipline it represents. Your discipline has defined an area of reality within which you as a student are to work.

What is required when a paper uses scientific knowledge to conduct research?

In the following, we provide a review of central terms in the sciences. By "central terms," we mean that scientific theories consist of different components of knowledge such as concepts, hypotheses, methods, models, etc. These are elements that you use in your paper. We want to explain what type of knowledge you make use of when you write – the argument that philosophy of science should be a part of your paper goes together with the fact that you use scientific components of knowledge in your research. But, first, a short introduction to what science is.

Science is ...

Science is a way of gaining systematic knowledge about reality. Researchers obtain new knowledge so that we may become systematically wiser about reality and our place in it.

Scientific knowledge is not produced isolated from the reality towards which it is oriented; the knowledge that is created in the sciences is anchored in particular social, cultural, and historical epochs. Scientific knowledge is created in varying social contexts in which, for example, researchers have worked together in a reflective community oriented toward the investigation of empirical reality. A reflective community means that a group of researchers advances certain methods for investigating reality to which they maintain a constant critical stance. That is, to reflect means the same thing as critically assessing why something works or does not work at the same time that the results achieved are incorporated into the overall knowledge production of a field or discipline. In scientific contexts, reflection means to contextualize one's own investigation within the knowledge and results of the discipline. Researchers publish their results in articles or books – or both – and it is this knowledge that you subsequently make use of in your paper. A good paper makes use of knowledge that is produced on the basis of the requirements of observability, reproducibility, stringency, etc.

By comparison, philosophy of science is *not* a discipline that produces knowledge about reality. Philosophy of science is a discipline that investigates scientific practice from historical, social, psychological, and philosophical angles and themes. Thus, the subject matter of the philosophy of science is the sciences themselves and scientific practice. As a result of this lack of "empirical connection," philosophy of science, according to certain definitions of science, is not itself a science but simply a discipline that, as is the case with philosophy, logic, and mathematics, investigates a particular form of knowledge – in this case, the scientific.

Philosophies of science engage in a methodological reduction

A certain sign of any sort of scientific activity is that *it is methodologically reductive*. This means that it investigates a *segment* of reality with the help of carefully selected methods, concepts, definitions, models, measurements, etc. The simplification of complexity is an ordinary trait of science and a precondition for being able to work systematically at all with reality. The underlying logic of reduction and the need to make the complex less complex stems from the expectation that there is a clear solution to any problem.

As a paper writer, you must repeat the methodological reduction in order to limit the scope of your research. This means that you must argue for what is theoretically and methodologically meaningful and not meaningful to deal with. Reality is reduced in scientific contexts because it is not empirically possible to research everything at one and the same time. You must limit yourself. It must be clear to your peers what you are leaving out of your research and why.

Thus, the philosophy of science is useful because it helps you to delimit your research. In empirical papers, it is used to justify *which* observations, experiments, archival materials, key indicators, measurements, interviews, cultural products, natural phenomena, earthquakes, epidemics, etc., you are researching in your paper and *how* you are doing the research. In theoretical papers, it is used to justify your choice of concepts and methods and to explain how they are suitable for creating understanding in your problem area.

Central scientific concepts

Below, we define some central concepts in connection with science. We mean by "central concepts" the theoretical components used in scientific papers. The point is that, by becoming familiar with these concepts, you have taken a first step towards incorporating considerations from the philosophy of science into your paper. When you know what words such as "theory", "concept", "method", "hypothesis", etc., cover, you can use these words in a defensible way from a scientific point of view.

What does a scientific theory consist of?: Terms that describe what scientific theories contain

Theories

You use theories to explain and research that segment of reality with which you are working. Theories consist of models, formulas, hypotheses, concepts, and methods. In other words, they contain different types of knowledge. Typically, theories are developed by either an *inductive* or a *deductive* approach:

Theories developed on an inductive basis

A theory that is developed on the basis of induction takes its starting point in data from which general conclusions are later drawn. If you are working inductively, you are concerned with a specific problem that you subsequently deal with and research theoretically, experimentally, and methodologically. For example, an inductive interview will take its starting point in what appears in conversation. As an interviewer, you do not try to steer the interview via a prefabricated questionnaire. Induction-based papers strive to work without a specific analytical strategy. By analytical strategy, we mean here a preconceived view of how something may appear and be known.

Theories developed on a deductive basis

A theory that is developed on the basis of deduction takes its starting point in a specific hypothesis, theory or concept that is later investigated methodologically and empirically. If you are working deductively, you take your starting point in a specific analytical method or analytical strategy, which means that your research takes its starting point in a preconceived theory or hypothesis that is to be tested empirically. For example, you have a preconceived or planned strategy that guides the research in the sense that the concepts you are using point out the traits and connections that are relevant for the problem you are interested in. You might also work from a questionnaire with fixed questions.

Concepts

You use concepts to delimit the topic you are going to research by indicating the traits, characteristics, effects, impacts, and connections you are interested in understanding. You use concepts to define linguistically the problem area you are going to investigate. Often, people investigate effects and connections, i.e., different types of relationships between factors – for example, between layers of soil and fossils, between parents and children, between students and teachers, between hydrogen and sulphur, between cash flow and consumption, etc. This means that the factors in whose connection you are interested must be defined before they can be investigated empirically.

Empirical concepts

Empirical concepts explain specific segments of reality without placing them in a larger theoretical framework. Empirical concepts are consequences of historical, discursive, economic, geographic, and social circumstances. Examples of empirical concepts are children of divorced parents, sclerosis patients, economic crisis, labour movement, inclusive public schools, etc. Empirical concepts do not need to be a part of a larger or more specific theoretical formation but can be used indiscriminately to explain actual phenomena.

Theoretical concepts

Theoretical concepts explain an abstract segment of reality, i.e., a context, a tendency, patterns, and the like. Theoretical concepts cannot be tested or studied empirically but can *lay the groundwork* for empirical testing. A good example of a theoretical concept is psychologist Lev Vygotsky's concept of *the zone of proximal development*. This is a concept that provides an abstract determination of how children develop in an interplay with their surroundings. Other examples might be force, mass, or acceleration. They are used in precisely the same way to discuss something empirical.

Data

Data are unlimited whereas empirical knowledge is limited. Reality is full of data, and when scientific theories turn to reality, they select certain data and omit others, thereby creating empirical knowledge.

Empirical knowledge

Empirical knowledge is the material you will research in your paper, and it may be qualitative, quantitative, or both. Empirical knowledge is formed when you use concepts, methods, hypotheses, theories, or assumptions on data in reality. The selection of empirical knowledge from data presumes a theoretical classification of what is useful to work with in relation to the context and the problem you want to research.

Methods

Methods are specific procedures used in a concrete investigation of reality.

- Quantitative methods are experiments, observations, measurements, questionnaires. They are based on numbers, calculations, measurements, and observations. There is a focus on how many, how often. Numbers and quantities make representativeness central.
- Qualitative methods are interviews and participant observations. They are based on the analysis and interpretation of observations, expressions, statements, cases, etc. There is a focus on *how* and *why*. Qualitative methods go into depth. Representativeness is not central since understanding and meaning count more.

In this book, we use the word "method" primarily about methods for selecting data, methods for analysis, and methods to evaluate, design/construct/create.

Methodology

Methodology is theory about method. I.e., the considerations you have about what characterises the method you are using, what it is suitable/not suitable for, etc., how you act as researcher, how you affect the research process, how you limit the "subjective pollution" of the experiment, and how subjectivity – in certain contexts – may be an asset and a necessity in the research process.

Research design

The research design is the general logic and procedure you use to do research. You use the design to imagine or visualise your entire course of study before you have done the empirical research. A large part of your study design depends on your research question since it will guide the choice of methods. For example, should you choose a questionnaire to reveal the relationship between two different departments in the public sector, or should you choose individual or group interviews?

Models

Models are graphic visualisations of (abstract) elements – for example, theories and methods, procedures, principles, and their mutual relationships. Models are good for making something concrete, operationalising something, or providing an overview.

- **Hierarchical models:** Explain dominance relationships or developments from something small into something larger, from something simple into something complex. Maslow's pyramid of needs is an example of a hierarchical model that shows the relationship between simple and more complex needs.
- **System models:** Explain how the interaction between parts of a system maintains the totality. These models are used to explain the development and organisation of society, families, children, mental illness, political systems, cells, communication, etc.
- **Type models:** Explain general features, traits or patterns. They are used, for example, in organisation theory and child psychology.

- **Stage models:** Explain processes with the help of fixed stages; development happens in leaps that cannot be reversed or skip stages. They are used, for example, to explain the development of cancer in stages or to explain child development (Freud's model of psychosexual stages (oral, anal, etc.), Piaget's model of a child's cognitive development).
- **Structural models:** There are countless examples of disciplines that make use of structural models, and they are often used to explain developments in everything from language (semantics) to the forms of organisms (structural biology).

Hypotheses

Hypotheses are assumptions or surmises about a connection or context among a number of factors. Hypotheses are often used in quantitative and qualitative methods. You may propose a hypothesis to your research question, and very often it will be formulated as an investigation of presumed connections. Many papers are based on hypotheses to be confirmed or refuted.

As a supplement to this schema, we elaborate on how a number of the components of knowledge we mentioned are often used differently.

Elaboration of theory, model, method and methodology

We write generally about theory in papers in chapter 10. This section deals with differences in the way the word "theory" is used. These differences are relevant for how theory itself defines words such as "method" and "methodology", and the connections it shows in models and, thus, how you can write in terms of philosophy of science about the theories you incorporate.

Theories

Scientific theories deal with a segment of reality. This segment does not arise randomly but is defined by a particular view of reality. As an investigator and user of scientific knowledge, you are interested in whether the theory, method or analytic model you are using fits with the topic of your paper and especially the connections in which you are interested. That is, when you are familiar with the problem area of a theory and understand its characteristics and the contexts in which it can be used methodologically, you can with greater probability choose the right components of knowledge for your research – which ensures your paper's professional and scientific level.

Theories explain different types of connections
Theoretical scope has to do with how far a theory has explanatory power over empirical data. A theory may cover everything from the description of unique findings to accounts of complex connections and relationships. The *scope* of a theory varies. Scope deals with 1) how much and what data the theory relies on, 2) how extensively the theory explains the world, and 3) the size of the explanatory force the theory has in relation to a specific topic. The philosophy of science distinguishes among minimal, medium, and large theoretical scope.

The scope is interesting for you as a paper writer because it points out what theory has brought to or omitted from, respectively, its investigation of reality. The scope explains something about how extensive the connections are that are being talked about. Below, we explain three degrees of scope, and our elaboration of the different theories shows that the theories you use in your research may incorporate greater or lesser portions of a field of research. You need to be attentive to which portions of the field of research are concerned because it has decisive influence on the theory's force of explanation. The narrower the scope, the less generalizable are the theory's results – at least, at first.

Theories with minimal scope create a provisional picture of empirical relationships. The explanatory power of such theories, therefore, is limited to an explanation of matters based on a restricted amount of empirical data. Such theories do not generalize and do not elaborate any context beyond the specific investigation. As a consequence, these theories do not permit general statements about complex connections between the data investigated.

Theories with a medium scope explain connections among various phenomena in different contexts. Theories with medium scope include smaller areas of reality but place the connections investigated in relation to other limited contexts and, thereby, explain more phenomena than theories with minimal scope. Despite the fact that theories with medium scope explain their empirical results in a larger framework of understanding, they do not produce coherent theoretical systems.

Theories with a large scope explain a large segment of the world and express it in general terms, create concepts that apply to all people, relationships, phenomena at all times.

Theories with a large scope can say something about so many things and such complex data that their use in specific areas is limited. Their explanatory power is often visualized in models.

Some theories can explain "everything" with respect to your paper's data, and others only part of it. This means that you can use theories on different levels and with different explanatory power in your paper. It would be appropriate for you to be explicit about the scope of the theories you are using.

Models

Models are a good example of the way scientific theories simplify and abstract reality in order to investigate it. Models are often good to incorporate into written papers because they make the work concrete by finding the right methods and concepts. For example, you can design a model that shows how you have organised the analysis of your paper's subject (empirical data, sources, theories, methods, or what have you). Or you can use a model to show which parts of your research question each of the selected theories and methods is used to investigate. In some disciplines, models are the subject of investigation – for example, in physics/chemistry, engineering, medicine, psychology, and economics. Two examples:

Some economists believe that the worldwide financial crisis in 2011/2012 was a result of financial institutions using models based on a too narrow modelling of risk. If, for example, an investment risk was assessed from a model that depicted economic reality as simple and predictable in a fixed cause-effect relationship, the model would not be able to place the risk assessment into a sufficiently complex context. Investment advisors, therefore, would advise on investments from mistaken conceptions of how the financial market behaved in a globalized world, which is characterized by its complexity. The model, therefore, did not reflect economic reality precisely enough.

The use of climate models that claim CO_2 emissions do not have any appreciable significance for the global climate may have fatal and irreversible consequences for our globe and survival if they are shown to be wrong.

The point of these examples is to make you aware that, if you use models in your paper, you have to be clear that models are simplified generalizations of the field of research that, in certain instances, reduce the complexity of reality in an inappropriate way.

Method and methodology

Methods may be specific research methods – such as, for example, mathematical or logical methods – and quantitative or qualitative methods. Methods may also refer to various analytical and design methods within, for example, engineering or mathematical fields. Method may also refer, for example, to teaching about sources of law, as is the case in legal education. Methods may also be formulated as research protocols for a specific experimental procedure.

Similarly, methodology can be used in different ways. Some use it synonymously with method. Methodological considerations explain why you have chosen the method you have. For example, it may be your choice of role as interviewer, how you shape your interview guide or the choice and type of informant. Or it may be thoughts about the interview situation itself, the transcription, the communication of results. It may also be that you discuss the significance of your findings for what is already known about the topic. In purely empirical projects, such considerations will be the highest level of philosophy of science. The methodological considerations also concern discussions of whether a method is valid, whether it is suitable for the view of knowledge and reality the theory has (see below). In theoretical projects, one may also encounter expectations and requirements that considerations about the view of knowledge and reality used by the theories be made.

Components of knowledge can vary in meaning

As a paper writer, you must be aware that, when you use scientific knowledge – regardless of whether it consists of concepts, methods, hypotheses or models, this knowledge is produced in a field of tension between knowledge and reality. What you need to take note of is that scientific theories vary in the way they use words such as "theory", "method", "models", "concepts", etc. The meaning depends on which type of knowledge they are talking about. For example, the technical sciences also use the term 'theory' about a hypothesis that is tested in a narrow, controlled context.

The point here is that, by focussing on the sense in which you are using one or more of the central scientific terms we have discussed here, you are well on your way toward a type of argumentation that is relevant for the philosophy of science in your paper. If you would like a deeper elaboration of the components of knowledge we have dealt with, you may go to the recommended literature on the philosophy of science.

How to use philosophy of science to substantiate the premises for a good paper

A central skill for a good paper is being able to define its boundaries. This will make the assessment of your paper easier, but it also ensures that the paper will be judged on the premises you have defined. If, for example, you write a paper about learning, you wouldn't be doing yourself any favours if you did not define precisely the type of learning you are investigating – by pointing out the concrete concepts and methods you are making use of. This minimises the chances that your examiners will have to guess what you even mean by the concept of 'learning' in your paper. Or if you would like to investigate a topic for which there is little scientific or professional material – for example, film sound – and, therefore, you are forced to merge a theory and conceptual framework together, you would again be on thin ice if you did not explain how the theories you have found precisely and concretely contribute to your analysis and assessment of the phenomenon 'film sound'.

Philosophy of science is also useful in cases in which several theories and methods are used in the same study. For example, a number of institutions of higher learning require students to use several methods – i.e., method triangulation – either by having the students use both quantitative and qualitative methods or by the incorporation of theories from different schools of thought such as, for example, hermeneutics and positivism. If, for example, the topic is the understanding of disease, an examination of the different basic assumptions or core values of these schools of thought will be an argumentation in the philosophy of science: In the case of hermeneutics, understanding and interpretation and, in the case of positivism, verification and objectivity. It can be as simple as this – at first, at any rate.

The paramount relevance of philosophy of science for paper writers is that it helps to define the framework of the paper through a justification of the paper's starting point, i.e., an argumentation for the connection between the problem area and the choice of method and theory. This starting point will undoubtedly have a connection with one or more of the basic approaches we shall examine in the following.

As a start for showing how you can formulate the premises of your paper from a philosophy of science perspective, we suggest here an activity that does not require comprehensive knowledge of either philosophy of science or scientific terminology. It only requires that you have an idea of what type of research you are going to engage in. It is the starting point of your paper formulated in your own words. This exercise is to draw you into the thought processes of expressing the premises of your paper and to make your understanding of the subsequent activities easier.

> **Activity: Justify the premises of your paper in your own words**
>
> - What characterises your paper? Is it theoretical or empirical? Or both?
> - What does it mean to say that it is, respectively, empirical or theoretical? How do you mean it is one or the other? Explain your weighting, write about whether it is mainly one thing or the other, and try to explain what has gone into the emphasis.
> - Point out where in your research your premises are expressed or can be seen. Write about the theories, methods, concepts you use and what you are using them for.
> - Are you interested in a topic that can be objectively measured and weighed or are you interested in a subject are that cannot be seen by the naked eye but must be investigated through its effects or impact? For example, we cannot see the factors behind global climate change; we can only observe its effects on the environment. Likewise, we cannot see gravity – we only know that it functions.
> - Argue for whether it is enough to use one or two theories and methods to carry out the research you have in mind, and take a position on whether there might be a need to involve more. The latter will typically be necessary if your project has a broad interface

In the next activity, the justifications for the premises of your paper are divided in terms of a theoretical and an empirical project, respectively. It is worth noting that a paper may easily be both empirical and theoretical. In this case, you should use considerations from both columns to promote your justification.

> **Activity: Justify your paper's theoretical and empirical premises. Use the box**
>
> | In a theoretical project | In an empirical project |
> |---|---|
> | **You focus on**
 - criticising/understanding/researching a practice through theories and methods
 - pointing out that a concept may have another meaning, function or role than was believed before in your field | **You focus on**
 - observing, experimenting in the laboratory or in the field
 - collecting data
 - elaborating, adjusting and optimising an already established experimental design |

• working with new juxtapositions of concepts in order to research an area about which there is not much knowledge in your field. This type of project is seen in the humanities and social sciences.	• forming hypotheses about other possible connections that can be investigated empirically and/or showing mistakes or deficiencies in a design. This type of project is especially seen within the natural sciences.
The challenge for you is to • justify your results empirically, i.e., by creating a clear connection to reality • operationalise the concepts and propose empirically-manageable hypotheses or point out how your results find use in practice.	**The challenge for you is to** • justify your results in a larger theoretical framework and orient them within the knowledge of your field at a more general theoretical level.
You must establish a connection • between the concepts and the investigation of the concept in reality. I.e., how do the concepts help you achieve an understanding of actual relationships?	**You must establish a connection** • between the limited segment of the world you have investigated and theories about your topic. You can clarify what a solitary finding says about the overall topic in which your research is inscribed.

The last two boxes on connection can be used in both types of paper. Your explanation of the connections you establish will depend on how you put your research into perspective. If you write a theoretical project, it may be a good idea to write about its practical implications; and, vice versa, it is a good idea to write about the theoretical/conceptual implications of an empirical project. In both instances, you are building a bridge between theory and practice. Remember that theory can be used in many senses, so you may put a hypothesis or a research design into perspective in an empirical project and, in that way, engage in a theoretical discussion. Another way to justify the premises of your paper is by indicating whether you are drawing on knowledge that derives from the natural sciences, the social sciences or the humanities, respectively. It is not unusual for many health and education fields to draw on knowledge from a number of disciplines, since they often make use of a number of different methods and theories.

The three basic research approaches

In this section, we examine some of the fundamental assumptions within the natural sciences, the humanities, and the social sciences. The fundamental assumptions are illuminated in relation to the primary purpose, interest, methods, goals and empirical data of these research approaches. This will give you a sense of the differences in the ways the three basic approaches define the central terms or theoretical elements we went through earlier: Theory, empirical data, concepts, hypotheses, models, method and methodology. You may use this division as a guide, for example, in your choice of theories and methods.

The basic assumptions of natural science

Phenomena in reality can be measured and weighed, and the phenomena positively exist. Therefore, it is possible to gather truth and valid knowledge about reality. Knowledge can be generalised and used to control, predict, and create prognoses about possible outcomes. For example, through a calculation of CO^2 emissions, you can say something about the greenhouse effect. Similarly, through calculations of the age at which women first gave birth, you can say something about the chances that women will give birth to children with chromosome abnormalities. There is a focus on reason and a prioritisation of rationality.

Purpose: Prediction and verification – there is a focus on explaining causality or cause-effect relations.

Interest: To determine and manipulate variables that can be calculated and verified.

Method: Based on experiments; i.e., that our relationship to the world is empirical and rational and based on what you can directly observe. The observer is fundamentally different from what he or she is investigating. Therefore, the possibility for subjective interpretations, influences, etc., is eliminated.

Methodology: Generalisable, measureable, controllable, and verifiable.

Theory: May be formulas but also coherent conceptual systems or models.

Goal: Lawfulness and improvement in efficiency, truth and objectivity, systematisation, rationalisation. Repetition and reproduction. General themes and uniformity.

Empirical data: Experiments, measurements, observations, verification, and prevention through control.

Researcher: Investigative, objective and cautious in the sense that subjectivity should be minimised.

The basic assumptions of the humanities

Reality is manifold, and it can be investigated but not measured and weighed and certainly not summed up in a formula. Knowledge, therefore, will not always be true but dependent on the context in which it is produced. For this reason, knowledge in one context cannot, without more, be used in another context. There is a focus on acknowledgement, interpretation, and understanding the opinions of others.

Purpose: Understanding and interpretation of the specific and the unique.

Interest: Interpretation of human-created products – especially texts and utterances. The ideographic, i.e., the unique (the singular case, etc.) is accepted as valid in itself; the unique – for example, the individual's experience or a singular historical event – has value in itself without thereby being able to be generalised.

Method: Interpretation and understanding of human-created products and of the subject's/individual's understanding, experience, opinion or attitude. Adherence to the manifold, unique, and singular. Researchers are themselves a subject; and, for that reason, they must take their own subjectivity into consideration when the results are processed. Subjectivity must not be hidden; it is an asset in the research.

Methodology: Dialogue-based (interaction between source and theory), communicative, explicative, interpretive. Subjectivity is an asset since preunderstanding exists in the researcher.

Theory: May be individual concepts, models, and coherent conceptual systems but will not or only very rarely be a mathematical formula.

Goal: Understanding, insistence on the unique and valuable in the individual case. Adherence to what is unique about the subject and a distancing from rationalization and generalization.

Empirical data: Cases, interviews, journal material, accounts, narratives, materials that can be interpreted and from which meanings may be derived.

Researcher: Exploring, understanding, empathetic, pragmatic.

The basic assumptions of the social sciences

Reality is complex; it can be measured and weighed, but it also contains contexts and characteristics that cannot, without more, be reduced to a formula. Thus, there is an interest in context, situation and lawfulness and general structures.

Purpose: Improvement and knowledge of social inequality and acknowledgement of social relationships. Enlightening, liberating and critically investigative, concerned with hidden power relationships and revealing contradictory values and conflicts. The focus is on proposing theories and methods that can transform human collectives, groups, and society.

Interest: Consciousness-raising and insight into oppressive relationships and altering conditions of inequality, critical and emancipatory of society.

Method: Quantitative and qualitative. Subjectivity must be acknowledged. The researcher's role must be thought through and reflected upon in the results since the researcher is a part of the same reality he or she is investigating.

Methodology: Critical and interpretive, analytic through active participation and interaction. Subjectivity is an asset, and dialogue and communication are the goal or ideal.

Theory: May be conceptual systems, models, and, in certain cases, formulas that state simple statistical connections.

Goal: To prevent social inequality via technical, administrative intervention in society and liberation from ideologically oppressive speech. To create better preconditions in order to ensure society's cohesiveness through the management of citizens. To understand general social trends and norms.

Empirical data: Numbers, measurements, interviews, observations, verifiable experiments.

Researcher/investigator: Critical, exploring, investigative, participatory and co-creator.

You can read more about the theoretical positions connected to, respectively, the humanities, the natural sciences, and the social sciences, *inter alia*, in Sonne-Ragans (2012): *Anvendt videnskabsteori. Reflekteret teoribrug i videnskabelige opgaver.*

Activity: Argue for the basic research approach of your paper

You can start by stating the reasons for the basic research approach of your paper where you feel you can do it best, i.e., start with the empirical data if that is easiest. The order of the factors does not matter. It's all about putting words down on paper. Write about which of the basic approaches you are inspired by in your own research, and write about your own paper's purpose, interest, method, goal and empirical data from the perspective of the three basic approaches:
- In which basic approach do the theories, methods, models you use have their starting point? Is the knowledge you are producing in line with the basic approach from which the theories, methods, models you use derive?

- Do the theories, methods, models have an unambiguous connection to a single basic approach or can you trace elements from several schools of thought?
- What is the primary purpose (or purposes) of the approach according to the theories and methods you use?
- What consequences do these affiliations with the basic research approach have for your research?

You might also want to try to write about how you yourself conceive your role in the empirical data, i.e., how you influence your research. Pay attention here to the fact that, in theoretical projects, you should be able to write about this in relation to your literature searches, the sources you are reading, the search terms you use, the theories you read, and the concepts you choose to focus on. Generally, considerations that touch on and ground your role as a practitioner of science, a researcher, are valuable from a philosophy of science perspective, and you can advantageously consult the bibliography (resources) to see what literature you can use to write about your ow role as a researcher.

In the following, we dig deeper into how you justify the premises of your paper. When you investigate a problem you have chosen yourself, you typically choose theories and methods you believe are relevant for investigating and understanding your topic. When you write about the characteristics, traits, development, effects, connections, etc., of the problem area (a problem area is a topic-limited area of knowledge that contains one or more research issues), you are describing the area of reality you want to research, and you are explaining at the same time how you will investigate it and what knowledge you are interested in. From the perspective of the philosophy of science, you are in the process of discussing your paper's *view of knowledge and reality*.

Basic evaluation criteria in the philosophy of science: A theory's view of knowledge and reality

Views of knowledge and of reality constitute the most central evaluation criteria in a research context. You need to incorporate them into your paper because these two terms have decisive influence on

- the data you select as the empirical basis for your paper
- the parts of the topic you omit

- the methods you assess as relevant in relation to the knowledge you want to produce
- the theories and hypotheses you use/propose to be able to investigate, analyse, discuss, and interpret your topic.

You as a paper writer must be familiar with various views of knowledge and reality because it is guaranteed that the theories and methods you employ derive from one or more of these positions – with the consequence that your paper, which makes use of this knowledge, will also be related to the basic positions on which these theories or methods draw.

When knowledge and reality are translated into the terminology of the philosophy of science, the concepts of *epistemology* and *ontology* are used.

Epistemology (view of knowledge)

What is knowledge, what counts as valid knowledge, and how do you gain access to knowledge?

Ontology (view of reality)

What characterises something as real? What must a phenomenon be in possession of to be able to be said to be real?

These concepts set the stage for the part of your paper that deals with the way theory builds a bridge between reality and knowledge.

Here is an activity in which you formulate in your own words the view of knowledge and reality in your paper.

Activity: Describe your problem area and the theories and methods you will use to investigate it

- How can the problem area you want to investigate be viewed? How do you know it exists? How is it manifested? Where? How often? What is the problem in particular you want to know about? How have you limited your research? What are you not dealing with in precisely this problem area?
- What methods, theories or concepts are you looking for within the field or adjacent fields in order to find (a) method(s) that are suitable for your formulation of the problem/inquiry/interest/topic?
- What concepts, theories, models, methods, etc., do you think of yourself? State the reasons why they can be used.
- What knowledge is crucial for you to be able to carry out your investigation?
- What affects the problem area? What is the area itself influenced by?
- Is the problem area clear to everyone, or do its traits and characteristics require you to interject explanatory concepts, hypotheses, apparatuses or models to investigate it? For example, you should consider the consequences of having to interpret in order to "see" your topic. If you must interpret, does this mean, for example, that, in an investigation of learning, you must assess whether you will interpret learning as it is expressed in direct behaviour or learning as it is expressed in the student's experience of learning. In the first instance, you must choose observations; in the second, interviews. These two different methods will set the stage for different analytical methods and modes of measurement.
- To what is the problem area connected or related? To what other topics/phenomena/events?
- What challenges are there in relation to investigating it?
- Is the problem area of your paper studied by other fields/disciplines? If so, which? In what way is the knowledge produced there different from the knowledge your field produces?
- What is your research question? What do you want to know about the topic? What understanding would you like to create?
- What methods do you eschew and for what reasons?
- Explain why you have chosen these particular methods, concepts, models or hypotheses to investigate the problem area? Create a connection between what you would like to know and the way you intend to gain the knowledge.

Two fundamentally different views of reality: Materialism and idealism

What comes first? Knowledge or reality? An idealist would say our concepts and ideas about the world. A materialist would say reality and that it dictates our concepts. The debate over which is correct falls outside your paper. What you need to focus on is that knowledge and reality are insolubly connected in the research process. As a writer, you express this connection when you argue for how your problem area relates to your choice or rejection of scientific theories, methods, models, etc.

With respect to your presuppositions for incorporating a view of knowledge and reality into your own paper, we would like in the following to point out two different views of reality that still intervene in the way knowledge is produced within the sciences, and they are: *materialism and idealism*. Materialism and idealism are different ontological positions and are also called realism and constructivism.

Materialism (realism)	**Idealism (constructivism)**
Reality *exists independent* of our knowledge of it. Reality exists prior to any conceptualisation of it. Thus, we can gain access to it as it is.	It is only possible to know reality through our concepts. Without them, we cannot know anything. Human consciousness carries the structures that construct the reality we experience.
Reality can never be dependent on the fact that there is a subject who thinks it. It exists regardless of what the human subject says or does. The consequence of this is that it is always the same reality scientific theories are speaking of. Despite the fact that the world can be experienced and described differently from different theories and disciplinary perspectives, this does not shake the fact that everyone refers to and is a part of the *same* world.	Reality is constructed through the methods, concepts, analyses, strategies we impose on it. This means, in turn, that we never have complete access to reality. At the same time, it means that we can be mistaken. Therefore, certain knowledge is not possible. As soon as our relationship to reality is mediated through theories, there is the possibility for error.
In order to navigate the different interpretations of materialism that exist, you may advantageously inquire into whether the theory sees reality as something about	In order to navigate the various interpretations of idealism that exist, you may advantageously inquire into whether the theory sees reality as dependent on or

which true and final knowledge can be achieved. If that is the case, then what we can know, we can see. Everything we cannot see, therefore, we cannot know about but only deduce our way to. Some materialist theories reject outright all forms of conceptual intervention, while others want to be open to the fact that concepts may have a helpful function in relation to a logical revelation of non-observable conditions.	determined by concepts. If reality is only dependent, there is a possibility that the theory is less constructivist since concepts do not become all powerful. If, on the other hand, the theory sees concepts as determining reality, we are dealing with a radical idealism with the consequence that everything that belongs to the human psyche – reason, language, thinking, concepts, calculations, etc. – will create the reality that can be experienced.

Pros and cons of the two positions

The advantage of idealism is its openness to the fact that what concepts refer to are real. Its strength is its conceptuality and that it leaves room for the investigation of things that fall outside of pure sensation and require conceptual processing. The traits idealism considers real do not need to have any extension in time and space, which is an advantage within the disciplines and fields in which interpretation is a part of the methodological foundation (as some believe. All fields, even the most mathematical and logical fields, interpret data and numbers). In idealism, real phenomena may be non-directly observable connections, relations, and contexts. Thus, as a view of reality, idealism is open to the notion that things that cannot be observed directly may be defined via concepts: learning, grief, innovation, atoms, natural selection, global warming, virtual networks, market-orientation, etc., are all phenomena that we study within different fields but which we do not directly see with the naked eye. Nevertheless, there is a general consensus that they exist. The knowledge you use in the investigation of such topics will always only be able to be expressed as a possible context or connection – through the use of interpretation.

The advantage of materialism is that it looks at the real as existing materially and not simply in the mind. Objects are not exclusively the result of our concepts. They exist outside our conceptual systems. Thus, an obvious possibility is created to embed phenomena in the natural, social, etc. order. The primary materialistic assumption is that the world is independent of the subject's ideas, thoughts, and concepts. The real is what we can see directly, and the fact that the subject can conceive the world, relate to it, and act in it had no meaning for the world's independent status. As a consequence, materialistic ontology prioritises the object, the external framework, and the world. This is reflected in the requirement for objectivity within the natural sciences.

A weakness in materialism is that it can be mechanistic and causal in the way it explains connections.

In this review, I have presented materialism and idealism as irreconcilable or absolute oppositions, but that is only to show what characterises the two ontologies. In practice, you will encounter new theories that often try to blend the view of knowledge and reality of these two -isms.

Activity: Taking your premises from the box above, explain why your paper is primarily materialistic or idealistic

- How do the theories in your paper define your problem area? What is their primary perspective of it?
- Does the problem area exist before we can observe it or is the problem area dependent on the fact that we have named it, defined it, and indicated how it becomes visible?
- How do you describe the theories' definition of the problem area? Or explain how what you want to investigate depends on human creations. Remember here that special measuring apparatuses, technical equipment or the like (such as special tests, microscopes, listening and measuring devices) should, in fact, be considered "constructs", i.e., something people have invented to observe something real.
- In what way does this constitute a problem in relation to your investigation of the problem area? What possible errors might "disturb" the problem area's traits/modes of expression?
- Do you use theories or components of theories that contain features of both materialism and idealism? What features are they? What problems or possibilities are there in drawing on theories, methods, concepts, and models that represent both views of reality?
- In what way does your choice of theory or method influence the problem area you want to investigate? For example, various phenomena such as stress, intelligence, protons, electrons are very vulnerable to the measurement strategy.
- What about your problem area entitles you to use components of materialist or idealistic theories only?

As an extension of this, I shall introduce three views of knowledge: *objectivism, subjectivism,* and *constructivism,* which affect the scientific production of knowledge as do the two ontologies. Objectivism, subjectivism, and constructivism are different epistemological positions.

Three fundamentally different views of knowledge

	Objectivism:	Subjectivism:	Constructivism:
	• Objects, events and reality exist independent of human conceptualisation. • Concepts refer to something real.	• Objects, events and reality exist by virtue of concepts held by human subjects. • Concepts do not necessarily refer to anything that exists objectively.	• Objects, events and reality are created in an interaction between humans/groups/society, which help create the concepts we use to understand things.
View of reality, knowledge and science	An objectively-oriented scientific theory means that • Reality exists independent of humans. • Science is ideology- and value-free, that which is known is simply there already.	A subjectively-oriented scientific theory means that • Reality depends on the way it is defined, interpreted and experienced by the subject. • Science is value-laden and ideological, since a subjective assessment constructs the reality that can be investigated.	A constructivist-oriented scientific theory means that • Reality is created between subjects: Knowledge is produced in the interaction between research and object, i.e., that knowledge is relational and interactive. • Science is value-laden and ideological since reality is defined in a social context and under the influence of social processes.
View of practitioners of science	• Subjectivity is to be eschewed, and the distinction between the subjective evaluation and objective facts must be maintained.	• Subjectivity is an asset in the knowledge process. The knowledge that is produced is guided by subjective understandings, conceptions and interpretations, which must be included in the results.	• Tries to couple the subjective and objective ideals of knowledge. • Knowledge uncovers regularities, structures and patterns in reality, but the subjective perspective must be made visible.

			- In particular, there is a focus on how the researcher or observer observes and influences the object.
Methodology and method	- Since the world exists materially, the methods that are used must explain the regularities, mechanisms and causality that organise observed reality. - Methods are quantitative and use statistical and mathematical calculations. - Testing of hypotheses, empirical investigation of reality, knowledge is objective, neutral and compelled by reason.	- Since the world depends on subjective interpretations, it is necessary to use methods that capture the subjective perspective and content that cannot immediately be observed and, for that purpose, qualitative methods are used in the form of interviews, observations, etc. - The investigator is a participant and involved in the investigation.	- Since what we can know about reality depends on intersubjective (between humans) processes, it is necessary to create transparency with respect to the knowledge process. Specifically, transparency is to be created in relation to the conclusions and interpretations that are given. - Transparency is a requirement and a guiding principle in the formation of data. Therefore, the investigator is visible.
Data	- Controlled experiments, testing of hypotheses, focus on the gathering of a lot of data.	- Interviews, narratives, discourse analyses, analyses of narratives; here, the case is deemed value-laden.	- Reveals the interests, communication relations and practices that control the gathering of data. There is a focus on connections, networks, relations and contexts; nothing can be investigated outside of the contexts in which they occur. A large part of the research involves revealing the implicit premises and assumptions that guide the knowledge that is produced.

In this review of the different views of knowledge, I have provided the -isms with content by pointing out their inherent premises. These premises are not necessarily given space in, for example, academic articles you might read in connection with your studies (that fall outside the genre), but they still exist. Note that even very data-heavy and experimental fields work to produce knowledge that addresses a topic that will always lie outside of the specific experiment. For example, research in chemical and physical processes – in fields such as physics, chemistry and biology – is generally focussed on producing knowledge about natural phenomena such as gravity, evolution, climate, planetary systems, the development of the universe, etc. The debates about such phenomena are guided by fundamentally different views. Think, for example, how our view of time has changed in the shift from Newtonian to Einsteinian physics. Our view of the development of animals and human beings changed radically when DNA was discovered. Thus, even these subjects rest on assumptions about reality that evade concrete observations. The considerations that evade concrete observations and that cannot be included in every practical or experimental context will always exercise influence over practice. In this connection, the philosophy of science is a tool that can help you get behind the immediate results of the theory, which is not to say that you should discuss them. It is enough simply to show that you are conscious that they are present. Concretely, this means that, by being familiar with these premises, you can create a critique based on philosophy of science of the theories and methods with which you are doing research.

Activity: Justify your paper's view of knowledge with the premises set forth in the box above

- On what view of knowledge does your research rest? How do you justify it? How is this expressed in your choice of method?
- What parts of the theory confirm for you that it has this view of knowledge? I.e., explain how the theory claims knowledge is possible and accessible through these methods.
- What can we not know according to your theoretical and methodological foundation?
- What constitute reliable sources of knowledge according to the theories you are using? What are unreliable sources?
- Explain the supporting concepts, models or assumptions of your paper.
- Are you going to create your own data or is the knowledge you want to get already processed empirically in a similar way? Are there important lessons to be learned from collecting the data yourself for the problem you want to investigate?

- What must you accept about the knowledge you are using in order for your paper to be said to live up to the requirements for validity: Have you used a method appropriate for researching what you want to research?
- Reliability: Have you used the method correctly in relation to your topic?

What does a paper writer get out of locating a theory in the context of their view of knowledge and reality?

- When you write about your paper's view of knowledge and reality, you provide your examiners with a clear yardstick for assessing the reliability and validity of your paper.
- When you write about how your theories, methods, concepts or analysis models fit within the framework of idealism or materialism, you put "meat on the bones" of your argumentation. Examiners will assess it as a positive quality in your paper that you can use these positions as a yardstick for the discussion of your paper's overall orientation.
- Your theoretical and methodological choices define your project's place within the field: In many educational programmes, a field/discipline is divided into different themes or branches. A nursing education, for example, is based on clinical decision-making and clinical management. Similarly, teacher education is divided into basic professional skills, pedagogical theory, and teaching skills. Psychology has been divided into cognitive psychology, educational psychology, clinical psychology, etc.
- To each of these academic divisions belong specific methods and theories that dominate the relevant knowledge within these divisions. It is important to be able to place your own paper within these academic divisions. It can be said that this is the first step toward stating the context of your paper in your introduction, cf. paper structure on pp. 329 ff.

Papers are enhanced when the choice of theories and methods is grounded in a view of knowledge and reality

After you have related your paper to a view of knowledge and reality and pointed out the primary features of theories and methods from the humanities, the natural sciences or the social sciences, the question then arises as to how you weave these considerations into your paper. In your discussion, you can argue the pros and the cons of your paper's basic philosophical affiliations in relation to your results, i.e., you can try, for example, to imagine the consequences of using methods and data from another field or you can compare different basic approaches to the role of the researcher in the research process and, in that way, discuss objectivity, reliability and validity. From your perspective, you can reflect critically on bringing in knowledge from the basic approaches on which you have drawn. Regardless of whether you do one or the other, you as a paper writer cannot "escape" taking a position on knowledge and reality. However, you do not need to expand the discussion to embrace the general pros and cons about -isms. The point is for your paper's premises always to able to be determined as either one thing or another.

Beyond the reasons already mentioned, it is important for you to be aware that the view of knowledge and reality plays a decisive role if you use knowledge from different disciplines. When and if you consider using knowledge from other disciplines, which is often the case, for example, in integrated papers, i.e., papers that are written within more than one field, you need to be able to assess whether the knowledge you are using in your paper is coherent from a philosophical position or whether the knowledge you are using is internally contradictory. For example, it may be difficult to argue for using a hermeneutical method of analysis in a multiple-choice questionnaire. If you are to combine theories and methods, you must be able to do it so that they can explain your problem without creating "holes" in your argument that are too big. You must identify which view of knowledge and reality you are making use of in your paper, and you will thus be capable of writing about these problems by putting them together.

Are you in doubt about where the philosophy of science fits into your paper?

In the course of your writing process, you may reach the conclusion that what you thought was the problem is not the problem in the sense you thought or that the theory or method you used was not as suitable as you thought. For example, you discover that you could have advantageously used other views of knowledge and reality. Or that your research proved to create new problems or to go astray. Don't panic. That is what happens when you are a practitioner of science and use knowledge on reality.

The solution is to describe what you think may have happened to create breakthroughs or deviation in your paper (in the discussion of method, for example). Might there have been a flaw in the measuring equipment, is it the result of your inexperience as an interviewer, or does it have to do with the fact that the theory you used focussed on other things than the topic you chose? You shouldn't be afraid that things have not gone as planned. As long as you can more or less competently point out and write about what went wrong and why.

Where do you write about your paper's view of knowledge and reality?

The answer to this question: A number of places! At a minimum in the pentagon's fourth corner (with theories and methods); but, since the consequences of your view of knowledge and reality spread to all corners of the pentagon, you can do it in all the corners of the pentagon.

If you are a beginner and would like to write an argument consistent with a philosophy of science – and think through your theories and methods – then you should do it in the pentagon's fourth corner, i.e., in the introduction's description of what you want to do, and in the theory and method section.

Another way to write about your view of knowledge and reality is by briefly pointing out and explaining whether your research question is materialistic or idealistic in theory and choice of method section. You can also underpin your aims in your view of knowledge and reality. This will give the reader a quick overview of your paper's philosophical standpoint and will, as a rule, suffice in many educational programmes as a good level of philosophy of science. As mentioned at the beginning of the chapter, you must remember to research what is expected in relation to the use of philosophy of science in your programme.

How do you write about your view of knowledge and reality when it is ambiguous?

A number of factors can make a view of knowledge and reality ambiguous for the paper writer:

First of all, there are different interpretations of what counts as valid knowledge and many views of how we can achieve and produce knowledge in an academic context.

Second, topics and research questions that cross scientific approaches require you to reflect on the extent to which the knowledge you integrate is able to be used in a justifiable way in the investigation of the problem you have chosen. Many problems are rarely solved with the use of knowledge generated within a single discipline, science or approach, which only accelerates the need for you to be conscious of how your problem area draws on the theoretical and methodological elements. You have to be conscious of the fact that, if your problem can be investigated with the use of theories and methods from other disciplines, fields and approaches, then you must justify the basis for your combination of these components in your paper, i.e., you have to point out the common denominator that allows you to use them to research the same section of reality. In fact, it is a consideration that will be deemed relevant in the philosophy of science context.

Third, it is often said that theories mix different degrees of idealism and materialism. What do you say specifically about this in your paper? If you are in doubt about where your theories primarily fit together in relation to a view of knowledge and reality, then you can point out where you find substantiation for the fact that they are both one and the other. It is not, as such, a problem for theories to blend insights because that is the case for many theories. It is only a problem in your paper if you do not address it and use the literature to substantiate your analysis of the theory. Therefore, you should avoid writing that a theory is *either* materialistic *or* idealistic but simply point out that you find features from one or both – and then you can point out the specific places in a given theory you believe create a basis for such a claim.

One general point is that you must make sure you do not write about these views of knowledge and reality disconnected from your paper's problem. Whether you write from a starting point in idealism or materialism, subjectivism, objectivism or constructivism, you should always relate it to the problem you are researching. You have to explain and demonstrate how the idealistic or materialistic is expressed in your paper and what consequences it has for your solution to the problem. As support for this, for example, you can use the schematic on basic approaches, pp. 209f.

Activity: Anchor your argument for your view of knowledge and reality in the literature

- Try to ground the theoretical elements in your paper on the premises of your basic approach and view of knowledge and reality. I.e., connect the theoretical elements to idealism and materialism and subjectivism, objectivism and constructivism.
- Find at a minimum one place in your literature where this grounding is clear. If it cannot be found in the primary literature, then look in the secondary literature.
- Show in your text where the substantiation of your view of knowledge and reality may be found. Is it in the concepts, methods, hypotheses, or the like?

Philosophy of science enhances your paper's argumentation

As we have mentioned, it is necessary to delimit yourself in academic practice. Therefore, it is also a necessary part of writing about the theories you use in your paper to include the philosophy of science on which they are based. Delimitation implies here, among other things, explaining where you are coming from, why and how, and substantiating how the limits you have "drawn" in your paper affect the results. As a paper writer, you use theories, concepts, methods, measurements in a thoughtful way in your investigation, and this requires a relevant assessment and discussion of the knowledge you are using *and* creating in your paper.

The knowledge you as a paper writer are using is produced by theories in the philosophy of science; and, in the context of a paper, this means there is an expectation that you understand the nature of the knowledge you are using. You have to show that you are familiar with the criteria that you are using to discuss and assess what you are writing about in your paper. You do this by documenting that you understand what you are using to understand reality.

You bring in philosophies of science with the aim of qualifying your paper in the way we have just described. In summary, you can say that, in a good paper, incorporating philosophy of science or writing about the philosophy of science in the first instance is the same as

- justifying and substantiating the knowledge you are using to do research, with a starting point in criteria such as your view of knowledge and reality and your choice of scientific approach
- locating your paper in the field of tension between science and reality
- using the knowledge of the field in a way that is relevant for the problem you are investigating
- explaining why a given method, form of measurement or theory solves – or works for – a practical problem. Or vice versa: Pointing out what makes something that normally works suddenly stop working. You would like to have evidence that malaria pills actually make the body immune to the bite of a malaria-ridden mosquito just as you would also want an anaesthetic you give a patient during the removal of a wisdom tooth actually to deaden nerve endings in the mouth. And not the foot.
- being able to assess whether the knowledge you have used from an academic and scientific perspective functions in relation to the problem you are investigating.

In this chapter, we have emphasised philosophy of science as a form of writing and assessment that enhances a good paper's argumentation for its academic premises. This means that it is a tool you use to think about the framework of your paper while, at the same time, it ensures that you write in an academically qualified way. When you write in a way relevant to the philosophy of science, your paper, your topic and the way you research are placed in the home court of research and the sciences.

How you tackle philosophy of science through a dialogue with your supervisor

It is a good idea to get supervision on the scholarly approach and the philosophy of science you use in your paper. You might, for example, ask your supervisor to point out papers he or she has supervised that have demonstrated a good level of knowledge about the philosophy of science or you can look for them at your university library.

The following activity will train you in what you to include when you are to write a presentation for your supervisor of your grounding in and discussion of philosophy of science.

Activity: Write a presentation for your supervisor

- Write the considerations and foundation in philosophy of science for your choice and delimitation of theories and methods. Use the activity in this chapter as preparation. Get your supervisor's response.
- Ask your supervisor what she/he expects or would advise you to write – with your specific project, research question, and subject field in mind.
- Ask whether your supervisor has papers that deal with the same subject. Get an explanation of what is good or bad about them.
- How do you yourself evaluate the best way to use philosophy of science? Where in your paper structure (see pp. 306f.) can you advantageously start?

Your supervisor can both react to and point out where your research design may have holes. In relation to your starting point in the philosophy of science and the discussions you want to include in your paper, your view of knowledge and reality will play a role anywhere there needs to be a justification for your selection of data, theories and methods and where there is any critique and discussion of theories and methods. Ask your supervisor how you can qualify your paper's philosophy of science by providing an excerpt that demonstrates how you intend to write about it.

In conclusion, we encourage you to look at the suggested bibliography. We have indicated the degree of difficulty and pointed out how the various works can enhance your paper by making philosophy of science a part of the pentagon's fourth corner or by integrating it into all five corners of the pentagon.

8. Sources in your paper

Sources are the part of the literature you choose to use in your paper – for example, data, theories, and methods. A field stores its knowledge, history, general understandings (theories) and tools (methods) in the literature. One way of demonstrating your disciplinary skills is through your use of sources.

> **What is a source?**
>
> "A source is not a source, before it is a source "for" something, and it is not a source for something until it is related to a question, no matter how vague this question may be".
>
> (Olden-Jørgensen, 2005, p. 49)

You can demonstrate independence – a central theme in this book – in your treatment of sources through your ability to
- search, find and summarise relevant material
- organise the material according to a theme
- relate your literature review to your own research question and to the data
- place your own work in relation to tradition and innovation, others' work, existing understandings and theories.

  (Delamont, Atkinson & Parry, 2004)

Sources' functions in and for the paper

Texts of the field can have different functions in your paper. Becoming aware of and showing in your paper why each bit of text is included is therefore a definite advantage.

> **Sources *for your* paper can be used as**
>
> - tools for information searches
> - sources of inspiration (e.g. to find problems, answers, perspectives)
> - a basis for general insight into and overview of the topic
> - models for your own work.
>
> **Sources *in* your paper can be used as**
>
> - the object – as primary sources to analyse, criticise, evaluate
> - state of the art – as a starting point and to preface your own work
> - support, evidence and documentation for the paper's claim
> - a methodological and theoretical foundation (also for the paper's philosophy of science)
> - a means for discussion.

Usually a distinction is made between three types of sources:

> **Source types**
>
> - Primary sources are the "raw" material which acts as data in papers, e.g. historical documents, cases, novels, letters, etc. ("what you write about").
> - Secondary sources interpret the raw material and are the "governing" theories: The concept and theory generators of any field that constitute the field's tools for analysis ("what you use to process (analyse, understand) the material and support your argumentation").
> - Tertiary sources summarise secondary sources and provide an overview of the disciplinary field, e.g. comprehensive textbooks, encyclopedic articles, wikis.
>
> (e.g. Booth et. al., 2008)

Applied sources

A fourth type of text can be used when writing a paper. For want of a better name, we call these "applied sources". Applied sources are the professional texts that apply, comment, interpret, expand, criticise and evaluate the field's theories and concepts on the basis of practice. For example, reports on practical experiments conducted on the basis of the field's perspectives, serious reviews, and discussions in the press, blog and Facebook entries. These texts are often written by the field's teachers and researchers and other academic writers, yet, these texts often have no scientific status. These practice-related, professional texts will often put primary and secondary sources into perspective and contribute to evaluating and nuancing these. However, applied sources cannot stand alone: They can serve as a possible supplement or source of inspiration.

The professionalism and scholarliness of sources

The professional and scholarly quality of the sources used in your paper can vary widely.

Sources listed according to scholarliness

- Peer reviewed books and articles
- Other academic texts, e.g. textbooks, surveys, monographs, PhD dissertations, theses
- General disciplinary works, e.g. debate books, research articles written by the practitioners of the field
- Popular articles
- Other "everyday texts", e.g. newspapers, magazines, brochures.

If an article is peer reviewed, it means that a professional in the field has carefully read and approved the article's research quality. Articles published in respected journals are usually peer reviewed. Naturally, papers can include sources that are not scientific. However, the point is that these must be used and evaluated on the basis of their professional and scientific status. This is also true of academic blogs and Wikis. Popular articles, in e.g. *Cosmopolitan* may make a good primary source, but not a good secondary source. Interviews quoting researchers and authors can be an exception. However, it is not only a question of who is writing but also whether it is a text that documents its information.

Why use secondary sources?

While some students use secondary sources too much and in too summarising a manner, other students are not willing enough to use their field's secondary sources, as they believe this hinders independence. Thus, they are disinclined to include others' texts and would rather present their own views. In connection with a course on the use of primary and secondary sources, we asked the 100 participating students to note down what they knew and were unsure of in regards to using sources in a paper.

Many mentioned that they disliked using secondary sources.

We recognise this (seductive) view from many talks with students. However, using others' text is the prerequisite for writing independently; not the alternative. Although some secondary sources can perhaps be reduced to "thoughts people have had", you cannot possibly replace the secondary sources of the field with your own thoughts or act as a secondary source in their place. Any thinker who is read and resonates within a field, thinks on the basis of the field's tradition and history, and these thinkers inscribe themselves in the field's long-existing dialogue, even though they may be in opposition to established thought. This is the ideal way of using the field's sources: Students must write on the basis of the field's immediate level of knowledge and discourse, and this must be reflected in their text. You should demonstrate independence in the *way* in which you analyse, interpret, discuss and evaluate sources (which you must naturally do on the basis of well-defined criteria, not simply subjective judgment). You do not demonstrate independence by refraining from using the field's existing sources. This is precisely what you must learn. You can overcome the dislike of "referring to what others have said", "repeating again" by using secondary sources in a way and context that clearly presents your own agenda. Secondary sources must form a coherent part of the structure of the paper's argumentation (see chapter 11).

Using secondary sources in papers – which and how

You must use secondary sources in most papers in most educations. The exception is small assignments, such as translation assignments or assignments where you must demonstrate your observation skills. Tertiary sources are good for providing an overview of the process. But you must always consider whether a tertiary source can be used as an actual source.

You must have a clear reason for including secondary sources – they must be relevant for the paper at hand. For assessing whether a source is relevant, you can ask the following questions:

> **Questions for sources**
>
> - What does the text say?
> - What can I use it for in my paper?
> - What is the text's aim?
> - Who has written it? A renowned bigwig or a newcomer?
> - Who is the author in relation to the field?
> - Which school of thought/tradition/method does he belong to?
> - What has been said of him and/or his work? Has the author been met with opposition?
> - How old is the text (and is it the newest edition?) Could newer texts have been published?
> - How do others (authorities) consider the text?
> - How sound and significant is the research on which the text is based?
> - How well-grounded is the argumentation?
> - Why should we (not) trust the text?
> - Where is it published? In a widely renowned subject-specific journal or something more informal – for example, a random Internet page?

The following examples show how to assess and use slightly dubious sources in your paper:

For a while, the most popular psychology book in Denmark was Jesper Juul's *Dit kompetente barn* [Your Competent Child], and as a result many psychology students wanted to include it in their papers. However, the author is not a researcher, academic nor does he have a degree in psychology. He is a trained chef and a psycho-therapist (which is not a recognised degree). His book does not include a list of sources and mostly consists of case studies and reflections, and can be categorised as pop psychology. Nevertheless, his practical experiences and reflections are relevant and longstanding and are thus not without substance. The question is now: Can the book be employed as theory about pedagogy and child psychology in the scientific field of psychology? We recommend that:

- You do not let this type of text stand alone or use it as theory (the pentagon's 4th corner). It can act as the object of analysis (the pentagon's 3rd corner). Popular publications cannot stand alone as a framework of understanding in a paper in higher education.

- You can use any material as data (primary sources) in a paper – including this book – and then analyse the data with a theory.
- You can make the pedagogical/psychological/therapeutic claims the book is based on the object of reflection, analysis, categorisation, etc., which can then become part of the framework of understanding alongside other theories.

When in doubt, you should always consult your supervisor and assess whether these kinds of "borderline" works should be included in your paper, and if so, you must define which status the work should be given and with accompanying qualification.

Considering the status of sources is relevant for many students, for example in the case of Wikipedia.

Wikipedia (the online encyclopedia) is a unique source insofar that many of its articles are written by professionals, are peer reviewed, and are therefore relatively reliable. Yet, a Wikipedia article cannot normally be used as more than a source for facts, and even facts must be carefully assessed.

Sometimes students are told that their sources are too superficial, for example if university students (maybe even in their later years of study) base research on concept definitions found in encyclopaedias and Wikipedia. Our advice is that the use of any tertiary sources and popular and non-peer-reviewed works must be arranged with your supervisor before your paper is due, as there are no established rules for using these types of sources.

How many sources? Your research question is the guide and measure for handling your sources

Students often ask us: "How many sources should I include?" Naturally, we cannot provide a specific answer as this depends on ... on what? First and foremost, on your research question, which determines which sources and which aspects of them you must use. The research question helps you

- search for and select sources
- relate your assessment of sources to your own research question
- place your own work in relation to tradition and innovation, the works of others, existing understandings and theories, the field's state-of-the-art
- determine the function of the source in the text
- place the source in the right place in the paper's overall argumentation
- assess and qualify the source.

A rule of thumb is that the sources should, first and foremost, be those
- that are newest
- that are written by the best possible researchers/professionals
- whose data, theory, method and/or argumentation are most thorough
- that provide a theoretical/methodological foundation for practice.

You can then attach special importance to these and supplement them with less important sources, by mentioning that other sources also support your chosen sources, e.g.: "Other sources (..., ...) agree".

Where are different sources placed in the pentagon?

This is a suggestion of where different types of sources can be placed in the pentagon:

1. Sources in which you have observed a problem to be researched or that document a problem.

5. (Sources from other corners which are mentioned in the order in which they appear in the research design).

2. Sources that document the need for the research and thus validate the purpose of conducting the research.

4. Sources that provide theories, concepts (models for understanding), philosophy of science and/or disciplinary methods (secondary sources).

3. Sources that are analysed or discussed (primary sources).

Activity: Insert your sources in the source pentagon

- Start from the beginning and write down your paper's sources
- Regularly revise in conjunction with searching and reading.

When and how should you refer to secondary sources in your text?

Sources must be

- introduced and qualified
- reproduced (in form of a summary, citation or paraphrase)
- analysed
- blended into the context of the paper
- referenced
- evaluated.

Students often ask where they should refer to sources in their papers?

Important sources, e.g. theory used in general and in all or large parts of your paper, should often be introduced in the introduction or even in an individual section at the beginning of your paper. But, remember that a theory this important should not merely be paraphrased; it must be described on the basis of how you use it, i.e. you must substantiate and qualify why you have chosen it.

Sources included for a specific purpose at some point in the paper, e.g. evidence of a claim in the argumentation, an example, etc., can usually be mentioned when they are used.

The extent and manner of including sources depends on the purpose. Some purposes require you to make space for a particular secondary source, others require less space. Secondary sources that help you solve your problem serve a very central purpose. In this case you must describe in detail what part of the text helped you and how. You can choose to quote and refer to the source.

If you greatly oppose the opinion of an included source, which is respected, well-argued, etc., you will have to describe the source thoroughly and thus refute it. See chapter 12 on argumentation.

Less significant sources can often be dealt with much less extensively. A brief summary of the points relevant to you will likely be enough. Or perhaps it will be enough to simply mention the given text in a sentence encapsulating its position in relation to you.

A good and relevant question to ask your supervisor is: "Do you wish to comment on the way I use the literature?"

Source qualification, source argumentation, source discussion and source criticism

You should present and perhaps be critical of your search, selection and analysis process in relation to the sources you have chosen. Any mention of sources in your paper basically forms part of the argumentation: "I refer to this source, because it can be used for ... on the other hand it can be criticised for ..."

Your source argumentation is affected by:
- What you have searched for and where; in which resources
- What and how much you have read
- With which delimitations
- With which search terms and in which language
- When the search ended
- What you have chosen to read instead of skimming abstracts
- Which theoretical selections you have made and what you have excluded
- Through which lens you have read the source.

Read chapter 5 on information searches.

In academic texts, claims are often documented with statements of authority. However, this form of argumentation must naturally be treated with careful consideration, as it is based on the ethos of the authority, i.e. credibility. In the academic world, evaluating the quality of a text on the basis of its argumentation rather than by whom it is written is the ideal. Nevertheless, in some contexts, it makes sense to trust the scientific statements and evaluations of acclaimed researchers from a given field. Their credibility as well as their argumentation guarantees the value of their statements as documentation.

Because your paper's argumentation is tightly bound to your chosen texts and the way in which you use these, you must be able to argue for your choice and use of sources in your paper. Again, the ideals are substantiation, argumentation and being willing to be self-critical and discuss how the limits of the research's method and width affects the reservations you may have about the points you make.

Qualify secondary sources

The most important secondary sources you include must be qualified in your text, i.e.

you must write why you use precisely these authors, and they must be commented on or evaluated by you or a "mouthpiece" you agree with. For example:

I choose to include X's views on Y, as X's views are relevant for my purpose because …

X has influenced several generations of thinkers' view of the matter …

So far, X is the only person to have written about Y …

X is an interesting contrast to … interesting because … according to Z, X is a significant theorist because … which Y also states about X.

Every time you refer to a source, you must note how it contributes to your research.

If you feel like we keep driving this point home, you are right: Many papers lack a clear indication of their sources' function. Often secondary sources and theorists appear to have simply fallen from the sky, and the reason why they have been included; the way they contribute to the research question and how the student evaluates their contribution is often implicit to the student and the supervisor. This implicitness may be caused by the fact that the supervisor has recommended and thereby qualified the source. The student has then accepted this recommendation without having any personal opinions about the source and without feeling capable of positioning the theorists in relation to his/her own project. If your supervisor recommends secondary sources, be sure to ask for the reason for these recommendations, and for want of something better, write down your supervisor's reasons in your paper. The best thing would be to write down your evaluation of the source's relevance in the context.

The following example (Film/Psychology, BA thesis, 12/A) shows how the choice of central sources is substantiated and qualified in relation to topic, research question (focus) and their function in the paper:

The paper's focus

We focus on computer culture based on the relationship between computer games, adolescents and late modern society. […] We examine whether the late modern state of society is reflected in the computer culture as well as how the games' design affect appeal and effect. We assume that a dialectic interaction exists between the structures of society and its cultural products – the openness of the games are a consequence of the late modern mentality, but simultaneously reproduce this.

> Relation between the paper's elements

> Research question (in form of a hypothesis)

[…] The reason for choosing Joseph Anderson's theory as the basis for analysis and as an interdisciplinary bridge between game theory and film theory is not chiefly due to the cogency of his theory.

> Choice of theory is substantiated in relation to the content elements

He has rather been chosen because he represents an open and debatable construction of theory, which can easily and justifiably be attached to other fields. Flemming Mouritsen's game theory has similarly been chosen on the basis of wanting an empirically based primary theory, which is not based on particular general theoretical preconditions.

> Clarification of the theories' function

These two theories are combined through the narrative concept of Giddens' social theory, which theoretically evaluates the way contemporary society impacts the individual.

> Combining two theories by means of a third

Giddens inscribes himself in the Anglo-Saxon tradition, which can be verified on the purely internal level of argumentation because of its empirical perspective, in contrast to modern linguistic-philosophical social theory, represented by certain thinkers (e.g. Jacques Lacan, Gilles Deleuze and Paul Virilio) (Kjørup, 1997, p. 270).

> Evaluation of the theories' function (usefulness)

As our project is dependent on the applied theories' explanatory ability and validity, we have focused on clear and well-defined concepts. This should not be understood as a stance, but rather as an assessment carried out on the basis of the project's theoretical form […]

> Substantiation for excluding otherwise plausible theories

> **Qualify your sources**
>
> - Introduce your sources (who are they, why are they relevant?) and qualify them (why have you selected this particular passage, what does it contribute to?). These qualifications can be kept on a purely descriptive level: "Here, I believe X illuminates aspect Y, as Z can be viewed through the lens of X". Evaluating X using adjectives will seldom prove beneficial.
> - Qualify sources even though they are drawn from a course curriculum or recommended to you by a teacher who therefore knows them already. When you qualify your sources, you demonstrate that you have understood the reason for using them and provided reasons of your own

The following example is a paper from economics (BA level, high mark), in which a central source is qualified in relation to the topic (volatility) and on the basis of the source's high status in the field.

Although the fact that volatility in the stock market is not constant has been known since 1963, this was first taken into account in an econometric model in 1982. At this time, Robert F. Engle introduced the ground-breaking ARCH (Autoregressive Conditional Heteroskedasticity) model for modeling time variance in volatility, with the view to predict future volatility.

> Writer places source in a disciplinary context in which it fills a "hole".

The ARCH model has formed the foundation for most models of volatility ever since, and has thus become a milestone. In order to predict volatility in different markets more precisely, the model has been elaborated several times since its initial conception. The most important of these expansions is ascribed to Tim Bollerslev, who introduced the GARCH-model in 1986, which is the most used model of volatility today.

> The source is characterised with big words, "ground-breaking", "milestone", which are substantiated subject-specifically (usually you should be careful when using words of assessment; however, it works out in this case).

> The writer emphasises the source's significance for later developments in the field.

As the name suggests, the ARCH model takes into account the time variance of volatility (*Heteroskedasticity*).

Qualifying sources is especially important when the source is a central model in the paper, as in this case.

Acknowledge, too, if you can, the contributions existing sources have made to the field and the understanding of the subject.

Work on a running basis to justify and qualify your sources – and be aware that you're assessment of them will change as you search and read more. You may find sources that change your understanding of the previous sources in the field!

When arguing in relation to sources, you must first have found the sources and have read or at least skimmed the parts you wish to include in your paper. Then you must pose your questions and give your first, tentative answers to these.

> **Activity: Focus on your paper's argumentation in relation to sources. Write keywords for:**
>
> - What knowledge exists in the field?
> - What has (seemingly) not been researched, knowledge gaps?
> - What is agreed upon, where do you see agreement?
> - What is disputed, where do you see disagreement?
> - What is your position on the sources' disagreements? What documentation and argumentation do you base these positions on?
> - How are others' contributions useful and relevant to the object of study?
>
> (Adapted from Lamberti & Wentzel, 2011).

This activity paves the way to your paper's statement about the sources on your topic – insofar as you are familiar with these. Consult your supervisor about this. Where does your supervisor identify opportunities for you to contribute your own argumentation as a student? And which knowledge and positions of the field are your supervisor familiar with?

Literature review: Materials, sources, state-of-the-art

What is a literature review?

A section with the title "bibliography", "literature review", "materials", "materials and methods", "sources", or "state-of-the-art" introduces many papers and reports. This is a review and qualification of the selected materials that form the basis for the investigation of your particular research question. Should you write a literature review in your paper? It is not a given because not all papers have one – especially not if they have, instead, a major theoretical section that reviews and relates theories and concepts to the research question of the paper or include on a running basis sources that are used in relation to the analysis. The literature review has to do with sources and materials about the paper's primary subject regardless of whether the subject is something material (for example, an app), or something conceptual, theoretical or the like (for example, the concept of democracy) (which are in the pentagon's corner 3). You can then choose to begin your paper with a – well-founded – review of limited, relevant materials that have to do with the paper's subject.

Why a literature review?

All papers are based on literature and materials – and what the writer uses the literature and materials for. To start with a famous quote: "Scholarship before research!" (Boote & Beile, 2005). This means that you must first study what others know and have done in a field before you can delve into your own investigations, analyses, arguments, and constructions in a knowledgeable way. It is this foundation and its connection with your own research question and study design that is the point of a general introductory literature review regardless of whether or not you want to call it your literature review.

The purpose of doing a literature review is
- to provide context for your investigation in the literature of the field
- to show that you are standing on the shoulders of what others have written and done, that you are familiar with it and can draw upon it meaningfully
- to provide a justification for the topic of the paper and the whole research design for the reader
- to distinguish your own work (perhaps, only a little) from what others have written, demonstrating that it is independent and relevant work
- to set up the argument of the paper by placing (positioning) yourself in relation to what already exists and what you think is lacking in the available literature and materials.

How?

You must clearly formulate the paper's focus, research question, and purpose (of course, always with room for change) in order to be able to research the literature narrowly for your paper and also to be able to write a literature review that sets up what the paper is investigating.

How much material and how many sources, and how many pages (perhaps, only lines) you should use on the literature review depends a lot on:
- The curriculum requirements for bibliography and materials, which must always be checked.
- The paper's length (do you have room for half a page or 10?).
- How much is really relevant for the rest of the paper: its starting point in the philosophy of science, theories and methods, its investigation, treatment of the problem, analysis, discussion and, if relevant, design/construction?
- What does your supervisor suggest?
- What is the custom within the field/programme level?
- How much do you have time to include?
- What do you want to emphasise and have learned from it?

You must be able to justify what you include – and what you have excluded. Let us say that, as a part of your paper, you want to design a new app with a particular purpose. Your literature review might then deal with
1. how other relevant apps are constructed to connect purpose and functionality (you choose which and how many apps, and you should justify your choices)
2. literature about the design possibilities and social functions of apps (you choose a number of articles, books, websites, etc. and justify your selection – perhaps, from a theoretical angle – and your exclusion of other sources – if they are prominent and the reader might have expected to see them).

Delimitation

If there are many apps and a lot of literature, you must limit what you will include in your paper on the basis of the important materials for your context, what is up-to-date (perhaps, set a time limit: materials that are at most 10 years old or crucial sources regardless of age), and, of course, what you yourself can manage to digest – even on an abstract level. See more about limiting literature searches, pp. 151ff.

One main rule: Do not include more elements in the literature review than you intend to use and, perhaps, take a position on either directly in the literature review or in later sections of the paper – namely, in the section on concepts and theories, data/materials, or analysis, or in the discussion section. You should avoid namedropping. That is noise.

The discussion section must contain a discussion of the most important, most relevant works – including their findings and concepts/theories/methods. Then, include literature you can use to clarify your own study's results and methods, etc. (see more on discussion and the relation of the discussion to the literature, pp. 235ff.).

What sources and materials can you include, and how?

Here, we have taken the example of apps because it *can* happen that non-academic sources are the object of the paper and must be investigated as a part of doing your own research. Regardless of whether the literature, the material you want to use as a foundation includes academic articles and books, websites or what have you, the literature/materials you mention in your literature review should include what you believe are the best, most relevant contributions to the starting point for what you want to do in your paper. And, here, you should use your supervisor or information specialist as much as you can.

If you have a somewhat larger number of materials, then consider grouping them together. It is tempting to group chronologically: "the first app was released in 20xx, and it …" and so forth, with highlights. However, a chronological construction of the background knowledge is only a good idea if there is a point to this historical development. Otherwise, the possibilities are

- theoretical – contributions within the same theoretical understanding
- methodological – contributions with the same method
- thematic – are there themes in the literature or materials that are also a part of your paper's topic?

If you group things together, you should provide subheadings that show how you see the contributions of the literature as groups. At any rate, it is always good to provide about one subheading per page.

The literature must be qualified in relation to your study

In what way do the individual contributions to the literature help your investigation

– or not? This can be done by qualifying each source you mention – for example, in this way:

> "Hansen found that … X, as she made use of method Y. In this paper, however, I use method Yy, and I did not get the same findings as Hansen."

or

> "The relevant app had a series of features that we want and is, thus, a step in the direction of fulfilling the desired functionalities, but no available apps have exactly these functionalities that we have specified. Therefore, on the basis of, *inter alia*, Jensen's and Petersen's writings on the significance of social communities, we suggest …"

or

> "as Hansen and Petersen argue in XX, p. yy, an important starting point for creating a connection between the app's purposes and functionalities is that one incorporates zzz, and we in our group do this in the following …"

– i.e., the literature review is used to qualify and acknowledge that you are standing on the shoulders of particular studies and to explain where there is room for your own investigation as a small piece of independent work.

Remember, too, along the way to relate the justifications, limitations, and points in your literature review to your research question. The research question must not be completely forgotten over several pages. So, be sure to relate what you have said to what you are investigating.

Discussing sources – advanced!

In the paper's discussion section, and in possible discussion sections throughout the paper, you should discuss (i.e., present arguments for and against)
- positions that are in disagreement, and/or which you find argumentation and documentation against
- what knowledge gaps exist – and perhaps why they have not yet been closed

- the way in which your own research corroborates or argues against sources – others' research as well as theoretical/methodological sources. Are other texts corroborated or contradicted?
- what can you say about the applied sources? Which perspectives do the sources include, what do they contribute to and what do they lack?

You can discuss sources by subjecting (often a single or a few) works to method discussion (in some cases this is called source criticism), just as if you were conducting a method discussion of your own research. Then you criticise the foundation of data, selection, analysis, the cohesion and logic of the argumentation, writer's bias, etc. This is part of the argumentation in regards to sources: "There are gaps!" (Implicitly: And therefore, the nuances offered in this paper are needed.). Discussing with other texts consists of being critical of their argumentation to evaluate their strengths for your own paper's argumentation. This is not to say that all primary and secondary sources used in a paper must be subjected to an extensive analysis of argumentation and critical review. However, the more importance a source is attached in a paper, the greater the requirement to provide explicit, critical evaluation of the source. Being able to produce this kind of review is one of the highest steps in Bloom's taxonomy.

Here is an example of a writer's discussion of sources in relation to the sources of the field known to him (although he has not read them all, he has read enough to have gained an impression of the existing sources and the field's gaps) (Film studies, BA, high mark):

∙ ∙

Recent decades have offered great theoretical progress. However, in many ways, the existing literature is still so conceptually fragmented, that identifying a comprehensive conceptual framework on which to base analyses is impossible. This lack of cohesion consists in the stark contrast between the concrete/practical processes of production, the way in which these are practiced in Denmark and other places, and the large number of philosophical/communicative theories which only summarise audio as part of our perception of films.	> Point of departure: The literature is fragmented and cannot explain the mechanics of/what goes on with in the audio of films
Based on my personal fascination and practical/professional experience from several years of working as a recordist, this paper will, by means of an interdisciplinary	> The fragmentation of the most important theorists is acknowledged

approach, attempt to unite the practical and theoretical disciplines in order to attain a less fragmented understanding of film audio. The theoretical discipline *film audio* is still a conceptually fragmented area, in which there is no single conceptual framework which independently explains techniques that maintain illusion, promote understanding as well as narrative tech.

Christian Metz formed the basis of modern film theory through his semiotic film theory which claims that auditive film perception succeeds because it is a semiotic operation, which is not affected by the mediated representation of sound. Mary Ann Doane argues that film's audio-visual duality is a material heterogenity, which risks being revealed, however practice seeks to blur this by means of techniques that maintain illusion.

David Bordwell's neo-formalist and functional categorisation of sound's acoustical perceptive qualities constitutes the best proposition of a systematic description of sounds narrative functions, however the approach is shallow and simplifying, and therefore Rick Altman elaborates on Bordwell's description of the relation between sound's reproduction and representation by means of auditive perception theory as well as acoustic, physical and practical observations that respect the complexity of sound.

The central creative intentions for the film's audio was direct it from a documentarian point of departure to fictional film. The paper illuminates how the film applies a number of techto fulfill this goal, including techniques that maintain illusion and promote understanding […] In its first use of sound, the film approaches Bordwell's definition of the art film's external norms through its use of subjective realism, authoritative commentary and ambiguity.

It is my hope that the reader of this paper will gain a greater understanding of the complexity of the audio-visual medium of film. The relationship between picture and sound and between reproduction and representation cannot be neglected or simplified without losing vital information about the audience's actual experience of the film. It is about time that broader film theory begins to acknowledge the processes of maintaining illusions that underlie any film.

> Bordwell can especially be used

… but he simplifies and therefore Altman must be included as a supplement …

… but by closely analysing a single film's audio (own research), the elements that are not explained in the literature become clear and reveal that audio cannot be analysed by means of the developed concepts ….

… and film theory should be encouraged to start acknowledging the complexity of the relationship between picture and sound.

Throughout the paper, the writer's starting point is that sources are fragmented, and that he must fill the knowledge gaps – knowledge gaps he has become aware of through engaging practically with his field.

Source criticism and review

Source criticism is defined here as a disciplinary tool that allows you to assess the quality of sources.

Checklists for source criticism

You have presumably made the acquaintance of checklists for source criticism in high school. Here is a checklist that can help you remember some of the recurring critical questions you should put to sources in academic contexts.

What should be your starting point when criticising sources?

- Credibility, e.g. closeness to the object or event
- Scientific and scholarly authority and status
- The foundation for explanations (methods and documentation: data and empirical facts) and their range (see chapter 7 on philosophy of science) in relation to the problem to be investigated
- The consistency of analysis
- The source's objectivity, impartiality
- Transparency of the source's angle and description of methods and procedures, and the source's critique of its own investigation, foundation in data, methods, etc.
- Contemporariness and currency, updating

In many fields, sources become outdated quickly. Regardless of how good a source is, it becomes less relevant if newer sources have updated the knowledge. You must also pay attention to whether the context of the source is very different from your own investigation because there may be problems in applying conditions from one context to a very different one or over many years. This kind of source criticism is relevant even in the information search phase.

You must always clearly indicate what your criticism concerns and your argumentation must be professional and factual.

Here is an example of a table for a systematic review of a physiotherapy paper (BA, top grade):

••

10.2. Results of literature review

The following section presents a schematic overview of the studies that meet the aforementioned criteria of inclusion. At the bottom of the table you will find a box entitled "review of methodological quality". In this box, the authors of this project have evaluated each of the four articles on the basis of the Danish Health and Medicine Authority's checklist for evaluating RCT-studies (see appendix 2). Nine out of ten of this checklist's criteria have been applied in part 1, as these concern methodological qualities. In each box, it is indicated how many of the nine criteria have been met in our view. After this it is indicated whether the results are deemed applicable to this project. Following this section, we summarise the results of these studies.

Study 1	
Title	Effects of Open-loop Feedback on Physical Activity and Television Viewing in Overweight and Obese Children: A Randomized, Controlled Trial.
Author(s)	Goldfield, G.S., Mallory, R., Parker, T., Cunningham, T., Legg, C., Lumb, A., Parker, K., Prud'homme, D., Gaboury., & Adamio, K.B.
Years of publication	2006
Keywords	Youth, Physical activity, obesity, sedentary behaviour, television viewing.
Journal	PEDIATRICS
Country	Canada.
Objective	To study the effect of open-loop feedback on physical activity, sedentary behaviour, body composition and energy intake in children.
Design	Randomised, controlled study.

Method	Thirty obese 8- to 12-year-olds were randomly assigned to an intervention group or a control group. Children in the intervention group who accumulated 400 counts of physical activity were allowed 1 hour of TV. Children in the control group had free access to TV.
Results	Compared with children in the control group, the intervention group demonstrated a significant increase in physical activity as well as a reduction in the amount of minutes spent in front of the TV every day. Furthermore, the group showed favourable changes in body composition and energy intake.
Reported restrictions	Few children, not enough obese or morbidly obese children to compare the difference between these groups. Short intervention period (8 weeks). No follow-up, and therefore no observations of maintenance and no goals for long-term effect.
Conclusion	Providing feedback on physical activity is a simple method of modifying the home environment to increase physical activity and prevent child obesity.
Evaluation of methodological quality	The method of this study was deemed of high quality (++). The study met the criteria in 8 out of 9 cases. The study's weaknesses: It is deemed problematic that the blinding method was not carried out in sufficient measure. However, it is described that the study's design and objective hindered this. The P-value of the study is set to $P<0,05$, and as the study is well described, the results seem probable. The results are deemed applicable to this project.

In the above studies, we find the randomisation and blinding method inadequate or descriptions of these lacking. The results are still deemed applicable as the authors of this project do not consider the above shortcomings to greatly influence the results and the processing of these.

In the paper, four studies are treated in this way. This is an example of systematic review based on explicit criteria. Evaluating and reviewing on the basis of explicit criteria is viable in all disciplines. If in doubt, consult your supervisor.

There are no checklists or methods that, with certainty, can distinguish good sources from bad sources. The quality of the source always depends on its use and situation. A banal short story in a weekly magazine may be used as data and form the basis for a discourse analysis of gender stereotypes, while it might not be of much use for forming theories within discourse theory.

Use of the source as a criterion

The fact that the quality of sources is determined by their use means that, every time you make use of sources, you must consider what it is you are using them for. The first thing you have to determine is whether your texts/sources are to be used to clarify your theoretical apparatus or whether they are part of your data. If you need examples or cases to analyse for your paper or texts that you want to analyse for content, then the quality of cases is to be determined by how you have selected and collected them. If, for example, you are working with a quantitative content analysis, the value of your data and sources is to be determined by whether you have been stringent in your literature search and systematically selected (and rejected) sources. Correspondingly, if you are working qualitatively with analyses of individual texts or special cases, the quality of the texts is to be determined by whether they are good examples of the points you want to work with in your analyses: Are you illustrating, for example, the rule or the exception? Sources must be useful in terms of what you want to use them for. On one hand, you use theoretical sources on your data/materials; on the other hand, you use theoretical sources on the data/materials. You let the data analysis comment on the concepts, theories and methods in order to discuss them: Were the concepts, theories and methods chosen good enough to analyse the material and to answer the research question? Were the sources strong as documentation and examples and to build an argument?

If the sources you want to include are part of your paper's research or literature review, theory section or philosophy of science section, it is important that you are familiar with the so-called "academic hierarchy of authority". Different fields of study have very different approaches to what kind of literature may typically be used. In the university world, the academic hierarchy of authority, *inter alia*, applies, while articles, textbooks, and other texts written by academics who do not work as researchers are used to a higher degree in, for example, university-level educations. In profession-specific fields, there are lots of articles and other texts written by professionals in the field – for example, professional articles and textbooks written by practitioners in the field: engineers, nurses, doctors, psychologists, teachers, social educators, etc. Often, they are not true researchers but professionals and practitioners who, through many years of experience, have acquired great knowledge about the field. Such articles and books are also used to a great extent in student papers – especially if there is no research literature in the given field. The decisive thing is not necessarily whether the author is a researcher or the text peer-reviewed but whether it is a text that relates to research and the newest knowledge.

Quality control as assessment criterion: The academic hierarchy of authority

The quality control of academic work provides yet another set of concepts for reviewing the quality of sources. Therefore, when you are reviewing the quality of sources for your research or literature review, theory chapter, etc., you must first ask whether the source has been through any form of academic quality control. This academic quality control typically consists of one or more researcher in the area having read the source and approved its quality. This process is called "peer review". Dissertations, monographs/anthologies, certain textbooks and articles in research journals go through peer review.

Books

Not all books are dissertations. Researchers also publish different types of books of which some are peer-reviewed and others are not. There are books in which the researcher is the single author (monographs) or that are collections of texts by different authors (anthologies). Here, you are trudging through a bit of a jungle. It rarely appears on the front page of a book whether it is peer-reviewed or whether it is not. In order for you to find this out, you must look into what sort of publisher put it out. If the book was published by a university press, it will probably have been peer-reviewed, while this is not as likely to have been the case if it was published by one of the purely commercial presses. But this is not always easy to figure out because publishers may have series that are not peer-reviewed and others that are. Sometimes, this appears in the book's colophon; sometimes, it does not.

Research articles
It is a little more complicated to figure this out with journals and articles. First of all, there seems to be an infinite number of them. Second, their quality and scholarly reach are very different. There are journals that print pretty much anything that is sent to them, while others are very picky and only take about one percent of the articles they receive. For quality journals, it is the case that researchers within the particular academic field are the editors or members of the editorial board. But the editorial processes may be quite different, and how much or how little value an article may contribute in the academic hierarchy of authority depends, among other things, on the journal's editorial processes. Lowest in the hierarchy are the journals that only have one editor who decides whether the article is to be published. Higher up in the hierarchy are the journals that have an editorial or review panel that undertakes peer review. The procedure implies that a proposed article is sent to two-three reviewers who, after reading it, decide whether the contribution is to be published. Nevertheless, even within peer-reviewed journals, there can be a great difference in quality. But again: It is ultimately the individual text you must review when you include it.

Theses, Ph.D. and doctoral dissertations
When you discuss peer review, you most often take the discussion of research articles as a starting point, but this is a little misleading. In reality, there is a kind of peer review when your examiner or your censor assesses your paper. Normally, people do not count master's level theses as true research texts; and, therefore, they do not belong in the academic hierarchy of authority. But everything from master's theses to Ph.D. dissertations to so-called doctoral dissertations counts as a piece of research if it is accepted. It is quite obvious in this context that a master's thesis is attributed less academic weight than a doctoral dissertation. It should always appear on the front page of such a document whether its level is a master's thesis, a Ph.D. dissertation or a doctoral dissertation.

Ideally, you will only include sources of high quality in your paper. But there may be reasons to include a dubious source. In that case, it would be a good idea to describe explicitly in your paper that you assess the source to be dubious, why you have decided to use it anyway, and how you will use it. For example, your theoretical foundation should not be based on a dubious source, while it might prove necessary to find cases, examples or, perhaps, tentative definitions of new words, etc., from widely different sources that are not necessarily quality assured. Speak to your supervisor about any possible dubious sources.

A good question for a supervisor is: Does my critique of X's (work, concept, study, theory, etc.) seem relevant and justified?

Pay attention to your teachers' critiques of sources in your lessons. Find out the basis of their criticism: What arguments do they have for their critique of sources, positions, studies, accounts that they nevertheless think are weighty enough to include in their teaching? Perhaps, you can use your teacher's examples of relating critically to sources as a model of a legitimate and fruitful foundation for academic criticism.

How should you represent sources?

When you include sources in your text, you should do so through quotation, paraphrasing, summarising, analysis, interpretation, discussion and evaluation of sources. These text types constitute the building blocks of all levels of academic writing; from first year practice papers to PhD dissertations.

The following section focuses on quotation, depiction and paraphrasing which are the basic text types for source representation. We discuss the remaining text types (of which the basic text types are often component parts) in chapter 11 on the paper's building blocks and structure.

Quote, paraphrase or summarise?

- *Quote*
    - when the exact wording is important, i.e. when the way something is phrased is just as important as the content – if not, paraphrase or depict
    - when you need the authority of the source
    - as evidence for textual analysis.

- *Paraphrase*
    - to reproduce the meaning when the exact wording is not important
    - when the source's style is unsuitable
    - when the source's focus is different than yours
    - to abbreviate
    - to demonstrate understanding.

> - *Summarise*
>   - to reproduce the core of the source
>   - to leave out unnecessary details
>   - to present the source.

See the following examples of quotes and see an example of a summary on p. 248.

It may prove necessary to explain the context of a quote if this is unknown to the reader.

Quotes

Quotes must be few and well-chosen.

Quotes can be used in many ways. A quote can act as an example if you are analysing a text. A quote can be the starting point of a discussion of a theory, or it can demonstrate a different take on the topic than your own. A quote can also act as documentation for something you are arguing for or it can illustrate the author's way of expressing himself.

Common to/for all quotes is that they should only be included, if they have a function. They must never be purely ornamental, but must be commented and evaluated.

Commenting on a quote is not the same as paraphrasing it. The reader will have read the quote, so unless it is extremely complicated, paraphrasing it would be wasting the reader's time. However, the read must be told why a quote has been included – what does it exemplify or document? If a quote appears without a commentary, it will seem like a clipping glued into a scrapbook. This form of quotation is unsuitable for research papers!

Some examples of relevant ways of using quotes:

1.

Through *everyday discourse,* the individual constantly constructs his/her conditions by drawing on experiences:

"What happens is that people casually and routinely construct formulations of such things (perception, knowledge, inference and so on) as part of everyday discursive practices …" (Edwards & Potter, 1992, p. 17)

The individual's use of himself as a condition can therefore be understood in the way actions, experiences and memory are constructed and connected. This makes me consider how everyday actions and routines can be understood as being constructed.

Here the quote is used to define a concept and the author of the concept's definition is important.

Directly after the quote, the writer's understanding of it is presented and then placed within the paper's context.

2.

Schema can be described as *"… a spatially and/or temporally organized cognitive structure in which the parts are connected on the basis of contiguities that have been experienced in time or space."* (Mandler, 1979, p. 263).

This means that schemas consist of neurologically based programs of constant active and pre-emptive expectations of input, which is why they simultaneously contain past and present qualities.

Here the writer's starting point is a quote in the source's original language, something which is often difficult to translate

– and the writer explains and interprets it for further use in the paper.

3.

Brack et al. (1992) provide the concept *time compression* as a type of therapy employing a therapeutic technique in which the client alternates between different temporal levels so that the client may be given the opportunity to understand the way his past is/has been constructed.

Here the quote is merely a simple concept, described for further use.

4.

[…] With his light, ironically entertaining style, he demonstrates that substantivisation is unnecessary and "less beneficial". However, in my view, he has skipped a couple of steps. He writes:

Here quotes are used both as the starting point for analysis, to interpret the wording and as documentation of keywords.

> Naturally, linguistic abstraction is not wrong in itself as long as it is used appropriately. This is not the time and place to discuss when abstraction is practical and when it is not.

A criterion that approves of substantivisation is here implicitly presented – *as long as it is used appropriately.* But when is it "appropriate"?

––

The number of quotes you should include differs according to the type of paper you are writing: Textual analysis, analysis of interviews, etc., use quotes as documentation, and therefore several quotes per page is appropriate whereas other types of papers use direct quotes as illustrations. Here a rule of thumb should be: Avoid more than one quote per page and quotes that are longer than 6-7 lines, as this result in a text that is too heavy and not independent enough. If you choose to quote directly rather than refer to the source, you should do so because the quote is famous; cannot be translated or expressed so well or illustratively that important meanings would be lost if you attempted to paraphrase it. You can also choose to quote your starting point and establish an opposition to the author's view. This can be rhetorically effective.

Quotation technique

A quote must be clearly marked in the text. A quote must always be cited correctly, even when the source itself is not completely correct. The following guidelines explain how to quote correctly:

- *Short quotes* (e.g., shorter than a line) must be put in quotation marks in the text
- *Longer quotes* must be typographically highlighted by means of indentation and line breaks (enter) before and after the quote.

See the examples above.

If you leave out part of the quote, you must indicate this with [...] or [...] in place of what you have omitted. The examples in this book demonstrate how to do this.

Paraphrasing and summarising

You can present the content of others' texts by either paraphrasing or summarising. We mention both here, as you may be asked to write either.

A *paraphrase* provides a close account of others' texts, chronologically and point for point. You need this if you are required to paraphrase a novel or film analysed in your paper.

A *summary* is a condensation of ideas and information in others' texts. When summarising, you can select parts of the text that are relevant to the given purpose and change the order these are originally presented in.

The following is an example of a summary.

5.2.1 Kasper & Dahl's research

Kasper & Dahl (1991) have created a similar overview of research methods in studies in the pragmatic area of research. 39 studies of inter-linguistic pragmatism are here presented to chart which methods for data collection are employed. Instruments for collection are classified in relation to the degree to which they guide the informants' answers and in relation to whether they examine the informant's understanding or his productive abilities. They conclude that more research using observational methods is needed as well as research into the validity of individual elicitation tech. Finally, they emphasise the need for further research into the way individual technique for collection can contribute to different questions of research.

You must not add anything new when summarising or paraphrasing. They must both be written in your own words and style, but you must remain faithful to the source's content and when distinguishing between the source's statements and your own comments. You can mix your exposition of sources with your own comments in a section, however metatext (see chapter 13 on language) is required every time you do so. This means literally stating: "My comment is …", "From this I deduce …", etc.

How to reference sources

Every time you draw from a source, whether you quote, summarise or paraphrase it, the source must be referenced. There are two main ways of doing this:

- *Integrated in the text* – the source or author is made an element of the sentence:
  - Hansen (1989) emphasises that ...
  - As a contrast Jensen establishes two new categories ... (2006).
- *Parenthetically* – sources are most often mentioned in a parenthesis and not as an element of the sentence:
  - In the study's conclusion it is emphasised that ... (Hansen, 1989).
  - Children's conditions have not improved because of reorganisation (Olsen, 2008).

Often the author's surname and the source's year of publication are enough to identify the source in a bibliography containing more detailed information. See the following examples.

Apart from being able to reference correctly, you must also be aware of the different conventions of different fields and disciplines. The amount and way of including source information in "hard" disciplines (natural sciences) differs from how sources are treated in the "soft" disciplines (the humanities and social sciences). This is due to the way knowledge of different branches of science is conceived and "constructed".

In hard disciplines, knowledge is considered indisputable – as long as theory, research methods and the scientific foundation are accepted within an established discipline. You add your results to the existing pool of knowledge, like a piece of the puzzle, and then continue looking for more pieces. You do not return to solved problems, but continue linearly from these.

In soft disciplines, knowledge is interpretation or possible understandings that must be described (quoted, depicted) as the starting point for the writer's argumentation and contribution to a deeper and more refined understanding. Here we are dealing with a continuing dialogue about the field's permanent (and urgent) questions. In soft disciplines, a subject area is not exhausted because it has been researched before. Results can be "re-negotiated"; you can return to the area viewing it through a different lens, and you can enter into dialogue and discuss with previous researchers. See also chapter 7 on philosophy of science.

These differences in the character of knowledge result in a (tendential) difference in the way in which knowledge is included and presented. Here are some typical examples:

From hard disciplines:
- A research of radon radiation on Bornholm (23) shows ...
- It has also been possible to apply the method to ... (Strand, 2004).

From soft disciplines:
- Hansen (1996) argues for a different understanding of the short story: (quote)
- As pointed out by Andersen in his dissertation (1999), Bakhtin can also be applied to linguistic analyses.

Below the principle differences are presented as opposites – in practice it is more nuanced.

Hard disciplines	Soft disciplines
• Research and method is at the centre	• The author's statement, intention and arguments on the topic are at the centre
• Quotes and longer summaries are rare	• Quotes and summaries are common
• Often a source is referenced without exact data	• The source's claim is thoroughly summarised or quoted
• The source is not integrated in sentences and the names of authors are often omitted (e.g., the source is referenced through numbers in parentheses)	• The author of the source is almost always mentioned and is integrated in the sentence, e.g. as the subject ("Hansen (1999) believes that ...")
• The source's claim is presented, often without further ado	• The source's statements are analysed, characterised, commented, explained, interpreted)
• The text mostly presents data from the source (using words like *describe, show, add, observe, develop, document, state*).	• Data from sources is often characterised (and even evaluated) in the text (using words like *argue, believe, assume, recommend, reject, overlook, mistake, exaggerate, misunderstand, claim, present, suggest*).

Which sources must be referenced?

Students often ask us which type of source must be referenced and which do not? We usually refer them to this outline:

What information must be documented and what information does not?

You *do not need* to reference sources of
- general knowledge, i.e. something everyone can observe
- knowledge which is accessible to everyone, e.g. encyclopedias which can be found at any public library
- your own observations.

You *must* include references for
- quotes, paraphrases, summaries
- claims, opinions, views presented in sources that are debatable
- events observed by a small number of observers
- statistics, images, etc.

The way in which you reference the source's information also indicates how you relate to and evaluate the source's statement. We suggest that you always use concrete and precise verbs – see the box "Summary verbs" below. And remember, if you question a source more or less directly (by using, for example, "alleges"), you must provide explicit arguments for your "implicit" evaluation.

Summary verbs

XX ...
- alleges ...
- analyses ...
- argues for ...
- claims ...
- compares ...
- concludes ...

- honfirms ...
- describes ...
- documents ...
- evaluates ...
- measures ...
- observes ...

- points out ...
- selects ...
- shows ...
- states ...
- suggests ...

etc.

> **Activity for varying summary verbs for the production or revision phase**
>
> Every time you include a source in your paper, try choosing a more specific summary verb than "writes".

As the writer, you must also own up to the amount of responsibility you take for a source's statement. This is illustrated well below:

> **Responsibility for statements**
>
> - The writer's responsibility: *The moon may be made of cheese.*
> - Shared responsibility, but mostly the writer's: *The moon may be made of cheese (Brie 1999).*
> - Equally shared responsibility: *As Brie (1999) argues, the moon may be made of cheese.*
> - Shared responsibility, but mostly the author of the sources: *Brie (1999) points out that the moon may be made of cheese.*
> - The author of the source's responsibility: *Brie (1999) argues that the moon ... According to Brie (1999), the moon ...*
>
> (Adapted version by Groom, 2000, handout)

The first example – in which there is no reference – is the most risky. Usually you cannot include a statement from a source without crediting the source in some way. Which option you choose must depend on your view of the source's statement; how much importance you attach to it in relation to your purpose, and how much you distance yourself from the statement's truth value.

You can explicitly indicate your (level of) agreement with your sources – and this is normally the wisest thing to do.

Distance to sources

Distance to sources is very important in academic texts. Crediting others' – and your own – contributions is crucial for "intersubjective controllability", i.e. enabling the reader to verify the information and thereby access the sources. There must always be a clear distinction between your statements and your sources' statements. It is better to indicate this bombastically, than it being uncertain whom information is to be ascribed. It is perfectly acceptable to write: "My interpretation is …" or "In the literature I have not been able to find expressed the idea that …" or "I will now introduce concept X, drawn from Y, which I have not yet seen applied in this context …, but in which I see the following perspectives …"

When a student does not explicitly participate and relate to sources, the paper will seem like it only presents the views of the sources or the views of the student (as in the first example in the box "Responsibility for statements"). In this case the student will end up hiding his light under a bushel and not be properly credited for his own independent contribution.

The examples of quotes above (pp. 246f.) demonstrate this distinction linguistically as well as typographically.

At the opposite end of the scale the lack of explicit distance to sources, will easily be conceived as plagiarism. I.e. the student pretends that the source's contribution is his own.

You are too close to your sources when you

- merely summarise sources and do not use them for anything
- use too many quotes
- do not clearly indicate when you are presenting the source's views or your own
- do not include enough of your own analytical text between quotes
- do not relate (in a selective, qualifying, evaluating manner) to your sources
- the source's language become contagious to your own.

Many students complain that detaching themselves from their sources is hard, and that they find it difficult to "assert themselves". If this is a problem for you, try following these instructions:

> **From summary to using sources**
>
> This is how to write using sources:
> - *Summarise* (quote or paraphrase) relevant text sections:
>
>   "He writes that …"
> - *Analyse:*
>
>   "I locate these elements in his writing …"
> - *Interpret:*
>
>   "I understand his writing in this way …"
> - *Use, apply:*
>
>   "In my context I can use what he writes to …"

If possible, start from behind with the last point. In this way, you will write your own material first and it will be easier to sort and only include what you need in the particular context. However, this requires that you are aware of your "context" and have formulated a research question. See the boxes "Sequence of analysis", p. 321, and "Discussion sequence", p. 325.

Contagion and plagiarism

You are also too close to your sources if you write in a "contaminated" language, i.e., if your source's language is contagious to your own writing, so you end up writing a form of masked quote. This is not quite as bad as "the mortal sin of academia": plagiarism, i.e. reproducing a source's information without referencing the source, but it is still unacceptable.

You are most at risk of "contagion" when you have not formulated a research question that prepares you to use sources for a self-selected purpose. It is even worse if your research question can be rephrased as "What do the sources (actually) say?". You will easily end up summarising too much and writing in a language that too closely mirrors the source's. The research question always – implicitly or explicitly – defines the function of sources, and how these should be treated. We discuss contagion further in chapter 13 on language, pp. 383ff.

It is always best to use original sources, perhaps in translation. Sometimes you may have to refer to a source via another source – this is often acceptable, especially in the first years of study. You must clearly indicate any use of secondary sources, i.e. you must make a reference to the original source as well as the one you actually use.

9. Data in the paper

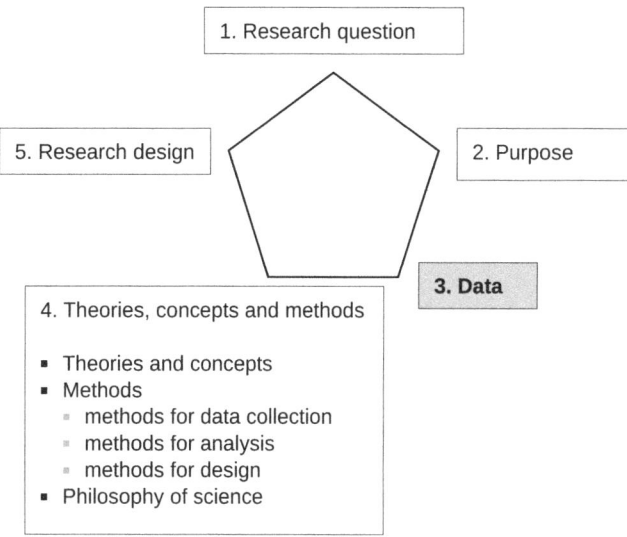

In this book, the term *data* covers all material that is methodically and systematically selected and classified and made the object of your research to which you can refer. This includes among other things:
- Texts (e.g., in the humanities)
- Observations (e.g., in the natural sciences)
- Numbers and statistics (e.g., in the natural and social sciences)
- Sources (e.g., in history)
- Cases (e.g., in the social sciences)
- Theories (e.g., in philosophy).

If possible, including data in your paper will always prove advantageous. It is best if data constitutes the object of analysis. However, for want of data, even small examples and illustrations of the phenomenon serving as the paper's starting point can concretise the phenomena you are writing about. The concrete (data) ensures that theories are not detached from their context, but that theory and data/practice are integrated. And you will use (and train in the use of) a number of different disciplinary methods and skills by writing papers that analyse data.

> **Advantages of including data in your paper**
>
> - Problem orientation will be self-explanatory and concretised
> - Data can be analysed, discussed and evaluated
> - If you have obtained the data, it is your own, and your position as subject and researcher will be strengthened
> - The paper will be easier to structure
> - Knowledge is contextualised and avoids taking on the form of general claims

Qualitative and quantitative data

Qualitative and quantitative data differ from each other. They therefore require different methods for analysis and result in different types of statements.

> **Qualitative data**
> Qualitative data is made up of the object of study's special qualities and features. If you have a limited amount of qualitative data, you must formulate the problem narrowly. For example, "on the basis of these four cases of ... we can analyse and interpret that ..." You should avoid making general statements on the basis of a limited amount of observations. However, you can make statements about the actual data you have examined.
>
> **Quantitative data**
> Quantitative data is data that can be put into numbers, quantities and sizes. If you have access to a large number of quantifiable items, you can formulate problems and conclusions that are more general.

Data does not have to be comprehensive. Data may be your own observations and reflections, for example, on an internship. Note that data can be produced by you as well as others.

Analyses can be based on a very small amount of data. These are qualitative analyses which analyse a small amount of material thoroughly and in depth. Data in smaller studies can demonstrate the complexity and context of a phenomenon. In the soft sciences, these small qualitative tasks are commonly written on different modules and semesters, while disciplines in the hard sciences more often conduct quantitative research and thus include larger amounts of data in papers.

Before choosing data: Research question and supervisor

Before you choose, collect and process data, you should have an idea of your research question (it can be loosely formulated so you can change it later).

There is a reciprocal relationship in the selection of philosophy of science, theory, methods and data and the research question (see chapter 4 on formulating research questions). Perhaps you want to write about a particular phenomenon or cultural product because it fascinates you and you want to know more about it. However, the decision of what and how much data you choose to analyse, depends on what interpretations you believe you can draw from the data. If analysing the translation of humour requires finding comic strips that are especially funny in both Danish and English, you need to select examples that are humorous. Your research would not benefit from including strips that are not particularly funny. In this way, your preconceived idea of the result of your analysis becomes important to your later choices. You could say that the argumentation of the research is crucial for the selection of data. If you know which research question will guide the research and which point you want to make, you must make yourself and your supervisor aware of the research question and point before choosing data.

It is important to consider whether the main point primarily relates to whether it relates to data or theory, phenomena, concepts, regularities or something else, which is then mean to be illustrated/exemplified/explained/challenged by the data. The point is crucial for selecting data.

If in doubt, you can conduct a "pilot study" where you consider examples for analysis and perhaps carry out a few test interviews, enumerations, categorisations, textual analyses, etc., to check whether the type of data you have chosen is at all interesting.

You should preferably have spoken to you supervisor. This is especially important if you plan on using people as data – in observations, interviews, questionnaires or designs/interventions. If so, you must be especially careful to uphold agreements made for using this data as your object of study. Your supervisor shares responsibility for this. The supervisor should always approve your plan for collecting and using data and methods before you start.

Always prepare collection carefully

Before you rush out to collect large amounts of data, you should check whether the collection itself requires methodological knowledge and a more focused research

question. The reason why we emphasise preparation and supervision before working with data, at least data involving people, is because we have supervised far too many students who were too quick of the mark, especially in regards to carrying out interviews and questionnaires
- without a question guide
- without having read anything about interview methodology
- without a research question on which to base interview questions.

Often this will lead to unfocused and useless data – and it will be hard to get to use the same people as objects of study in later and more focused interviews, observations, experiments, teaching, care, treatment or whatever the I's starting point may be. Therefore, we always advise that you, in advance, formulate as complete a research question as possible, read methodological literature that prepares you for the data-based work in question, and present a temporary data and method section to your supervisor.

Furthermore, data often requires systematic documentation of how it was collected. Consider archeological finds. In Archeology, you do not simply start digging without knowing what you are expected to look for and how to treat finds.

A certain knowledge of method is necessary before collecting data. If you cannot explain the reasoning behind the way data has been collected, the paper's methodological argumentation can be undermined. If you intend to use data you have personally collected, you must be familiar with the following:

Methodological prerequisites can be knowledge of

- methods for collection and analysis, based on theoretical criteria, and generally how descriptions and analyses of "actual reality" are consciously or unconsciously based on (theoretical) categories.
- methods for observation, both as a detached spectator and as a participant in observations, recordings and transcripts
- interview techniques and the formulation of interview guides
- how to document data during and directly after collection
- methods for categorisation
- ethical considerations

When people form part of your data, you need to carefully consider your procedure in terms of contacting them, providing them with information about the study and ethical considerations, see the table p. 266.

Here, physiotherapy students describe their selection of informants for a BA thesis on physiotherapy for the homeless (12/A) (MDN = the organisation Make a Difference Now). Note the table of data at the end of the excerpt.

Our purpose of spending time at the homeless centre was communicated to the centre through MDN. The centre took great interest in our BA thesis, but emphasised that contact to the users must be respectful and take their best interests into account.	Observance of ethics relating to participants
Data was collected when MDN was at the centre. MDN's visits to the centre were not planned out beforehand. Their starting point was to have a physiotherapist present at the centre once a month who would give between one and six treatments.	Reason behind the frequency of visits to the centre
As the field was new to us, we scheduled three extra visits to the centre with the aim of expanding our background knowledge. Furthermore, the extra visits constituted an important part of building mutual trust between the homeless and ourselves. This trust is important when accommodating homeless people's possible distrust of health professionals, see the background section (p. 3).	Trust is built up between the participants and writers of the paper
When researching a new field, it can be hard to determine in advance, who and how many people to include in the data. However, selection is made on the basis of the researcher's assessment of who can provide the most comprehensive answer to the problem area (Hovmand & Præstegaard, 2002, p. 46).	Selection criteria – with reference to methodological literature
During the collection of data, it is a good idea to regularly revise the selection of informants in relation to the problem area as you gradually acquire more knowledge. Sufficient data will seldom be obtained with fewer than six to eight informants, while more than 20-30 would make processing data an overwhelming task (Hovmand & Præstegaard, 2002, p. 46).	Selection is adjusted – within the framework of methodological literature

To ensure sufficient amounts of data, informants were selected on the basis of the criterion that they must use MDN. The informants thus consisted of homeless who received physiotherapeutic treatments each of the three times we collected data. This selection strategy is termed random strategic selection (Malterud, 2003, p. 60). We excluded non-Danish-speaking homeless people receiving treatments. This criterion was based on an assessment of our own limited language abilities. After consulting with the centre's employees, we also excluded mentally challenged homeless people.

Selection criteria supported by methodological literature

Criterion of exclusion based on own limitations, which is perfectly fine

Yet another exclusion criterion

Thus, data consisted of the following informants (see table 1):

First time No.	Gender	Age	Participated as an informant/ Informant no.	Symptom	Reason for not participating
1	-	-	No	-	Did not wish to be part of the BA thesis
2	♂	63	Yes/Informant no. 1	Pain above the lumbar vertebrae and bilateral pain above the hips	
3	♂	46	Yes/Informant no. 2	Pain above the lumbar vertebrae	
4	♂	41	Yes/Informant no. 3	Pain in the vertebrae, locked costa, strained shoulder	

| 5 | - | - | No | - | Because of criteria of exclusion – did not speak Danish and was not considered mentally able |

It is easy to follow this account of how in this paper data was selected and how the writers made contact, built trust and adjusted their procedure according to what proved appropriate.

Criteria for choosing data can be:

Choosing cases

- **Criteria:**
    - Exemplary (cases that demonstrate the ideal)
    - Representative (cases the demonstrate the typical)

(Avoid random selection and choices made from convenience).

- **Which and how many cases?**
    - Cases must be selected on the basis of a purpose, research question and theories/methods
    - One case can be enough to demonstrate the qualities of something, if it is critical, extreme, unique and especially informative (however, you presumably cannot generalise on the basis of a single case)
    - More cases can be used to show differences, contrasts or patterns. Coincidences are reduced.

- **The selection of cases must be qualified and possibly discussed.**

(Based on Neergaard, 2001).

Substantiation, rationale and selectivity are ideals of the research genre, and choice of data is precisely one of the elements of research that must always be substantiated by the writer.

Activity: Substantiate and prioritise your choice of data

- Why do you want to use this data?
- List the data you plan to include according to priority. If your data consists of more than one object, which would be the best piece of data, and why is this piece the strongest in your paper? What does the remaining data contribute to?
- How can the processed data contribute to the paper's points and argumentation?

After choosing/studying case(s)/data you can

- choose method(s) that are particularly suited for processing your data
- specify your research question
- find other evidence (documentation, studies, data, sources) that supports/challenges your data
- argue for your choice of cases
- describe the benefits and disadvantages of the chosen case(s)
- consider whether your choice of data has theoretical consequences for your research

---

Presenting data in your paper's introduction

Just like theory and method, data must be presented in your introduction, possibly in a special data section if there is much data to describe and argue for. This applies whether you are talking about your own or others' data-based research.

Activity: Write about your data

- What kind of material does your data consist of? Cases, texts, etc.?
- In the introduction: How comprehensive is the material? How many, how much?

- How has it been selected? Which criteria?
- And in the method section: With what and how will the material be categorised and analysed?
- Which status does it have in your paper? Is it representative or purely illustrative?

Including data as documentation in your paper

In different methods and fields, different conventions apply for how and how much data to include in the text or as appendices, and whether it should be quoted and/or be summed up in a table, how comprehensive it must be before a summary becomes interesting etc.

You should preferably read analyses using the same methods to find out what others have done, read methodological literature and consult your supervisor and/or teacher(s) of the field's method.

In general, data is quoted frequently in the analysis section of data-based papers/academic research. Following a close analysis, preferably with many quotes, the meaning of the data must be interpreted and summarised in light of the paper's concepts and methods. This can be written in cohesive text or be presented in displays, illustrations and tables depicting the interpretation of data.

The following example is from political science (BA level, grade 12/A). In this case, the data consists of a text: *NATO's Strategic Concept of 1999*, which, after being analysed, is interpreted on the basis of a theory about narrative dimensions, summarised in this display at the end of the paper:

The past narrated as	The present narrated as	The future narrated as
The positive narrative: Community of values Civilisation	Democracy Civilisation	**The hopeful future:** Stability The spread of democracy and western values
The negative narrative: Rearmament and deterrence		**The bleak future:** Unstability Unrest

We highly recommend making displays while you collect data in order to keep track of the large amounts of data.

When using data, you must take all of the gathered data into account (or else explicitly exclude the parts of the data that are irrelevant in the context) and seek to explain finds that do not fit into the paper's explanatory models and methods and general argumentation.

It is your treatment of the data, and not the data in itself, which serves as documentation for the paper's collected argumentation.

As soon as you have an idea of what concepts, theories and methods to process your data with, i.e. as early as possible, it is a good idea to write a mini-data analysis.

Activity: Write a mini-data analysis

- Write what you use to analyse/process data
- Write a short analysis (a couple of lines or a few pages) of a single, delimited piece of data. As often as possible, mention the concepts/parameters used for analysis.
- Write a conclusion to the analysis: What does it show? How does this analysis form part of the paper's overall argumentation?

Data can be discussed in discussion sections

You should evaluate your data when discussing method (reservations, nuances, qualification).

Is it suitable, sufficiently comprehensive, telling, representative, etc.? You should also evaluate whether the data can be explained by the theories and methods used in your paper, and whether your specific data entirely or partially confirms or disproves the theories' general statement. Even if the data is chosen and collected by you, the important thing is to provide an honest evaluation of the material's evidential power in relation to the paper's argumentation. If, after conducting your research, you discover that other data or the same data gathered or processed differently would have led to more interesting results, make note of this better data. In this way, you contribute to furthering the enterprise of academic research.

Remember not to draw general conclusions on the basis of small amounts of data. Your data and applied theories/methods must be able to support your conclusion:

> **Conclusions on the basis of small, qualitative studies/research**
>
> - Your conclusion must be based on the data itself, the phenomenon it illustrates and the applied theories/methods
> - You cannot and should not generalise on the basis of one or few cases! Your research question must be narrow if you only include one or few cases.
> - However, perspectives can be general (but with reservation)
>
> (Partially based on Neergaard, 2001)

Collecting and using human data

Many disciplines in higher education deal with human data: in interviews, observations, pedagogy, treatment, care, etc. This should preferably be educational and comfortable for everyone involved: informants, their organisations, students, writers of papers and supervisors/educational institution. No informants should feel uncomfortably exposed or exploited in uncontrolled contexts. The research ethical guidelines that apply to researchers also apply to students.

In the following, we present recommendations on how to use people as data in papers, lightly edited from the guidelines of Sociology Department at Copenhagen University. The following are suggestions for research ethics that students from BA to MA level can/ought to abide by. It is a good idea to discuss these suggestions in your own department where there may be particular conditions you must be aware of.

> ### Anonymisation, confidentiality and ethics
>
> - Information must be stored and treated in such a way that no third party can come into possession of it.
> - If the student gains access to non-published material belonging to an institution, company or organisation, this material can only be used with the institution's, company's or organisation's full knowledge.
> - Usually persons, institutions, etc. must be anonymised – unless they do not wish to be anonymised and the student agrees with this assessment.
> - If anonymisation is not possible, the project must be made confidential. A confidentiality clause entails that only [the third party, i.e. informants] the student, supervisor, external examiner and agents that treat a potential complaint about an exam, can read the project – or parts of the project.
> - The research must be carried out with consideration for individuals as well as the group, organisation, institution or company involved in the research and its results.
> - Qualitative methods and especially qualitative research interviews must be conducted with consideration for the common methodological precepts for conducting qualitative interviews, including a sharpened vigilance and prudence when dealing with topics considered sensitive or delicate by the informant.
> - Observations and informants' statements must be treated in a way that ensures that neither the informant nor identifiable persons mentioned by the informant are unnecessarily brought into disrepute. A study and its results must not be unnecessarily offensive or harmful neither in regards to the identifiable persons' integrity nor the public reputation of particular groups.
> - Possible dependence on one or the other party in the planned project can be in conflict with research ethical principles and must be taken into account.
> - The regulations of the data protection agency must be observed in connection with survey-data.

The third party is the informants or the organisation with which the student has an arrangement (possibly an internship agreement).

It is important to communicate the final results to informants and their Institutions as well as during the writing process have informants provide feedback as to whether or not they acknowledge the information and context they feature in. The Sociology Department writes: "In principle, scientific activity is based on open knowledge sharing which must be respected to the greatest extent possible". Therefore, communication in itself is important and students are given the following advice:

Agreements and contract with the third party

- The agreement is made with informed consent
- It is recommended that students and informant sign a contract
- It is recommended that communication to informants and others is specified in the contract

---

Many educational institutions have guidelines like these. Some also include contracts to be signed by informants and their organisations/institutions and the student. Check whether your department has a contract on its website – if not you can draft one yourself. Consult your supervisor about which agreements you can make before you contact a third party.

This brings us to how to *contact* the people whose data you wish to include in your paper. It is a good idea to ask your supervisor to look at a draft of the e-mail you intend to send them (writing is often wiser than calling as you can include this e-mail as an appendix to your paper).

Activity: Plan the information, contact and communication to informants and their possible institutions

- Who must be informed, sign a contract, etc.?
- What is the agreement about?
- When should you do so?

Present drafts of these kinds of letters and agreements to your supervisor to discuss whether you are abiding by the principles of research ethics – and do so before sending anything!

The writer's rights with regards to data

- The written product resulting from collaboration with the third party is the intellectual property right of the student. If several students have collaborated on a written product, they share joint copyright of the product. Only the student(s) can give permission to a possible limitation of this right.
- Insofar as the student and third party wish to enter into agreement about transferring these rights, this is solely an agreement between the student and the third party, and not extraneous to the Department of Sociology, as the Department has title of the papers required to be handed in for assessment according to the regulations.
- On the basis of the procured material, students have a right to use this for other presentations than the written product in question, for example in interviews with the media, feature articles and popular articles.
- The student reserves the right to withhold the project's results until the end of the project. If in agreement, both parties can make different arrangements about this.
- … the third party [the informant] cannot invoke the right to change the text of the paper
- The freedom of research is also inviolable for students – this includes the freedom to formulate a scientifically substantiated critical stance.

(From Sociology, University of Copenhagen, website)

10. Theory, concepts, methods and research design (= the method of your research)

This chapter heading mentions "method" twice. We distinguish decidedly between a paper's *research design* and its *research methods*. The research design is principally unique to the paper in question. With each new research question, you should construct a new research design, i.e. procedure for examining the material that is the object/data of the paper. We will return to this later in this chapter.

In the pentagon, the methods of different fields and the paper's research design are placed in each their corners: 4 and 5 respectively:

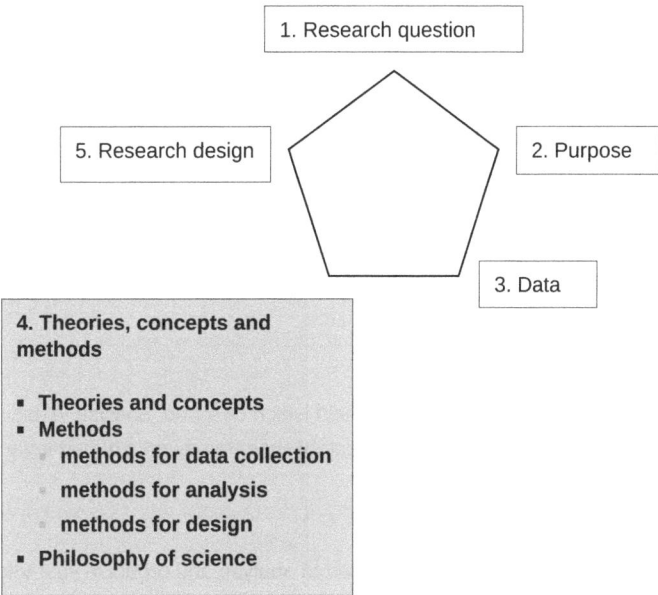

In addition, theories and methods must often be placed in and justified from the philosophical framework within which the paper is written.

> **Definitions**
>
> Theory and research methods are a field's tools for gathering and selecting data and discussing it. This is why curricula often require theory and research methods. In this chapter, we describe how to meet these requirements in papers.

In the good paper, it is crucial to include the field's concepts, theories and methods because by using the field's tools

- you demonstrate the ability to analyse and use the knowledge of the field
- you relate the field's tradition and foundation to the data that theories and methods are applied to
- argumentation becomes academically trustworthy – because theories and methods are crucial to a paper's argumentation (see chapter 12).

Theory and method sometimes do not have to be included in first year practice papers. However, in later years of study, the curriculum usually requires that research papers, projects and theses include and explicitly deal with either theories or research methods – most often, both. Simply storing them at the back of your mind or drawing on them implicitly is not enough. Here are definitions of some central concepts:

> **Central conceptual definitions**
>
> **Theory**
> System of ideas (or assumptions) within a field which describe, analyse, explain and predict the phenomena of the field and which establishes frameworks of understanding for the field.
>
> **Concepts**
> The keywords (often drawn from theory) used to analyse and organise your information.
>
> **Models**
> Models are graphic Illustrations of (abstract) elements – for example, theories and methods, procedures, time, principles, and their mutual relationship. Models are good for making things concrete, operationalising and providing an overview.
>
> **Methods**
> The methods of the field are specific or general (=used in a number of fields), are often

theory based and constitute tools for concrete tasks, e.g. collection, categorisation, analysis, interpretation, evaluation of data, design (construction, processing, etc.).

Research design
The research design is the design of the inquiry, the connection between the research question and the methods used for data selection and analysis, discussion, evaluation, design, etc.

Data
The object of study and the material you can refer to (observations, statements, texts, sources, etc.).

Some disciplines include many concepts and theories. This is especially true of the soft/dry disciplines. However, in these disciplines papers will not always include method sections and students will often look nonplussed when asked about their methods. Other disciplines include numerous methods, but less theory. This especially applies to the hard/wet disciplines. Here researching, among other things, consists of using systematic methods for collecting, classifying and evaluating data. Other disciplines are rich on both theories and methods, e.g. social and medical sciences, pedagogy, psychology and many others.

Theories in your paper

Theories can serve different functions in your paper:

Possible functions of theories in your paper

- As the foundation for method (analysis, categorisation, evaluation, etc.)
- As the explanation of research results (interpretation, validation)
- As background, set of values (a theoretical current or school of thought)
- As data (object of study)
- As discussion, comparison, contrast
- As authority (supportive argument).

Theories generalise and encompass many, sometimes all, phenomena of the same type. If you are interested in a theoretical question or a general description of a phenomenon rather than the phenomenon itself, you can decide to write a purely theoretical paper. If you want to know something about special, individual phenomena and individual manifestations of phenomena, you can choose specific examples and apply theories to them.

Concepts are often drawn from theories

Commonly, only parts of theories, rather than entire theories, are used. E.g. you draw out key concepts and models representing important categories in the theory and apply these to your analysis. So "theories in paper" will often mean "selected concepts from theories".

Concepts are thus terms for disciplinary contexts, perspectives, categories, etc., which can be used to analyse and systematise disciplinary objects. A student analysing a novel uses the concepts "narrator level" and "plot level" to organise his observations about the text. You may come across papers that do not appear to include explicit theories and methods. However, even in papers that seemingly lack theory, it is necessary to use concepts drawn either from the field's underlying theory and unspoken and implied assumptions and prerequisites, or concepts constructed on the basis of the studied material.

You must define concepts and state why you use them in your research

If there can be any doubt, discussion or alternatives, the paper's concepts must be defined. Concepts you have constructed or use unconventionally must be especially be carefully defined. In all cases, it is a good idea to describe what you use concepts for and how you use them. The following example is from sociology (BA level, high mark):

••

Research question

What is the connection between knowledge and society, and which role should knowledge play in a democracy?

Which answers can be drawn from Habermas' theory on discourse ethics and American Pragmatism respectively?

2. Concept definitions

The main question includes two central concepts: knowledge and democracy. These two concepts will guide and delimit my interpretation of pragmatism and discourse ethics. To begin with I define knowledge simply (and tautologically) as "knowing something, being certain of something" (Grant 1996: 110). I have chosen this vague definition because the theories contain detailed and thorough definitions of knowledge, and because these are determinative for which role knowledge can and ought to play in democratic processes.

Democracy […]

• •

Note the phrase "to begin with". In this way, the writer indicates that one of central concepts in the paper will be elaborated on later. Developing and nuancing an understanding of a concept as a result of the paper's argumentation is an excellent approach.

Problems with a paper's theory

When including theory, some papers make the mistake of
- summarising too much theory or too many theories which are not used later in the paper
- "sneaking in" theories that are neither relevant nor suitable in the context
- not including any theory at all
- not relating theory and data to each other
- introducing several theories without relating them to each other.

If you include theory without being able to explain the function of each theory section and each line, you will end up with a knowledge-telling paper. This only shows that you are familiar with the field's theories and methods, and not that you are capable of using them in a professional way. The important thing is to bring theories and methods into play with either data, with each other or both (i.e., using them for analysis, discussion, synthesis, evaluation).

Too much or too little theory

If you begin with theory, you may end up forcing it upon your material to make the theory "fit". These kinds of papers include a number of claims drawn from a theoretical universe where the most important or only evidence is references to the literature, and the paper will contain numerous broad and generalising statements.

Choice of theory for research papers

Students often ask the following questions in regards to using theory in papers:
- How do you find out which theories are relevant to a field? How do you choose and how many theories do you need?
- What determines whether a theory is good and useful?
- Do you need to use the entire theory?
- What if there is no theory?
- Can you use theories and methods from other fields and sciences?
- What if the theory is much older than the data?

Important guiding principles for theory in papers are that all theory is subject to the research question; the data and the paper's argumentation; and restrictions in terms of length and time. When the research question is in place, you look for concepts, models and theories you believe have a particular angle and can explain (parts of) what you want to learn.

It is important that you are fond of and respect the disciplinary tools you employ. Spending your studies battling issues and trends you consider outdated, irrelevant or destructive may teach you criticism, but will not necessarily provide you with constructive tools/methods for later work. When studying your field's tools, you should get the feeling that you are storing these tools in your professional toolbox; tools you can use productively when you start working.

Usually theories are introduced in class. However, if for example you choose subject area which falls outside the content of these classes or if you dislike the current theories included in your field's curriculum, you may have to conjure up other theories from somewhere else.

You must substantiate your choice (and possible rejection!) of theories. A defining feature of research papers is substantiation and presenting reasons for all choices (even if these were made with help from your supervisor). The following is an example of substantiating the choice of models (theories) from Political Science (BA level, passed):

After this we will continue the discussion emphasising a *further* democratisation and the *desirability* of a such, taking as our starting point the model of direct democracy.	The chosen model
The reason why we have chosen this model rather than the classic Athenian or Republican model is that a distinction is normally made between two main categories of democracy models: competitive democracy and participatory democracy (Bille, L. 1997: pp. 10-12). The distinction between these two categories roughly amounts to the distinction between representative and direct democracy (Hansen, P.N. et al. 1997 pp. 64-66).	Reason 1
As indicated above, we have chosen to include the model of direct democracy as a heuristic tool, as it is considered to differ markedly from the liberal model and therefore can illuminate other aspects of democratic theory. This is furthermore because one of the characteristics of direct democracy is that the people have great and direct influence on political processes. And as the original meaning of democracy is the people's rule (Hansen, P.N. et al. 1997 p. 64), we imagine that this can be considered a more democratic system of government than the reprelsentative model.	Reason 2
We shed light upon this, using parameters from Alf Ross' definition of democracy. This choice will be elaborated later in the paper.	Indication that the reason will be elaborated later

And this example of the choice of concepts and theory is from a paper from teacher training (BA, high mark):

Choice of theories

Before considering the structure of lessons, I will consider which theories and methods I find best suited for Geography class. […]	Disciplinary relevance Pedagogical key concepts the starting point of selected theory

In my view, there are certain factors that must be present in order for lessons to succeed, namely motivation, engagement and coherence between the material and pupils' own experiences. For this reason, I have chosen to describe what I consider to be the optimal learning process partly by means of Constructivism, including David P. Ausubel's emphasis of motivation. Furthermore, I have chosen to include Wolfgang Klafki's theories of cultivation, partly because of Geography's qualities as a subject of cultivation, and partly because the amount of material requires me to work from the exemplary principle. Finally, I have also briefly described hermeneutics as the methods described in the hermeneutic circle are suitable for forming an overview of a number of contexts, something which applies to Geography lessons when considered as a coherent course of teaching.

Choice of theorists substantiated on the basis of their explanatory power and usefulness.

Activity: Choice and substantiation of theory

You must always be capable of answering the question: Why have you chosen this theory for researching this problem?

Describe what you use your theories (and their concepts) for, e.g. to:
- explain observations
- be transformed into models and methods for e.g. analysing
- discuss with
- evaluate on the basis of
- argue for design.

Also substantiate your choice on the basis of:
- topic/problem/context
- use/function in the paper
- supplement
- news/currency
- acknowledgement.

Justify choices and delimitations on the basis of
- research question
- purpose
- data.

In your paper's introduction, substantiate your choice of theories, central concepts and models used for analysis and for processing material. These should also be discussed in the discussion section and/or throughout the paper, as your reason for choosing a particular theory must ideally be seen in light of the chosen theory's interaction with the problem, materials, methods and philosophical framework.

How to find theories

We sometimes hear students say that there are no theories explicitly related to the given subject area they want to study. However, this will typically be the case, e.g., if the object of study is so new that it has not yet been analysed – for example, a new novel, case, film, exhibition or something similar. In these cases, you may have to be the first person to use a particular theory to understand the given phenomenon. If there "are no theories", you should borrow theories and concepts from related areas to explain the phenomena. Here are some possibilities:

> **Activity: Find theories**
>
> - Ask you supervisor. To some extent, your supervisor should be able to guide you through the jungle of theories relevant to the field. Present keywords to your supervisor: What do you need theory for – and what should it explain?
> - Conduct a systematic literature search using your topic's keywords (possibly combine these keywords, see chapter 5 on literature searches). This will provide you with titles and abstracts of articles and books, which may reveal how the topic has previously been approached theoretically – but nothing more: Using theories that have not previously been used in a specific context may prove interesting as they could bring about new perspectives.
> - Examine theories and methods of other fields. Related fields may use theories relevant to your own discipline. The librarian at your research library may be able to help you.

Theory section

Most papers will need to introduce the concepts and theories applied to material or used as a basis for discussion and argumentation. You may need to analyse theory or method with a theory, or carry out theoretical discussions or syntheses of several theoretical contributions. Structuring theory depends on the purpose of your theory section, i.e. on your research question. The theoretical/conceptual universe is most commonly constructed from several or many building blocks, applied to data/material and then discussed in relation to the material and/or internally. The challenges of the theory section consist of

- keeping descriptions brief, writing succinctly
- being guided by the research question and not getting too close to sources – neither in terms of structure nor language
- including it in a functional way, i.e. not let theoretical passages standalone without using or considering them
- integrating it with the material/data or the discussion each element of the theory is meant for.

Lacking explicit integration between theory and data, i.e. too long chunks of detached theory, is one of the most common problems of writing papers at all levels of study.

Therefore, when writing your theory section, you can make use of a preparatory table providing an overview and which focuses on function and integration. A paper can naturally include more than four theories, but you can adjust the table according to your needs.

Activity: Substantiate and integrate elements of theory				
Insert you research question here:				
Element of theory (or concept)	Theory element (or concept) 1, name	2	3	4
The **central statement or keyword** from the theory (that I need):				
The theory I **need for** (analysis, discussion, design, etc.):				
The theory **adds** to my research's theoretical universe:				
I need **x number of lines/pages** to introduce/account for the theory:				
I will **integrate** the element of the theory **with data/materials, research question, method** by (indicating the theory's function in relation to, by exemplifying, concretising):				

In short: Consider how to ensure that your inclusion of theory is substantiated, coherent and necessary in your particular research context. If you are ever in doubt of whether something comes across as unnecessary namedropping our best advice is:
- Delete or elaborate!
- Get feedback.

Method and method section

A research method is a systematic procedure which can be explicated so the reader is able to follow (replicate) the study and can reach the same results by following the described premises. Method and systematism are the core of science. Sometimes methods are drawn from theory and in an interplay with the philosophical framework of the paper.

The different fields offer methods (tools) for all the phases of research: for
- collection of information
- analysis and description of the information
- interpretation of results from analyses
- evaluation of interpretation
- creating professional designs.

Methods may be:
- Tests
- Methods for literary analysis
- Archeological methods
- Statistical methods
- Methods for source criticism
- Ways of analysing argumentation
- Methods for troubleshooting, fault-finding methods
- Methods for interviews and questionnaires
- Methods for construction, design, presentation, treatment, care and teaching, implementations.

... to mention but a few.

The following pentagon model of a bachelor's-level paper in nutrition and health was awarded a 12/A. Notice the fourth corner as it illustrates that different methods for collection can be applied to the different stages of answering the research question.

"Food Waste – From knowledge to action"

1. Research question
"How can the problem area of food waste be communicated in writing via Samvirke's published as well as electronic magazine with the aim of decreasing consumer's waste of food?"

2. Purpose
"As a health professional I will analyse the background for consumer's food waste as well as question how the problem area of food waste can be communicated to Samvirke's readers to make them act on the basis of this information. Furthermore, I will attempt to identify different options for decreasing food waste through this project. I hope that this BA thesis can be applied as a working model and/or inspire other professionals working in related fields."

3. Data, phenomenon
- Own data from internship at Samvirke
- Analysis of FDB-report on food waste: *Vi smider ikke mad ud!* [We do not throw out food!]
- Data about Samvirke's readers and reading of Samvirke
- Own data from interviews with selected Samvirke employees
- Own vox pop data from consumers with different food wasting patterns
- Own web articles written during internship.

4. Concepts, theories, methods
Theories and concepts:
- Gallup's compass model: Samvirke's 5 archetypical readers
- Theory about processes for changing opinions and action competences: Model "Stages of change" (Dalum).

Methods:
(Methods for gathering data)
- Kept a systematic log during internship
- Interviews with employees at Samvirke
- 4 consumer vox pops

(Methods for analysis)
- Analysis of target audience

(Methods for design)
- Strategic communication
- Ingemann's circle model for popularisation
- Web articles based on communication strategic models and theory about popularising articles.

5. Research design
"… target audience analysis of Samvirke's readers. Here I will examine the target audience's relationship to food waste and how they define food waste in their housekeeping. I will apply humanist theories on action competences and processes of change as well as employ the model "Stages of Change" (Dalum et al. 2000, p. 47) to locate the stage Samvirke's readers are at in terms of acting and reducing food waste […] My starting point is Samvirke's archetypes and the sources interviewed during my internship. Finally, I will use theories about written communication and journalistic writing for published and electronic media as a basis for my strategic communication." …

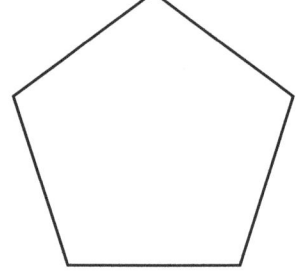

This good paper includes so many methods because of its ambitious research question which poses the question "how can communication be carried out?" i.e. how can a design be created on the basis of an analysis?

Naturally, different fields prefer different methods: Different fields have different objects of study which must be treated differently. Different schools' specific ways of analysing demonstrate their particular (theoretical) understanding of the field's objects. Part of studying a specific discipline or subject is therefore to familiarise yourself with

- the prevalent methods of your field
- what they can be used for and in which situations
- how to carry them out in practice
- to try out as many methods as possible.

You develop invaluable disciplinary competences by trying out different methods. You have to be able to do things, not just know things. As a student, you are stronger as a writer of papers – and as a professional in the labour market – if you have conducted interviews, done analyses based on a theoretical approach, tested the field's construction and design options, and done so after reading relevant methodological literature, consulting a supervisor and possibly a method teacher. You should seek out your field's methods and get to know as many as possible. If there are no supervisors or courses that teach discourse analysis, statistics, qualitative interviews, picture analysis, case methods or any other method you wish to apply to answer your research question, look for one on the Internet or, if you have time, in other fields or educational programmes. Lectures are sometimes open to anyone, even if you are a student at a different university.

Methodological literature should play a crucial role in your studies. Your supervisor and librarian can help you find methodological literature relevant to your research question and material, and which is also suited your study programme and level.

Activity: Write a method section

- Describe each of the methods used in your research separately.
- Substantiate: Based on your material, research question, the philosophy of science underpinning the paper, time limit, prerequisites and other resources, why have you chosen this method?

- Describe how you apply the method in your research context. In principle, your description must enable other researchers to replicate your study.
- If you need more methods: How do these relate to each other (e.g. observations of XX and interviews with YY?).

Usually discussion of method is not included in the method section but in the discussion section at the end of the paper. However, in connection with your choice of method, you may note any limitations that may not have been able to be avoided even though, despite everything, it was the most appropriate method.

Method sections and method discussion is of varying lengths – from extremely short (methods are implicit) to forming a large part of the paper. This is the case in many hard disciplines; where method sections and method discussions nearly constitute the entire paper, save for the introductory literature section leading up to the research.

In terms of process, it is a good idea to draft the method section as well as the discussion of theory and method as early as possible before determining specific ways of conducting your research. As soon as you have an idea of which method(s) to use, you should draft your method section – and discuss it with your supervisor.

Turning a theory into method (analytic tool)

A field's theories and methods are often closely connected. It would be possible to depict a theory in a model demonstrating the main elements (concepts) of the theory and their interconnection. This model can then form the basis for a procedure in which these elements are used in a suitable order for analysing or characterising. Theories, for example, are depicted in models which are used for analysis. When theory is not visualised in a model, the writer (and others!) can often benefit from making their own "model of the theory" and using it as a template for their method. You can extract dimensions from the theory and turn these into analytic tools. Here is an example of how theory can be transformed into an analytical framework and operational method:

A student writes a paper about whether a particular novel can be considered a *Bildungsroman*. She intends to use two different theories about the *Bildungsroman*. These two theories characterise the *Bildungsroman* differently. Turning theory into an analytical method firstly consists of extracting central dimensions from the theories (written as coherent text and not necessarily placed in boxes ready for analysis). These are the dimensions of the *Bildungsroman* in abbreviated form:

Moretti's theory of the *Bildungsroman*:
- future oriented
- time is the most important dimension
- the goal is happiness
- home-out-home model
- balance between individual and society
- the maturation of the individual.

Erikson's theory of the *Bildungsroman*:
- not future oriented
- space just as important as time
- the goal is insight and cognition
- the protagonist acquires history not necessarily identity
- development, but not always towards happiness, maturity or balance.

Following this, she analyses the chosen works based on the distilled dimensions. Her interpretation is a statement of whether the works contain features of the *Bildungsroman* in 1. the traditional sense and 2. the modern sense.

Breaking down theory (or parts of a theory) into analytical dimensions often form the methodological backbone of a paper. Each analytical dimension becomes a lens through which to read your material closely. Each analytic dimension can form a heading of a section in the paper's chapters of analysis.

Where in the paper do you write about theory and method?

Theoretical elements can be found throughout the paper. These are the most "loose" elements as they can serve many different functions (see above p. 271). However, we present some guidelines in the following.
- The paper's main theory and main method should be introduced and validated at the beginning of the paper – often, in a separate theory and method section.
- Concepts from the main theory and method must be used throughout the paper
- Supplemental theories and methods used locally for specific purposes can be included throughout the paper and be introduced when used

- Main theories and methods should be discussed and evaluated late in the paper, but before the conclusion.

Introduce theory in the introduction or theory section

The concepts, theories and methods or the parts of these you wish to use in the rest of the paper, should normally be accounted for in the paper's first sections. It is often enough to present theories and methods in the introduction, especially in shorter papers. However, in longer papers and dissertations, you will need entire sections, one for theory and one for method. Separate theory sections can be a good idea, especially if the theory involved is
- large
- unknown and therefore requires introduction
- from other fields
- a combination of theories
- a controversial theory you must argue for.

This account must be selective: Do not include more than what you use. And you need to create links to points made later.

And in its modified form, this is the concept I will later use for …
When understanding phenomenon X, aspect A of theory 1 is worth emphasising because …
I will later show that …

Dividing your account of theory, analyses and discussion into these sequences makes it more manageable:
- Theory, data, analysis, or
- Theory 1, theory 2, discussion of theory 1 and 2.

However, your account of theory and presentation of concepts can be mixed with your analysis – as long as you are careful and avoid blurring the lines between different elements. And, preferably, your supervisor must approve of this! Some – e.g. literary disciplines – prefer it when theory is woven into the analysis and avoids becoming too heavy and separate in the paper as a large theory section at the beginning. A literature professor once said about theory: "There is nothing worse than a big, heavy theory section followed by an aesthetic product being cheerlessly violated by theory". The most important thing is simply that the basis for analyses and discussions are made visible to the reader – even if this reader is not a supervisor, acquainted or familiar with the writer's theoretical landscape.

So, our advice is: Ensure that the entire basis for your analysis is presented and accounted for, and ensure maximal closeness between your account of theory and concepts and analysis. This closeness can be established by keeping the account brief and by regularly alerting your reader what you intend to use the theory for: "This concept will later be included in …"

Where in your paper should you present critique of theory and methods?

Critique of theory and method should be presented *before* analysis if you intend to use these theories and methods in a modified form later. You can place criticism *after* analysis if you use theories and methods in their present form and later wish to criticise them based on the experience drawn from using them.

Many papers include separate method sections and present a discussion of method at the end of the paper if the method played an important role. This applies if the method used is interviews, observation of participants or questionnaires. So, before analysis:

> I wish to use method X, but have had to modify it by means of Y because I found it inadequate in relation to my material on the following counts …

And after analysis:

> After the analysis of X, I have reason to present the following criticism of the method …

Discussion, evaluation and critique of theory

Discussion of theory and method and criticism of method heighten a paper's quality because you explicitly reflect on your own and other's argumentation. In a paper, critique often consists of short passages and single sentences, but these are nonetheless crucial. Many students are especially respectful of theories. But a theory is merely one suggestion of how parts of reality can be understood. As a student or researcher your main obligation is not to theories, concepts or methods, no matter how great they and their authors are, but to attempt to see clearly, open your eyes and understand how theories and methods function in a given context. It may then prove necessary to modify, criticise or expand on these theories, concepts and methods.

You are always welcome to evaluate concepts, theories and methods on the basis of your own research question – and evaluate whether these tools are applicable to the context you have chosen to focus on.

Evaluate theory on the basis of

- your research question
- its explanatory power and coverage in regards to the phenomena you are researching. Can the theory explain the data?
- applicability in relation to the functions (see p. 271) you have chosen the theories for, e.g. as a foundation for method
- internal consistency (is the theory coherent without internal contradictions?)
- reasonable objections raised by other theories
- the writer's chosen disciplinary/philosophical foundation.

This is an example of how two students (communication) criticise theory using other theories and thus indirectly argue for supplementing the theory:

Critical remarks

Sepstrup has been applicable as his model provides a useful tool for our analysis. However, Sepstrup's limits consist in the fact that his model appears to be based on an almost behaviourist understanding of the information process, in which stimulus from the sender results in an almost predictable receiver response. Sepstrup is inspired by the American social psychologist William J. Mcguire (1989, p. 43-66), who originally developed a 12-step model of the information process.	Introductory acknowledgment of the theorists' applicability to this context The model's limitations

According to other theorists this information process is not that simple. Kim Schrøder (1984, p. 30) for example, argues that *content* is subordinate: The important thing is how the receiver *experiences* the content. Schrøder	A different theorist with a more nuanced understanding
(1993, p. 71) discusses how reception research is interested in the receivers' way of creating meaning as it takes place in the decoding of a specific media text, and that the receiver's experience of a media text must be seen in relation to the receiver's total lifeworld.	A different theorist with a more nuanced understanding
This enables a broader understanding of the information process. This understanding draws attention to the fact that the information process, like the learning process, cannot be reached alone through stimulus – response activity, because the information process is far more complex and includes factors such as interest, experience and knowledge. This understanding of the information process makes it difficult to plan campaigns on the basis of Sepstrup's general model.	… and the simple model is hard to apply to the practice the research question focuses on
Good communication processes require the ability to engage with the way the media product is understood, experienced and interpreted by the receivers. Kåre Nielsen (1993, p. 48-60; 135-162) directly states that we must consider the receiver's previous knowledge, i.e. experiences, learning processes as well as authority.	Finally, a different theorist offers an important suggestion of which dimensions to consider.

••

Here, Sepstrup's model is criticised through two other theorists from the field. We understand that the writers agree with this criticism. Finding others' criticism and using their formulations as support is both common and viable. You can also criticise theory without ascribing the criticism to others; namely, by presenting arguments and reasoning which reveal the theory's limitations in the given context on a more general disciplinary basis.

The following is another example of systematic criticism of theories from teacher-training (BA). The writer begins by criticising on the basis of his own broader pedagogical understanding and then includes "the purpose of primary and secondary school" (trump card!) to support his criticism of theory.

However, in my view, merely regarding students as closed systems that must be invaded by outside surroundings to learn anything, gives rise to important criticism. The affective aspects of teaching are not taken into account nor in relation to the social aspect. The community of the class is only considered a surrounding factor for pupils' learning and is not considered to have any intrinsic value.	Criticism of the theory's lacking "degree of coverage" in a teaching situation (in class)
If the theory is understood literally, it operates from a very narrow view of learning and concept of communication. Practical-musical learning processes are for example not included in the theory, and neither are communication with pictures, objects, etc. Both concepts must be interpreted broadly in order to fulfil the purpose of primary and secondary school and the stipulations of History as an educational subject.	Criticism of the theory's lacking "degree of coverage" in relation to learning processes and the primary school's purpose and the subject
The theory is not useful for stimulating pupils' ability to engage themselves, which is mentioned as one of the purposes of history. According to the theory, it is impossible to identify with others – to experience as another. The individual system's own filter of understanding will "be in the way".	Criticism of theory based on its usefulness to a pedagogical concept from the subject's teaching purpose (empathy/engagement)
On this basis, I conclude that purely using constructivism as a theoretical foundation for teaching history does not alone give rise to misgivings, but is impossible if the guidebook is to be complied with.	Summing up: Criticism of theory in relation to subject-specific teaching and official teaching guidebook
Furthermore, I personally distance myself from the mechanical role of the teacher implied in this theory. Its lack of affective and social aspects leads to the dehumanisation of pupils. This view is disastrous for pupils as well as teachers.	Personal criticism based on implicit, fundamental view of humanity Evidence for these strong words would be welcomed here!
The operative constructivism is partially a useful and fruitful theory of learning for teaching history, for example, in connection with historical narratives. However, the theory has its limitations. In brief, my conclusion is that teachers can draw inspiration from the theory, but that it does not constitute a comprehensive foundation for teaching history overall.	Following such strong criticism, it is necessary to explain what the criticised theory can be used for (and what the writer has used it for) in relation to the subject/discipline and work as a teacher.

Often, criticism of theory consists of constructively expanding and modifying theory, supplemented by others' theoretical contributions so construction of theory takes place.

In the following example of criticism of theory, the writer suggests an expansion of the theory. Furthermore, the assessor comments that the criticism could "carry more weight" – implying that the expansion of the theory could be supplemented (from the conclusion of BA thesis, Danish, including the assessor's comments).

> Incorporating intonation would be a valuable way of expanding the theories. When working with conversations I have often been inspired by the tone of what was uttered, and it is greatly insufficient that this is not included as an active element in the theories. Intonation can be crucial for which implication or intention we are dealing with, and whether it is an initial implication. In face-work, intonation is especially important. The same utterance can be harmless or extremely face-threatening depending on intonation.
>
> Assessor's comments in the margin:
>
> "the criticism of the theories' lacking treatment of intonation could easily carry more weight – after all, the theorists claim that the theory is especially suited for vernacular language"

Discussion, evaluation and criticism of methods: Research method

An important purpose of writing a paper is that the writer *takes a stand* – also on his/her own methods, research design and procedures; that he/she discusses these, is critical of and learns from them. Furthermore, this stand must be communicated to readers/assessors.

A section in which you are critical of your own methods may be called "method discussion" or "criticism of method". It is a question of degree, and it is up to you to choose the heading that best conveys the content of the section.

As mentioned previously, writing a paper has two footings: 1. literature and 2. your own research. This is why papers can include a literature section about literary methods as well as a discussion of both the included literature and one's literature search. The model below illustrates this.

In chapter 8, we treat bibliographical method, discussion and criticism.

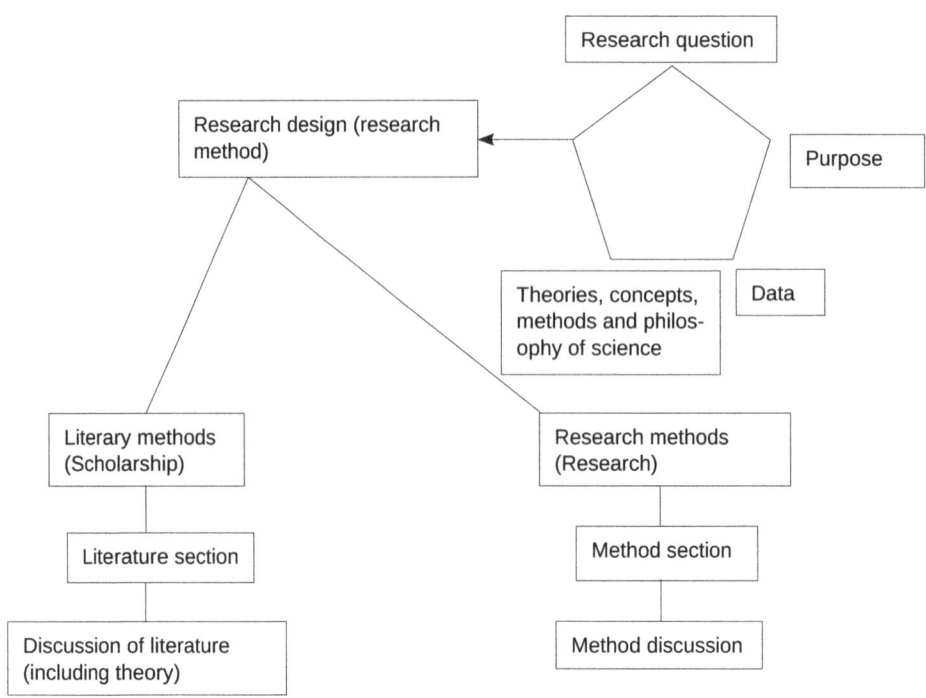

In this section, we write about the research method and the method discussion and criticism of method in your own research. "Method" here means all applied methods – methods for data collection, calculation, analysis, classification, design, etc. In principle, you should evaluate every method you use and soberly make note of what could have been better, i.e. more systematic and which could thereby have led to more tenable results – within the limits of the paper in question and level of study etc.

In the discussion section (or in a section entitled "criticism of method" – which is rarer) you gather possible objections against the methods used. However, you should also include the reasons why these methods have proven fruitful – hence the title "discussion". You discuss the pros and cons. This is where you consider how professional your research is. By evaluating and criticising your own method, you anticipate any reasonable objections your reader may have – objections that may affect the strength of your conclusions. If you can criticise the scholarly foundation of your own study – and you normally can to one extent or another, you must argue that this research method is nevertheless satisfactory and the extent to which it is "good enough".

In this discussion with yourself, you may consider the circumstances in which the research design used may nevertheless lead to claims that are entirely valid and how you could try to support and legitimate your choice of research design (and, thus, the scholarly methods used therein). Finally, you must assess and state how certain you are of the validity of the claim once the methodological problems and the methodological advantages are taken into consideration – i.e., you must qualify how certain your conclusion is.

Activity: Write a discussion of method

1. Answer the research question.
2. Mention the most important documentation.
3. Explain any unexpected results, conflict with other results and studies.
4. List limitations and points for criticism in your research methods – where it is relevant.
5. Back up your method, explain its strengths.
6. Point out anything new you have contributed and how you would qualify your results – have you suggested something or proved it?

It is difficult to criticise your own method, and it seems like an obvious thing to do to cover up mistakes that might easily have been avoided. However, it is honesty and a willingness to bring up possible critiques that pave the way to qualification – and to academic credibility (ethos). It is less OK to argue glibly and not to deal with possible objections. If you do not yourself discuss possible critiques in your paper, you invite exactly those critiques.

What do you do if it is really hard to argue for your conclusion – and for the methods you have used? This happens, of course, because research can go wrong in many ways – and in ways so unclear that you can hardly become wiser from them. Our best advice is:

- Write about your research design and methods and the difficulties with the method, and write about what might instead be a better methods and research designs.
- Get supervision – as early as possible, and find out what other methodological options you have.

Here is a long and good example of a comprehensive and thorough method discussion from political science (BA thesis, high mark):

••

Our use of case studies as a method for our analysis of the reorganisation of the Ministry of Economy and Business Affairs has had different consequences for the results of our analysis.

The descriptive and explorative case study of the restructuring process proved fruitful for acquiring concrete knowledge of a delimited area. Through our many data sources, we have first of all collected much detailed information of the reorganisation process itself, which was not otherwise available. By supplementing the written source material with our own interviews, we have acquired good and more nuanced knowledge of the events and contexts, which enabled our description of the course of events. Secondly, we got a step closer to getting below the surface of official and conventional knowledge through our semi-structured interviews with the department's employees, as we were introduced to thoughts and opinions in the department which were not reflected in the press or the Ministry's own papers.

The writers defend their research method which consists of several methods. In the method literature, supplementing methods is considered to strengthen the research (this is called method triangulation). However, the composite research method is also substantiated on the basis of the goal to acquire "good and nuanced knowledge of" and "getting below the surface".

However, it is possible that our case-based procedure based on our own interviews as primary sources has led to us being dazzled by the success of the restructuring. Despite having selected informants from different parts and levels of the organisation in order to ensure as nuanced a picture of the reorganisation process as possible, we must point out that all respondents had a very positive attitude to the idea of project-oriented work as well as the restructuring process itself. There is a lack of more critical perspectives of the process, and it is regrettable that the interviews do not present the reservations that existed in the Ministry according to the press and the employees.

1st criticism of method: Reservations about the informant's opinions (="bias") which are not representative of what is described in other sources – the press.

We will briefly mention another criticism of our data. In reference to our theoretical starting point, interviewing actors from the Ministry's surroundings to uncover the attitudes and reactions to the department's situation and reorganisation could seem like an obvious approach. On the other hand, starting from a neo-institutional mindset, we could

2nd criticism of method: Informants' own interpretation of the events have implicitly provided input to the research: And objective informants would possible

also argue that the way the organisation has understood and interpreted signals and impulses from its surroundings has been crucial. It has been crucial to the way the Ministry reacted to its surroundings and the way the Ministry itself viewed and defined requirements and expectations.

The most controversial aspect of the case study method is the question of whether this kind of study, in terms of research, has another and broader value beyond the treatment of the particular phenomenon – in this case, the reorganisation of the Ministry.

Our case analysis has resulted in significant information and understandings of the course of events of a specific reorganisation process in a particular department in the Danish central administration. Our method has activated many actors and fundamental mechanisms within a specific context. However, the case study of the Ministry's restructuring can also be seen as an "extreme" case, which directs attention to some universal reference points for organisational change in a public context. In this way, attentive case studies draw attention to general conditions, which initiators of reforms should pay attention to when the aim is an organisational initiative for change.

However, on the basis of this case study, it is neither possible nor in agreement with the neo-institutional paradigm to present universal precepts for the ideal reorganisation process in light of the specific and context-dependent situation.

have provided a different picture than the one obtained by studying the actors' interpretation of a course of events. This is a classic criticism of method.

3rd criticism of method: The ability to generalise on the basis of one case is problematised – also a classic objection to small, qualitative studies. If the case includes unique features that are not present in other examples, what can we even learn from them? A relevant objection to case studies.

Here formulations become vague: "fundamental mechanisms", "some universal reference points", "some general conditions" – the plural tense is used and this results in vagueness and broad claims. A better justification of the research method's value would be to concretise and exemplify here.

∙∙∙

In this example, the writers' criticism of method is based on their selection of interviewees and the resulting limitations on a generalisation of these persons' statements: Certain opinions have not been included. This is a good criticism of method. But the authors do not comment on, e.g., their own interview guide or their methods for interpreting and analysing what was said. We are not saying they or you should, but there are more ways method could have been criticised in this paper. Naturally, you should only criticise points you actually consider deserve criticism and are relevant so that the reader can agree with the conclusions and the strength with which these conclusions are presented. In this example, we get a sense of the writers' awareness of methods and criticism of method – they have read the relevant methodological literature and this is one of the paper's great strengths.

To a great extent, criticism of method is rooted in reappearing questions – just like source criticism (see p. 238).

Evaluate methods based on

- what the method's results can be used for in light of the research question, purpose of the research, data/object of study and context.
- what limitations and sources of error have affected the use of the method
- what results you have achieved by using the method

Validity and reliability

What you are assessing is the method's validity and reliability and, thus, how valid and reliable the results are.

The method's validity is the certainty with which a method measures what it is intended to measure. The method's reliability is its ability to be repeated, i.e., that the method shows the same result every time.

A group of archeology students wrote the following in their criticism of method:

> Fish remnants were not found in the village, but this could be due to the fact that the holes in the sieve we used were too big to catch fish remains. From this it is not possible to determine whether human beings on Amager ate fish in the Mesolithic.

Here we see that the method for collecting finds is crucial for which conclusion students can draw. It is good that they mention the size of sieve, as this is an important piece of information for uncovering the truth in this case and to alert subsequent researchers to the methodological implications of studying human being's eating habits from so long ago.

Activity: Write a method discussion and a criticism of method

- Make a bullet list of your own objections and criticisms of your own research design and methods – what objections could others raise about your methods?
- Pick out the methodologically weakest link (if you find this difficult, involve an opponent or your supervisor). Write down this weakness and explain why/how it has arisen.
- Write down why you use the methods despite your criticism: How will you substantiate your choices?
- Describe how your criticism of method affects your conclusion. Are reservations and hedgings required?
- Which methods would you suggest for the same piece of research now? How can you take your criticisms into account next time you write a paper/do similar research? What would work better?

Having reservations about conclusions because of methods' limitations is the order of the day. If in doubt, exposing your research's methodological weaknesses is a good idea. Or if you are uncertain of how to put this in writing without undermining yourself, consult your supervisor or suggest exchanging method discussions and criticism of method with your class.

The paper's research design, the procedure

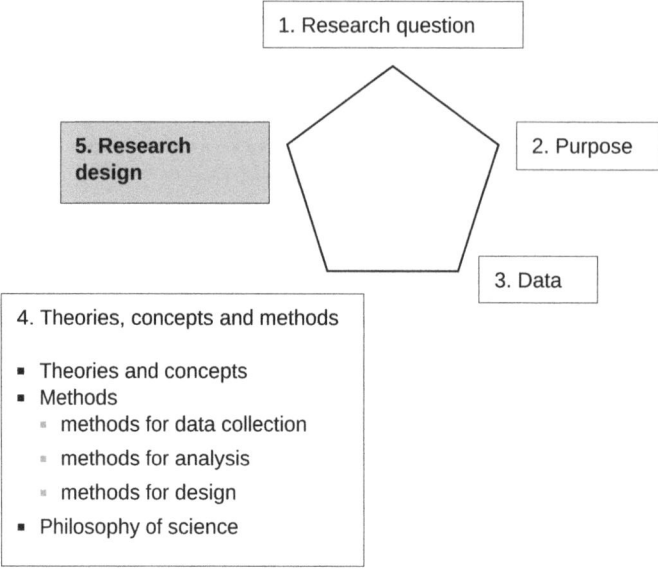

The paper's research method constitutes the *collected procedure* or research design of your entire paper's research. Research design encompasses both the research of literature and your own research and can usually be found in a section called Procedure or Structure "Structure".

Often, the research design is composed of several of the field's methods, which are the tools of the field. In purely literature-based papers, it will consist only of methods for treating literature.

Research design is often described using this formula: "First I do this …, then I do that …, subsequently I do this …, finally I do that …". Here, both research words (I collect, I interview, I cultivate the culture of bacteria, I examine, I calculate) and text types (I summarise, I analyse, I discuss, I conclude), etc. are used.

The research design is central to the research nature of the study, which naturally makes it important. This is why we suggest that you make it explicit, also when writing in fields where this is neither required nor expected.

From research question to theory and method and research design – in a linguistic sense

When choosing theories and methods (as well as any premise based on a philosophy of science), the research question also determines which theory/theories and methods to use. The following example (p. 298) is from Sociolinguistics, Danish. It demonstrates how the research question's concepts recur in the description of the research design; here entitled "Structure". (Our CAPITALISATION of concepts).

You should also note the use of text types (see pp. 315ff.) in the phrases: "present", "on the basis of", "consider", "research", "delimit", "analyse", "discuss", "reflect", "conclusion". This indicates clearly what the author "is doing" in the text.

Use your supervisor for selection, use, qualification, discussion and criticism of theory and method

Your supervisor must see and be given the opportunity to supplement or help you delimit your choice of theories, concepts, methods and data for your paper – preferably as early in the writing process as possible. If you supervisor offers suggestions, ask him or her to substantiate why this exact suggestion would be important to your paper and consider whether you agree. Far too many times we have asked students why an unsubstantiated theory was included in a paper and received the answer: "Because my supervisor suggested it, but I didn't quite understand what he meant, so it ended up being slightly detached from the rest of the paper". Suggest which disciplinary tools you wish to use and then ask for your supervisor's, fellow students' and others' reactions to your suggestions and to how well these are interconnected.

All sections in which you describe your methods, use theories and methods and criticise and discuss theories and methods are particularly good to talk to your supervisor about.

1.2 Research question

Taking as my starting point a qualitative longitudinal study of how Canan establishes references to the past in her utterances, I wish to examine the relationship BETWEEN FORM AND FUNCTION IN HER LEARNER LANGUAGE. Based on this study, I will then discuss the relationship between SYSTEMATIC AND ASYSTEMATIC (FREE) VARIATION in Canan's learner language. In this connection I will furthermore reflect on the parts of the VIEW OF LANGUAGE AND ACQUISITION on which I have based my analysis of learner language.

→ From concepts from the research question to theory and method

1.3 The paper's structure

The second part of the paper constitutes the paper's theory section. In this part, I present the VIEW OF LANGUAGE AND ACQUISITION on which I base this paper, taking as my starting point Holmen (1996). **The third part** of the paper is the paper's method section. Here I consider how the relationship between FORM AND FUNCTION IN LEARNER LANGUAGES can be studied using Sato (1990) as my point of departure. The paper's **fourth part** is the paper's analysis section. After presenting the data, I delimit the utterances referring to the past with relevance to my study of Canan's indication of past. I then analyse the relationship between FORM AND FUNCTION in data in the 2nd and 3rd grades respectively. In the **fifth part** of this paper, I discuss the relationship between SYSTEMATIC AND ASYSTEMATIC (FREE) VARIATION in Canan's learner language taking my analysis as my starting point. In this connection I reflect on parts of the VIEW OF LANGUAGE AND ACQUISITION on which I have based my analysis section. The paper's **sixth part** contains the paper's conclusion.

→ Theory and method all in one
→ Theory as a basic view (explanatory model)
→ Theory as the basis for method
→ Concept definition

→ Discussion on the basis of theoretical categories

The **appendices** of the paper consist of two main parts: The first part (appendix 1,2 and 3 i.e. A1, A2, A3) consists of printouts of analysed conversations. I have not personally made these printouts. Second part of the appendices (remaining appendices) refers to my delimitation of utterances relevant to my analysis of the relationship between FORM AND FUNCTION in connection with Canan's indication of past references (the appendices are introduced more thoroughly in section 4.2.-4.2.4).

→ Methodological information

2.1 Holmen's view of language

[…]

11. The paper's structure and elements

To structure is to divide your content, relate the separate parts to each other and put them in order: Which elements make up your paper, how should they be subordinated each other and what order should they appear in? Working with structural elements is both a tool for processing and part of the finished product.

In this chapter, we focus on the structuring of papers' main sections and academic text types (e.g. analysis, discussion, evaluation). At the end of the chapter you will find a brief guideline for the formal sections, i.e. front page, contents, introduction, literature list, index. Read about source and literature lists in chapter 8.

When and how to structure

You can write down the first structural elements as soon as you have formulated a temporary research question to base your literature search on. A fully developed structure requires that you can answer these questions:
- *Division:* Which elements must be included to answer the research question? Which sub-questions must be answered before you can answer the research question's main question? The information must be divided into connected "clusters".
- *Relation:* How are the elements interrelated in the paper's main reasoning and argumentation? The connected information must be placed in relation to each other.
- *Order:* Where do the elements appear in the paper's reasoning/argumentation? Elements must be placed as prerequisites for and consequences of each other.

When structuring your paper, we suggest you use
- the research question
- the general structural conventions of research articles (which we will examine in the following)
- the principal research design (see "The research paper's standard structure" on p. 303 for an overview"), which always includes sections about the object of

study, disciplinary systematisms (theories and methods), the research itself, its results, etc.
- a bird's eye view to raise you above the worm's eye view's multitude of details
- possible curricular requirements for the paper's elements.

These structuring tools can be used individually as a line of approach, but are in practice inherently linked.

Here are a couple of examples of classically well-structured papers, each awarded a high mark (First, in the sociology of religion, MA-level).

Title: Muslim Websites in Denmark

Research question: "How do muslims in Denmark communicate their faith on the Internet?"

Table of contents
1 Introduction	1
1.1 Problem	2
2 Methodological considerations	2
3 Theoretical framework	4
4 Islam and Moslems in Denmark	6
5 Analysis of websites	8
5.1 www.islam.dk	8
5.1.1 The website's iconography – Islam at the centre	8
5.1.2 Chat, mailing list and quiz	9
5.1.3 Texts	10
5.1.4 Links	12
5.1.5 Summing up	12
5.2 www.khilafah.dk	13
5.2.1 The website's iconography – the caliphate at the centre	13
5.2.2 Audio and video	14
5.2.3 Texts	15
5.2.4 Link	17
5.2.5 Summing up	17
5.3 www.kritiskemuslimer.dk	17
5.3.1 The website's iconography – debate/critique/principles at the centre	18
5.3.2 Texts	19
5.3.3 Links	21
5.3.4 Summing Up	21
6 Summary of communication patterns	21
6.1 Patterns for communication of faith	22
6.2 Communicative patterns on the internet	23
6.2.1 Computer mediated communication	23

6.2.2 Audio and video	24
6.2.3 Texts	24
6.2.4 Links	25
7 Conclusion	25
8 Literature	26

- - -

Note how the writer moves from the general problem, theory and method to concrete analyses, and then moves back "up" to a general summary (chapter 6 in the example). Also note the systematism of the subsections of the analysis.

Here is another example of a table of contents that is governed by the research question. Note how the research question's topics and concepts appear throughout the table of contents (Teacher Training, professional bachelor).

- - -

Topic: Children's faith and how it affects Religious Education

Research question: How can Religious Education at intermediate level in a late-modern and secularised society take into account pupils' own religious views?

Table of contents	
Introduction	2
Research question	3
Method and delimitation	3
Concept definitions	4
The religious dimension	4
Religious views	4
Secularisation	5
Late modernity and adolescents	5
System and life world	5
Late modern society	6
Adolescents of the time	7
Summary	8
Religious Education as a subject	10
Analysis of the subject's objects clause	11
Qualified self-determination	12
Learning *about* and *from* religion	13
Summary	14
Adolescents' religious views in late modernity	14

Studies about adolescents' religious views	15
Own data about pupils' religious views	17
Summary	19
The teacher's role in Religious Education	20
Summary	22
Discussion and perspective	23
Conclusion	24
Bibliography	26

Use the research question as a structural guideline

The structure of a paper points from the research question in the introduction towards the answer in the conclusion. As previously mentioned, the research question is a statement about the paper's content, and the structure is a statement about the form of the content.

When structuring, it is a good idea to begin with the most central aspects – the aspects that must be included to answer the main research question. Following this, ask yourself: "Based on the aspects I have decided to make central to my paper, which prerequisites am I required to present to the reader?". Structuring from the centre (which will often be found in the middle or at the end of the finished paper) and towards the more peripheral parts is a good idea, and better than structuring chronologically from the introduction, chapter 1, chapter 2 and so on. The result of this will too often be that prerequisites expand and the paper becomes predominantly summarising and descriptive. The structure's design must indicate that the paper is knowledge transforming, not merely knowledge telling.

Structure is determined by genre

In fact, the *research text* genre has quite a bound structure which spans departments and fields – both in terms of the elements that must and can be included, and the order in which they usually appear. This is a clear advantage to the writer, who can follow these conventions and focus on content. Thus the research paper's structure is not completely optional, but is, in most cases, a variation of this standard structure:

> **The research paper's standard structure**
>
> - Observation of a "problem in the world"
> - Problem, problem field
> - Literature review, review of literature in relation to the problem
> - Research question, a relevant, disciplinary question
> - Method, procedure to reach a solution
> - Theory and philosophy of science to explain and substantiate the method
> - Collection of data
> - Processing, analysis of data
> - Result(s), solution (or attempted solutions)
> - Evaluation, discussion of results (solution)
> - Conclusion in relation to the research question
> - Perspective, relevance in the field and "in the world".

The research structure reveals the "ideal" research design (=the paper's general method) as the foundation for the paper's structure. By "ideal", we mean the edited and revised design – in practice the process is seldom linear. The goal is that the reader is able to follow the research process, reasoning and argumentation, so he/she can accept the results and conclusion.

The structure is meant to (1) demonstrate what you want to study (topic description and research question), then (2) explain why you want to study this, and with which method(s). Then (3) account for what others have said about the topic and which possible objections can be made against this. Then (4) state where you position yourself in your own research, which you then (5) carry out. Following this you (6) conclude and answer your research question: What does your research show in terms of the object and the theories and models used to study the object and (7) what are the limits and perspectives of your own method. Lastly (8) emphasise interesting finds, their implications, limitations and perspectives.

Each element forms an action which is carried out in your research. These elements are also present in the standard "table of contents" of research texts:

> **Standard structure**
>
> - Abstract
> - Table of contents
> - Introduction
> - Theory, method, "state of the art"
> - Research
> - Results
> - Discussion
> - Summary
> - Conclusion
> - Recommendations
> - Literature
> - Appendices and references.

The experimental, empirical papers of the natural sciences follow the standard structure most consistently. These papers are often called IMRAD (Introduction, Methods, Results and Discussion). This example (Biology, BA thesis) follows the IMRAD template, and section 1-3 constitutes the introduction.

1.0 Introduction	3	
1.1 Purpose	3	
2.0 The beach crab, *Carcinus maenas*	4	
2.1 Colour variations in *Carcinus maenas*	7	I
2.2 Acid Mine Drainage (AMD) and Restronguet Creek 83.0 Cd, Cu, Ni, Zn and As' bioavailability and speciation	10	
3.1 Absorption of spore metals	11	
3.2 Absorption and handling Cd, Cu, Ni, Zn and As	12	
4.0 Materials and methods	14	M
5.0 Results	15	R
6.0 Discussion	21	D
6.1 conclusion	28	
References	29	

The papers of other fields – especially the main fields of textual interpretation such as the humanities, theology and, at times, the social sciences (this also includes continental papers, see p. 61) – are partly structured as a softened variation of the standard structure, and partly according to the slightly different structure of papers that discuss theory and papers that present designs (e.g. the professional bachelors). Below the principle differences are shown:

Macro structures			
Analysis of data	Discussion of theory	Design/ Construction	Evaluation
↓ Introduction with research question ↓ Basis: Presentation of theories, concepts, methods, philosophy of science, research/results from practice, state-of-the-art ↓			
Presentation of data	Analysis of discussion theme	Analysis of theoretical, methodological practical rationales behind and prerequisites for construction, design (i.e., *why*)	Presentation of the object and criteria of evaluation
Analysis of data	Discussions of different positions	Descriptions of precepts for new designs (such as specification of requirements) (i.e. *how*)	Analysis and evaluation of the object
Results, interpretation, possible disucussion	Summary/ deliberations/ interpretations	Possible pilot/test experiment	Results, discussion
↓ Possible evaluation, discussion and critiquie of method/theory ↓ Conclusion, possible perspective			

The higher your level of study, the greater the expectation that you include all the elements relevant to your paper's context. The necessary, central elements recur in all fields.

Activity: Adjust the standard structure to your own paper

- Cross out any sections that are irrelevant to your paper
- Add relevant sections
- List the material you have for each section in the column on the right
- Rearrange the order of sections if this is better suited to your paper
- Keep it up to date and revise your structure regularly.

Introductory sections - Presentation of material/topical work, author, topic - Context (background, history, subject-specific context) - Observation - Problem - Research question - Hypothesis - Delimitation - Structure	

Method and theory section
- Presentation and validation of
    - research method
    - theory
    - concept definitions
    - conventions and practices of the discipline
    - premises from philosophy of science
- Presentation of data.	

Analysis section - Analysis of data (or theory, concept) I.e., (source statements, Interview data, statistics, measurements) - Results, partial/sub interpretations - Comparisons - Summaries - Partial conclusions.	

Discussion section - Discussion of results - Evaluation and critique of method - Substantiation of methods.	
Conclusion section - Claim - Points - Confirmation/disconfirmation of hypothesis - Interpretations - Evaluations - Designs.	

Perspective sections
- Perspectives
  - Empirical, practical, professional
  - Theoretical, conceptual, methodological
  - Consequences, implications
  - Future.	

The fact that the genre is bounded may be seen as an advantage as you can simply choose to follow the template and spend more time on content. You can naturally break with some of the less important conventions. If you are able to, you can for example account for theory while analysing (use of theory). However, crucial conventions, such as introducing research tools before/while analysing, are indispensable as the text's prerequisites and foundation are not understandable without these conventions. One writer who tried inverting the structure failed: Chapters 1-3 in his paper constituted analyses of works using concepts that had not been defined beforehand, and then followed two chapters introducing theory, a discussion of theory and a perspective. This order did not make it possible for the reader to ascertain whether the analysis was carried out on an academic basis.

If you want to break with conventions, you must be familiar with them, to ensure that you break with them consciously and deliberately, and you should discuss doing so with your supervisor before handing in your paper.

The structure contains elements of the argumentation

Another feature of the research paper is that it constitutes an argument as a whole. For this reason, the structure must also contain the elements necessary for a reasoned argument. This aspect is so important that we have dedicated an entire chapter to argumentation in papers, where we show the connection between the paper's pentagon, structure and argumentation. See chapter 12, especially p. 363.

The model below illustrates the connection between the paper's basis as expressed by the pentagon model, the basic structure for research and argumentation in research.

The pentagon's corners as represented by: ->	Structure	Argumentation
The introduction presents the research question, purpose, material, concepts/theories and methods, and the research design.	**Introductory sections** • Introduction of material/topic • Observation • Problem • Research question • Hypothesis • Delimitation • Structure • Literature search, possible account of literature search and use.	• Context • Literature search, collection, selection and use.

In the method and theory sections the disciplinary tools are presented.	**Method and theory section**
	• Introduction and validation of
	  ▪ theory
	  ▪ concept definitions
	  ▪ research method with all disciplinary methods.
		• Research method.

In the research/analysis section, disciplinary tools are applied to the data.	**Procedure section** - Analyses of the object of study - Results, partial interpretations - Partial conclusions.	- Documentation.
Here you discuss the results of the meeting between theory/methods and data.	**Discussion section** - Discussion of results in relation to own methods and literature (critique of method, support, evaluation) - Discussion of literature, source critique.	- Research discussion - Discussion of literature.
Here you return to the research question.	**Conclusion section** - Claims, points, conclusions - Confirmation or invalidation of hypotheses - Interpretations - Evaluations - Designs.	- Conclusion with reservations.

Here you return to the purpose of the research.	**Perspective section**
	- Usefulness
	- Meaning
	- Consequences
	- Future
	  - in relation to the object of study
	  - in relation to the literature.
		- Context.

General – concrete – general, up-down-up

Usually, the research text will move between the two poles, general and concrete. You are expected to apply the field's general ideas (theories) to concrete material (and that concrete material in return will give rise to considering the field's general views). A frequent movement in the paper as a whole as well as its separate parts, especially analyses, is this:

Structure principle: up-down-up again

- Up: general material (philosophy of science, theory, model, method, history, context, structure
  ↓
- Down: diving into concrete details, analyses
  ↓
- Up: returning to a general level again: details, the analysis is placed in relation to the general material.

The following is an example of a table of contents from Political Science (BA, high mark), which is a variation of the standard structure. All the elements are there but have been organised differently to better suit the writers' presentation of their research. Note how the structure shows the paper's move to a bird's eye view in section 5.2 and 5.3, where the writers reflect on their choice of theory and method and offers a perspective. It is a good sign that the paper both moves "down" into detailed analyses and "up" into method discussions and perspectives.

• •

Topic: "The restructuring of the Danish Ministry of Economy and Business Affairs – an analysis in a neo-institutional perspective"

Table of contents
1. Introduction.. 1
1.1 Research question... 2
    1.1.1 Clarification and delimitation 2
1.2 Method... 3
    1.2.1 Theoretical point of departure 3
    1.2.2 Case methodological considerations 6
    1.2.3 The paper's data sources 7
    1.2.4 Reading guide – the paper's structure 8

2. Theoretical framework	10
2.1 Neo-institutionalism	10
2.1.1 The institution as the pivotal point	10
2.1.2 Behaviour and interests – action logic	12
2.1.3 Organisation and surroundings	13
2.2 Organisational changed in a neo-institutional perspective	15
2.2.1 Types of change	15
2.2.2 Decision process in relation to change	16
2.2.3 Motives for change	17
2.2.4 Relation between the organisation, surroundings and changes	18
2.3 Operationalisation of theory and analysis method	20
3 Case: Ministry of Economy and Business Affairs	23
3.1 History and data of the Ministry	23
3.1.1 The merger	23
3.1.2 The Ministry today	24
3.2 The Ministry in its official capacity	25
3.2.1 The nature of the Ministry's tasks	25
3.2.2 The Ministry's organisational context	27
3.2.3 The Ministry's normative foundation	27
3.3 The restructuring process	28
3.3.1 Idea and problem diagnosis	29
3.3.2 The deliberation phase	31
3.3.3 New formation and completion	31
4 Analysis	34
4.1 Surroundings	34
4.1.1 International surroundings	34
4.1.2 National surroundings	35
4.2 Organisational level	37
4.2.1 Objective and strategy	37
4.2.2 Role of the project unit – signals and communication	38
4.2.3 The employee profile	40
4.3 Individual level	42
4.3.1 Interests and motives	42
4.3.2 Action logic	43
4.3.3 Frame of reference – barriers and possibilities	44
4.4 Summary and characterisation	46
5 Conclusion and perspective	50
5.1 The restructuring of the Ministry	50
5.2 Methodological considerations – strengths and weaknesses	51
5.2.1 Reflections about/of/on choice of theoretical basis	51
5.2.2 Reflections on the case-study as method	52
5.3 Perspective	53
Literature	55
Appendix 1: Interview guide	
Appendix 2: Organisation diagram	

(This paper also appears on *Scribo – Research Question and Literature Search Tool* (2012) as an example of a research question)

The paper's shifts between general and concrete can be illustrated as below (after Paulsson, 1999, p. 47):

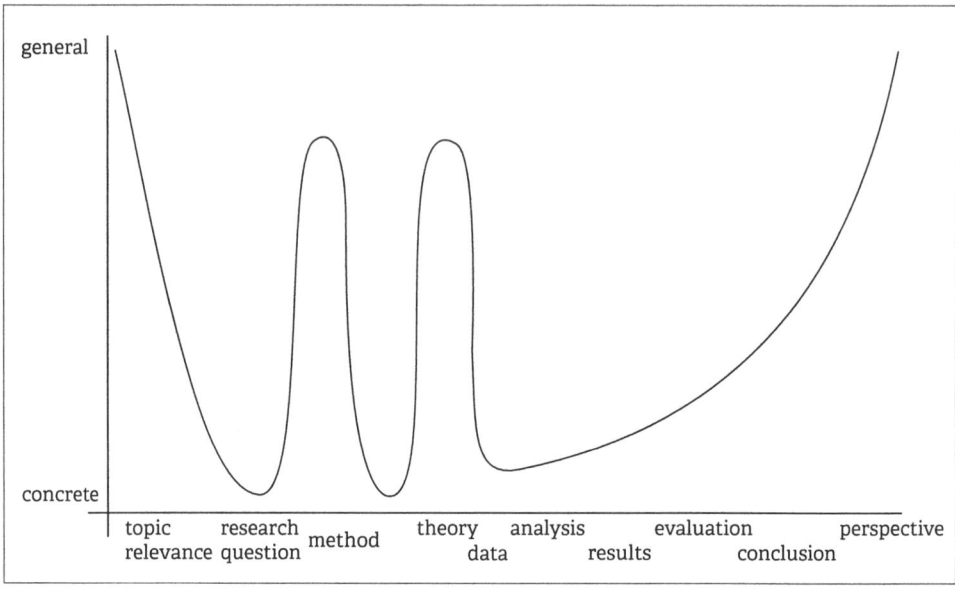

Papers and research texts start "up" among general perspectives, problems, purposes, theories. Then they move "down" to the analysis' smallest, exemplifying details, whereupon the text moves back "up" again by returning to the applicability of the theories and methods, uses, the perspectives in greater and future contexts. The paper about Mannerism (see pp. 117f.) is an example of this. Sometimes, we come across papers that end "down" in analyses and never really point up and forwards again.

End your paper at an upper, general level
Take into account that you must end "up" on a general, interpretational level that puts your paper into perspective – at least in the conclusion's and perspectives concluding remarks. However, you can also add sections called, e.g.:
- "The practical examples' implications for the theory"
- "Discussion of the method's general applicability for X type of studies"
- "The principles behind future designs".

In regards to the paper's argumentation, this means that a paper will not simply end after having presented detailed documentation for its argument, but instead end by presenting the argumentation's claim in light of methodological discussions and possible counter arguments, support and reservations – thus placing the argument in a relevant context. The difference between a 7/C and a 12/A can easily depend on whether or not the paper ends "down" in the analyses' detailed documentation or "up" at a linking, theorising level.

Consider your paper from a bird's-eye view – 3 activities

When problems arise in connection with structuring larger material, these are often caused by the writer not trying to or being unable to raise himself above the details and consider the paper as a whole, or because central elements in the final structure are still missing. We suggest the following three activities, all of which have as a purpose to provide an overview of the paper, so that you can see where the various textual elements belong:

Activity: Write a mini paper or a mini bachelor's/master's thesis

Write down what you want to include in each section of your finished paper. For a bachelor's/master's thesis, this pilot should not be longer than 4 pages. For a larger paper, 1 1/2 pages at the most. You must not use expressions like "I want to write that …" as you will end up providing concrete information and details. Instead use formulations such as "In this section I want to account for …", "In this section I will analyse/argue for/evaluate etc. X". You can use "The research paper's standard structure", p. 303 as an overview.

Activity: Describe the structure of the paper's overall argumentation

A structure with rationales is an exposition of the main sections of the texts which describes the function of each section in the text. I.e., every time you mention a section, you should add "in order to". Furthermore, a structure with rationales can be used later when introducing the paper's structure in your paper. See the section on introductions, pp. 329ff.

> **Activity: Work on a structure with rationales**
>
> A structure with rationales is an exposition of the main sections of the texts which describes the function of each section in the text. I.e., every time you mention a section, you should add "in order to". Furthermore, a structure with rationales can be used later when introducing the paper's structure in your paper. See the section on introductions, pp. 329ff.

However, the result of all these activities must be considered temporary drafts which will need to be changed later in the writing process.

The structuring process takes place throughout the entire writing process

As mentioned previously, it is perfectly normal to change a paper's structure while writing, e.g. by adding subsections as you discover a need for them – and by removing sections that are not in line with the paper's focus or which contain repetitions. Usually the final structure will grow organically. Revising your structure can be a way of achieving a logical progression in your paper. Here are two suggestions for how to start structuring:

> **Activity: Start structuring immediately**
>
> Start gathering structural elements as soon as you have chosen a topic
>
> Make a first draft of the entire structure as soon as you have written a reasonable research question and filled out a pentagon model.

> **Activity: Take the standard structure as your starting point**
>
> To begin with, fill out the standard structure (pp. 306f.) and find out whether you are able to add content to form. After this, adjust it to your own paper.

Structuring problems

Students experience structuring problems for two main reasons, and these problems

arise at either end of the writing process – either at the beginning or end of the writing process:
- Structuring problems at the beginning of the writing process are often caused by attempting to create a structure before having any material to structure. (Asking students to bring a finished structure to the first supervision can thus be unwise, whereas there is nothing wrong with asking students to provide a suggestion for a structure). If your supervisor demands to see a structure early in the writing process, possibly in addition to a research question (which many supervisors actually do), you can instead offer to write something else which similarly provides an overview, such as a quickly written, temporary introduction (see p. 331).
- We can safely say that forcing a structure – attempting to create a finished structure before having enough content and, especially, before having a research question – is one of the most common sources of frustration when writing a larger paper.
- Structuring problems late in the writing process when there is loads of material is caused by the writer being unable to identify the function of information in the paper. The writer lacks a focus, an "organising point" (Neman, 1995). This is often because the research question is too broad, not precise enough or is entirely lacking, which will make it hard to control the structure. When experiencing structuring problems, you should return to your research question and check whether it actually requires research. If it is merely an indication of topic, you risk ending up with a "textbook structure" with many parallel chapters without progression.

The structure is a tool, but can end up impeding effective writing if
- you feel unable to write before the structure is in place
- you feel obliged to follow it without being willing to change it as you obtain new results through your research and understanding
- you believe the structure also dictates the structure of your work process, i.e. the order in which the text should be written.

Text types – the building blocks of the academic text

Academic and research texts are built on a number of set text types, i.e. textual building blocks (e.g. Björk & Räisänen, 1996, pp. 18-19). These text types are not subject specific, but exist in texts and research genres of all fields:

Text type		
Skill	Text type	Explanation
Synthesise (use independently for own purpose, restructure)	Construct designs, theorise, evaluate, assess, argue, discuss, interpret, guide, put into perspective	• Complex text types that build upon less complex text types • Require greater skills and independence
Process (mechanically)	Compare, analyse, classify, categorise	
Understand	Explain, characterise, convey, define, exemplify, identify	
Replicate	Account, paraphrase, narrate, describe, summarise, summarise	• Simple text types that do not require command of other text types • Require limited skills and can be written mechanically.

Text types can constitute entire chapters or a 10-line section. They are often combined, interweaved and are prerequisites for each other. E.g. argumentation will often be part of a discussion and evaluation; summaries and description constitute necessary documentation for the analysis, and the analysis is a prerequisite of interpretation etc. Note how the text types are equivalent to Bloom's taxonomy and the SOLO taxonomy for learning objectives (see pp. 47-48), and how they constitute speech acts carried out in practice.

In the following, we will characterise the most important of these and provide instructions on how these can be written.

Definitions

A special text type is *definition*. Defining sections can be as short as a couple of lines and as long as several pages, depending on the amount and importance of the concepts used in your paper. In all cases, disciplinary concepts in the research question must be defined. Concept definitions are particularly important when the meaning of a concept is under dispute in the field. Normally, definitions are drawn from subject specific sources; especially theories (remember to reference sources). However, if there are no established definitions of a particular concept, you must convey your exact understanding and use of the concept so the reader is left in no doubt. Definitions must be as precise and unambiguous as possible.

Sections that define the paper's most important concepts will appear early in the paper, either in the introduction or possibly in a separate section for just this purpose. However, you may have to define concepts throughout your paper.

Summarising and paraphrasing paragraphs

You can convey the content of others' texts with a *summary* or a *paraphrase.*

In both cases you must not add anything new, and you must write these in your own words and style. However, you must remain faithful to the source in regards to content and the distinction between the source's statements and your own comments.

A *summary* is a condensation of the ideas and information of others' texts. Here are some guidelines for writing a focused summary for a paper:

Summary for a paper – guidelines

- Do not necessarily follow the original text's structure. When summarising you are supposed to select the parts of the text that are relevant for your particular purpose. So changing the order is perfectly fine.
- Indicate that you are writing a summary by using summary markers, e.g. "x emphasises/ evaluates/suggests/argues for" etc.
- Separate the summary (the source's information) from your own comments, explanations, conclusions – even though these are intermingled. It is possible to mix summaries of sources with your own comments, but every time you do so, it requires metacommunication (see pp. 378ff. about academic language). Metacommunication is simply to write: "My comment is …", "From this I deduce that …", "I would term this …" etc.
- State – especially if the summary is long – the summary's purpose, its relevance in the given context and its possible focus point.
- Qualify – especially in the case of secondary literature – the original source (see chapter 1 on the use of literature). How important is the source?

A *paraphrase* is a close reading of others' texts in chronological order, point by point. This is necessary when, for example, paraphrasing a novel or a film analysed in the paper. Unlike summaries, paraphrases are meant to provide an overview of the original source rather than present it selectively.

- As a general rule, you should only paraphrase if the entire original source is important in the context. If not, it is better to summarise and only include what you need. Normally you present your own comments after a paraphrase.
- When paraphrasing a text closely, you run the risk of writing with contagion, i.e., your language may become too similar to the language of the original source. This is in no way approved of in academic circles; we will consider this problem further in chapter 13 on academic language, pp. 383ff.

Descriptive, characterising paragraphs

Description and *characterisation* provide important facts about a topic, a condition, a person, an object, or a process all of which can form the object of your research. The important thing is that the selection and division of these descriptive texts are relevant to their purpose.

Characterisation is to draw out the characteristics, the object's special features, and thus leave out any characteristics shared by or identical to other objects.

In field reports registering e.g. concrete archaeological finds, description and characterisation are often the predominant text types. Here are some guidelines:

- Clarify what the description etc. is to be used for, and outline the perspective and the criteria for your particular selection of information and possibly how you have categorised it.
- Categorisation and classification are key words, and you must investigate the field's possibilities: Which theoretical systems exist in the field? Which disciplinary perspectives are useable?

Narrative and descriptive paragraphs

These text types reiterate processes, e.g. historical, narrative or processual. The narrative is the story, whether it be fictitious or historical. In a paper, these processes often constitute the object of study or function as documentation. You must describe historical processes to demonstrate a development, you must recapitulate a novel's course of events to analyse or document a development. But structure can also serve as the foundation for an entire paper, e.g.

- past
- present
- future (however, often only in the conclusion and perspective).

The basic structure is the chronological structure. For readers, the chronological structure can be the most boring, and you should only choose it if the chronological structure serves a purpose in terms of understanding and interpretation.

Usually *narrative* will only contain factual information, "what happened", while a description will also describe context and causation.

Use *descriptions* when context and causation are more important to the paper than the information itself. And then focus on and emphasise this in the text.

Papers based on a narrative structure risk resembling the way children tell stories: "and then …, and then …, and then …" The trick is to divide your work process and assemble it in phases that are both useful for your research and simultaneously acceptable within your field. Listing a succession of kings will rarely be interesting in itself, but a division that groups the kings according to period will to a greater extent enable you to make a general statement. (But be aware that not using the chronological structure may prove more fruitful, even when dealing with historical events. You could for example treat the kings according to characteristic features).

The narrative text type has become more common in, for example, social scientific papers analysing companies on the basis of an internship. Narrative and description form the basis for analysis and interpretation later in the paper.

Comparative, juxtaposing paragraphs

Much research work is concerned with identifying differences and similarities between two or more topics, texts, conditions, statements, etc. An important task is to systematise data, and comparing and juxtaposing is about identifying what can be put in the same "boxes" and what must be put in different "boxes". Among other things, the purpose of finding similarities is to find statements that can support a particular view: You analyse different theories to find common features that can serve as documentation for an argument. You examine the common cultural and historical features of some authors and the individual psychological differences between them.

Comparison and *juxtaposition* are often the prerequisite for being able to evaluate objects.

Some good advice:
- When comparing it is important to indicate which elements and dimensions you wish to compare. Just as in analyses, these dimensions are drawn from theories or disciplinary concepts.
- Afterwards, you can compare each element individually and use the result of the comparison/juxtaposition to support your argument.

Analysing and interpreting paragraphs

In our experience, students (and supervisors) find analysis and discussion the hardest text types to define. However, these text types are the principle elements of the good paper, which is why we will examine them carefully in the following.

An *analysis* systematically divides a topic, a text, a case, material, etc. into its component parts.

Different fields have their own methods and concepts for analysing the field's topics – analysis is usually carried out through a subject-specific lens: One/several theories, models or even a single concept.

Sometimes an analysis focuses on one object, e.g. a literary text or a musical piece. In these cases, the purpose of the analysis is often to find what you might call the object's structure – its constituent parts and how they interact – in order to discover an underlying meaning, i.e., reach an *interpretation*. Analysis can also be to compare two objects and attempt to discover significant differences between them – on the basis of their similarities. Sometimes the object of analysis can be several objects that together form a large area. In this case, the aim is to look for a system, i.e., how the objects are related to each other and how they are similar or differ from each other.

Analysis is an important disciplinary skill in all fields; however, it is never a goal in itself. Being able to analyse an object is an instrumental discipline: It is a prerequisite for presenting independent statements, contributing to research or carrying out other tasks within the field. Usually an analysis is not interesting in itself. What is interesting is the way you use the analysis to interpret its results.

From analysis to interpretation

Analysis:
- To examine an object/text etc., by separating, dividing, classifying and distributing it in its component parts.
- Analysing must be done on the basis of at least one disciplinary systematism: concept(s), theory(ies), method(s).
- On the basis of the disciplinary systematism(s), you focus on selected elements of the object/text.

↓

Interpretation:
- The results of the analysis are categorisations that can be made the object of explanation/interpretation/overall understanding of the analysis' object.
- Interpretation can be used to answer (part of) the research question.
- After interpreting, consider the disciplinary systematisms (the analytical tools): Were they appropriate for showing something important? Were they limited in any way?

Good analyses:
- Many and well-chosen elements and documentation
- These are clearly structured (use sub-headings)
- Lead to an interpretation that is correct and important
- The disciplinary systematisms are suitable for the purpose.

Sequence of analysis

1. Lead-in (introduction, motivation) to quote, summary, paraphrase, material (description, observation, etc.)
2. Quote, summary, paraphrase, material
3. Analysis (explanation, reading, interpretation)
4. Evaluation (use, contextualisation).

(Adapted from a model by Renate Recke, Institute for Nordic Studies and Linguistics, 2004)

Here is a short example of an analysis sequence from Social Science (BA, high mark):

According to the following definition, the case must be critical:	Lead-in, introduction
"… a case is chosen on the grounds that it will allow a better understanding of the circumstances in which the hypothesis will and will not hold" (Bryman, 2001: 50).	Quote
In this respect, critical means that we have chosen our cases to ensure the best possible conditions for testing the five hypotheses about teaching. The goal is thus not only to test to which degree the hypotheses are right or wrong (part 1 and 2 of the research question), but also to examine which conditions make them right or wrong (part 3 of the research question).	Use in paper in relation to research question.

Discussion sections

A *discussion* throws light on a topic by contrasting different viewpoints and arguments, often with the purpose of reaching a new viewpoint through combination and synthesis. The discussion can be the supporting/load-bearing/leading element in a paper ("discussion paper") as well as form the discussion section in any paper, for example the discussion of method, i.e. a discussion and critique of your own method, or constitute a discussion of different points of view in a paper that centres on analysis.

Here is an example of a discussion section (Danish, BA-level in teacher training, philosophy of science):

… thus both positions consider the narrative as constitutive of the self's construction of identity.	The discussion topic is introduced
In regards to the tension between individual and community, Ricoeur stresses a synthesis between the two positions. The individual cannot think of himself without also thinking of the other, which is embedded in the title: *Oneself as Another*. However, the self is also rooted in himself as an individual; for example, as a biological and physical phenomenon rooted in the world. For Gergen, the world is not physical as an objective entity, but something that must be constructed collaboratively. Thus, in Gergen's view, the self only becomes a self by virtue of the narratives it constructs within the norms of the social community	Ricoeur's and Gergen's views are contrasted in a discussion

it is invited to participate in. Thus, Gergen's theory of relation is a strong social theory, in which the self *is* the narratives that construct the community. This results in different views of the concept of identity. Whereas Ricoeur views identity as a synthesis between idem and ipse, in which identity is created in the dialectic between that which stays the same over time and that which is different and which is articulated through the narrative, Gergen does not view identity in the same way, and thus he does not operate with a core-self.	Their views are summarised
[...]	
In my view, they each offer an important insight into the problem I have chosen to research. Gergen encourages diversity … and even though I cannot agree with him about … he still provides… In the end, however, Ricoeur's suggestion that … provides the most nuanced description of identity in my view …. and thus, in pedagogical work, through the narrative principle, constitutes an ideal to aim towards.	The writer participates in the discussion The writer evaluates the positions The writer points to the perspective and use of the discussion.

In most fields, papers purely based on discussion are relatively rare (the majority of papers are analytical papers using data) and mostly appear in fields where theory plays a big role, such as philosophy, psychology, ethnology, etc. You can structure discussions on the basis of this model:

A discussion can include these elements

- Introduction of the discussion's topics, a research question that specifies what the paper will discuss and an introduction of the "discussion's parties" (authors, theories, texts)
- Establishing the discussion criteria or categories that form the basis of discussion ("to keep the discussion on-topic")
- Analysis of the discussion parties (texts) on the basis of the criteria/categories
- The discussion itself: juxtaposition of opinions, arguments, contrasts, positions, thesis/antithesis
- Result of discussion: the discussion's rationale, consequence, conclusion, compromise, combination
- The purpose of the discussion: use, context, perspective, consequence, resulting precepts for design.

In a paper, the starting point of a good discussion section is thus an analysis of the elements that will be discussed – perhaps from a different perspective than the one of the discussion's parties – and the paper can be concluded with synthesis, evaluation, perspective and/or design.

Examples of discussion questions in papers

- *What-questions* (the paper's focus will be placed on summarising):
  - What is the discussion about? Which parameters are discussed and what are the viewpoints? Which positions are represented, and what are their arguments?
  - What are the similarities and differences between the discussion's positions?
  - How has the discussion developed over time?

These questions are placed on the lowest level of Bloom's taxonomy and the SOLO taxonomy, and are often enough for essays on the first year of study, but insufficient when writing a BA paper or dissertation.

- *Why-questions* (focus will be on analysis, explanation, interpretation, understanding of the discussion elements):
  - Are these really the parameters, the theorists write about?
  - Does the foundation of their discussion explain their dispute?
  - Are the interests (vital, cognitive, etc.) of the different parties explained?
  - Is it clear what/who has influenced the discussion's parties?
  - Is the dispute fundamental or only apparent?
  - Is there an underlying agenda in the discussion?

- *How-questions* (focus lies on synthesis, evaluation, consequence, suggestions for design, action perspective):
  - Is it possible to mediate between opposite views? How is this possible and which fundamental disagreements will endure?
  - Can the viewpoints supplement each other or are they fundamentally opposed to each other?
  - Where (in which contexts) is each of the positions applicable and substantiated?
  - What are the consequences of this discussion? (Choice, design, perspective).
  - Can a third viewpoint annul the entire discussion?
  - Could the discussion be enriched by other arguments, points of view, examples, etc. (possibly from an entirely different discourse)?
  - Can the contributions to the discussion be qualified as more/less significant, relevant (and if so in relation to what), is the discussion ongoing, finished or unending?

"What do I think?"

Deliberation or the result of discussion – both in regards to discussion papers and discussion sections in papers – does not necessarily have to include a "what I think"!

Your options are to
- present your professional opinion, followed by disciplinary arguments, documentation, possible concretisation
- sum up the discussion (answer the research question), consider the discussion in light of the research question
- explicitly declare yourself undecided, hesitant, still participating in discussion and dialogue!

Discussion sequence

- introduce the discussion topic
- present the positions of the involved parties
- consider, mediate and conclude
- possibly participate.

In the conclusion of a discussion section or discussion paper you must include
- the result of the discussion
- the purpose of the discussion: what can this discussion be used for?
- the possible (disciplinary, historical, social) consequences and perspectives of the discussion.

Reflecting sections

Reflection means merging, for example, theory and practice, past/present/future, cause and effect, appearance and explanation in a way that is less systematic and more personal than a conceptual, theory-based or methodical analysis. Reflection should be based on the field's theories, concepts, criteria and views. However, reflection does not have to be systematic or structured as analyses should be. Reflection is not a text type as such but is linked In particular to discussion, interpretation and perspective.

Reflection will often be relevant and desired, for example, in practice oriented papers of the professional bachelor programmes, such as internship reports.

Seeing as reflection will often be tied to concrete descriptions and accounts of a course of events, it may prove practical to include a separate section entitled "Reflection on …" in connection with these descriptions. In your reflection, we recommend mentioning at least one disciplinary concept demonstrating the disciplinary angle of your reflection.

Here is a model for writing a reflection:
1. When you consider/observe/experience xxx
2. and look at it through a particular (xxx) conceptual lens,
3. you can consider/think about/reflect on
   - how you can explain xxx or
   - whether the causes/effects are xxx or
   - what the options for acting in this research/professional context are.

(Rienecker, Stray Jørgensen & Gandil, 2016, p. 185).

Evaluating sections

A *professional evaluation* considers the value of something on the basis of criteria accepted in the field. Ideally the research paper is expected to contain the writer's evaluation of
- others' texts and their contribution to the research of a disciplinary problem (see chapter 5 and 8 on how to evaluate sources)
- own research, and what can be concluded on the basis of its documentation and method.

As mentioned earlier, the ability to evaluate is placed high on Bloom's taxonomy and the SOLO-taxonomy (see pp. 47-48). We have also mentioned normative/design oriented research questions as the foundation for strongly independent research papers. However, when including evaluating comments in their papers, many new students experience critique from their teachers: "Subjective! Loose claims! I need substantiation! I have no interest in your personal opinion!" There are thus right and wrong ways of evaluating. See the section "What do I think?", p. 325.

Academic evaluations are made on the basis of clear, disciplinary criteria. *Non-academic evaluations* are made on the basis of personal, undocumented and unsubstantiated opinions, or by adopting others' evaluations without critical detachment.

You can follow these guidelines when evaluating in your papers:

Evaluation sequence

- Specify what needs evaluating, e.g. topic, viewpoint, text, phenomenon
- Mention the criteria of your evaluation, e.g. theories, concepts
- Be concrete and criteria-based when evaluating, not simply good/bad
- Argue for your evaluation.

Discussion and critique of method

You will find two forms of discussion in a paper, quite analogous to the two sides of argumentation:

1. Discussion with the literature and between positions that are represented in the literature (read more in chapter 8 about sources and the discussion of text types, p. 322)
2. Discussion with yourself about the tenability of your own research and the extent of your conclusion seen in the light of the research design.

When you discuss your own research design, you argue back and forth about the methodological reservations others (e.g., examiners) could raise and how the relevant reservations and objections can affect the strength of your conclusion.

This is where you actually assess the academic validity of your research. And if you can criticise it – and you normally can to one extent or another – you must nevertheless argue that the research design is satisfactory and the extent to which it has been "good enough".

In this discussion with yourself, you may consider the circumstances in which the research design and the methods used may nevertheless lead to claims that are entirely valid and how you could try to support and legitimate your choice of research design (and, thus, the scholarly methods used therein). Finally, you must assess and state how certain you are of the validity of the claim once the methodological problems and the methodological advantages are taken into consideration – i.e., you must qualify how certain your conclusion is (cf. the example later in this chapter in the section "Argumentation is shown in the structure", pp. 363f.).

> **Activity: Write a discussion of method**
>
> 1. Answer the research question.
> 2. Mention the most important documentation.
> 3. Explain any unexpected results, conflict with other results and studies.
> 4. List limitations and points for criticism in your research methods – where it is relevant.
> 5. Back up your method, explain its strengths.
> 6. Point out anything new you have contributed and how you would qualify your results – have you suggested something or proved it?

Thus, when you criticise your research method, you make explicit the reservations you have about the validity of the conclusion that follows from the research method you have used. It is here you can criticise your own choice of method and your own implementation of the method and indicate any possible weaknesses in your argumentation that derive from the method. It is difficult to be impartial, and it is tempting to cover up mistakes that might easily have been avoided. But, as it was mentioned earlier, honesty and the willingness to expose what is open to critique that is the path to qualification – and to academic credibility (ethos). It is less OK to argue glibly and not to deal with possible objections. If you do not yourself discuss possible critiques in your paper, you invite exactly those critiques.

What do you do if it is really hard to argue for your conclusion – and for the methods you have used? This happens, of course, because research can go wrong in many ways – and in ways so unclear that you can hardly become wiser from them. Our best advice is:

- Write about your method and the difficulties with the method, and write about what might instead be a better method.
- Get supervision – as early as possible, and find out what other methodological options you have.

Design and perspective paragraphs

Creating designs means suggesting or recommending how to act (or produce, innovate) in a specific situation. Designs can consist of very concrete instructions, e.g.

therapeutic guidelines, suggestions for changing working procedures, pedagogical recommendations. In professional bachelor programmes, papers will often contain concrete proposals and instructions for the profession's practice. However, research texts and papers will often only contain suggestions for designs by pointing out what ought/can/should be done in continuation of the research's results. These designs can apply to society in general or to the specific field: What has not yet been researched? Where should the understanding of existing theories be changed? Etc. These kinds of softer designs often appear as perspectives that raise awareness of how something is significant or has consequences for other contexts. Being able to identify the outcome of your academic work is a valuable skill.

Our guidelines for perspectives are as follows:

Perspective – sequence

- Specify what (e.g. results, conclusions, evaluations) needs to put into perspective
- Specify which contexts the perspective applies to
- Point to what you believe to be/should be the significance and consequences of your research (e.g. new research topics, new practice)
- Indicate how different people (e.g. authorities, teachers, professionals) should relate to your research.

Introduction

The introduction and conclusion are especially important sections because they frame the actual treatment of content and disciplinary work. These sections provide the reader with a framework of understanding containing the prerequisites for and the results of the research documented in the text. At worst, the main section would become incomprehensible without these sections, but also lack credibility as context would be missing.

Furthermore, the introduction and conclusion place the paper in its field and draw a problem into the paper's laboratory to examine it; and lastly the conclusion sends the results of the research out into the world again, whereupon the perspective demonstrates their significance.

The introduction as a template

The information presented in the introduction is general, provides overview, prerequisites and framework.

We dedicate much time and space to introductions as they form an especially important part of any text. This is because the reader's expectations to the text and its author are established in the introduction, as well as because people always pay more attention to the beginning and end of any process. However, in academic texts, there is the added factor of the writer explicitly describing the intentions and rationale of the text, and the method and literature search of the research, i.e. the prerequisites on which the remaining text rests.

It is often said that introductions should not be written before the actual text is completed, i.e. when everything else has been written. But another possibility is to write a draft of the introduction and revise it as you go, and naturally, especially once you have finished. An early draft will make your starting point clear to yourself (and others, e.g. a supervisor) and can be a support if it does not become a restriction.

In the introduction of research papers and dissertations include

- Topic, problem area
- Research question (substantiate)
- The purpose of the research
- Possible point of view
- Concept definitions
- Possible hypotheses
- Method(s) (substantiate your choices)
- Choice(s) of theory (substantiate your choices)
- Possible data (substantiate your choices)
- Delimitation
- The paper's research design.

The elements do not have to be presented in this order. Larger papers often include several theories and methods, and therefore include separate theory and method sections. However, it can still be a good idea to briefly mention the most important theories and methods in the introduction. And when you justify your choice, it is the paper's philosophy of science on which it is based.

The template is precisely that; a template. There will always be elements in this template that do not apply to your paper. Introductions can contain more or less information than suggested by the template. For example, method is often implicit in papers in aesthetic fields, and hypotheses are rarely seen in the Humanities, and theories rarely seen in a number of hard fields. However, to the extent possible, the corners of the pentagon should be present in the introduction, e.g. as in this table, which can form the starting point for working on your introduction:

Activity: In your paper's introduction include		
Topic, problem area/definition, possible context and example		
Research question (-substantiate)		
The purpose of the research		
Concept definitions		
Possible hypotheses		
Choice(s) of theory, philosophy of science (substantiate your choices)		
Method(s), philosophy of science (substantiate your choices)		
Data, philosophy of science (substantiate your choices)		

Delimitations	⬠
The paper's procedure and structure	⬠

The example below is taken from a BA thesis about computer games and through headings shows how the paper's introduction includes (most of) the elements:

- Introduction
- The paper's focus
- Research question
- The paper's method
- Concept definitions
- Theoretical position
- Reading guide
- Research thus far
- The computer as a medium
- Screen violence and society: A question of opinion.

This example also demonstrates that you can vary the exact phrasing; the important thing is that each element is present. After having read the introduction, the reader should have a clear idea of what the writer is going to do, why and how. Furthermore, it is important to substantiate your choices to the greatest extent possible. If you do not, the paper's elements will seem indisputable and as if they have simply been conjured out of thin air. Presumably this happens because the explanation was given orally during a supervision meeting. But you must be able to read the text without the oral context. The ideal is explication, definitions, precision, selectivity and transparency in all choices and all steps.

The introduction reflects the entire paper

Much research has been carried out on the introductions of papers and research articles because this is where the genre's features are clearly shown. Furthermore, the introduction constitutes a microcosm of the entire paper – all of the paper's most important elements and speech acts must be mentioned briefly. A Swedish, empirical study on the structure of introductions in good and poor papers respectively from fields as different as comparative literature and biology proves especially interesting to students writing papers. This study concluded that the introductions of good papers shared these features:

Students who are sure of genre demonstrate this in the introduction

They
- demonstrate awareness of the genre's aim and functions
- meet the programme's requirements in regards to theories and methods
- have a research question or thesis (macro-position) from page 1
- include standardised elements in the introduction
- introduce central terms and referents (central sources) in the introduction
- use (or vary) the standard structures for papers.

(Blåsjö, 2000)

It is especially worth noting that the good paper's introduction includes disciplinary references, i.e. at least one theorist or disciplinary text on which the paper is based is presented early on, even on the first page. If no texts or theorists (methodological works can also be used) are mentioned, the writer has not established himself in a disciplinary universe, and the suspicion will easily arise that the paper is unscientific and placed on a common-sense level.

Another well-known study of introductions has shown that readers expect three classic moves in an introduction:

Moves in Research Paper Introductions

Move 1: Establishing a research territory
  a. by showing that the general research area is important, central, interesting, problematic, or relevant in some way. (optional)
  b. by introducing and reviewing items of previous research in the area. (obligatory)

> **Move 2: Establishing a niche**
>   a. by indicating a gap in the previous research, raising a question about it, or extending previous knowledge in some other way. (obligatory)
>
> **Move 3: Occupying the niche**
>   a. by outlining purposes or stating the nature of the present research. (obligatory)
>   b. by announcing principal findings. (optional)
>   c. by indicating the structure of the RP. (optional)
>
> (Swales & Feak, 1994, s. 175)

The conventions of the genre find their rationales in the purpose and deeper meaning of the genre. You can deviate and create variations based on the fundamental pattern, but this requires awareness of the basic pattern and what you hope to achieve by experimenting.

We commonly see (new) students make the mistake of introducing the field (describing what applies within the field, the chosen period, etc.) instead of primarily introducing their own research. This is caused by contagion from the textbook genre, which does exactly this. Overall, however, the research article provides the most reliable genre model and will, in most cases, present a fully formed pentagon within the first few pages.

We will now consider each element of the introduction separately:

Choice of topic, problem definition, motivation and research question

The writer introduces his topic, his personal (but not private!) and scientific reason for writing about it. Which disciplinary perspectives are found in this topic? By adding a couple of lines "selling" the topic to the reader, the writer can strengthen the reader's motivation to view the paper in a positive light. This has been done convincingly in a paper from Department of Education (MA thesis):

> The growing prevalence of the evidence concept and its ability to hierarchically predict the degree of certainty in research-based knowledge on the basis of applied research methods, is the reason why I am interested in examining the evidence concept in relation to Psychology in this dissertation; a field which has not been captured in terms of the evidence concept's hierarchy of knowledge to the same extent as the areas mentioned. In this thesis, I will therefore …

Writing "it's an interesting topic" is not enough. This is a subjective, emotional statement, which, furthermore, is global and unspecific. This kind of statement leaves readers none the wiser. The writer must be able to couple reason with emotions and explain why the topic can be considered interesting from a disciplinary point of view as well as why it can be considered interesting to others than himself.

Hypotheses

A hypothesis is a prediction of the answers you expect to find (in contrast to a research question). A hypothesis is a statement about

- there being a connection between variable a and b (possibly c, d etc.) and
- the nature of this connection (often: "I expect a negative/positive connection between a and b").

If you have one or more hypotheses, you need to look for material to confirm or refute these. In your paper, you then write what the material has shown about your preliminary hypotheses and to which extent. You may end up having to conclude that the preliminary hypothesis has been disproved.

A hypothesis does not necessarily have to be included in a paper, but can be if prompted by the material and author's angle, and if insight into the topic gives rise to this. This is especially the case if the paper aims at examining disciplinary assumptions/hypotheses/theories. Explicit hypotheses are far more common in papers from Social and Natural Science than in the Humanities.

Where do hypotheses come from? From e.g. previous research or guesswork, common sense or from the press, in short: We get our hypotheses about How the World Really Works from everywhere.

Hypotheses are mentioned right before or just after the research question: "As my hypothesis is … I will now ask the following question …", or "The question is … as my preliminary hypothesis is …" In this connection, you explain what has led you to this hypothesis, i.e. from where your surprise stems.

When working on the basis of a hypothesis, you work deductively rather than inductively. Often a hypothesis will ease the collection of data and reading of literature. If, for example, you wanted to examine the question "how do interaction patterns in families with and without domestic violence differ?", it is far easier to select data with a hypothesis than without one. Without a hypothesis, you would have to register all data and then start looking for patterns.

Just like the research question, you can start formulating hypotheses from the start, even from the very first day of working on your topic. Although one subject area can give rise to many hypotheses, it is wise to keep to a few and, preferably, simple hypotheses in each paper. Do not worry if you have no hypotheses. It is perfectly acceptable to enter the field with an open and questioning attitude – at times, this is the best approach.

The paper's purpose

The research question is subject to the paper's purpose. Whereas the research question is the question you would like to answer, the purpose constitutes the reason for asking the question: What are the theoretical and practical interests (for you and your peers, the users, the public) of solving the question? Many confuse purpose with research question. It is most convincing when both a research question and a purpose are described in the introduction. See chapter 4, p. 112 on formulating research question for an example of the difference between research question and purpose. Purpose and research question each take up a corner in the pentagon.

The purpose is the general statement of what you hope to gain with your text, what it can be used for (perhaps, in your studies and even in your later work). This is a big requirement, which is why student papers often do not include a purpose. However, the more you think about and pursue your purposes throughout your studies, the more meaningful the work becomes and the less writer's block you will experience. The writing process is furthered by thinking about and writing down the purpose of writing about this material from this exact angle early in the process. The reader will also be motivated if your academic work has a good purpose.

Point of view

Often, you will not have to write explicitly about point of view. However, you may choose to view the field from a particular point of view (e.g. from a Danish point of view or from the point of view of either sender or receiver, the buyer or the seller, etc.). Explicating the point of view can thus help narrow down the literature search and make the text more clear.

Theory

A theory is a system of tenets (or assumptions) within a field which can be used to describe, explain and predict the field's phenomena.

You must write which theories and concepts you intend to use in your paper, and you must substantiate and qualify your choices. Why is the chosen theory suitable for examining this exact problem? You should also note how the different theories employed relate to each other: Do they supplement each other? Are they contrastive? How are they to be used in the paper?

Method

You must mention the methods use in your research, and your choice must be substantiated. However, deliberation and critique of method does not belong in the introduction. You should consider including special sections in the paper for this form of methodological discussion, either after the sections in which the method has been used or in a special section for critique of method. See chapter 10 about method.

Philosophy of science

Some people choose to write a separate section with a subheading on the paper's premises and foundation in a philosophy of science, while others include the philosophy of science in justifying their choice of theories, methods, data and research question. There are different expectations, requirements and customs in different courses. So, it is important here to investigate the options and customs locally.

Concept definitions

If your research question contains disciplinary concepts that can be defined differently, you must state which definition (or combination of definitions) applies to the way you use these concepts. Concept definitions are often related to the theories you work with. However, if you cannot find useable definitions, you will have to define or combine your way to definitions of central concepts. It is important that the reader knows how *you* use the words encapsulating the theoretical and methodological focus of your research. In the good paper "central terms" are defined at the very beginning (Blåsjö, 2000). A striking feature of good papers is their emphasis on concept definitions and precise terminology in general. If you can keep it brief, this can either be placed in the introduction, or else in a separate concept definition chapter at the paper's beginning (if much discussion and contemplation is necessary).

Read more about how to treat theories, methods and concepts in chapter 10.

Data

If you have chosen to describe and analyse so-called empirical data – e.g. certain texts, statements, etc., you must introduce your chosen data in your introduction.

Delimitation

When introducing your delimitations, you often merely need to write a line or two about the material you do not treat, especially the material the reader may have just reason to expect you to include. Each corner of the pentagon can be delimited, but especially

- *data* can be delimited according to time, space, persons, works, phenomena, etc.
- *theoretical systems* (concepts, theories, methods) can be delimited by stating which otherwise relevant parts of them you choose to exclude.

The more important and central the excluded parts seem, the more crucial substantiating your delimitation becomes. Your delimitation will come across especially strongly if the delimited material is explained as being less relevant to the examined problem. It is implicit that delimitation is always required because of time limits.

The paper's research design and structure

In larger papers it is common to account for the paper's structure: Why are these parts included (especially the parts whose function is not immediately obvious)? You can also explain which principle underlies the paper's structure. You should not simply describe what will appear in the paper – if the reader has read the table of contents, this is redundant.

Introduce your project, not your reservations

A general piece of advice on introductions: Introducing what you are going to do, why and how is enough, without excusing and regretting what you had to exclude. Critique of method, general overviews of philosophy of science that are not specifically related to the paper, and disciplinary doubt do not belong here. Deliberations, counter arguments and refutations are important elements of a paper (see chapter 12 on argumentation); however, they are rarely appropriate when placed in introductions. This is where the reader's expectations are created, and these must be as positive as possible. You should completely avoid expressions that signal uncertainty or reservations such as: "In this paper I will attempt to ..." Just do it! The common excuse of limited space or time is no good either and a teacher's comment will often be: "If so, you have not delimited or narrowed down your research question enough!" Reservation, caution, moderation and self-critique belong at the end of a paper in discussions and conclusions. In general, excuses are an inappropriate speech act in papers.

Conclusion

Like introductions, conclusions have a standard structure. Return to the pentagon and the argument model and evaluate the entire basis of your research as a foundation for your conclusion
- whether the answers you have found have been nuanced appropriately
- whether the purpose of the research has been met
- the data and documentation used – were they relevant, sufficient? What conclusions can be drawn on the basis of these?
- the theoretical systems (theories and methods) used to examine the problem and data: what were their strengths and limitations in this context?
- the suitability of the research design
- and the general argumentation in light of objections and reservations on one hand and substantiation on the other.

The conclusion must relate to the research question

Note the conclusion *must* take into account the research question presented in the introduction. Furthermore, you must also evaluate your method and the documentation for your answer, for example, in a discussion section immediately before the conclusion if you have written a larger paper.

Here is an example from a MA thesis on Didactics in Danish (Department of Education, high mark):

•••

Research question:
Is it possible to employ the process folder as a formative method of evaluation, and thus as documentation, when analysing and interpreting a novel in the 6th grade, taking the methods of reception aesthetics as the starting point and simultaneously avoiding a compromise of the cultivation ideals of the subject Danish, which are not black and white.

From the conclusion:

Through this case study I have found that the process folder as a formative method of evaluation is constructive, but cannot stand alone in connection to the goals of cultivation I have set. […]

The process folder is thus not adequate in relation to documenting the cultivation ideals of Danish and a compromise is inevitable. However, under different conditions it could perhaps be possible to document cultivation *without* compromise. The process folder would then have to be supplemented by other tools of evaluation, such as a video log.

Activity: In the conclusion you can include

- You can write your conclusion based on this template. (NB! Remember that templates are for inspiration only. The elements can be varied.)

- Write the answer/conclusion/point (briefly and in broad outlines).

- Relate the conclusion to the research question/thesis.

- Relate your conclusion to your purpose(s).

- Write what the answer is based on (documentation, analyses, choice of method, philosophical premises).

- Briefly repeat points from your discussion and critique of method and evaluate the validity of your conclusion.

- Comment/evaluate/suggest alternatives in regards to the usefulness of the employed methods/theories/concepts.

- Put you research into perspective by pointing to greater/future disciplinary contexts, uses, contributions, significance, consequences – or do so in a separate perspective section.

Remember that conclusions do not have to be clear or strong – we are not dealing in black and white or yes-no answers. A nuanced conclusion "on-the-one-hand-and-on-the-other-hand" is an equally important and worthy result. Many papers, especially in soft disciplines, do not deal with a world of hard facts.

Write your conclusion as you go

Being unable to write your conclusion before you have finished your research is to be expected. However, you can still write your conclusion as you go and use it as a temporary aim that can be changed if your research points in a different direction.

Working on your conclusion is a particularly good idea if you are generally aware of which answer the paper will presumably reach and for example have a hypothesis of which you are reasonably confident.

Continuous activity: Regularly work on your conclusion
Keep your conclusion up to date and revise it while writing. Evaluate whether any part of your research gives rise to adjustment and revision.

Perspective

In the perspective, you consider the significance your results/conclusions have or should have for the future, whether it is research-related or practical – "out in the world". In smaller papers a perspective can be contained in the conclusion. However, it is a good idea to clearly indicate a perspective, e.g. by using a sub-heading. See suggestions of how to structure a perspective on pp. 328f.

The paper's formal sections

A larger paper consists of these formal sections around the main sections:

> **The paper's formal sections**
>
> - Formal requirements before the main section:
>   - Front page
>   - Table of contents
>   - Resumé, abstract.
> - Main sections of the text:
>   - Introduction
>   - Body
>   - Conclusion.
> - Formal requirements after the main section:
>   - Appendices
>   - Notes
>   - Bibliography/list of sources and literature.

Note that forewords are not normally included in a paper unless you wish to thank e.g. test persons and special informants or draw attention to special circumstances surrounding the paper's prehistory or origin. You should not thank your teachers and supervisors; they are being paid for their services.

Formal sections (e.g. introductions, conclusions, index and abstracts) are meta sections that provide readers with:

- overview (e.g. the table of contents, abstract)
- identification (e.g. front page)
- documentation (e.g. bibliography/literature and source list, appendices, notes)
- orientation and use (e.g. abstract, parts of the introduction and conclusion)
- references (e.g. note sections).

In the following we present guidelines for writing some of these sections (they are described in more detail in Stray Jørgensen, 2014a).

Front page

The front page is the first thing the reader sees. The front page must captivate the reader and will provide the information needed for orientation as well as all the most important practical information about the paper. A good front page presents the topic, content and practical information for identifying the paper.

Information on the front page

- Title and subtitle
- Name(s) of author(s)
- Hand-in date
- Department
- Publishing institution
- Paper type
- Field
- Supervisor
- Illustration.

A short title can be good, but may prove too short and unspecific. Often expanding the title, e.g. using a specifying subtitle or pre-title will be an advantage as this gives the reader a clear indication of your focus.

Table of contents

The table of contents constitutes the final version of the paper's structure. If papers are longer than 4-5 pages, you must include a table of contents with page numbers.

The good table of contents does not alone reflect the material, but also how you treat it. It must reflect the features of the good structure:

A good table of contents

- shows and maintains focus and research from start to finish
- refects the disciplinary systematisms and the paper's research design
- progresses logically from one element to the next
- shows the emphasis of content elements
- contains precise and meaningful headings, with conscious use of research terms like "analysis/discussion of"
- includes page numbers.

Use headings to demonstrate the structure

One quality is subtitles in the shape of whole sentences which contain the section's point. Subtitles thus serve the same function as introducing a section with a point-sentence. Chapter headings show a development in themes and research throughout the paper. Writing point-headings demonstrates a greater degree of textual processing than using "empty" words like "Discussion". This is not enough, as it means nothing to the reader. Instead you should clarify what the discussion is about. You can even expand on the heading "Conclusion" – although this is what the majority call the conclusion section.

> **Activity: Formulate the table of contents to aid readers**
>
> - Show how you use data/theories through subtitles
> - Use text types and speech acts consciously in chapters and subheadings, but also describe the content of summaries, analyses, discussions, etc. (Analysis of …)
> - Do write subheadings using sentences rather than just individual words. Statements and questions are both useable.

In the table of contents, formulating headings in whole sentences is a good idea. In this way, they become much more expressive and informative than short headings, e.g. names, elements or periods. A fully articulated structure – both throughout and in the finished paper – is also a good idea. An example is the chapter headings in *Winnie the Pooh*: "Chapter 1, in which we are introduced to Winnie the Pooh and some bees", i.e. a formulation which informs the reader of the chapter's content and possibly its function in relation to answering the research question. Another good way of structuring section headings is by using questions, which indicate that an answer will follow, and the use of text types (speech acts) which characterise the form of the disciplinary information, e.g. "Analysis of …", "Discussion of …", "Evaluation of …". See also pp. 300f. on examples of good tables of contents.

Appendices

Appendices are material which cannot or should not be included in the paper's main text. This could for example be interview transcripts, copies of whole articles, internet print outs, brochures, calculations, schematised survey results, larger text samples, etc.

The purpose of appendices is to document what you write in your paper and provide the especially interested reader with supplementing information. You should only include material in appendices if including it in the actual text is unpractical. For example, if its form and content (size) is hard to incorporate in the text. Another reason could be that it should not be read or seen in connection with the body text because it is a supplement or a special form of documentation for the exceptionally interested reader.

You can determine whether material should be included as an appendix by assessing whether you need to refer to it in the actual paper. Do not include the material unless you feel absolutely compelled to refer to it.

Here are some practical guidelines:

Guidelines for structuring appendices

- Appendices must be provided with a title, number or letter and possibly explanatory text.
- Many appendices must be gathered in an appendix section with page numbers (like the rest of the paper).
- The appendix section must be organised and easy to navigate using the appendix outline, either presented before the appendices and/or in the table of contents.
- When referring to appendices in the main text, use precise references to appendix number and page number.
- Do not include appendices that have not been mentioned in the body text.

Notes, note sections and references in the text

Notes (footnotes etc.) are comments and references that do not form part of the body text These provide additional information about or elaborate on the actual text. They can also refer to other sections in the text, the appendices, the bibliography, etc.

Notes can appear
- in the text (parenthetical notes)
- near/by the text (footnotes)
- after the text (endnotes in a special note section).

Parenthetical notes must be as short as possible to avoid disrupting the reading flow. On the other hand they must be exhaustive enough for the reader to use them without problems. You must find the proper balance. Short notes can refer to literature, appendices or other parts of the text:

(Hansen, 1994, p. 16)

(see also, p. 22).

This is a common way of referencing. If you reference the same author in the next note, some write "ibid." The important thing about referencing is consistency.

Footnotes must be clearly separated from the main text. You can use a smaller font size, less spacing, indentation and/or a horizontal line above the note. Only use footnotes for short, necessary explanations and comments, which cannot be incorporated in the main text. Footnotes should be no longer than 2-3 lines.

Endnotes may include any long explanations and comments you were unable to fit in the body text as endnotes. However, out of consideration for the reader, you should avoid larger notes and note sections as a general rule.

Footnotes and endnotes may be generated in all word-processing programs, but you may edit the configuration.

Abstract

In some programmes of study, at least in BA and MA theses, you will be required to write an abstract, perhaps even in a foreign language. It is important that your abstract is as informative as possible. We offer these guidelines:

An abstract must

- be able to be read independently by peers, who are not experts in the area, searching for information
- be short (for a dissertation a rule of thumb is not to exceed one A4 page)
- help the reader decide whether or not to read the text
- in broad outlines communicate

    - topic and problem
    - research question
    - purpose
    - important theories/theorists
    - research design and methods

    - content
    - results
    - conclusion and recommendations
    - extraordinarily important points.

- be provided with text identification: title, author, publishing institution, year, etc. (in regards to copying the abstract).

Furthermore, the abstract must include any field terms under which the paper will be registered in, for example, a literature search.

Note that the abstract covers all corners of the paper's pentagon.

12. The paper's argumentation

As we wrote in the chapter about genre and quality criteria, argumentation is a cornerstone of research texts. This chapter presents an argument model which you can use as a *processing tool* for building your arguments and as a *production tool* to evaluate your and others' (your sources') argumentation.

Argumentation in papers and other genres

In chapter 1 about genre and quality criteria we accounted for the way in which research papers differ from the classic essay, the textbook and the popularising article. A crucial difference between the research paper and these other genres is argumentation. In the other genres, it is possible to argue in ways that should be avoided in a research paper.

In a personal essay, you can document your claims using personal feelings, experiences and opinions. Here you can comment on how love affects people on the basis of your own experience, possibly with a few anecdotes drawn from world literature – or perhaps from your nearest circle of acquaintances. You approach the topic unmethodically and draw documentation from where ever possible.

In textbooks and popularising articles, argumentation does not necessarily occur. Here claims can be presented without actual documentation and validation. "Eric of Pomerania was born …", "The muscle musculus sternocleido-mastoideus is located …", "The preserved works written by Plato himself consist of …" The purpose of these texts is not to convince, but to lecture, and therefore argumentation is not necessary in these genres.

When papers do not meet expectations, it is often because they too greatly resemble these other genres. They draw documentation from personal experience such as in the classic essay. Or they present claims without arguing for them or without documentation, just as in (some) textbooks.

Argumentation in research papers

In your paper, you argue by documenting the claims and points you present in your paper, e.g. in the form of academic authority, others' research and/or your own research. However, your paper must also, as a whole, constitute a single argument for the overall disciplinary claims you reach in your conclusion.

This can be expressed by the following argument model, originally developed by the argumentation theorist Stephen Toulmin (1974) who aimed at understanding everyday argumentation. Toulmin's model can also describe research papers and their structure. The model for the anatomy of a paper's argumentation looks as follows:

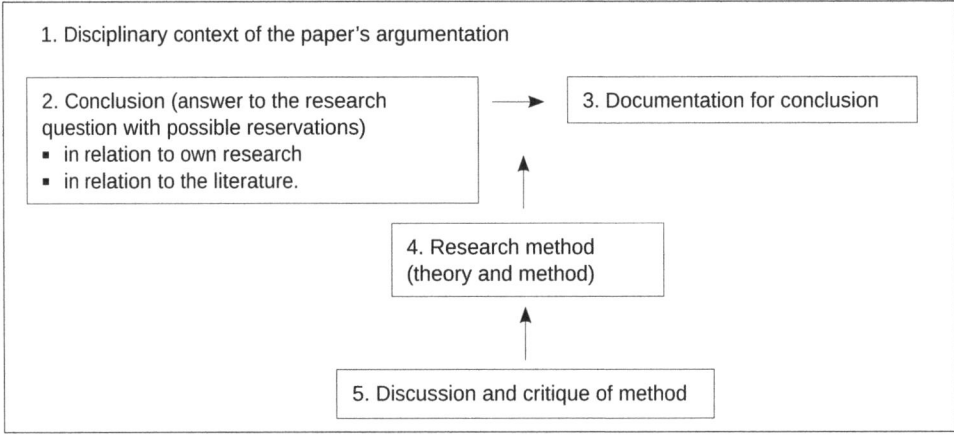

The boxes contain the elements that must be included in a research paper. The point of this chapter is to describe what to fill in these boxes, how they correspond to the paper's structure and elements, and how to the model can be used when writing a paper.

There are four good reasons for using the argument model when writing a paper. The model advocates that you
- *argue* rather than merely postulate or demonstrate
- *focus* i.e., make/keep your general point clear
- *structure* systematically towards your point (conclusion)
- *critique*, i.e. evaluate and discuss your and others' argumentation.

What you may not do is postulate. You postulate when you do not have sufficient or relevant documentation for you claim(s). On the other hand, if you have loads of documentation (e.g. analyses, your or others' research, statements by academic authorities), but have no overall point or claim to substantiate, you merely demonstrate having knowledge rather than using knowledge. Neither of these constitutes argumentation, but are typical pitfalls to avoid when writing papers.

In chapter 1, we wrote that research writing consists of two aspects:
- Knowledge of the field's literature ("scholarship", "being well-read", "others' material")
- Carrying out own research ("research", own use).

The higher the level of study, or rather the closer a text is to dissertation level, the clearer it becomes (ideally, as this is not always the case) that two types of argumentation are needed: 1) a literature argumentation ("they write"), and 2) argumentation drawn from your own research ("I research"). In comparison, essays and short assignments (see chapter 3) predominantly contain literature argumentation.

If the entire argumentation apparatus is fully unfolded – which is not the case in all papers – the paper will contain two different tracks which can include parallel sections on literature and research methodology, discussion and critique.

Literature and research – the two tracks of argumentation	
Literature search method applies to methods used for literature search and selection on which the paper is based (the scholarship of the paper).	*Research method* applies to all methods related to the object of study on which the paper's research is based. However, the research method will often be a combination of several disciplinary methods, e.g. the method of selection, data collection, analysis, evaluation and design.
Literature argumentation constitutes the writer's points about (part of) the field's literature.	*Research argumentation* constitutes the points the writer presents on the basis of the paper's research.

Literature discussion discusses the content of secondary sources (theories etc.) included in the paper and constitutes the method discussion of your own literature method.	*Research discussion* is a methodological discussion and critique (critical appraisal) of your own research.
Literature discussion (critical appraisal)) discusses the included literature (in relation to your research).	Critique of own and others' methods.

Discussion and critical appraisal are placed on a continuum – you determine whether it constitutes "discussion" or "critical appraisal" depending on how strongly the critique is phrased.

This does not appear in all papers! You may only need a chapter on method to account for all methods, and a discussion section in which all methodological questions are considered and where argumentation takes place.

Introductions should always introduce literature as well as research (some disciplines call it "Materials and methods"). Conclusions should similarly bring out points related to your own research as well the literature constituting your starting point – possibly in that order. This can be illustrated as such – note how the two forms of argumentation constitute two parallel tracks underlying the paper's research design.

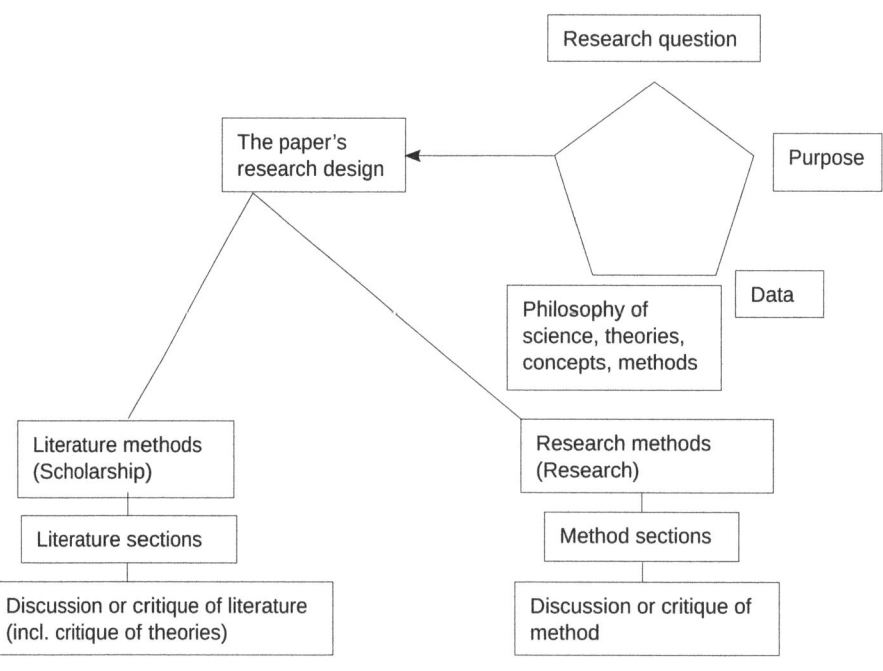

Principally, there are thus two connected forms of argumentation in research papers. We only come across fully developed and explicated argumentation in relation to both literature and own research in exceptionally good papers. Less than this is therefore acceptable. In most (fields') papers, research is predominant, while literature argumentation often constitutes the condition for and is subject to research argumentation. Research argumentation is thus superior, and the main points of most papers are focused on the object, data, material, while points about literature and sources are subordinate. This chapter is about research argumentation.

In the following we consider the paper as a single argument, and you must therefore assess whether your main argument or point is based on literature (e.g. as in essays, reviews or other types of papers) or research, or whether your paper includes two equally important argumentations. If your paper is purely based on literature without any actual research of your own, some parts of this chapter may be less relevant to you. We describe literature argumentation in chapter 8 about sources.

That research texts by "nature" are argumentative texts can also be illustrated by this dialogue-based representation of a research paper's argumentation (adapted from Toulmin by Booth et al., 2008). Here you must remember to include both literature and research argumentation in the dialogue:

> **Activity: Write and think about your paper's argumentation as a dialogue**
>
> What is your point?
> "I claim that …"
>
> What evidence do you have?
> "I offer as evidence …"
>
> Why do you think your evidence supports your claim?
> "I offer the general principle …"
>
> But how about those reservations?
> "I can answer them. First …"
>
> Are you entirely sure?
> "Only if …and as long as …"
>
> No reservations here at all?
> "I must concede that …"
>
> Then just how strong is your claim?
> "I limit it …"

Keeping the above dialogue in mind is a good idea when writing a paper: Which objections could my reader have to my claims, statements, research design, both in regards to literature and my own research, and how can I meet and accommodate these?

Argumentation forms part of the unfinished disciplinary debate

A paper is a contribution to the research debate, in which you as a student are able to present your disciplinary claim and enter into a dialogue with the field's practitioners about the disciplinary problem and how to solve it. Participating in this dialogue is thus not about being right or presenting a final answer that ends the discussion: It is about presenting your arguments and, insofar as these arguments are valid, contributes to providing a solution, an answer, a new understanding in collaboration with others. In principle, your paper's general argumentation constitutes a counter argument against previous contributions to the given debate – or support, nuance, elaborate, etc. others' contributions.

What should your paper argue for?

You should begin to consider what you would like to argue for early in the working process, as well as contemplate which general claim or point you count on presenting in your conclusion on the basis of your research. From this you will be able to formulate a preliminary research design, i.e., choose literature, theory, data and method. In this way, you focus on what you want to say and how to create credible arguments for it early in the research process.

This is not cheating. Often you will have an assumption, a hypothesis of what you believe you will discover in your paper, or else you would not start writing it. But naturally this hypothesis may gradually change as your research progresses. It is therefore important to continue to adjust either your research design (philosophy of science, theory, data, method) if it turns out to be irrelevant in regards to your point. Or you must adjust your main hypothesis if you discover that it, or the assumptions you had about the nature of the problem, turn out to be wrong or different that you thought.

> **Activity: Write the most important sentence or point in your current conclusion and adjust it regularly**
>
> - Write no more than one line and no longer than one minute to keep your general claim clear.
> - Adjust your main claim as your research progresses.
> - Compare your claim (conclusion) with your question (research question) and adjust either your research question or conclusion to ensure that question and answer correspond.

The next section is about constructing your research design in such a way that your paper becomes a cohesive argument.

Your paper as a cohesive argument

When we apply the argument model to papers, it looks as the following. Note that the paper's entire argumentation is framed by a context. In the following model, we have included the concrete elements that can be put into the argument model's boxes as well as added boxes with evaluation criteria for the individual elements of the argumentation:

Activity: The paper as a single argument – fill out the form

1. Disciplinary context for the paper's argumentation

What is the paper's research question and purpose?

Evaluation of claim, e.g.:
- is it subject-specifically *relevant*?
- Does it prepare the ground for argumentation?
- Is it formulated as a *clear* and *distinct* general question (or hypothesis) at the beginning of the paper?

Evaluation of documentation e.g.:
- Is the evidence *relevant*?
- Is the entire claim *substantiated*?
- Is there *too much* or *too one-sided* evidence?
- Is it probable, i.e. are the analyses of data conducted correctly?

2. Conclusion (answer to the research question)

What is your paper's overall claim?

3. Documentation for the conclusion

Which data/material do you analyse, discuss, use to substantiate your claim?

4. Research method

Which methods do you use in your research?
Which theories and concepts do you use?
What is your overall research design?

Evaluation of research method e.g.:
- Is the method *credible*, i.e. is the choice of method(s) acceptable?
- Is there correspondence between the choice of theory, method(s), data and the paper's claim?

5. Discussion and critique of research methods

Which strengths and which limitations are present in the choice of method(s)?

Which validity and which reservations are connected to the research results?

Evaluation of discussion and critique of research methods, e.g.:
- Is the discussion of methods *critical* of both methods and the results of the research?
- Is there correspondence between the critique presented in the discussion of methods and the *reservations* expressed in the conclusion?

You can fill out the argument model for your own paper. Your research question should go in box 1, which constitutes the frame for the entire research process. In box 2 write your preliminary conclusion, i.e. general claim as it appears at a given time in your research process. In box 3 note which data and additional documentation you include and analyse as substantiation for your claim. In box 4 write your method(s). Finally write any objections there may be against your methods and your results, their strengths and wants in box 5.

The main elements to include in the model are:
- Disciplinary context
- Conclusion
- Documentation
- Research method
- Discussion and critique of method.

We will now examine these in the above order:

Disciplinary context

The paper's entire argumentation is embedded in the disciplinary context, which establishes the framework for the argumentation. This context consists of a number of elements that do not form part of the paper's argumentation. However, the purpose of these elements is to legitimise the disciplinary relevance and justification of the research, and these elements explicitly place the paper's main argumentation within the field. Most importantly this includes:

- Pointing out disciplinary gaps, a problem, and a short account of what your research (paper) contributes to the disciplinary problem.
- An outline of the "state-of-the-art", i.e. what is currently known within the field and which disciplinary discussions and unclarified aspects exist within the chosen problem area. This is the beginning of the paper's argumentation with regards to the literature. The central issues are which literature is important and which gaps or unresolved/inadequately resolved issues the writer identifies in the examined literature.
- An explanation of why there is a disciplinary or general need for solving or clarifying the problem in the research question, and who may benefit from reading the paper and the results of the research.

The need for disciplinary argumentation is created or arises from disputes and unresolved issues within the field. You must explicate and clarify these disputes and unanswered questions in your introduction, as you thus make room for yourself, your disciplinary argumentation and your research. And you must point out how and with what you will fill these "knowledge gaps" or how you will incorporate them into the ongoing discussions, on the basis of disciplinary legitimate criteria.

In the introduction, you begin to establish your disciplinary ethos, i.e. your professional credibility through

- identifying a disciplinary problem that is relevant to your field
- displaying knowledge of the field's existing knowledge, research and disciplinary discussions
- treating sources soberly and critically/analytically
- demonstrating that you can conduct disciplinary research with a suitable research design
- setting the scene for disciplinary argumentation.

In assessment and exam activities, such as writing a paper, your disciplinary ethos will start out low because you have not yet demonstrated knowledge. Your ethos must be established and constructed through your use of credible and relevant documentation for your statements, claims and points (e.g. own or others' analyses and research, disciplinary authorities' statements, basic disciplinary knowledge), and through continuously sober and factual treatment of sources.

Conclusion

In your conclusion, you write the entire paper's main claim and answer to the research question. It is the claim you have substantiated through your research throughout your paper.

Conclusions in papers do not have to be long

In chapter 1 we noted what independent contributions a paper can make to the "big house of science". We also wrote that a very small stone or even a lump of mortar can be considered contributions. The claim presented in the conclusion is the paper's contribution. Consequently, this claim can be small and yet crucial.

Here are some examples of claims presented in conclusions from a number of papers from different fields:

> … principally it is possible to document results in Danish lessons without coming into conflict with the cultivation ideal of primary and secondary school. At the same time, however, you must be aware that intention rather than method primarily determines whether … (Teacher training, BA).
>
> When the translator can explain why the source material is humorous he is making conscious the process of translating humour. The value of translating consciously is that the choices that the translator makes are not based on intuition but on arguments which rest on knowledge and understanding of humorous comic strip material. (English, BA project).
>
> The emergence of the political consumer can be seen as a result of new conceptions of values and prioritisation of the population in what can be called a post-materialistic society. (Political Science, MSc).
>
> For my part I believe there can be no doubt as to whether chariots constituted a status symbol among rich noblemen at the end of the pre-roman iron age (Archeology, BA).
>
> Although Said can be criticised for theoretical problems, there is no doubt that *Orientalism* has helped throw light on the connection between Western knowledge production and the accepted truth about the inferiority of the Orient (European eth, MA).
>
> In relation to test and diagnosis, it requires determination of the sub occipital muscles' default value. The results of the pilot test of ultra-sound scans indicated that practice and experience will enable the use of ultra-sound scanning as an impact goal in clinical practice. (Physiotherapy, BA).

Naturally each conclusion was much longer, but these statements constitute the papers' central claim, which the papers' inquiry and research documents and argues for.

The perspective contains points about the literature and your own research

After the conclusion follows the perspective, which places the claim in a broader context. The perspective is a part of the paper's general argumentation, and it places the claim in a greater disciplinary context. This perspective will often contain the contours of a new research question or argumentation made relevant by the argumentation that has just been carried out. This points towards the next study and next contribution to the scholarly debate. An example:

> A research question from a teaching BA (10/B) asks the following:
>
> "Which special-pedagogical challenges can a teacher as the leader of a classroom face when inclusion is a condition in a regular 5th grade class?"
>
> The writer's last sentence constitutes the perspective:
>
> "This paper has led to further questions. Is it time to change field terms and rename special-pedagogy inclusion-pedagogy?

Documentation

Documentation is the necessary foundation to enable the reader to accept the conclusion if the documentation obtained is methodologically sound and relevant. This applies to both the literature and documentation/material/data connected with your own research.

Determining which documentation is best depends on the target audience (the field's readers), the text's purpose, problems and traditions within the field and, thus, the expectations of the reader. In practice, you will have to use the documentation that is available and explain why it is the best among the available documentation.

Documentation can be

- your own research, e.g. analyses of texts, cases or historical sources, field analyses, observations, qualitative interviews, quantitative interviews, statistics, experiments, surveys/questionnaires
- others' research, e.g. analyses of texts, cases or historical sources, field analyses, observations, qualitative interviews, quantitative interviews, statistics, experiments, surveys/questionnaires
- statements of academic authorities, e.g. theories, concepts or definitions
- the basic knowledge of the field
- combinations of these forms of documentation.

(Adapted from Hegelund, 2000, pp. 16 and 24)

What can you use as documentation – and for what?

Determining which type of documentation is most convincing depends on the claims that are made and the philosophical context in which they are presented. However, a few good rules of thumb are:

Use your own research as documentation
- when you contribute to the field's collected knowledge. It will build on top of the work that authorities and others' research have already contributed to.

Use authoritative statements and others' research as documentation
- when you need to construct an academic foundation for your problem and substantiate its relevance
- when you account for "state-of-the-art", i.e., "what we currently know"
- when you account for your use and definition of concepts
- when you construct an academic foundation for your claim/conclusion
- when you construct an academic foundation for your choice of method.

(Based on Hegelund, 2000)

Generally, researching something there is already comprehensive and credible knowledge of simply to document it with your own research is unnecessary – unless you wish to document it using different material or on the basis of other methods.

Your own methodologically sound research can form the most convincing documentation in a paper. When you are able to generate new knowledge by conducting research, you demonstrate academic skill as well as independence. You demonstrate that you are not limited to referring to knowledge presented by others, but that you are able to search for answers to relevant academic questions by carrying out methodological research (based on Hegelund, 2000).

Placement of theories and methods in the paper's argumentation

Methods' and theories' position in the argumentation and thus in the paper's structure can be hard to determine. When considering a paper as a single argument, theories and methods can easily appear in different positions of Toulmin's model and thus serve different purposes in the overall argumentation.

Theories can appear as:
- Documentation in the shape of authoritative statements to support your own statements
- The object of study – in a theoretical paper (if so theory is placed in the pentagon's 3rd corner)
- The foundation for the method employed
- Legitimatisation of the method employed
- Critique of the method's (general) applicability
- The core values of the entire research (corresponding to the position presented in the paper's introduction).

Methods can appear as:
- Research methods (which form part of the general research design)
- The object of study (if so method is placed in the pentagon's 3rd corner).

Research argumentation

The research argumentation is the part of the paper's argumentation resulting from your own research – however, it also forms the argumentation for what you have chosen to study as well as your method for studying it. The research argumentation states: "You reach b by researching a in xyz ways". There is no special section for this, as it permeates the introduction, method, discussion and conclusion/perspective.

Research design and procedure

Both in relation to literature and your own research, methods are what connect documentation and conclusion. If you employ acceptable and properly applied methods for examining both literature and object, you will be able to reach a conclusion from the documentation.

The research design and procedure is a set of academic methods collected and combined to research the particular problem that constitutes the paper's starting point. Regardless of which research methods, specific academic methods and literature and literature searches you employ, they must be acceptable according to the governing research ideals within the particular science or scientific school. Here you must consult your supervisor to calibrate expectations.

A paper's research design and procedure, for example, can be made up of methods for interviewing, transcribing and analysing. In the paper's method section, you should carefully account for and substantiate the research method so that it is as transparent and easy to replicate as possible. A condition for accepting the conclusion is that the reader can follow the method.

Use the argument model in your writing process

Filling out an argument model for your own paper in the beginning, during and at the end of your writing process is a good idea. If you have or strive for both literature argumentation and research argumentation, you should fill out a model for each argumentation form, you can simply use keywords depending on how far you have come in your writing process.

A filled-out argument model provides an overview of the paper in terms of coherence, relevance, how different elements are emphasised, whether there is correspondence between questions and answers, and whether the appropriate reservations have been made in regards to research design and scope. A filled-out model can furthermore indicate how realistic your project is: Is it possible to document the argumentation as planned – both in relation to your time limit and the available documentation?

It is a good idea to show your argument model to your supervisor to clarify these questions. You can also show it to your study group/fellow students to get feedback on your paper's research argumentation.

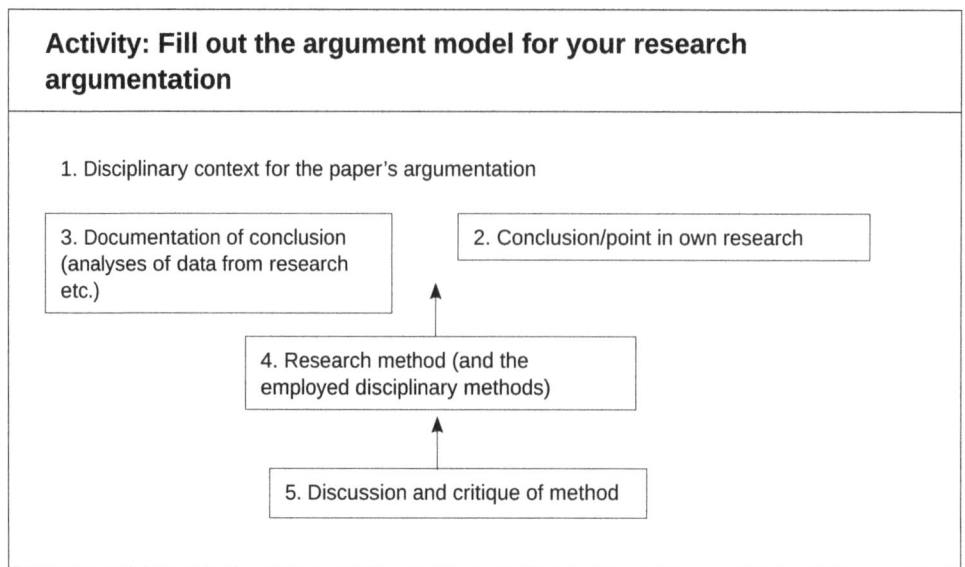

An example of discussion and method critique (professional bachelor's degree, nursing):

> According to Kvale, the validation of a study is tied to [...] the credibility of the informants' descriptions and securing the meaning of what is said (41, p. 276). During the interview, I have attempted to follow up on conflicting statements, to ensure that interviewees really meant what they said. Here it must be added that the neuropsychological difficulties of informants suffering from apoplexy affected and impeded their answers. One of these informants [...] was highly emotional during the interview and demonstrated clear signs of depression. This worsened her speech impediments, and her answers were therefore short with few spontaneous outbursts and thorough descriptions. In this case, I could have chosen to re-interview her. However, I decided not to for ethical reasons. I sensed that the informant used much energy to make herself understood, and I did not wish to cause her unnecessary strain. I chose to interview the informants about their experience of the rehabilitation process after their discharge. Taking into account the cognitive problems of apoplexy patients, this could have consequences in relation to their ability to recall their experience of the rehabilitation process. However, due to my time limit I chose not to conduct interviews at the time of the informants' discharge. Instead I presented the informants with the rehabilitation plan for apoplexy sufferers during the interview to assist their memory.

When you have filled out the models either using keywords or cohesive text, you will have text fragments that can be included in a number of important sections of your paper: Introduction, literature review, method section, conclusion, discussion of method and abstract. These sections frame and express your paper's overall argumentation. It is a good idea to write these sections early in and during your writing process, and it is important that these sections are clarified and sharpened at the end of your writing process.

Argumentation is shown in the structure

It is possible to identify the function of each individual element in your paper. And if you compare this to the standard structure, everything will come together forming a synthesis. The next table shows how the elements of argumentation appear in the research papers' standard structure. This table is slightly simplistic, but makes for a good starting point.

Where does argumentation appear in papers across departments and fields?	
Structure	**Argumentation**
Introductory sections - Introduction of material/topic - Observation - Problem - Research question - Hypothesis - Delimitation - Structure - Literature, possible description of literature search, review and use of literature.	- Context - Literature, literature search, selection and use

Method and theory sections
- Introduction and foundation in philosophy of science
  - theory
  - concept definitions
  - research design including all academic methods.
	- Research design

Analysis section • Analyses of the object of research • Results, partial interpretations • Partial conclusions.	• Documentation
Discussion sections • Research discussion: discussion of results related to own methods and literature: critique, substantiation and evaluation of method • Discussion and critique of literature.	• Research discussion • Literature discussion
Conclusion section • Claim, points, conclusions • Confirmation or invalidation of hypotheses • Interpretations • Evaluations • Designs.	• Conclusion with reservations
Perspective section • Perspective, consequences, implications with regard to 　◦ empirical, factual, practical, professional matters 　◦ theoretical, conceptual, methodological matters 　◦ implications for further study and research.	• Context

The argumentation's boxes are thus filled out by the paper's structural elements.

In this chapter, we have shown how the argument model can be used to analyse and "control" your paper. However, as previously mentioned, you can also use the model to generate ideas and material by putting material, theories, sources, discussions, etc. into the model on the basis of your research question and by continuously updating and revising the model.

Argumentation in language

Use argumentation signals

Signals of argumentation are small words such as "therefore", "seeing as", "because", "although", "conversely", "also", "but". With these you can linguistically signal argumentation, coherence and cohesion.

Objectivity

A paper is a contribution to an academic debate, which the field's proponents have previously contributed to. However, the debate is not about "winning" and being right, but rather about contributing relevantly and usefully to the development of the field's knowledge. The best thing is thus to consider your chosen sources and your own results in a sober and nuanced way. By presenting your own and others' work as soberly as possible, you demonstrate academic maturity and thus heighten your ethos – your credibility. You should therefore completely avoid caricaturing the debate by exaggerating the excellence of those who are "right" and the ignorance of those who are "wrong".

You can also demonstrate your sober treatment of sources and your own research in your language. In academic texts, you must be wary of using expressions and phrases that are loaded and normative, and which are not sufficiently documented, e.g. "TV's large masses of unassuming viewers …", "The works is based on an incontrovertibly original foundation", "This should even make today's politicians …"

These statements are loaded and normative and do not belong in academic texts, but are connected to other genres mentioned in chapter 1, e.g., reviews or feature articles or even textbooks. The requirements to language and style in academic papers are elaborated in chapter 13 on "Clear and academic language".

13. Clear and academic language

In higher education, the most important quality of a paper is its academic content. However, there are good reasons for mastering good and academic language, as language expresses and co-creates content. With language, you signal the professionalism you possess and develop as well as the professionalism and scientific standards of your papers and research. When asked to characterise good papers, most teachers mention language, and when BA and MA theses are assessed, spelling and formulation are taken into account as well (see examination regulations 2010, § 24).

In this chapter, the language of papers is considered from the following two perspectives. Language in an academic paper must be
- academic – not necessarily varied, beautiful or appealing
- clear – not necessarily difficult.

Furthermore, an academic paper's language must be correct, i.e., it must abide by accepted conventions of spelling and punctuation. We will not treat correct language in this book, but in the bibliography, you can find references to books, encyclopaedias and electronic resources which provide instructions on correct language.

Subject specific – and often supervisor specific – norms for good academic language are not treated in this book. Here we treat the general interdisciplinary language norms which are connected to the genre "the research text". However, professional competence and written work are closely linked because research is expressed through language. Therefore, it is crucial that students acquaint themselves with the specific language codes, traditions and norms of their field and the academic discourse community of which they are part. You can do so by asking your supervisor about his/her quality criteria for language and by reading good papers and research texts from your field.

First of all: Language changes from think text to draft text to product text

In this chapter, we describe the language of the finished paper ready to be handed in, i.e. the product text. It is an important point that the language requirements for the finished product text, which will be read by others, do not apply to the language used during the writing process in idea text and draft text. The purpose of language in the writing process is to produce content and support the thought process. If you focus on writing well-formulated and correct language from the start, you run the risk of getting bogged down. I.e., you should postpone any concerns about the finished paper's language until you start revising – after content and structure are in place.

Text to supervisor, project- or feedback group

In the writing process, however, it is important to distinguish between think text and draft text when sending text to your supervisor, project- or feedback group. In think text, you use language as a tool for thinking. You brainstorm, develop ideas, write practice text, i.e. text to get you started, text that touches upon your topic, text that may not yet be focused on any particular points. You should not send this type of text to your supervisor or group for textual supervision and feedback. It will be difficult for your supervisor and fellow students to give you qualified feedback on loose, writer based text. Furthermore, being sent a text which is not aimed at a reader can be a frustrating experience as well as a source of irritation. However, if you present this form of text in e.g. mind maps, tables, overview models (e.g. the pentagon), it can be suitable for discussing ideas, thoughts, connections and possible content with your supervisor.

The text you send to your supervisor, your class or group for textual supervision and feedback should neither be a "think text" nor a product text but something in between, also known as a draft text. This is text that has been through an initial phase of processing, but which is not yet fully worked out, and is in need of improvement in terms of language and content, which is where supervisor and fellow students can help. In draft text, you demonstrate professional competence in your language through relatively cohesive reasoning leading to academic points and by using field terms, concepts, definitions, etc., which prove central to the research. It is a good idea to inform your supervisor (and other readers) to which degree the text is edited, so the reader can focus on the important aspects. Also see the section about supervision in chapter 14. The following table shows which text types are best suited to different readers throughout the writing process.

Text	Sender	Reader
Think text	Writer	Writer
Draft text	Writer	Supervisor Project group Feedback group
Product text	Writer	Supervisor/ External examiner

The rest of this chapter is about the requirements for language in the finished paper, i.e., language in the product text.

Clear and academic language

The first and most important thing about language that we tell students in higher (academic) education is that it must consider both research text conventions and academic usefulness. Language is meant to render the paper's research and results credible in the academic debate, i.e. it must be credible to peers so they can use and build on it.

> **In the name of research, papers must communicate information**
>
> - clearly, unambiguously and in a way that enables replication – the reader must understand what the researcher does, and the reader must be able to check up on the information
> - objectively – the reader must be able to reach the same results following the same procedure
> - cohesively – the reader must be able to follow the reasoning and argumentation
> - economically and exhaustively – the reader should neither be disturbed by irrelevant information nor should information that could change the results be withheld.

If these requirements are not met, it is possible to dispute the paper's research and academic character. Apart from these absolute genre specific requirements for language, there is also a number of desired – often important – requirements of a general, communicative nature. These promote the text's readability, legibility, comprehensibility, clarity and correctness. There is good advice in the following.

Clear language in papers – a virtue rather than a requirement

We see many texts that perhaps meet the research requirements, but are far from clear. Some students believe that academic papers should be written in an especially complex and abstract language – but this is not the case. You may write about complex and abstract topics which are hard to understand in themselves – this is unavoidable. However, you should then be even more careful to write about complex matters without adding to their complexity.

A compilation of the language requirements for academic papers is shown below:

Clear and academic language – characteristics and examples	
Characteristics	**Examples**
1. Precise, unambiguous, and replicable	- Use references, definitions, the same terms for the same things - Give evidence for your claims (e.g. statements from academic authorities, others' research, own research). - Use research metacommunication (indicate how you use your sources and why). - Use field terms and subject specific terminology. - Avoid generalisations, undue abstractions, clichés, figurative language and colloquial language. - Use academic text types ("summarise", "analyse", "discuss", "evaluate", etc.).
2. Objective	- Avoid loaded expressions, assessments without academic argumentation, agitating phrases. - Avoid unprecise and unconcrete text types (e.g. "denigrate", "worship", "popularise"). - Avoid contagion from your sources.

3. Cohesive	- Write with a focus, a theme, one thing at a time, be governed by points. - Write with progressions (known before unknown, concrete before abstract, introduce new themes and concepts). - Use argumentational and structural markers ("therefore", "because", "also", "hereafter", "partly", "first of all").
4. Economic, exhaustive	- Avoid irrelevant information (fillers, repetitions, broad knowledge, warm-up text). - Introduce all relevant information (avoid implicit understandings or withholding information).
5. Clear	- Subject and verb should appear within the first 5-6 words. - Avoid long sentences of more than 20-25 words. - Use "I" and verbs in the active when you do or say something in the paper. - Avoid unnecessary nominalisation (e.g. "demonstration" vs. "xx demonstrates"). Read more about nominalisation on p. 396. - Use a reasonable amount of textual metacommunication (how your text is structured and why).
6. Correct	- Abide by the accepted conventions of spelling and punctuation.

In the following, we will elaborate and exemplify the requirements for clear and academic language on word, sentence and section level. We will start on word level.

Choose precise, unequivocal and argumentation terms

According to the definition of a research paper, the text is expected to
- *research* an academic problem, ideally to produce new knowledge
- *use* the theories, concepts and methods of the field to analyse, explain, interpret, evaluate, etc.
- *document* information, sources, research process, reasoning and
- *argue,* i.e. be unequivocal and precise to enable replication.

The good paper's language must demonstrate this, and it does so with "research term categories":

Research term categories

Investigation terms

Investigation terms demonstrate that material is being processed and analysed. Investigation terms:

- present the writer as an active researcher in the text, i.e. with the "professional I", but also through text types in which "the I" is implicit: "choose", "delimit", "conclude" or the corresponding nominalisations: "choice", "delimitation", "conclusion"
- constitute the research text types: "analysis", "interpretation", "combination", "characterisation", "categorisation", "evaluatation", etc. See the box about acceptable and unacceptable speech acts (text types) on p. 27.

Knowledge transforming terms

Knowledge transforming terms show that the field's theories and methods are used to carry out research and how they are used. Knowledge transforming terms are:

- concepts from the theories and methods of the field: "tool words"
- research metacommunication that shows how the writer chooses and uses theories and methods in a goal-oriented way: "use ... to", "choose ...to", "be substantiated with", "explained on the basis of", "analyse ... to".

Documentation terms

Documentation terms unequivocally demonstrate what is being researched, with what and how. Documentation terms are terms that:

- define and specify, e.g. "i.e."
- demonstrate connections, reasoning and argumentation, e.g. "so that", "therefore", "the argument for this is ..."
- show who is responsible for the text's different statements, e.g. with references that clearly mark statements from sources, see the box about summary verbs on p. 251.

Contrastively, in a research paper, you should *not* include:

- text types that assess subjectively without documentation and argumentation, e.g. "I think/believe/presume/claim" etc. without being followed by the word "because".
- opinionated terms, terms that imply evaluation without documentation and argumentation, e.g. "claim", "well-conducted", "excellent"

- figurative words and metaphors that are not defined, e.g. "crazy about", "dancing style"
- ambiguous terms that can be interpreted, e.g. "desire to move forward"
- "imposing words", i.e. words that impose an attitude or opinion on the reader, such as "naturally" and "you see"
- different terms and concepts for the same content.

Precise and unequivocal terms

The language in a paper should relate and stick to the case under investigation and the field by means of subject-specific terminology, i.e., the terms and expressions employed within a given field. Ideally, subject specific terminology should be precisely and unequivocally defined terminology within a field. The demand for precision in papers also applies when the field does not provide useable concepts and terms, and the writer himself must find suitable concepts for his research.

A general rule is to choose the most precise and concrete word or expression in the context following the maxim: "Call it a 'spade', not an 'excavation tool' – granted that you are in fact talking about a spade". For both writers and readers, many problems in papers are caused by the text being vague or unclear.

> **Imprecise terms are**
>
> - when persons (both writer and agents) in the text are hidden behind passive constructions ("in the paper the data is analysed"), "one"-formulations, plural terms ("all", "children", "some"), general concepts ("man", "the client")
> - When the writer's textual actions are vague: "I wish to pin down", "illuminate", "draw nearer", "look at", "go into", "touch upon", "do a reading of"
> - when large, broad concepts are used without concretisation, e.g. "communication", "discourse", "literary understanding", "pedagogical"
> - when information is devalued with "rubber words": e.g. "sufficient", "often", "as possible", "a reasonable amount".

Also see the box about problematic research questions, p. 136 and the section later in this chapter about the use of "I" in papers, pp. 395f.

When should you define concepts, terms and expressions?
The benefit of subject specific terminology is exactly that it does not have to be specified and defined every time you use it. The meaning can be presupposed. The problem thus becomes when a word can be considered unequivocal and precise and when it cannot. In practice this boundary is often unclear: When must you define a term, and when can you reckon on it being part of the reader's subject specific vocabulary? The general rule is that you do not have to define the field terms that belong to the field's central vocabulary and whose meaning is firmly established.

Here are some rules:

Terms that must be defined in the paper

- Expressions and concepts drawn from other fields, schools, theories, disciplines
- Special, recurring key concepts, especially if they appear in the research question
- Concepts used by others but which must be expounded and interpreted
- Expressions you wish to specify and define more than usual, e.g. because you want to use them unconventionally
- Every day words you wish to include in an academic context.

Be especially sure to explain words which perhaps are unequivocal within a particular field, but which have a different meaning in others. "Discourse" is for example used differently within different fields, and a word like "care" means something different to nurses than to pedagogues.

Carefully choose the subject and verb of a sentence

It is important to think about the subject and verb you choose for a sentence. When the text's agents, the active parties, are made the subject and their action the verb, sentences do not alone become more clear; by using subject and verb consciously, sentences also become more precise and concrete.

The subjects – what is in focus?
Consciously choosing your subject will demonstrate your focus and starting point of your text (MacDonald, 1994). Take a look at these sentence openings:

> ### Subject – what is in focus?
>
> - **The phenomenon, object, text**
>   - The children in the studies express different …
>   - *The Grapes of Wrath* exposes …
>   - Excluding the social and stepping into loneliness is …
>   - Male Pakistani immigrants try to adapt themselves …
>   - Experiences with death often have identical elements and processes …
>   - Empathetic sense is a quality …
> - **Research**
>   - A comparison of the two studies shows …
>   - The results show …
>   - The analysis… points to …
>   - The arguments are …
> - **The writer**
>   - use Ziehe's concept to …
>   - have chosen to compare the analyses on the basis of …
>   - We must necessarily consider it an expression of …
> - **The field (sources, knowledge, theories and method)**
>   - Williams (1990) has argued that …
>   - Existentialism's most important contribution is …
>   - System theory offers …
>   - Bourdieu's concept …
>   - Brix' method …

The examples show how the subject accentuates the writer's focus. All subjects can exist together in academic texts, but they can and should be consciously selected on the basis of what you want to emphasise, draw attention to or draw information from: The objects, research, writer or field.

The verbs of the sentence must be specific

The clarity (and precision) of your writing can be increased by specific action verbs that, as concretely as possible, convey what the subject is doing or subjected to. Good verbs are for example: argue for, evaluate, specify, define, accentuate and focus on. More general and inane verbs are, for example, "says", "writes", "states".

Some more advice on clear sentences

- Place the subject early in the sentence (preferable within the first 5-6 words)
- Use the position of the subject consciously
- Keep subject and verb close to each other
- Write old and known information before new
- Write few sub clauses and preferably place them after the main clause.

The good paragraph's beginning, middle and end

The good paragraph follows these rules of thumb:
- The paragraph begins with a topic sentence (indicating the topic of the section), metacommunication (which is linked with former sections and ascribes status, significance and function to the section's information), a concrete verb
- The middle of the section retains the theme using keywords and demonstrating the reasoning and connection between connective words
- The paragraph is concluded with a point sentence indicating the paragraph's "result", and possibly metacommunication which ascribes status, significance and function to the point, pointing forward in the text.

Knowledge transforming language often places the topic/problem at the beginning of the paragraph and is combined with metacommunication which ascribes status, significance and function to the information. See for example this extract from an introduction from a well-assessed paper written in Public Administration at Roskilde University:

> "Our choice of theory is primarily based on the theorist Nicholas Barr. We use his book: *Economics of the Welfare State*, from 2004. Barr is relevant to the project as he includes several theories which are concerned with the economic aspects of the welfare state's tasks. Among other things, he treats efficiency in the economy and the difference between different finance models of the welfare state's expenses.

We thus use him to underpin part of the employed data. He is relevant to us, as he provides an economic theoretical foundation on which to base discussion. In other words, this theoretical approach enables us to discuss what is meant by effective health services, which incentives apply in different welfare models and different ways of organising the health care system. We are given the opportunity to evaluate whether one model is better than the other, and we are given a clear starting point which enables us to be critical of our own approach."

The very first sentence makes the paragraph's theme clear, i.e. the writers' choice of theory. This theme is adhered to and expanded on in the rest of the paragraph with information about how it is connected to the rest of the paper, reasons for the choice of theory and its usage, etc. In conclusion, the section presents the possibilities the choice of theory gives rise to later in the paper in relation to the writers' own position.

Use academic keywords to demonstrate coherence in the section

The finished paper must be cohesive so the reader can follow both the reasoning and argumentation. The reader must be able to see how the information is connected. Here is an example from Russian. In the text, note the expressions

- change
- ambiguity
- system change
- theory (+ explain, predict).

We have capitalised the academic keywords.

This concrete case of SYSTEM CHANGE CAN BE EXPLAINED alone by taking the linguistic system as the starting point, i.e. as an evolutive LANGUAGE CHANGE. As described in the previous section, this CHANGE is conditioned by AMBIGUITY in the output the language user has at his disposal when establishing his grammar by means of abducting observed language usage. In the specific case, this AMBIGUITY consists in the fact that nouns with final -o can be either declinable or indeclinable, as mentioned above. THIS AMBIGUITY can then result in a SYSTEM CHANGE. According to THE THEORY, this SYSTEM CHANGE occurs before CHANGES IN LANGUAGE USAGE can be observed. The governing linguistic norms may even completely prevent its manifestation. However, according to THE THEORY, a language user who is unfamiliar with the linguistic norms will be led by his productive system, which can EXPLAIN why workers in the 1963 study applied the indeclinable variant more frequently than philologists. Furthermore, THE THEORY PREDICTS that the frequency of the new variant will gradually increase as the norms are harmonised with THE NEW SYSTEM. This can EXPLAIN why philologists display a higher frequency of indeclinable variants than workers and sluzjasjie in the new questionnaire.

• •

Abbreviated, this section can be read as such: THE CHANGE IN LANGUAGE is conditioned by AMBIGUITY which has resulted in a SYSTEM CHANGE which can BE EXPLAINED by THE THEORY.

In addition to the mentioned keywords, the writer also uses the terms: "norms", "language user" and "declinable/indeclinable" to tie together the section.

More advice about clear sections

- Begin by indicating the section's main point and theme and connect the section to earlier ones
- Let the theme emerge clearly from the heading
- Adhere to the theme and secondary themes by using keywords
- Only include information relevant to the theme
- Round off the theme and point to subsequent sections
- Demonstrate internal connections using sentence connectors (e.g. and, it, he, she) and structural markers (e.g. therefore, hereafter, partly)
- Retain the same style and tone throughout
- Use the relevant amount of metacommunication.

Write metacommunicatively

Metacommunication is an important feature of research language. Metacommunication shows how the writer uses, evaluates and organises the content, and guides the reader's attention. These functions are important in academic writing because they connect the text's academic information to the professional forum to which both writer and reader belong (Hyland, 1998). You could say that metacommunication attaches academic information to the reader, to the field and to each other in the text.

Metacommunication (also known as metalanguage, metatext, metadiscourse or structural markers) means "text about text". While most of a paper is concerned with the topic, part of the text is not about the topic, but rather about the text itself. For example, a sentence that anticipates what will be discussed in the following section, a summary of the central content of the preceding section, or a specification of how the information can be used.

This is our advice:

Write metacommunicatively

Metacommunication constitutes signals in the language about the use, status, purpose, relations, type, attitude, emphasis of academic information. I.e.:
- Introduce and point out what is in focus
- Communicate how you use sources, theories and methods
- Indicate who is speaking – your or your sources
- Make transitions
- Show back and forth
- Connect sections
- Show changes in topic
- Mark the level (primary category – secondary category) and order
- Mention what function and status information has in the text
- Mention speech acts (see pp. 26f.) and text types (see pp. 315ff.).

Metacommunication can be expressed on several textual levels:
- Metasections, e.g. introductions to chapters and summaries
- Metasentence, e.g. thematic sentences indicating a section's topic and purpose
- Metawords, e.g. conjunctions/connector words
- Metapunctuation, e.g. colon or bullet points
- Metatypography, e.g. accentuation using italics or underlining.

The following table is based on the British researcher Hyland's (who specialises in academic communication) studies of a large number of dissertations from different fields (Hyland, 1998):

> ### How metacommunication creates textual coherence and cohesion
>
> - Connectors which show the connection between sentences and sections in regards to argumentation and meaning, e.g. "but", "therefore", "hereafter", "furthermore", "in contrast to"
> - Markers of textual status which indicate speech acts and position in the text, e.g. "to conclude", "finally", "in the following analysis", "then … will be examined", "the reason is …"
> - Internal textual references, e.g. "as previously mentioned on p. 7", "also see example a"
> - External source references, e.g. "according to x", "(y, 1998)", "z emphasises"
> - Explications, explanations, e.g. "that is to say", "e.g.", "such as", "to put it differently".
> - Reservations about statements, e.g. "maybe", "this is possibly the case when …", "to a certain degree".
> - Emphasis that indicates the writer's assessment of a statements validity, e.g. "actually/in fact", "definitely", "clearly", "obviously".
> - Attitude which indicates the writer's relation to his own or others' statements, e.g. "surprisingly", "my objection is", "I agree with"
> - Addressing the reader to guide the reader's attention, e.g. "note that", "from this you can see that …".

Research metacommunication

Especially important is what we call *research metacommunication*. This is where you relate how and with what you research your problem.

> ### The functions of metacommunication in research texts
>
> Research metacommunication
> - connects the paper's information to existing, academic knowledge
> - demonstrates how scientific, academic theories, concepts and methods are used in the research
> - places the research's (partial) results in the field's on-going discourse and debate
> - supports the paper's reasoning and argumentation
> - points out information's function in the text and marks out speech acts
> - interconnects different pieces of information.

Another form of metacommunication in academic papers is what we call *textual metacommunication*.

Textual metacommunication

Textual metacommunication is communication about how your paper is structured and coheres. Textual metacommunication is especially prominent in a paper's main introduction and throughout papers in the sub introductions and conclusions that tie together sections and chapters.

Textual metacommunication
- relates how a paper is structured and why
- presents text types and intentions
- connects sections and chapters
- sum up preceding text and introduces forthcoming
- shows how information fits into the text's overall meaning.

Here is an example of the use of research and textual metacommunication from a paper from Psychology (MA-level, high mark). Following this we present our comments.

- -

> In this connection you could thus ask the question: If the two mentioned foci border on other sciences, how does the science of psychology fit into the problem definition? I will consider this question more closely in the following section.
>
> ### 3.2. AN ACTION THEORETICAL UNDERSTANDING OF THE INDIVIDUAL
> The above discussion points to the need to understand how general tasks **concretely** appear and are understood, to be able to determine Helhedshuset's [an institution] problem area in a way that is meaningful to users.
>
> In this connection – and as a temporary answer to the question I raised at the end of the last section – you can claim that the object of Psychology has traditionally been situated and studied at the concrete, personal level.
>
> When the person(s) are made the preferred locus for intervention, this is naturally connected with the fact that personal problems have traditionally been viewed as the question of *how* the person understands and uses his conditions and opportunities. There is therefore reason to investigate how the conception of this problem can be changed and expanded through a contextual understanding.
>
> Inspired by Giddens, Mørch points out that the individual realises societal conditions by "using him- or herself" (Mørch, 1993, p. 27). I.e., that by acting, you draw on previous experience and personal prerequisites […].

> The point is that routines must be understood on the basis that the person does not alone develop his own routines – or perhaps he does so – but that personal space of action must be understood on the basis of the inclusion of and reliance on existing routines and forms of action.

In this text, the writer has done all he can to clarify what happens in the text. There are

- sentences that relate the passage to the paper
- sentences that explain what will happen next
- sentences that sum up what has happened
- headings
- clarifying divisions of sections
- repetition of keywords
- typographical accentuation
- substantiation of the researched area
- identification
- explanations.

Many papers would likely receive a higher mark if they used more metatext. Research into the assessment of papers' quality shows that students' use of metatext is attached great importance (Prosser & Webb, 1994; Cheng & Steffensen, 1996), as the writer thereby demonstrates overview of his own work. When reading papers, assessors time and again think to themselves: "Why has this section been included?", or "Is this example supposed to be a contrast or a parallel to the preceding?" In these cases, metatext – even a single word – could have provided clarification and prevented misunderstanding and annoyance. Metatext is generally attached greater importance in Anglo-American research cultures than in Continental.

Metacommunication thus helps complete a text, which in its own right is well-structured and rich on substance, but does not replace substance and structure. If the text is well-structured it would be a pity if the assessors struggle to follow it because of a lack of metacommunication.

Too much metacommunication?

However, there are papers with too much metacommunication. If you are constantly told, in great detail, what is going to be written next, what has just been said, and if this is then repeated at the end of the section, there is too much metacommunication. The effect can be that the metacommunication appears as fluff compensating for a lack of substance in the sections about the topic itself. The effect can likewise be that the text becomes heavy and redundant to read. Readers of academic papers (supervisors and external examiners) read, and have read, many academic papers. Furthermore, many of them are trained writers of research and academic texts. Thus, they are greatly familiar with the genre, which is something you as a student must take into consideration when deleting and adjusting metacommunication in your revision.

Activity: Use metacommunication to further knowledge transformation

- When you draft: Overdo your use of metacommunication to force yourself to relate to your paper's academic foundation, to the reader and the paper's structure and coherence
- When you write the finished text: Remove superfluous metacommunication so it does not exceed the academic information.

Detachment and contagion in language

For many students maintaining a suitable distance to their sources is a particular problem. If their language too closely resembles that of the source, this is called contagion. And if you forget to reference the source, this is called plagiarism, an academic mortal sin.

Typical pitfalls in regards to too closely resembling your sources are if
- you are not sure of which parts of and how to use a particular source in your paper. You will thus end up working on the source's conditions rather than your own and your paper's
- you have not quite understood what you have read and thereby "borrow" formulations for your own text
- your source or theorist writes in an abstract and complex way and your writing therefore becomes similarly abstract and complex.

> **Activity: Avoid contagion from your source(s)**
>
> - Clarify your purpose for including the source(s) as well as your concrete application of the particular source in your paper
> - Begin by writing the surrounding text of which the source will form part
> - Put away the source when you start writing and begin by paraphrasing the parts of the source you need in your paper using your own words – possibly writing in colloquial language at first (this can be rephrased later)
> - Do not write product text about something you do not understand. Start by writing think text about the parts of the source you do and do not understand.

Here is an example from philosophy (BA-level) in which the paper's language (too) closely resembles that of the philosopher Søren Kierkegaard:

> The subjective determination of truth thus concerns the relationship, the way in which the individual establishes relation to the truth, rather than the truth itself being something outside the subject and independent of the subject. Whereas the ideal for objective reflection is the object of thought processes, "truth as object", the relationship and its "how" is the gravitational point of subjective reflection. That "the truth in this and its mouth can become untruth" in this sense originates from the subjective determination of truth's accentuation of a "how", and thus from the circumstance that the subject, who does not relate to the object with its entire being, cannot be said to step in relation to the truth and thus cannot be said to understand. Whereas it is possible for the individual who considers the truth "objective" to remain wholly unaffected by its object, i.e. in a special sense remain indifferent to the truth, it is the establishing of relation to the object with its entire being that is crucial to Kierkegaard's subjective determination. It is thus "only this recognition that concerns existence as something significant, significant recognition".
>
> The "how" of subjectivity is the relation to the significant; fervour. Insofar as this "how" remains unstressed in favour of the "what" of objectivity (the object in itself), recognition remains insignificant to the subject as an existing being and recognition unimportant.

It is extremely hard to see where Kierkegaard begins and ends, and where the writer's analysis and interpretation of Kierkegaard appears. Furthermore, many of the formulations, which are not presented as quotes, are far removed from contemporary written language, resembling Kierkegaard's style, e.g.:

- "as being something outside the subject"
- "originates from"
- "with its entire being"
- "wholly unaffected"
- "establishing relation to the truth"
- "remains insignificant to the subject as an existing being and recognition unimportant".

Watch out for "hidden" translations from foreign-language sources!

By Ida Klitgård

As a student, you cannot get around using foreign-language sources such as, for example, theory books, critical works, internationally-published research articles, foreign-language pages on the Internet, etc., and there are incontrovertible problems in reading and understanding difficult academic material in a foreign language that puts things in a completely different way than you would in your native language. This section will illuminate the necessity of being linguistically aware when you are working with foreign-language sources since you can easily risk falling into situations in which you write poorly because of "hidden" translations from what you are reading into what you are writing. Consequently, you lose your own "voice" in your paper, and you put your credibility as an academic reader and writer at risk.

English into Danish – Anglicisms

This is the case, for example, with English, which uses heavy nominalizations (the formation of nouns from verbs and adjectives) and dense, compact and concise structures more frequently than Danish. However, if you undertake a study in which Danish is the primary language, you must still paraphrase, summarize and discuss in Danish what you have read in a foreign language – preferably, without it being noticeable in the paper. Unfortunately, it is often noticeable in the language of Danish university papers that there has been an interlinguistic exchange of information, knowledge, thoughts and ideas from one language to another when the student sits down at the keyboard. And it is not only a matter of "hidden" translations of difficult terms and theoretical concepts but also even linguistic structure. This results in unintended bad translations from, for example, English, which are called *interferences* (a muddling influence) or so-called *Anglicisms*, which include "any linguistic phenomenon that derives from or is stimulated by English and which appears in communication in another language" (Farø & Gottlieb, 2012).

Anglicisms and loanwords

Anglicisms, for example, may be entirely ordinary words and phrases but also the use of two words in compound nouns that we in Danish would write in one word – such as, for example, *gene test* instead of *gentest*, and the use of an apostrophe before a genitive -s such as, for example, *Jensen's Bøfhus*, which has finally been corrected in written Danish to *Jensens Bøfhus*. These disturbing elements should not be confused with different types of *loanwords* that have been completely accepted in Danish such as, for example, the direct loanword/foreign word *powernap*; the borrowed meaning of *orm [worm]* in the sense of a computer virus; the pseudo-loanword *stationcar*, which does not exist in English but is our idea of an English-language concept; and borrowed translations such as, for example, *posedame* from the English term *bag lady*.

Here are examples of some unfortunate Anglicisms in two bachelor's-level projects:

Example 1: Direct translation

···

Den daværende emir, Sheik Khalifa bin Hamad Al Thani, red på pengebølgen og levede et liv i luksus, som ansigtet udadtil for et land, der fremviste en ekstrem form for excessiv rigdom

···

The expression "excessiv rigdom" breaks with the Danish idiom (fixed expression) and indicates a direct translation from the English phrase "excessive wealth". If you google the student's expression in Danish, there are no hits other than links to that paper at the relevant university library. In standard Danish, you probably would have written "en ekstrem form for overflod" or "enorm rigdom" or something similar.

Example 2: Direct translation

> Ved "Air Quality Act" i 1967 blev staterne for første gang tvunget til at leve op til satte *standarter*

Here, the formulation "satte standarter" is again directly translated form the English "set standards". This does not sound Danish since, instead, you would typically say "vedtagne standarder". The word "satte" has entirely different associations, and "standarter" is spelled wrong. With a "t", it refers to a banner for a knight whereas in Danish – as in English– it is spelled with a "d". Thus, there is some confusion and a lack of language consciousness about how we formulate things in Danish.

Example 3: "Mental translation"

> Oversætteren invadere [sic] og udtrækker information af originalen for at kunne oversættelse [sic] hvilket kan *efterlade* ham/hende *med* en følelse af tristhed efter både succes og fiasko

This example comes from an abstract in Danish of an English-language text and distinguishes itself from the previous two in that the unidiomatic expression "efterlade x med følelsen …" is undoubtedly translated from the English "leave x with the feeling …", but the interesting thing is that it does not appear anywhere in the original text. The student has done a sort of "mental translation" in his/her head since he/she has formulated what he/she was going to write in English – but with the intention of writing it in Danish. Thus, a muddled translation has crept into the text here. In Danish, we would have said something in the direction of "få ham/hende til at sidde tilbage med følelsen af …".

Example 4: "Self-translation"
This example comes from an abstract written in Danish connected to a bachelor's-level project in English. This is a direct translation from the student's introduction to the abstract:

> *Terror angrebene* som fandt sted den 11. september, 2001 i Washington DC og New York City kom som en stor overraskelse for Amerika, som siden *enden af* den kolde krig havde været den eneste stormagt i verden.

The corresponding text in the English introduction reads:

> *The terrorist attack* on September 11, 2001 in Washington DC and New York City came as a big surprise to America, which had been the only superpower in the world since *the end of the Cold War*.

Here, we have the problem mentioned before with compound nouns (in Danish, it is written "terrorangrebene"), and a direct translation of the English expression, "the end of", which we would say in Danish "afslutningen på".

Example 5: Definite and indefinite form

> Denne opgave undersøger hvordan institutionel racismes sammenhæng med *stemmeret* har ændret sig siden borgerrettighedsbevægelsens storhedstid i 1960'erne, og det bliver konkluderet at på trods af åbenlyse forbedringer i *sortes* stemmeret, findes institutionel racisme stadig i nutidens USA

This example shows the problem of using an indefinite form in English over the definite form in Danish. In English, you would say here "institutional racism" while, in Danish, we would say "den institutionelle racisme". In English, it is called "the right to vote" or "voting rights" and the corresponding idea in Danish uses the definite form "stemmeretten" in this syntax, but the student was confused and avoided the definite form in Danish. The same is true of "the blacks' right to vote" or "voting rights for blacks", which mistakenly becomes in Danish "sortes stemmeret", where we can see the contagion of the indefinite form in Danish. Here, we would have written "de sortes stemmeret".

"Colouring and discolouring"

The Danish language in all these examples is quite deeply coloured or, rather, discoloured, by a basic tendency toward so-called "hidden" translation from the original text to your own text – both consciously and unconsciously. Therefore, it is important that you are linguistically conscious when you use foreign-language sources. Be careful about "translating" from English to Danish, for example. And use your critical linguistic sense for the colourations and grey tones in the finished product in the motley world of near-plagiarism if you get too close to the original's formulation.

A question of credibility

Hidden translations into incorrect language breach the requirement that one should be able to hear the different voices in a paper. Who says what when? Is it the source that is speaking or the student? With such interference from a foreign language to Danish, you as a student lose your voice and, thus, your credibility as an independent, critical analyst of statements, language, and discourse. Therefore, you should take this widespread but almost hidden problem very seriously when you write papers – especially when a large part of the curriculum and bibliography is in English.

Checklist for writing papers on the basis of literature read in a foreign language

- Be aware that there is not always a 1:1 translation from one language to another.
- Be aware that there are many linguistic-cultural nuances of meaning in words, expressions and structures. It is your job to investigate and choose between, for example, using good dictionaries, the Internet, etc., in both the foreign language and the language of the paper.
- Be wary after your reading and thinking process of formulating your ideas in a foreign language when you write about them in the language of the paper – abstract from the source and think things through from the start in the language of the paper before you take notes or write any final text.
- Use the same techniques for abstracts and paraphrasing from one language to another, but think in particular about the meanings of the words when you summarize in your own words.
- Use metalanguage in your papers to explain that you have given special consideration to the meaning of the words, concepts and representations in the different languages.
- Turn on the spelling and grammar check in your word-processing program as you write. Then you will catch more of these mistakes along the way.
- Always let your text "cool off" before you submit it, so you can see and hear any awkward formulations with fresh eyes and ears when you read your paper aloud for editing.

To conclude this chapter's exposition of what characterises clear and academic language, and before ending this chapter by examining students' typical questions about language in papers, we present an activity for checking your clear and academic language – or for a fellow student to check your language for you:

Activity: Check your clear and academic language

Choose some pages from your paper, for example, from your introduction or method section, and check or get a fellow student to check your clear and academic language on the basis of the following control questions:

- Do you use the field's expressions, terms, concepts?
- Is your terminology precise? Do you specify and define expressions and concepts? Do you use the terms consistently?
- Do you indicate which text types you use?
- Do you separate yourself from your sources in language and tone? And are your source references precise and correct?
- Do you make use of research metacommunication? I.e. indicate which theories, methods and concepts you use, why and how?
- Do you make use of textual metacommunication? I.e., indicate what you plan to do in your paper, why and how?
- Is your text logical, progressive and cohesive from research question to conclusion?
- Have you structured your sections so you introduce one theme at a time, add a new aspect, elaborate on the new and conclude with a point (rather than continually presenting new material without processing it)?
- Is your syntax clear and do subject and verb appear relatively early in sentences?
- Is your choice of words clear and concrete and do you avoid unnecessary or unsubstantiated abstractions and implicit meanings in your introduction of concepts, theorists?

In the following we answer a number of questions about precise, sober and academic language frequently asked by students.

FAQ

Use of evaluating terms?

Using descriptive adjectives, for example, "the qualitative method", is not a problem and papers can neither do without nor avoid this. However, the use of evaluating adjectives is often debatable, for example the expression: "the excellent method". A statement like this requires explicit argumentation. As a general rule, you can only evaluate if you have prepared a thorough foundation through formulating and validating your criteria of evaluation. Even then moderation is preferable, using terms like "viable" rather than "excellent". Personal opinions and evaluations *without* relevant substantiation are not valid in a paper. See also the non-viable speech acts, p. 27.

Variation in language?

Many students ask whether they should vary their language. In other text types, such as free compositions, feature articles, debate books, etc. (which are also written by academics and teachers), variation is often an ideal. However, in academic papers, precise, sober and neutral language is the ideal, because in these texts not only topic, but also the way the writer has obtained results and the basis for the writer's views are at the centre. This does not mean that there is no room for any personal expression, but variation must under no circumstance occur in the system of terminology used in the paper. Personal style must furthermore not get in the way of research writing.

Literary language

When describing the qualities of language, some teachers – especially in literary and other aesthetic fields – will model these on the vivid, supple, personal, flourishing language influenced by the fictional texts that are the object of study. But, watch out. Although language that provides an experience without sabotaging the academic requirements will pay off in terms of assessment. However, it is difficult to outline general criteria and guidelines for what a teacher and external examiner consider good, over the top or unacceptable. It is important to strike the proper balance. However, in the academic paper being precise by using the same terms for the same concepts is more important than aesthetic concerns. Students writing literary papers must for example remember that metaphorical language by nature is ambiguous, unless the meaning of each metaphor is explicated.

Popularising language

Students who wish to write in a more popularising (journalistic) style must be careful not to overstep the conventions of academic language. If an academic wishes to leave the ivory tower, this is both fine and commendable; however this is not appropriate in academic papers and dissertations. The popularising genre is the place for this. As mentioned earlier in this chapter, there is nothing wrong with writing in a readable and reader-friendly way. However, the paper must not become unacademic as a result. In general, "cool"/"cheeky", vernacular language can easily affect the reader's impression of the paper's seriousness, as in the example below from a paper in economics.

> After a short restitution from the First World War's political and economic hangover in the mid-1920s, the world economy flip-flopped again in connection with the great crash. Germany was hit especially hard because the country was already placed in a vindictive, economic leg-lock as a result of the Treaty of Versailles.

As the example above shows, language can become too popularising and signal colloquial "looseness". However, you need to find the right balance, as readers (the ones we know of) want language that is accessible without being imprecise and vernacular.

Spoken language, everyday language, slang?

In principle, you should strive towards timeless language. This means language that is not marked by narrow, current language usage, e.g. slang and other words bound to a particular contemporary historical occurrence. You should for example not use the word "awesome" in a paper (unless you make the word itself the object of study). Apart from being an evaluating expression it is also a subcultural expression, i.e. it belongs to the language spoken within a small group (adolescents). It is thus implicit, which an academic text absolutely must not be, save for subject-specific terminology. Furthermore, it is, by all accounts, a context-bound expression which, with time, will become outdated in line with "righto" and "tickety-boo". And in contrast to journalism, academic texts do not strive towards being a passing fad/a nine day's wonder, but aim at lasting importance. This is why language in papers must be neutral, timeless and aimed at academic readers.

For these same reasons, you should also avoid using spoken and everyday language in your papers. Spoken language is too imprecise and context-bound in its immediate form. In spoken language, there is neither physical nor temporal distance between sender and receiver. Spoken language, therefore, is far more context-bound. It forms a contrast to written language, which must be able to stand alone and which cannot be further elaborated. See this example from linguistics in which there is a distinct use of spoken language, and where the choice of topic is substantiated by personal, everyday experiences and reasons:

13. CLEAR AND ACADEMIC LANGUAGE

> I have been interested in the Danish glottal stop ever since I became acquainted with it […]. My interest was strengthened when a friend from South Funen called me [maj]. Taken out of context, it was impossible to distinguish which word she said, and I did not react. I tried to teach her to say [maj/] with a glottal stop, but it was impossible for her to learn. (The glottal stop is created by a powerful airstream which brings the vocal chords out of balance, so a short pause or an irregular weakening of the voice occurs). If this ability was not learnt in childhood, it can be difficult to acquire. Together we discovered that if she lengthened the vowel it sounded more like [maj/] and I reacted when she called me. This experience made me want to examine whether people without the ability to produce glottal stops generally are unable to express the difference between minimal couples. Can the distinction be heard on the basis of context and thus lead to understanding? Or do they express the distinction by for example lengthening the vowel, as my friend did?

As the example shows, that every day and situational experience is favored above disciplinarity to such a degree that when the explanation finally appears, it is put in parentheses.

Difficult language

Language in an academic text should however not be unnecessarily hard or abstract. Here is an example of difficult language (Psychology, BA-level):

> There are several implications involved when it comes to contextualism. First of all, personality features are understood as situational in contrast to individual. The actual processing structures we use for carrying things out are created in a transaction between individual and surroundings, in which the individual processes the current situation by comparing it to inner experiences established in conceptual systems, and thus experiences options which in turn are decisive for the direction of the chosen action. This sequence of influence-process-action, I have called the individual's negotiation of meaning in the introduction. Secondly, the individual is viewed as active in this sequence of influence-process-action. Thirdly, the individual can be changed; or rather the individual is constantly changed through the perpetual negotiations of meaning in relation to the experiences of life.

Of all the texts we have looked at, the above is among the more concept heavy and abstract. Is the difficult language of this text then a good or a bad thing? We can weigh the pros and cons: Some would believe that this kind of language enables terminological precision, which can be difficult to achieve in clear, everyday English. The language signals inside understanding of teachers' and other peers' conceptual universe. Furthermore, by making the text compact, words and space are used economically. And also, being able to write in this style can seem impressive.

The cons, which we consider crucial, are:
- Abstractions are the number one enemy of clarity. Appropriating the text will be hard and take a long time for the reader. Many readers will have to concretise while reading: "What does this actually mean?" There is thus a risk that readers will envision different concretisations than the writer had in mind – thereby precision is removed.
- If the writer does not concretise throughout, it may cast doubt on the extent to which the writer really understands what he/she writes.

To simplify the language in the above example, we would advise that you:
- Concretise at least once: E.g. exemplify what a "sequence of influence-process-action" could be.
- Break up the long sentence from line 2 to 7. There should be at least one additional full stop.
- Translate the following words to (more) common words: "implications", "process structures", "transaction", "establish conceptual systems". As far as we can see, none of these are necessary field terms.

Again, we wish to drive this point home: You are not required to write complex language at any stage of higher education, but you can if you want. You have to compare the pros and cons, requirements, wants and abilities to each other. You should especially avoid abstract and syntactically/grammatically complex writing, if you're not in full command of the language. If you attempt to build a linguistic multi-storey building with towers, spires and domes on a weak linguistic foundation, the entire construction will come crashing down. The combination of poor grammar, long sentences and abstractions will seem as if a 15-year-old schoolchild and a 50-year-old professor have taken turns writing.

Using "I", active and passive

Students often ask whether using the word "I" in papers is ever allowed. Or students tell us how their supervisor has forbidden the use of "I" on the grounds that it is not objective. We have experienced students doing peculiar things in papers to avoid this. Earlier, this "I"-taboo was widespread, however, it appears to be declining. There are no good scientific arguments for a general ban against using "I". In fact, using "I" is sometimes the most prudent thing to do. It is especially appropriate in introductions and conclusions, where the text's selecting and evaluating subject (the writer) appears: "Here I choose to take as my starting point Bourdieu's ideas of ..." In reality, when describing what you e.g. research, select, analyse, summarise, cite, discuss and conclude, "I" is the subject of the sentence. The alternative to an "I"-subject is constructing passive sentences that obscure the subject: "As Bourdieu's ideas are taken as the starting point ..." This is unnecessary. Writing "I" when you make choices in the text is perfectly acceptable. You demonstrate objectivity in your selection and treatment of material, not by leaving out the subject in the text. If you refrain from using "I", the distinction between your own and others' material will become unclear. If your teacher is of a different opinion, ask him/her to substantiate this view.

Some believe that passive constructions are a thing to strive for as they express objectivity. Others have repeatedly been told that: Active language is better than passive language! If either of these is expressed as an absolute command, they are both wrong. An acclaimed American work about academic writing, Booth et al. (2008): *The Craft of Research* suggests:

- Use the passive when you want to accentuate general designs that others can replicate, e.g. "the observations are analysed and then categorised according to the model".
- Use active verbs and "I" when writing about the speech acts and other actions you have carried out in connection with your research, i.e., "I employ, select, suggest, conclude, argue for, show, claim", etc.

Here is an example from pedagogy which shows how a student, to an excessive degree, attempts to keep himself out of his/her paper.

....

> In the papers first part the methodological considerations on which the paper is based are discussed. The paper's two theoretical perspectives are discussed with a view to reach a specification of the theoretical factors that may influence the quality of teaching. In the

second part of the paper, the data is analysed with an aim to evaluate the theoretically founded factors' significance for the quality of teaching. Furthermore, a single factor is added as a result of the interviewees' emphasis of its importance. In the paper's third part a number of factors that are significant to the quality of teaching are specified. Here a specific angle to the problem represented by a model of the interrelation of the factors is suggested. Finally, the suggested angle of approach is commented on and a conclusion is drawn about the paper's problem.

• •

This text is furthermore characterised by an extensive use of nominals, that is, verbs turned into nouns, e.g. "specification" instead of "specify", "emphasis" rather than "emphasise". This may contribute to a text becoming further abstract. We will expand on this in the following.

Nominalised style? – both yes and no

Academic texts are often written in so-called nominalised style. This involves a great degree of abstraction and compression of information which in turn can make texts difficult to read and understand.

As mentioned above, nominals are nouns made from verbs, for example, using the suffixes -ing, -tion, -al, -ment or from adjectives using the suffixes -ity or -ness. These words replace a sentence. (They are also known as sentence replacements):

- "Evaluation" replaces the sentence "x evaluates y".
- "Expectation" replaces the sentence "x expects y".
- "Usefulness" replaces the sentences "x is useful for y".

In itself, nominalisation enables leaving out both the subject and object that would have been mentioned in a full sentence. The condition is then that the reader must deconstruct the implicit information by mentally working out the sentence that would have been. Our advice is to write all concrete information in sentences rather than using nominalisations insofar as this is possible and justifiable. However, academic texts are precisely about the general and phenomena that are not dependent on concrete subject and objects. Therefore, nominalisations may sometimes be the correct approach (just as the passive tense can be suitable at times). Furthermore, nominalisation works well for summing up. If you described research in one section, it is perfectly fine to refer to this as "the research" in the following section as it does not run the risk of becoming unspecific.

"What do you think?"

In academic papers, your research is at the centre and throughout your paper, you contribute new knowledge or new angles to the academic problem. This is why personal opinions have no place in academic texts. In academic texts, your opinions must be based on disciplinary analyses, theories and research – your own or others'. On this basis, you can then evaluate. The following is an example of an academic evaluation from a good paper in Political Science:

> Binderkrantz' and Christiansen's analysis shows that classic economic organisations with corporative resources, wage earner, employer and corporate organisations take up most space in the media. However, the three newspapers prioritise the coverage of these organisations differently (Bindercrantz & Christiansen, 2010: 37, 42), *which could suggest* that they are already a brand that appeals to some media. Simultaneous with these organisations' partial dominance is the ideal organisations which are significantly represented in political areas such as environmental and legal politics (Binderkrantz & Christiansen, 2010: 41). *This could suggest* that ideal organisations know how to brand themselves within political areas, which traditional NGOs may neglect. As mentioned previously, the ideal organisations were characterised by not seeking "collective goods, which would benefit the organisation's members selectively and materially". (Binderkrantz & Christiansen, 2010: 35) (Our italics).

In this example, the writer evaluates in a valid way by using the formulation: "… could suggest …" The evaluation is based on a study conducted by theorists within her field.

As a contrast, this following example is from a paper in art history, in which personal opinions are left standing alone without disciplinary substantiation and argumentation:

> Here it is important to emphasise the positive, but naturally remain conscious of the development to strengthen women in the arts. However, it must be said, that the art scene has come far since Barr's table mentioned earlier. This does not mean that women and men should be equally represented at museums, as this idea would result in one-sidedness, but naturally this does not mean that it could not happen. Art is a living organism infixed into a pluralistic world with soul, sparks and autonomous freedom.

In the box below you can see examples of where to find substantiation for your views.

Substantiate your evaluations

In research and other academic texts, you need to substantiate your evaluations. Substantiation can be found in

- subject specific descriptions
- subject specific analyses
- theories

- the views of professional authorities
- others' research
- your own research.

What can you do?

If your supervisor, teachers or assessments repeatedly tell you that your written language is not good enough; that it is imprecise, unclear, marked by spoken language, heavy or complex, you have to make a special effort to improve your language. Not just for the sake of writing papers and future assessments, but also for the sake of your career once you graduate. Most jobs list good, clear and correct written language as a central competence.

Improving your written language can be a long and tough process because the related problems often go way back. First and foremost, it is therefore important that you are prepared to spend time on improving your written language. Among other things this entails that you

- read others' good papers
- ask you supervisor about his/her criteria for good language in papers
- set aside time for textual revision and proof reading
- use fellow students or a writing/study group
- ask you supervisor/teacher to give you feedback on your language
- read books and participate In courses about good, academic language
- use Internet resources (such as web dictionaries)
- read research and academic texts from your field
- participate in courses about good, proper language.

14. Supervison, independence and ownership

Supervision provides help and feedback to aid you in writing a good paper. As a student writing a longer paper you will be offered supervision, and – more importantly – supervision is something you will use.

Supervision can be aimed at the paper's
- subject-specific aspects
- research, methods, theories, philosophy of science, data, argumentation
- textual composition,structure, language
- research process, writing process
- professional and practical orientation
- ethics

and probably much more.

Being supervised and assessed when writing a paper is practice for being able to write within professional discourse, within scientific and scholarly criteria and within a supervisor's and assessor's administration and weighting of academic and scientific criteria.

Being able to use and receive supervision is a skill in itself! It is therefore extremely important to have the courage to ask your supervisor which parts of your work are good and where you should do things differently to ensure that you gain the best competences possible from supervision.

However, the condition is that you can acknowledge your supervisor's criteria and the validity of his/her feedback. If you are unable to do so, you should consult your supervisor.

The fact that supervisors often function as assessors can complicate supervision for both student and supervisor. On the one hand supervision becomes a situation in which you must perform well: The supervision and assessment situation results in the writer's ownership of his/her own text being brought under pressure because the supervisor's statements are considered overly important. On the other hand, the supervisor's dual role can mean that the supervisor must be withholding in terms of how far into the process he/she will supervise and how straightforward he/she will be.

How much supervision can you receive?

The amount of supervision differs in different educations and at different levels of study. In some places, early papers are not supervised. BA projects, professional BA theses and papers/projects/theses at the master's level are usually supervised. In some programmes, supervision only takes place in groups. You must investigate how much supervision you are allotted and in what form.

Activity: Investigate how much supervision you can receive when writing your paper and in what form
Consult the curriculum or ask your teacher/supervisor.

If you are not supervised or if you would like more supervision, you can investigate alternatives to supervision. See page 411 later in this chapter.

Independence and ownership

Some – both teachers and students – consider supervision a restriction of the student's independence when writing, and thus the student's ownership of the finished paper is similarly restricted. This is untrue – for a student should not simply assume and do exactly what the supervisor says. Independence is when the student uses supervision consciously and critically.

You can demonstrate independence by consciously planning, preparing, making presentations for and relating to the supervision, partly evaluating the supervisor's suggestions in relation to your concrete paper and research question as well as material and literature, and partly by making your own decisions. In brief, you should consider supervision to be a resource in line with other tools (e.g. theories, methods, guidelines), printed and electronic resources and information specialists that can all help you research your problem and write your paper.

Having ownership of your paper, the product of your work process, is to feel that your paper is yours and that you fully and completely vouch for its content, because you have made use of supervision in an independent way.

The following is based on the view that writers should have – or acquire – as great a degree of ownership of their work and text as possible, while at the same time independently being open to as much of the supervision's forward-looking planning and backwards-oriented feedback as possible.

Good supervision

Supervisor and students are most likely to be satisfied by their collective process if
- they have an expectation of and agree on what and when and remember to adjust appointments if need be
- both parties are prepared for – and process – all meetings, and treat each other as busy people
- it is clear that the ownership of the paper is and remains the student's, all decisions are to be made by the student
- the criteria on which the supervisor's input and feedback are based are clear
- it is possible to have many readers and people who can provide feedback (e.g. (a group in) a class, in the classroom) so the writer is given plenty of response and the text does not become private and overly sensitive to feedback
- the students begin writing the paper in good time allowing sufficient time for implementing the supervisor's input. Too much supervision takes place right before a paper is handed in, and at this point it is often too late to revise on the basis of supervision.

These are high ideals and you can get by with less. However, as a student you can play a part in fulfilling these ideals in supervision. Fundamentally the preconditions of good supervision are an understanding of what is discussed and how, and good practice in keeping appointments and agreements. The crucial thing is to be in agreement as to whether the way you proceed is acceptable and fruitful on a disciplinary and personal level.

Seek information about supervision

As a student, you should generally be informed about the possibilities, limitations and other conditions that apply to supervision when writing papers in your programme of study:
- Ask during classes and study guidance.

- Read the curriculum.
- If possible, read the supervisor's website or written information material.
- Listen to older students.
- Get started early – and be flexible. Supervision is a collaboration.

You need to know the timeframe for supervision; whether a supervision contract must be signed, whether there are particular dates and forms of supervision etc. that you must be aware of. For example, deadlines, and whether parts or all supervision takes place in the classroom as a group activity.

If your supervisor is published, skimming his/her written work is a good idea. This will tell you much about the supervisor's own writing abilities and ideals for academic writing as well as tell you much about the supervisor as a professional in general. Academics often google each other before collaborating.

First meeting – as early as possible

If you are entitled to or are able to receive supervision, you should try and get as much supervision as early in your writing process as possible – even if you have not written a great deal. Sending your supervisor drafts already before the first supervision is a good idea, and we therefore advice that you write as much as you can – within a short period of time! – before the first supervision. Read more in chapter 2 on the writing process.

For your first supervision, it can be wise to send e.g. the following:

Presentations for the first supervision can include

- Topic and draft of the research question (possibly more than one)
- The most important concepts you aim to use
- Suggestions for theory(ies), method(s), data and philosophy of science
- Possible points for a structure – if you are able to
- Temporary bibliography or plan for literature search, possible search terms, etc.

You can document this information and perhaps send them to your supervisor as a
- filled-out pentagon model (even if all corners are not filled out)

- a draft of the introduction
- a problem description (see p. 121)
- use *Scribo* (Rienecker & Bay, 2014) which is a tool for formulating research questions and conducting literature searches.

You should always include a bibliography of the literature you have found so far.

However, you may have to present an idea more loosely and orally if this is the most feasible way of moving forward.

Your initiative!

When it comes to your paper, it is your responsibility take the lead in regards to research question, methods, concepts, theories, data and literature and which search terms and databases you plan to use. Your supervisor's task is to respond to your ideas as well as supplement and narrow these down.

In our view, you should not do much more than write clarifying text, which aims at presenting ideas which the supervisor can respond to before the first supervision. You should meet your supervisor for an introductory talk as soon as possible, or else your work may become overruled If your supervisor is unavailable or does not answer your emails for a couple of weeks, you should consult the student counsellor, supervising coordinator or director of studies to ask whether you should be assigned a different supervisor.

Preparing for supervision

Always attach a covering letter listing the items you would like to discuss in supervision.

If your supervisor does not know you, it can be a good idea to send a list of the papers you have written previously, and possibly the methods you have used – in short, a student CV. Is there any other information your supervisor might need in order to provide good supervision? E.g. your expected deadline, whether you have any particular ambitions for your paper, whether you have any special (lack of) prerequisites?

Calibrating expectations

Talk to you supervisor about the way supervision can be carried out, what you will send and what deadlines you wish to set etc. Find out what you supervisor expects from you: how processed and revised should your work be and how long can texts for supervision be?

Provide all text for supervision with

- a covering letter in which you point out your agenda for supervision as well as what you need supervision for
- an updated research question – if you have one – for example placed in the header of each page
- a temporary structure indicating where drafts belong in this structure
- a timetable: what are you working on and when?
- an indication of the status of drafts, from introductory ideas to almost fully revised text (see p. 83 on the status of work(ing) papers)
- page numbers
- file and path name with your full name/the names of each group member
- the paper's hand-in date.

Part of preparing for supervision is to keep a log of questions you wish to ask. Every time you are in doubt about either content or form write it down and bring these questions to your supervisor.

Activity: Preparing for supervision

Three questions to prepare for supervision

1. What do you seek supervision for/about?
2. What have you done to answer any questions you want your supervisor to answer?
3. Who else have you asked?

The point is that, the person who wants supervision must do as much preparatory work as possible, for example, by finding answers in texts and discussing with fellow students and others. You then send the result of your own preliminary work to your supervisor. But: Do not spend so much time preparing that supervision begins too late. Then it is better to be less prepared.

Emailing your supervisor

Many supervisors receive texts from students they have never spoken to before, who "just" want a response to the attached files without a cover letter. Supervisors need contextual information as well as agreement on how email correspondence should be carried out. Otherwise supervisors run the risk of being sent half completed and finished papers all year being expected to be able to open all types of files, print out and react wherever and whenever, perhaps without ever hearing back from the sender. If supervision via email is to work, students (and supervisors) must "behave", also known as online etiquette. Concrete supervision sessions via email can best be framed in a written or oral agreement.

Agreement in connection with supervision via email

There must be an agreement regarding
- what can be supervised via correspondence
- the max. amount of text (or questions) you can send per supervision and in total
- pointing out what the supervisor should especially provide feedback on and which kind of comments the writer wants (comments on content, text, language)
- the status of the work sent (see p. 83 on the status of working papers)
- whether the supervisor should print files or be sent printouts
- how long the writer should expect to wait for an answer, also in connection with weekends and holidays
- what counts as supervision in the total number of hours allotted to each student – e.g. does a short answer to a question count?
- the student's feedback on supervision.

Email is suitable for feedback, especially if you already know and trust each other. Email is less suitable for asking questions and developing a longer dialogue. However, email supervision is best when the writing process is underway rather than at the very beginning. However, email supervision can be necessary if you are far away from the educational institution.

We often hear students complain about supervisors who do not answer their emails, and we hear that some teachers receive so many emails that they give up. Use office hours/telephone hours to establish contact and then ask if you can email him/her. Some supervisors do not wish to supervise via email, and you will have to respect this.

If you receive supervision by email, you must remember to respond to it. In a conversation, the supervisor can get a sense of how you receive his/her supervision, but in email supervision, the supervisor will only get a response, if you answer his/her email and input.

Several supervisions

If only a short course of supervision is made available, e.g. over two sessions, we suggest that you spend

- one session on the paper's content on the basis of a short presentation prepared by you (so you can get feedback on your content and research design ideas and forward planning)
- one session on how to carry out your plans (structure and formulation, i.e. feedback on your draft text, even just a few pages).

In each supervision discuss any questions you may have regarding content, form and process with your supervisor.

Good text for supervision

As a main rule, supervision should move in a top-down direction, moving from the text's general guiding points down to the text's lower levels, just as drafting and revision do not benefit from being greatly detail oriented at the beginning of a project. You should therefore also make sure that the text you present and the questions you ask in supervision enable your supervisor to give you feedback on the way you use your field (theories and methods). Because of this, the most knowledge transforming parts of your paper are best suited for feedback – which is why it is wise to start writing these parts as early as possible so you have enough time to use them in supervision.

Good text for supervision can for example be

- analyses of data, interpretations, discussions, method sections and methodology discussions
- philosophy of science section

- sections in which theory and data are brought into play with each other
- drafts of the introduction and conclusion
- sections you are uncertain of or have brought you to a standstill.

It is important to ask your supervisor whether the academic content and form of your project generally looks reasonable. Your supervisor cannot approve or guarantee that you will acquire the most relevant competences or the highest marks, but your supervisor can keep you on track in terms of qualifying your research and your writing as good and academic.

Feedback from macro to micro level (top-down)

The important thing is to get feedback on the right elements of your paper and in the right order. First and foremost, it is therefore best that the text's higher levels are commented on first and the lower levels later:

Macro level: The paper's content, literature and research design (pentagon: research question, purpose, data/material, concepts, theories, methods, entire research design), philosophical premise.
↓
Meso level: Argumentation, textual elements (such as analyses, discussions, structure, documentation, sources).
↓
Micro level: Individual facts/calculations/arguments/textual elements, language, formalities: source references, notes, bibliographies, etc.

There may be a need to talk about and get feedback on everything. But, as mentioned earlier, the macro level is more important and ought to be discussed in supervision early on. There is no reason to discuss details if the general aspects are not yet agreed upon and before a plan conducive to good work has been made. If supervision is spread over several sessions, it should move from macro to micro level, from research design and content to presentation and form. If only one supervision session is offered, it should focus on how the writer can work on the basis of a realistic research design in a good and qualified manner. As a rule, it is wise to prioritise a top-down approach. If you only have an hour's supervision, it does not make sense to talk about 16 different dimensions of writing a paper. As a writer, you can perhaps act on four-five different, significant inputs from your supervisor.

In addition to the crucial aspects: literature and material, research design, research question and choice of method, etc., it is also a good idea to discuss

- the paper's general argumentation
- treatment of data, especially when collecting human data. Through method descriptions and letters/emails to contact persons, your supervisor must be informed about all contact made through the educational institution.

Again, the student must research, read and write, analyse and calculate – and, most of all, define where supervision is needed: What are the challenges for you? Which questions can only your supervisor provide answers to?

Naturally, the supervisor always co-defines the focus of supervision meetings and written exchanges. However, it is the writer who initially must point out themes for supervision.

If you as a writer find that parts of the paper's macro level are unfinished later in the writing process, you will have to return to and inform your supervisor about this.

Forward-looking and retrospective feedback

You can use both retrospective and forward-looking feedback on all the text's levels and elements. It is more useful to be told what you can do (better) than being told what you have done and then personally having to assess how you should proceed. If you are only given feedback on what you have written, ask for suggestions, examples, etc., of what you can do to improve your future work.

The supervisor and the – your – good paper

Many students – and supervisors – relate how supervisors do not praise students in supervision out of fear of being "held accountable". It has happened that students have complained about average or bad marks following what they experienced as positive feedback. If your supervisor praises you, consider it a local statement that in this context, in this text and with this reader your work has been successful. The supervisor can never promise or guarantee anything! (Which is why "approval" is a doubtful concept). If your supervisor has reservations or critiques, you must take this seriously and consider it an occasion to learn about how your drafts come across.

How to receive critique

If your supervisor has *reservations in regards to content*, consider whether you can take your supervisor's objections into account by including suggested texts, or include your discussion with your supervisor in your paper as an academic discussion.

If your supervisor *suggests other/more/special literature,* ensure that you understand why your supervisor believes the suggested literature is relevant and a necessary supplement to your project.

If your supervisor *criticises the form or language of your paper*, ask for concrete examples of which sentences/words give rise to critique and in the light of which criteria. Be prepared to hand in text that has been proofread more thoroughly, preferably in time for the next supervision, even if you need others to help or improve your own competences. It is your responsibility to ensure that your language does not disrupt reading or understanding. Experience shows that supervisors find it very hard to concentrate on the content if there are many mistakes and problems in a paper's language. But if there are "gaps in your language", inform your supervisor about this in the cover letter and let him/her know that you are aware of the mistakes and will correct these before handing in your paper. Or else you risk that you supervisor will only correct language and spelling mistakes.

The general writing process, formalities, references, and how to conduct literature searches are all areas the student must become acquainted with through for example books, net resources or courses organised by research libraries. At the end of this book we recommend a number of resources.

Ask yourself what works in your drafts and what could be improved. If you have put in the work, you should not fear that your work is inadequate. The point of the activity is to learn something new, not to present finished products. It is the finished, handed-in product that is assessed, not the process. For most students the process is messy, dubious and full of stabs in the dark and mistakes, and any experienced supervisor is aware of this.

Comments about what could improve future work are always relevant, also after a paper has been handed in. You cannot rewrite a paper (unless you fail), however, learning how to do better in a similar situation is still useful. Ask your supervisor for this kind of feedback and ensure that giving you feedback becomes meaningful to him/her by reporting back which suggestions and comments you have used and proceeded with.

Working through supervision

Take notes or record/log supervision. Write down what you have agreed with your supervisor and send a summary of the main points to your supervisor. In this way, you are both up to date with the paper's status.

Activity: Summing up supervision

After each supervision, note:

How should you proceed? Write a prioritised list:

1.

2.

…

Note points for the next meeting, possibly supplementing these points later:

-
-

Get feedback on all papers – and give feedback on the feedback

As mentioned previously, feedback that is more detailed than a simple mark is important if you wish to learn as much as possible from writing papers. All feedback, both on drafts during supervision and on the finished paper, is potentially important for your learning in terms of both content and writing. Therefore, you should ask for feedback, also on your finished paper.

It is important for supervisors to know how a student receives and uses their feedback – also, if the feedback did not prove useful. Get into the habit of writing notes to your supervisor after each meeting, e.g. following this template: "I have proceeded with/have not proceeded with … and … and/because/but …"

No supervision or unhelpful supervision?

For many students, bad supervision manifests itself in apathy, e.g. if there are too few or too many normative comments or directions based on the supervisor's hobbyhorse. If you do not feel you get enough supervision, begin by examining the norms on your particular level of study by consulting your student counsellor. What is the custom – and what is possible at this point?

If your supervisor is out of town or too busy, ask: When would you have time? And make an appointment. If your supervisor is out of town for a long time and has not made any arrangements with you concerning this, contact your study head and point out that you need supervision and that you need it before this and this particular date. Ask the study head to put you in contact with your supervisor or if possible appoint a different supervisor.

If you feel (over)steered to employ specific texts, methods, angles, etc., and if this affects your motivation in a negative way, it is important to discuss your supervisor's arguments and present your own arguments and reservations. When writing a paper, advice and suggestions are only useful if you can and want to incorporate these and if these can be incorporated well. The writer must be able to claim ownership of all plans – even if the ideas came from others initially.

Dissatisfaction can be used constructively if you, throughout the writing process, draw attention to how you would like supervision to proceed and make sure that the supervisor is provided with the necessary contextual information of what is possible and important to you in connection with the paper in question.

Alternatives to supervision

It is important that students work as goal-oriented as possible on making the proposed supervision of papers useful and fruitful for themselves.

If you cannot get the supervision you want, make use of the best possible alternatives:

> **Alternatives to supervision**
>
> - Ask fellow students to give you feedback, establish writing groups, or engage in a dialogue thread on project writing in the online course room
> - Read about writing papers
> - Find papers written in the same field/with the same supervisor – preferably with assessment/mark
> - Ask questions during lectures, ask whether general supervision can be offered to the class or in the online course room
> - Find a different supervisor – if possible.

Think also about group supervision, dialogues in the online course room and how you might otherwise make use of your classmates for feedback and the discussion of common challenges. When it comes to supervision, the most fruitful approach is, on one hand, aiming to gain as much from the supervision as the supervisor will allow, while on the other hand being or becoming capable of writing without supervision if it should ever become necessary.

15. Recommended literature for writing papers and on study skills

Read more about …

Examples of papers

Braintrust Base. http://braintrustbase.com/. Here, many examples of papers from many disciplines may be downloaded.

Research papers in general

The Craft of Research (Booth et. al., 2008, 3rd ed.). One of the best and most inspiring books on academic writing known to us! It illustratively, concretely and very instructively reviews all parts of the process of researching an academic topic in connection with writing – from choice of topic to research question, information searches, argumentation, drafting, revision and language in relation to the academic reader. It applies to all fields, all levels and all types of academic theses.

Writing process

Writing with Power (Elbow, 1981). Insightful – albeit slightly chatty – classic about "the new writing process" by the grand old man of creative writing. Many good suggestions for writing processes.

Understanding Writing Blocks (Hjortshoj, 2001). Very recognisable descriptions and good proposals for action.

Research question

Scribo (Rienecker & Bay, 2014). Interactive tool that guides the writer through the first phases of the writing process; generating material, formulating a research question and searching for literature. *Scribo* is based on this book's chapters on research questions and literature searches. At scribo.dk, you can discover how the programme works and whether your educational institutions has a license so you can use the programme for free.

Searching for and incorporating information

Academic Infoseek. coursera.org/learn/academicinfoseek – this is an open online course you can sign up for. The course introduces you to the basic elements in academic information searches from the preparation of a search strategy and an evaluation and documentation of your search results.

Biblioteksvagten. biblioteksvagten.dk – biblioteksvagten is a nation-wide inquiry service of Danish libraries. Here, you can get answers to factual questions, help with a search strategy, references to books, articles, web resources, etc.

Scribo (see above).

Stop plagiat nu. stopplagiat.nu – a web tutorial that explicate some of the general rules that apply to academic integrity. You are presented with definitions and examples of plagiarism and can test your knowledge of plagiarism.

Studiemetro. studiemetro.au.dk – Studiemetroen is an academic study tool you can use in connection with writing papers, literature searches and other study-related work methods. Here, you can find specific advice, inspiration and exercises. The material is divided into: requirements for university papers, writing university papers, studying and academic searches.

Søgetips til Google. libguides.mit.edu/google.

UBtesten. ubtesten.dk – UBtesten is an e-learning tool that focuses on literature searches and information management in connection with your subject. UBtesten helps you test and improve your search abilities and select academic information, and use it in an academically correct way when you write your paper.

Zotero – zotero.org – is a free programme for organising references and bibliographies.

Argumentation

Academic Writing. A University Writing Course. (Björk & Räisänen, 2003): Chapter 4 provides concrete guidelines and advice on how to write argumentative texts. A number of examples of argumentative texts are analysed, and excercises are suggested.

The Craft of Argument. (Williams & Colomb, 2003) "is designed to help students integrate the skills of writing, critical thinking, and arguing so that they can write arguments that are clear, sound and persuasive".

Popularising papers

For the Article Writer – How to Win Acceptance by Psychology Journals: 21 Tips for Better Writing (Sternberg, 1993) – public.iastate.edu/-treg/resev550/550-notes/notes-pdf/21tips.pdf. Excellent – mentions all important aspects listed in bullets on 4 pages.

Study skills

Study Skills Handbook (Cottrell, 2013). The best-selling book on study skills in the UK – a highly inspiring book series on study skills with Cottrell as the main author. We recommend the Study Skills series by Stella Cottrell.

Bibliography

Angélil-Carter, Shelley (2000): *Stolen Language? Plagiarism in Writing*. Abingdon & New York, Routledge.

Bereiter, Carl; Scardamalia, Marlene (1987): *The Psychology of Written Composition*. New Jersey and London, LEA.

Biggs, John; Tang, Catherine (2007): *Teaching for Quality Learning at University*. 3rd ed. Maidenhead: Open University Press.

Bitsch Olsen, Poul (2013): *Videnskabsteori i samfundsvidenskaberne – på tværs af fagkulturer og paradigmer*. 3rd ed. Frederiksberg, Samfundslitteratur.

Björk, Lennart; Räisänen, Christine (1996): *Academic Writing. A University Writing Course*. 2nd ed. Lund, Studentlitteratur.

Bloom, Benjamin (1974): *Taxonomy of Educational Objectives: The Classification of Educational Goals*. New York, McKay.

Blåsjö, Mona (2000): *Uppsatsens yta och djup – Studenters skrivutveckling mellan B- och C-uppsats*. Stockholm, Institutionen för Nordiska Språk.

Boote, David N.; Beile, Penny (2005): Scholars before Researchers: On the Centrality of the Dissertation Literature Review in Research Preparation. In: *Educational Researcher*, Vol. 34(6), (aug.-sep. 2005), pp. 3-15. http://www.jstor.org/stable/3699805. (Accessed 5.11.2017).

Booth, Wayne C.; Colomb, Gregory G.; Williams, Joseph M. (2008): *The Craft of Research*. 3rd ed. Chicago, University of Chicago Press.

Cheng, Xiaoguang; Steffensen, Margaret S. (1996): Metadiscourse. A Technique for Improving Student Writing. In: *Research in The Teaching of English*. Vol. 30(2), pp. 149-181.

Cottrell, Stella (2013): *The Study Skills Handbook*. 3rd ed. New York, Palgrave Study Skills.

Dahler-Larsen, Peter (2002): *At fremstille kvalitative data*. Odense, Odense Universitetsforlag.

Datatilsynet: datatilsynet.dk/offentlig/kort-om-persondataloven/. (Accessed 5.11.2017).

Davies, Martin (2011): *Study Skills for International Students*. New York, Palgrave Study Skills.

Delamont, Sara; Atkinson, Paul; Parry, Odette (2004): *Supervising the Doctorate. A Guide to Success*. 2nd ed. Maidenhead, Open University Press.

Elbow, Peter (1987): Closing My Eyes as I Speak: An Argument for Ignoring Audience. In: *College English*, Vol. 49(1), pp. 50-69.

Elbro, Carsten; Nielsen, Per (1996): *Videregående læsning – Processer, overblik og forståelse*. Copenhagen, Dansklærerforeningen.

Elsevier (n.d.): *A guide for writing scholarly articles or reviews for the Educational Research Review*. https://www.elsevier.com/__data/promis_misc/edurevReview-PaperWriting.pdf. (Accessed 5.11.2017).

Farø, Ken; Gottlieb, Henrik (2012): Coole Songs Downloaden – om engelsk påvirkning af dansk og tysk. *Sprogmuseet.dk*. http://sprogmuseet.dk/ord/coole-songs-downloaden-om-engelsk-pavirkning-af-dansk-og-tysk/. (Accessed 5.11.2017).

Feak, Christine; Swales, John (2009): Telling a Research Story – Writing a Literature Review. In: *English in Today's Research World*, Vol. 2. Michigan, University of Michigan Press.

Forsknings- og Innovationsstyrelsen: fi.dk/publikationer/2002/vejledende-retningslinier-for-forskningsetik-i-samfundsvidenskaberne. (Accessed 5.11.2017).

Galberg Jacobsen, Henrik; Stray Jørgensen, Peter (2013): *Håndbog i nudansk*. 6th ed. Copenhagen, Politikens Forlag.

Gandil, Trine L. (2005): *Eksamenshæftet. Mundtlig og skriftlig eksamen på universitetet*. Frederiksberg, Samfundslitteratur.

Graff, Gerald; Birkenstein, Cathy (2006): *They Say/I say – The Moves That Matter in Academic Writing*. New York, W.W. Norton & Company.

Groom, Nicholas (2000): Attribution and averral revisited: three perspectives on manifest intertextuality in academic writing. In: Thompson, Paul (ed.): *Patterns and Perspectives: Insights into EAP writing practice*. Reading, School of Linguistics and Applied Language Studies, The University of Reading.

Hedelund, Lis; Stray Jørgensen, Peter (2004): *Mundtlig eksamen med skriftligt materiale/synopsis*. Frederiksberg, Samfundslitteratur.

Hegelund, Signe (2000): *Akademisk argumentation – skriv overbevisende opgaver på de videregående uddannelser*. Frederiksberg, Samfundslitteratur.

Hillocks, George (1987): *Research on Written Composition – New Directions for Teaching*. Illinois, NCRE and Eric, USA.

Hyland, Ken (2002): *Teaching and Researching Writing*. Harlow, Longman.

Hyland, Ken (1998): Persuasion and Context: The Pragmatics of Academic Metadiscourse. In: *Journal of Pragmatics*, Vol. 30, pp. 437-455.

Hvass, Helle; Stray Jørgensen, Peter (2014): *Synopsiseksamen og andre mundtlige eksamensformer med skriftligt materiale*. Frederiksberg, Samfundslitteratur.

Jensen, Leif Becker (2000): *Ud af elfenbenstårnet – fortælleteknik for fagfolk der vil skrive en god historie*. 2nd ed. Frederiksberg, Samfundslitteratur.

Juul, Jesper (1995): *Dit kompetente barn*. Aarhus, Schønberg.

Lamberti, Pia; Wentzel, Arnold (2011): Konferencepræsentation, præsenteret på konferencen Postgraduate Supervision, Stellenbosch.

MacDonald, Susan Peck (1994): *Professional Academic Writing in the Humanities and Social Sciences*. Carbondale and Edwardsville, Southern Illinois University Press.

MacDonald, Susan Peck (1987): Problem Definition in Academic Writing. In: *College English*, Vol. 49, s. 315-331.

Murray, Rowena (2011): *How to write a thesis*. 3rd ed. Maidenhead, Open UP Study Skills.

Nass, Bine; Ravn, Signe (2010): *Bacheloropgaven – en guide til lærerstuderende*. Copenhagen, Gyldendal.

Neergaard, Helle (2001): *Udvælgelse af cases i kvalitative undersøgelser*. Frederiksberg, Samfundslitteratur.

Neman, Beth S. (1995): *Teaching Students to Write*. New York, Oxford University Press.

Olden-Jørgensen, Sebastian (2005): *Til kilderne! Introduktion til historisk kildekritik.* Copenhagen, Gads Forlag.

Paulsson, Ulf (1999): *Uppsatser och rapporter – med eller utan uppdragsgivare.* Lund, Studentlitteratur.

Petersen, Nikoline Jacoby; Østergaard, Sille (2010): *Projektsamarbejde med organisationer og virksomheder.* Frederiksberg, Samfundslitteratur.

Prosser, Michael; Webb, Carolyn. (1994): Relating the Process of Undergraduate Essay Writing to the Finished Product. In: *Studies in Higher Education.* Vol. 19, pp. 125-138.

Pædagogisk Center Samfundsvidenskab (PCS) KU: Filmvejledninger til studieteknik. http://samf.ku.dk/uddannelser/studiestart/studieteknik/filmvejledninger/. (Accessed 5.11.2017).

Rienecker, Lotte (2015): *Problemformulering på videregående uddannelser.* 4th ed. Frederiksberg, Samfundslitteratur.

Rienecker, Lotte; Bay, Gina (2014): *Scribo,* version 4, see scribo.dk. Frederiksberg, Samfundslitteratur.

Rienecker, Lotte; Stray Jørgensen, Peter; Gandil, Morten (2016): *Skriv artikler. Om videnskabelige, faglige og formidlende artikler.* 2nd ed. Frederiksberg, Samfundslitteratur.

Rønn, Carsten (2006): *Almen videnskabsteori for professionsuddannelserne. Iagttagelse Viden Teori Refleksion.* Copenhagen, Alinea.

Schriver, Karen (1987): *Teaching Writers to Anticipate the Reader's Needs: Empirically Based Instruction.* PhD dissertation. Carnegie Mellon University.

Sharples, Mike (1999): *How We Write. Writing as Creative Design.* London and New York, Routledge.

Skov, Annette (2014): *Referér korrekt! Om udarbejdelse af bibliografiske referencer.* http://iva.ku.dk/refererkorrekt/. (Accessed 5.11.2017).

Skov, Signe (2007): *Sprogtest 1 + 2.* http://hum.ku.dk/uddannelser/vejledning/sprogtest/ (Accessed 5.11.2017).

Skov, Signe (2008): *Bundne opgaver – hjemmeopgaver og eksamensopgaver på videregående uddannelser.* Frederiksberg, Samfundslitteratur.

Slotte, Virpi; Lonka, Kirsti (2001): Note-taking and essay-writing. In: Rijlaarstam, Gert m.fl. (eds.): *Studies in Writing. Volume 7. Writing as a Learning Tool. Interating Theory and Practice*. Dordrect, Kluwer Academic Publishers.

Sociologi, KU. http://www.soc.ku.dk/uddannelser/bokse/troogloveerklaering/forskningsetiske_problemstillinger.pdf med bl.a. "Standardaftale for samarbejde mellem studerende, Sociologisk institut og tredjepart" og tjekliste. (Accessed 5.11.2017).

Sommers, Nancy (1980): Revision Strategies of Student Writers and Experienced Adults Writers. In: *College Composition and Communication*, Vol. 31(4), pp. 378-388.

Sonne-Ragans, Vanessa (2012): *Anvendt videnskabsteori – reflekteret teoribrug i videnskabelige opgaver*. Frederiksberg, Samfundslitteratur.

Stray Jørgensen, Peter (2014a): *Formalia i opgaver på videregående uddannelser – serviceafsnit, layout og typografi*. 2nd ed. Frederiksberg, Samfundslitteratur.

Stray Jørgensen, Peter (2014b): *Klart sprog i opgaver på videregående uddannelser*. 3rd ed. Frederiksberg, Samfundslitteratur.

Stray Jørgensen, Peter (2014c): *Notatteknik for studerende på videregående uddannelser*. 3rd ed. Frederiksberg, Samfundslitteratur.

Stray Jørgensen, Peter (2014d): *Talegaver. Mundtlig formidling for studerende på videregående uddannelser*. 3rd ed. Frederiksberg, Samfundslitteratur.

Stray Jørgensen, Peter (2004): Videnskabelige ord – sproglig rådgivning i videnskabelighed. In: Jørgensen, Henrik; Jørgensen, Peter Stray (eds.): *På godt dansk. Festskrift til Henrik Galberg Jacobsen i anledning af hans 60 års fødselsdag 4. februar 2004*. Århus, Wessel og Huitfeldt, pp. 181-190.

Stray Jørgensen, Peter (2001): Metakommunikation og videnskabelighed – om praktisk skriverådgivning på videnskabeligt grundlag. In: Jarvad, Pia m.fl.: *Sproglige åbninger. E som Erik, H som 70. Festskrift til Erik Hansen 18. september 2001*. Copenhagen, Hans Reitzels Forlag, pp. 311-320.

Stray Jørgensen, Peter (with the assistance of Thomas Harboe) (2007): *Studielæsning på videregående uddannelser – læsestrategier og læseteknikker*. Frederiksberg, Samfundslitteratur.

Stray Jørgensen, Peter; Rienecker, Lotte (eds.) (2011): *Studiehåndbogen – for studiestartere på videregående uddannelser*. 2nd ed. Frederiksberg, Samfundslitteratur.

Stray Jørgensen, Peter; Rienecker, Lotte; Skov, Signe (2011): *Specielt om specialer. En aktivitetsbog*. 4th ed. Frederiksberg, Samfundslitteratur.

Swales, John M.; Feak, Christine B. (1994): *Academic Writing for Graduate Students. A Course for Nonnative Speakers of English*. 2nd ed. Michigan, University of Michigan Press.

Toft, Trine (2012): *Informationssøgning til bachelorprojektet for professionsbachelorer*. Frederiksberg, Samfundslitteratur.

Toulmin, Stephen (1974): *The Uses of Argument*. Cambridge, Cambridge University Press. (1st ed. 1958).

Wegener, Charlotte (2016): *Skriv med glæde*. Frederiksberg, Samfundslitteratur.

Williams, Joseph M.; Colomb, Gregory G; (2003): *The Craft of Argument*. 2nd ed. Longman, Chicago.

Young, Art (1994): *Writing Across the Curriculum*. Washington D.C., Blair Resources for Teaching Writing, USA.

Index

A
abstract 346
academic essay 31, 95
academic language 367ff.
- abstract 393
- clear 370
- contaminated 383
- difficult 393
- distanced 383
- imprecise 373ff.
- literary 391
- nominalised 396
- popularising 391
- spoken language 392
- varied 391

active forms of verbs 395
analysing paragraphs 320
analysis 320ff.
analytic tool, theory as 282
anglo-american research tradition 61ff.
appendix 344
applied sources 220
argumentation 50, 347ff.
- and paper structure 308, 313, 352f., 355, 363
- as a dialogue 352
- documentation of 358ff.
- placement of theories and methods 360
- procedure 361

article search 147
assignment question 101
assignments 222

B
bibliograph 170
bibliography
- supervision 170

Bloom's taxonomy 46, 48f., 316
- research question 127

Boolean operators 157
brainstorming 76f.

broad writing 79
brochures as sources 221

C
cases, choices of 261
chain search 167ff.
characterising paragraphs 318
choice of topic 67, 334
citat 246
citation search 167
closed questions 138
coherence 380
comparative section 319
concept definition 337, 374
concepts 191, 269ff.
conclusion 339, 356, 364
- section 307, 364

constructivism 206, 209
contagion 254
context of the paper 363f.
continental research 61f., 64
continental writing tradition 65
core concepts 152
cover page 342
criticising theory 285ff.
curricular reading 171

D
data 191, 256f., 271, 338
- analysis of 305
- choice of 257
- collection 257
- conclusion 264
- discussion of 264
- documentation 262
- presentation 262
- qualitative 256
- quantitative 256

databases 147
delimitation 132f., 338
description 318
descriptive paragraph 318

423

design, create
- research question 305
design, creative 328
disciplinary context 354f.
disciplinary search words 377
discussing sources 235
discussion 320, 322ff.
- discussion and criticising methods 327
- questions for 324
- section 307, 364
- sequence, formulation of 325
display 76, 79ff.
documentation 358
- words 372
draft 83
- for supervision 406
- status 83
- writing 81

E
early research question 122
empirical concepts 191
empirical knowledge 191
empirical premises 198
empirical project 198
endnotes 346
epistemology 204
essay 95ff.
- academic 30
- personal 30
evaluation 326
- section 326
- terms 390
everyday language 392

F
fact bases 146
feedback 88, 407f., 410
field terms 137
files 177
focus 45, 109
footnotes 346
formal requirements 341ff.
full text 147

G
genre map 30
genres 21, 32
Google Scholar 146

H
hard disciplines
- research questions 115f.
- source reference 250
headers 343
health databases 159
heoretical premises 198
homework assignments 95
humanities
- basic assumptions 201
hypothesis 193, 335

I
I 395
idealism 206
independence 42, 100, 399
index search 163
information search 148
internet search 151
internet sources 221
interpretation 321
introduction 329ff., 363
- for research papers and theses, template 330
- standard introduction 125
introductory section 363
- writing 75

J
journalistic language 391
juxtaposing paragraphs 319

K
knowledge telling 97
- telling papers 43ff.
knowledge transforming 43ff., 97, 126, 372
- transforming papers 44
- transforming terms 372
knowledge, views of 209

L
learning goals 46, 48, 126
learning outcomes 47
letter to supervisor 403
library catalogues 146
literature review 231
literature, see sources
literature search 145ff.
    – articles 147

M
main question in research question 133
materialism 206
metacommunication 51, 372, 378ff.
    – research 380
method 270, 279ff., 336, 360, 361
    – and theory section 306, 308, 363
    – critique of 285, 289, 361, 363
    – discussion 364
    – evaluation 294
    – section 277
method methodology 195
methodological reduction 189
methodology 192
methods 192
mind mapping 76f.
models 192, 195
motivation 334

N
narrative 318
    – paragraphs, narration 318
natural science
    – basic assumptions 200
nominalisation 396
non-stop writing 76, 78
notes 83
    – contextualising 180
    – keeping 177
    – knowledge transforming 180
    – section 345
    – underlining 179
notes for your paper (as opposed to lecture notes) 176
notetaking 171ff., 176ff.
    – strategies 171

O
objectivism 209
observation, research question 124
one-week assignment 95
ontology 204
open questions 138
ownership 399f.

P
paragraph, clear 376
    – comparison 319
paraphrase, paraphrasing
    – paragraph 244, 248, 317f.
parenthetical notes 345
pentagon, research paper 32f., 122
    – literature and information search 148
    – research question 224
    – souce pentagon 225
perspective
    – paragraph 329
    – section 307, 309, 364
philosophers of science 187
philosophy of science 183
phrase search 161
PICO model, the 152
plagiarism 383
point-first 130
point-last model 130
point of view, an introduction 336
popularisation 75
popularising language 391
    – papers 31, 95
practicum
    – reports 30
practitioners af science 187
presentation of paper design to supervisor 402
primary sources 220
problem 110ff.
    – area 112
    – definitions 112
    – description 121
    – identification 111
    – related words 110
problem area 205

procedure 269, 270ff., 296, 338, 360
- discussion of 289
- section 306, 309, 364
process, project planning 89
product orientation 83
professional, the research paper writer as 42
progression 100
project 22
project planning 89
prospective chain search 168
purpose of the paper 95, 113, 336

Q
qualitative data 256
quality criteria 21, 28, 40, 53ff., 96
quantitative data 256
quotation 244

R
random literature search 150
reader
- consciousness 88
- oriented drafts, writing process 83
- oriented writing 44
reading 70, 171ff.
- purpose 173
- selective 174
- skimming 173
- speed 176
- strategies 171
- ways of 173f.
realism 206
reference 241ff., 249f., 345
- articles 243
- books 242
- journals 243
- to sources 248ff.
referencing style 249
reports 22
requirements 24
research 24
- design 308
- genre 23ff.
- genres 23
- language 367f.

- metacommunication 380
- method 269
- on revision 84
- on writing process 74
- paper design 74, 125
- structure 308
- words 372
research approaches 200
research design 33f., 52, 192, 269f., 289, 296, 298, 303, 338f.
- argumentation 352ff.
- research question 109
research paper, genre 21, 30
- writing process 67
research question 109, 111f., 127f., 334
- an overall argument 129
- approval 142
- broad 130
- check 140
- conclusion 339
- creating 127
- examples 117ff.
- good 117ff., 142
- interpretation 127
- levels 127
- literature search 149
- main question 133
- narrow 130
- poor 119
- precise terms 135
- Scribo 125
- speech act 139
- summary 127
research question's broadness vs. narrowness 130
retrospective chain search 168
revision 85ff.
- criteria 88
rhetorics of research 41

S
science 188
scientific knowledge 188
scientific theories 190
Scribo, research question 125
search engines 146f., 163

search language 157
search profile 151, 164
search profile schema 156
search terms 153f., 157
    – thesaurus 163f.
search tools 146
search words 377
    – literature search 138
secondary sources 22f., 226
selective reading 174
sentence words 396
sequence of analysis, formulation 321
set exams 96f.
skimming 174
slang 392
social sciences
    – basic assumptions 201
soft disciplines
    – research question 115f.
    – source reference 250
source critique 227, 238
    – 236
source references 248f., 251
    – hard disciplines 250
    – soft disciplines 250
source representation 244
source review 238
sources 219ff.
    – distance to 252
    – how many? 224
    – primary 220
    – qualification 227f., 230f.
    – research question 224
    – secondary 220
    – tertiary 220
    – types 220
sources in papers 222
speech acts 26f.
    – see also text types 26
spoken language characteristics 392f.
state-of-the-art 231
structure 82, 301, 363
    – and argumentation 358, 363
    – and elements in papers 299
    – and writing process 81
    – of the paper, introduction 338

    – standard 303f.
    – up-down-up 310
structure 300f.
structures, macro 305
structuring, problems 314
subject in sentence 374f.
subjectivism 209
subject specific terminology 373
subordinate concepts 154
summary 244, 248, 317f.
    – summary section 317, 346
    – verbs 251
superordinate concepts 154
supervision 399ff.
    – alternatives 411
    – calibrating expectations 403
    – no supervision 411
    – preparing for 403f.
    – working through 410
supervisor
    – and the good paper 408
    – email 405
    – literature and information search 150
synonyms 152
systematic literature search 166

T

targeted audience 24, 84
terminology 373
terms
    – in research question 112
    – plural 136
    – precise 371ff.
    – subject specific 136
    – unequivocal 371ff.
tertiary sources 220
tests 31
textbook genre 334
text types 244, 315ff., 372ff.
theoretical concepts 191
theoretical premises 198
theoretical project 198
theory 190, 193, 269ff., 336, 360
    – choice of 274ff.
    – deductive 190

    – discussion 305
    – functions of 271
    – inductive 190
    – outdated 274
    – problems with 273
    – research question 297
    – where in the paper? 283
thesaurus 163
thesis statement 130
topic 120
    – classification systems, literature search 149
    – sentence 376
topic index 163
Toulmin argument model 348
truncation 162
tutorials 163
types of material 145

V
verbs in sentence 374f.

W
wh-words, research question 124f.
Wikipedia 146, 150
working paper 83
    – questions 135
writer based 88
    – prose 75
writer's block 82
write to think 75ff.
writing process 67, 73, 106
    – argument model 361

About the authors

Lotte Rienecker has an MSc in Psychology. She has worked in the fields of academic writing, writing theses, PhD dissertations and articles, research problems, supervising and university education since 1990 at, *inter alia*, Copenhagen University, Aarhus University and the Technical University of Denmark. She has authored teaching materials and is now an educational developer at Roskilde University.

Peter Stray Jørgensen has an MA in Danish Language, Communication and Literature. For a generation, Peter has worked at universities and institutions of higher learning in the fields of academic writing, writing theses and PhD dissertations, supervising, university education and study techniques. He is now a textbook author, a consultant on university education and a lecturer.

Signe Skov holds an MA in Danish and Pedagogy. She is a PhD student at Roskilde University in educational research, where she is researching the genre of PhD dissertations. Since 2012, Signe has been employed in the university's teaching and learning unit, EAE, where she is an educational developer. Previously, she was employed as a writing consultant at Copenhagen University and as an assistant professor at University College UCC. Among other things, Signe is the co-author of *Specielt om specialer – en aktivitetsbog* (2011) and the author of the handbook *Læringsorienterede kursusdesign* (2015).

Vanessa Sonne-Ragans has an MSc in Psychology and received a PhD in Developmental Psychology from Copenhagen University in 2007. She teaches and supervises bachelor- and master's-level students in the psychology department at Copenhagen University. Vanessa lectures in applied philosophy of science at Copenhagen University and has been appointed as an external examiner in psychology. She is also a consultant to private industry and the author of the book *Anvendt Videnskabsteori. Reflekteret teoribrug i videnskabelige opgaver* (2012).

Lotte Thing Rasmussen has an MA in Communication (Journalism) and has been employed as a research librarian in Media and Communication at the University

Library of Southern Denmark (SDU) since January 2010. At SDU, Lotte has, *inter alia*, taught university students information searching and paper-writing for seven years, and she has also engaged in a number of different collaborations at SDU on academic writing.

Charlotte Wien is the head of the Research and Analysis Section of the University Library of Southern Denmark. She has a PhD degree in Information Science and is the author of the book *Introduktion til informationssøgning – om navigation på informationshavet* (2006). Charlotte has 20 years of experience in research and teaching at the University of Southern Denmark.

Kirstin Remvig has been educated as a teacher and possesses an MSC in Information Technology (Web Communication). Kirstin is employed as an information specialist at the University Library of Southern Denmark (SDUB), where, among other things, she offers courses in information searching and reference management as well as IT tools relevant to study and research. Kirstin also participated in IT-didactic research and development projects in connection with SDUB's portfolio of courses.

Ida Klitgård has an MA, a PhD, and a DPhil in English and Translation Science. Ida is an associate professor in English at Roskilde University and has taught, *inter alia*, English literature, translation, and academic English. Among her publications, for example, are a doctoral thesis on Danish translations of James Joyce's *Ulysses* and a range of international articles on translation and, more recently, on writing academic English.